Affect in Language Learning

CAMBRIDGE LANGUAGE TEACHING LIBRARY

A series covering central issues in language teaching and learning, by authors who have expert knowledge in their field.

In this series:

Affect in Language Learning

edited by

Jane Arnold

CAMBRIDGE
UNIVERSITY PRESS

PUBLISHED BY THE PRESS SYNDICATE OF THE UNIVERSITY OF CAMBRIDGE
The Pitt Building, Trumpington Street, Cambridge CB2 1RP, United Kingdom

CAMBRIDGE UNIVERSITY PRESS
The Edinburgh Building, Cambridge CB2 2RU, United Kingdom
40 West 20th Street, New York, NY 10011–4211, USA
10 Stamford Road, Oakleigh, Melbourne 3166, Australia

First published 1999

Printed in the United Kingdom at the University Press, Cambridge

Typeset in Sabon 10/12 pt   CE

A catalogue record for this book is available from the British Library

Library of Congress Cataloging-in-Publication Data

Affect in language learning / edited by Jane Arnold.
     p.   cm. – (Cambridge language teaching library)
   Includes bibliographical references and index.
   ISBN 0–521–65041–0 (hb: alk. paper). – ISBN 0–521–65963–9 (pbk.: alk. paper)
     1. Language and languages – Study and teaching – Psychological aspects.
2. Affect (Psychology) I. Arnold, Jane, 1944– . II. Series.
P53.7.A37   1998
418'007–dc21   98–30812   CIP

ISBN 0 521 65041 0 Hardback
ISBN 0 521 65963 9 Paperback

This book is dedicated to Earl Stevick. For many foreign and second language professionals, much of our information about language teaching has come to us from his work. But, more importantly, our attitude towards language teaching, our relationship with the people in our classrooms and our vision of what we would like to achieve as language teachers have all been influenced by his thinking. And I stress the word *thinking* – deep, experience-based thinking – because in Earl Stevick's writing what predominates is not the little statistic, although it may also be there to inform us, but the big idea to inspire us. In his dialogue with the reader, we find ourselves in the presence of a philosopher and a master storyteller, as well as a great language teacher and teacher trainer. For many of us Earl Stevick's work has been not only a significant factor in the origin of our interest in the affective aspects of language learning and teaching but also a continuing source of wisdom for our minds and our hearts as we strive to develop our students' second language abilities and their potential as human beings. It has touched and enriched our lives.

Jane Arnold, Seville, 1999

Contents

Contents

Contributors

Naoko Aoki, Osaka University
Jane Arnold, University of Seville
H. Douglas Brown, San Francisco State University
JoAnn (Jodi) Crandall, University of Maryland, Baltimore
Verónica de Andrés, WINGS, Buenos Aires
Zoltán Dörnyei, Thames Valley University
Madeline Ehrman, Foreign Service Institute, US Department of State
Grethe Hooper Hansen, SEAL (Society for Effective Affective Learning), UK
Viljo Kohonen, University of Tampere
Angi Malderez, University of Leeds
Gertrude Moskowitz, Temple University
Rebecca L. Oxford, University of Alabama
Herbert Puchta, Graz University
Joy Reid, University of Wyoming
Mario Rinvolucri, Pilgrims, Canterbury
John Schumann, University of California at Los Angeles
Claire Stanley, School for International Training, Brattleboro, Vermont
Earl W. Stevick, Lexington, Virginia
Adrian Underhill, International House, Hastings

Acknowledgements

Cambridge University Press, the editor and authors are grateful to the authors, publishers and others who have given permission for the use of copyright material in the text. Every effort has been made to identify and trace sources of all the materials used. Apologies are expressed for any omission.

'Why There Can Be No Best Method for Teaching a Second Language', pp. 38–41 from *The Clarion, Magazine of The European Second Language Association*; Figure 1, p. 49 from *Working with Teaching Methods: What's at Stake?* by Earl Stevick © Heinle & Heinle; 'I like you, you're different', 'Fortune cookies', 'How strong I am', pp. 190–1, from *Caring and Sharing in the Foreign Language Class: A Sourcebook on Humanistic Techniques* by Gertrude Moskovitz © 1978 Heinle & Heinle; Figure 1, p. 252 from *Visionary Leadership Skills* by R. Dilts © Meta Publications, P.O. Box 1910, Capitola, CA 95010, USA.

Preface

> The term 'feeling' is a synonym for emotion, although with a broader range. In the older psychological literature the term 'affect' was used. It is still used to imply an even wider range of phenomena that have anything to do with emotions, moods, dispositions, and preferences.
>
> (Oatley and Jenkins 1996:124)

As an English teacher in Singapore, Bob is concerned with creating materials that are of relevance to his students' lives in order to increase the motivational effectiveness of his classes and to develop his learners' potential on both linguistic and personal levels. Janice, a textbook writer and teacher in the UK, feels it is important to communicate positive messages in the classroom to enhance students' self-esteem since their beliefs about their abilities strongly influence their performance. In his intermediate-level English classes in Argentina, Vicente considers very carefully his treatment of errors in order to maintain a relaxed atmosphere in which his students are not afraid to speak. Meg, a researcher in the USA, has found that personality factors are closely related to how language learners' feelings affect their learning behaviours. As she trains ESL teachers in Australia, Donna encourages them to expand their awareness of the person behind whatever method they use in the classroom. Working in very different contexts, all of these educators are involved with affect in language learning.

When dealing with a topic as varied as the affective aspects of second and foreign language learning, we can recall the well-known fable of the blind men who come across an elephant. One touches a leg and says, 'Ah, ha. An elephant is like a column'. Another touches the trunk and says, 'No. An elephant is like a thick rope'. A third, touching a large, rough ear, says, 'Oh, that can't be. An elephant is like a carpet'. Each, touching only one part, conceived of the whole in a very different way. None was entirely wrong in his perception, and yet none really understood what an elephant was.

Likewise, the affective domain in language learning can be approached from several quite different but not mutually exclusive perspectives, such as the mainly theoretical, the empirical, the humanistic or the experiential. This book aims to bring together some of the many varied facets of the whole picture for the reader. Both novice and experienced second and foreign language teaching professionals can find much in *Affect in Language Learning* to guide their classroom practice. Similarly, those involved in the planning of language courses, materials developers and students of applied linguistics can benefit from a greater knowledge of the role of affect in language learning.

Specialists in language teaching often do not agree about the relative importance of theory and practice. Writing of educators in general, Howard Gardner, Harvard professor and creator of the influential theory of multiple intelligences, notes that 'theorists wish that their methods could be instantly transferred to the untidy and unpredictable classroom, while practitioners search for the generative power of an appropriate theoretical base for their techniques' (Gardner 1993:120). In this book the place of both theory and practice is recognized since neither should be ignored when dealing with language learning. Thus, a basic theoretical introduction to each topic is generally provided, and then some practical applications for the foreign and second language classroom are included.

The authors in this volume are not proposing that attention to affect will provide the solution to all learning problems or that we can now be less concerned with the cognitive aspects of the learning process, but rather that it can be very beneficial for language teachers to choose to focus at times on affective questions. Countering allegations that these matters are not part of teachers' obligations, Underhill (1989:252) points out that 'teachers who claim it is not their job to take these phenomena into account may miss out on some of the most essential ingredients in the management of successful learning'. Indeed, from one point of view we are abdicating our responsibility if we do not address these questions. Bruner (1996) reminds us that if our educational institutions do not deal with values and affective issues, such as self-esteem, which are the basis for healthy value systems, learners will turn to a myriad of 'anti-schools' that will certainly provide them with models – though very probably not the most socially desirable ones.

Affective language learning fits within what appears to be an emerging paradigm that stretches far beyond language teaching. There is evidence from a wide variety of fields which indicates that attention to affect-related concepts is playing a very important role in the solution to many types of problems and in the attainment of a more fulfilling way of life. British law enforcement officers are making use of contributions from Neuro-Linguistic Programming to be more 'affectively' sensitive.

Olympic ski teams and other sports participants incorporate visualization techniques as a regular part of their training to put themselves into optimal affective states. Stress management programmes are blossoming in business centres all over the world. British architect Norman Foster is known for designing buildings which, while using the most advanced technology, are especially adapted to transmit feelings of tranquillity and well-being to the people who will use them. Violinist Yehudi Menuhin, working with MUS-E International, a multicultural educational project, has pointed out that education today is directed towards training learners' thinking rather than their emotions. He stresses that there is a need to create a voice to give a vehicle for emotion and calls for a change in the present educational system (Fancelli and Vidal-Folch 1997). Fritjof Capra (1982) has documented further signs of this paradigm shift in areas such as physics, medicine, psychology and economics.

In very diverse areas of experience there is a growing concern for humanistic approaches and for the affective side of life. Perhaps the common ground upon which all rest – both in language learning and the greater whole of society – is a desire to contribute to the growth of human potential.

In this book *diversity* is indeed a key word. Diversity in the areas of learning experience covered. Diversity in the backgrounds of the contributors – geographic diversity (from Europe to North and South America and Asia) and professional diversity with contributors involved in foreign or second language research, teaching and teacher training in state and private educational facilities, on primary, secondary and tertiary levels. Yet within this variety there is a communality among the authors, a sense of unity in the commitment to a type of teaching that makes the book in a very real sense the product of a gathering of friends.

After the first chapter, in which Jane Arnold and H. Douglas Brown present an overview of affective factors related to language learning, our incursions into the domain of affect are within three main spaces. The first deals with aspects located within the learner, such as memory or personality traits, the second is mainly in the realm of the teacher, and the third brings us to the interactional space, where the resources at our disposal are put to use. However, these 'spaces' are, of course, not elements which can be topographically circumscribed. The chapters within them are rather like dunes in the desert which shift positions around a few permanent oases that serve as orientation. In the concluding chapter, Joy Reid takes a brief look at several general issues, including learning styles, an area that has been touched on in several parts of this volume, and points to directions for future research.

After each of the three main parts there is a list of questions and tasks. This is offered as a way to bring the reader into dialogue with the authors, either through individual reading or in classroom group discussion. Hopefully, additional questions will be raised and will lead researchers to illuminate new areas of affective language learning.

With whatever I have done to prepare *Affect in Language Learning* – thinking, planning, writing, editing, revising – work and pleasure have, at every moment, been indistinguishable, indeed a perfect example of flow. At different stages in the maturation of the volume, I have been fortunate to have received a good deal of assistance. In the Mesón del Moro in Seville, in what were once Moorish baths, working lunches, first with Mario Rinvolucri and later with Doug Brown, provided the occasion to reflect on the direction the volume was to take and to clarify aspects of its development. Grethe Hooper Hansen injected enthusiasm and vision into the project when she was in Seville in 1995 for a conference on Humanistic Language Teaching. At the same conference I had the undeniable pleasure of spending many hours throughout the week conversing with Earl Stevick about the book and language teaching and learning in general. All four have provided invaluable continued support. Both at the 1997 TESOL Convention in Orlando and later, Madeline Ehrman offered many useful suggestions. My colleagues in the English Language Department at the University of Seville have also helped in several ways; a special thanks to Mary O'Sullivan. My gratitude also goes to Tim Murphey and Leo van Lier for their helpful ideas and to Tammi Santana and Jo Bruton for proofreading. Financial support for aspects of the preparation of the book was made available by the Junta de Andalucía.

Alison Sharpe at Cambridge University Press provided encouragement from the very beginning. Had it not been for that, this book might have been just another good idea which never got off the ground. Mickey Bonin's editorial assistance in the later stages and comments on the manuscript from the reviewers were most appreciated.

Facing the beginning of the third millennium, all evidence points to the fallacy of Pangloss' advice to Candide; this certainly does not seem to be the best of all possible worlds. Thus, change is advisable, though not easy. Margaret Mead said, 'Small groups of thoughtful concerned citizens can change the world. Indeed it is the only thing that ever has'.

It is my hope that this book, written by a number of thoughtful, concerned authors, may contribute to the process of change by reaching out to a special group of people – the worldwide language teaching community.

Part A   Introduction

1   A map of the terrain

Jane Arnold and H. Douglas Brown

Introduction

The term *affect* has to do with aspects of our emotional being; however,
as Fehr and Russell (1984:464) have noted, 'Everyone knows what an
emotion is, until asked to give a definition'. Damasio (1994:145) makes
a distinction between the terms *emotions* (changes in body state in
response to a positive or negative situation) and *feelings* (perceptions of
these changes). Besnier (1990:421) refers to further categorization but
brings up reservations from the anthropological point of view about
cross-cultural validity of distinctions. In the present context, affect will
be considered broadly as aspects of emotion, feeling, mood or attitude
which condition behaviour. In this chapter we will be looking at a wide
spectrum of affect-related factors which influence language learning.

It should be noted that the affective side of learning is not in
opposition to the cognitive side. When both are used together, the
learning process can be constructed on a firmer foundation. Neither the
cognitive nor the affective has the last word, and, indeed, neither can be
separated from the other. Damasio has shown how evidence indicates
that even on the neurobiological level, emotions are a part of reason
and, as he demonstrates, fortunately so. In years of clinical and
experimental work he has been able to observe how the absence of
emotion compromises our rational capacity. He affirms that 'certain
aspects of the process of emotion and feeling are indispensable for
rationality' (Damasio 1994:xiii). Neural scientist LeDoux sees emotion
and cognition as partners in the mind. He notes how, after years of
behaviourist dominance, cognitive science once again made it respect-
able to study mental states; and he insists that now it is time 'to reunite
cognition and emotion in the mind' (1996:39). LeDoux goes so far as to
say that 'minds without emotions are not really minds at all' (1996:25).
Although psychologists have traditionally considered emotion to be the
Cinderella of mental functions, today a reversal of this trend is evident.
Oatley and Jenkins (1996:122) affirm that 'emotions are not extras.

They are the very center of human mental life ... [They] link what is important for us to the world of people, things, and happenings'. And there is a growing body of evidence that points to the significance of our emotions in maintaining our physical well-being; Goleman (1997:34) presents research which indicates that 'the afflictive emotions tend to make one ill and wholesome states of mind tend to promote health'.

A broad understanding of affect in language learning is important for at least two reasons. First, attention to affective aspects can lead to more effective language learning. When dealing with the affective side of language learners, attention needs to be given both to how we can overcome problems created by negative emotions and to how we can create and use more positive, facilitative emotions.

In the presence of overly negative emotions such as anxiety, fear, stress, anger or depression, our optimal learning potential may be compromised. The most innovative techniques and the most attractive materials may be rendered inadequate, if not useless, by negative affective reactions involved with the language learning process. Anxiety, for example, can wreak havoc with the neurological conditions in the prefrontal lobe of the brain, preventing memory from operating properly and thus greatly reducing learning capacity (see Stevick this volume). Fortunately, language teachers are becoming increasingly aware of the importance of negative emotional factors and of ways to handle them.

Looking at the other side of the question, stimulating the different positive emotional factors, such as self-esteem, empathy or motivation, can greatly facilitate the language learning process. A moment's reflection, however, leads us to the conclusion that in many situations much more attention is given to the question of negative emotions. For example, Damasio (1994) identifies five major emotions, under which others are subsumed: happiness, sadness, anger, fear, disgust. Goleman (1995) also groups the emotions in basic families: anger, sadness, fear, enjoyment, love, surprise, disgust and shame. In these and other classifications, the majority of the emotions would generally be seen as negative. While striving to resolve the at least numerically more predominant negative emotions, one should not lose sight of the importance of developing the positive. Motivation, after all, is better guided by a move towards pleasure and what Csikszentmihalyi (1990) calls *flow* than by a move away from pain. Even Skinner (1957) claimed consistently more efficient long-term retention under conditions of positive reinforcement than avoidance of aversive stimuli.

A second reason for focusing attention on affect in the language classroom reaches beyond language teaching and even beyond what has traditionally been considered the academic realm. Daniel Goleman

(1995) has convincingly presented his case for an 'expanded mandate' for all educational institutions. He points out that, especially since the eighteenth century, in Western civilization we have concentrated on understanding the rational, cognitive functions of our mind, while misusing or denying whatever falls within the realm of the emotions or the non-rational. One of the consequences of this situation is our current 'emotional illiteracy'. 'These are times,' Goleman states, 'when the fabric of society seems to unravel at ever-greater speed, when selfishness, violence, and a meanness of spirit seem to be rotting the goodness of our communal lives ... There is growing evidence that fundamental ethical stances in life stem from underlying emotional capabilities' (xii). He puts forth as a solution 'a new vision of what schools can do to educate the whole student, bringing together mind and heart in the classroom' (xiv) and shows how many educational programmes are already dealing very successfully with the emotional mind.

This expanded mandate can be fulfilled in all subjects across the curriculum, and foreign and second language learning is no exception. In a language classroom which focuses on meaningful interaction, there is certainly room for dealing with affect. Ehrman (1998: 102) states that 'it has become increasingly evident that the purpose of classroom learning is not only to convey content information'. In this context, Stevick (1998:166) speaks of bringing to language teaching a concern for 'deeper aims', for 'pursuing new "life goals", not just for reaching certain "language goals"'. As we teach the language, we can also educate learners to live more satisfying lives and to be responsible members of society. To do this, we need to be concerned with both their cognitive and affective natures and needs.

The relationship between affect and language learning, then, is a bidirectional one. Attention to affect can improve language teaching and learning, but the language classroom can, in turn, contribute in a very significant way to educating learners affectively. Ideally, we keep both directions in mind.

Language teaching reaching out

Just as language teaching has become increasingly open to information from vital feeder fields (for example, psychology, psycholinguistics, sociolinguistics, education and neuroscience), in the same way we have been witnessing in recent years a broadening of aims for the foreign and second language classroom. When pointing out the advantages of teaching thinking skills in the language classroom, Chamot also stresses the importance of collaborative learning. She notes that collaborative language work helps to develop Gardner's interpersonal intelligence, which 'is characterized by the ability to understand and respond effectively to others' (1995:4). This is definitely a step in the direction of emotional literacy. Freudenstein (1992) has argued that in our increasingly aggressive world, teaching peace has a vital role in the language classroom. *Idiom*, published by NYSTESOL, devoted an entire issue (1993–94) to peace and environmental education, and *English Teaching Forum*'s October 1993 issue was dedicated to 'Environment and ESL'.

Along with this diversification of objectives for the language classroom has come a new view of the language teacher. From the point of view of affective language learning, *being* is just as important as *doing*; a good language teacher *knows* and *does* but most essentially *is*. This does not mean that language teachers no longer need, for example, a firm command of the language being taught or proper training in language teaching methodology. It means that these skills will be much more effective if teachers are also concerned with their own emotional intelligence, as this can make a great deal of difference in the language learning process from the point of view of the learner.

Drawing on Sartre (1956), van Lier (personal communication) comments that in teacher training he finds it useful to set teacher development within a broad spectrum of experience. (See Figure 1.) *Having* relates to the knowledge (of subject matter and pedagogy, of self and others) and resources teachers have available, *Doing* to their skills and their abilities to construct learning opportunities, and *Being* to their personal qualities, their vision, and their sense of mission.

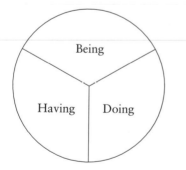

Figure 1 Areas for teacher development

Millett points out that when teachers focus on their students' learning, they 'begin to see that if they want to improve their teaching and become more aware of the learning, eventually they have to work on themselves' (interviewed in Johnson 1997:20). Thus, as part of their professional training, teachers can benefit from working on their personal development. As they come to know themselves better, they will also be able to understand their students better and lead them towards more significant learning and growth. As Griggs (1996:232) puts it, 'this awareness [of self] and belief in human potential is a transformative power in itself. It lays a firm basis for learning and working effectively and connecting deeply with the self as well as with others'.

The influence of affect in educational contexts

Interest in affective factors in education is not new. Already implicit in the writing of Dewey, Montessori and Vygotsky in the first part of this century, it gained importance with the growth of humanistic psychology in the 1960s (see Maslow 1968; Rogers 1969). Not unlike Goleman today, Rogers was pessimistic about mainstream educational institutions: 'They have focused so intently on the cognitive and have limited themselves so completely to "educating from the neck up", that this narrowness is resulting in serious social consequences' (Rogers 1975:40–41). Among the most notable applications of humanistic psychology to education was the Confluent Education movement, whose theorists, such as George Isaac Brown (1971) and Gloria Castillo (1973), stressed the need to unite the cognitive and affective domains in order to educate the whole person. With related aims, the Human Potential Research Project was founded by John Heron at the University of Surrey in 1970.

In the late 1970s and 1980s foreign and second language teacher trainers and writers expressed similar concerns. Stevick, Rinvolucri, Moskowitz, Galyean, among other representatives of Humanistic Language Teaching, were searching for ways to enrich language learning by incorporating aspects of the affective dimension of the learner. It has been stressed, however, that humanistic language teaching does not propose to replace teaching the second language by other activities, but rather to add to the effective language teaching going on in the classroom, where information and formation can co-exist (Arnold 1998).

Many of the major developments in language teaching during the past twenty-five years are in some way related to the need to acknowledge affect in language learning. The methods coming to the fore in the 1970s – Suggestopedia, Silent Way, Community Language Learning, Total Physical Response – take into account the affective side of language learning in a very central manner. (Description and evaluation of these methods can be found in Asher 1977; Curran 1976; Gattegno

1972; Larsen-Freeman 1986; Lozanov 1979; Richards and Rodgers 1986; and Stevick 1976, 1980, 1990, 1996, 1998.)

Communicative Language Teaching (CLT) has had pervasive influence on language teaching in all its phases (syllabus design, materials, teaching techniques ...), and it too gives affect its due. CLT emerged in the late 70s as a reaction to structuralism and to methods such as the audiolingual which neglected important affective aspects of learning and which were not successful in teaching learners to communicate. 'Communicative Language Teaching appealed to those who sought a more humanistic approach to teaching, one in which the interactive process of communication received priority' (Richards and Rodgers 1986:83). Unfortunately, in some cases, CLT has been reduced to the implementation of certain types of activities, without engaging learners in real communication (see Rinvolucri this volume).

The Natural Approach, developed by Krashen and Terrell (1983), takes affect into consideration in a prominent way. One of the five hypotheses in Krashen's theory of second language acquisition is the affective filter, and Natural Approach classroom activities are designed to minimize stress.

Curriculum design in recent years has also been influenced by humanistic-affective currents of thought. In the past many experts on language teaching have tended to emphasize the language over the teaching, the *what* over the *how*; and theoretical linguistics has often occupied space that might more appropriately be given to insights from the field of education, for example. Van Lier (1994:341) states clearly: 'I would like to see the field of SLA anchored in education'. As a way to cure the 'classic schizophrenia' of an understanding of SLA which moves back and forth between education and linguistics, he has proposed the development of both domains through what he and others have called 'educational linguistics'. Current researchers in the area of curriculum design have developed undeniably humanistic learner-centred models (Nunan 1988; Tudor 1997), which show the necessity of focusing more on language learners and their experience rather than simply on the narrower field of non-learner related linguistic corpora.

Indications that learners themselves would welcome a greater focus on humanistic content in language classes are not lacking. A study of reading topic preferences among advanced level students of English in Spain showed that from a broad selection of reading texts, including the main types found in most EFL/ESL textbooks, those most highly ranked related to personal development (Avila 1997). Similarly, Moskowitz (this volume) has documented the favourable response of foreign language students to humanistic language activities.

A learner-centred language curriculum takes affect into account in many ways. Participation in the decision-making process opens up greater possibilities for learners to develop their whole potential. In addition to the language content, they also learn responsibility, negotiation skills and self-evaluation, all of which lead to greater self-esteem and self-awareness.

In an affect-relevant study on adult learners applied to course planning, Brundage and MacKeracher (1980) found that better learners look to their own experience as a resource, set learning objectives in consonance with their self-concept, process through several channels and have learnt how to learn. As learners, they are influenced by their feelings and do not learn when anxious or stressed. Learning for them is most effective when it is personally relevant and when information is presented through different sensory modes.

Among the recent developments of significance for language learning are those from the fields of psychology and neurobiology, and both acknowledge the role of affect. For example, Stevick (1996) discusses research from psychology on one of the most vital aspects of language learning – memory – and links it very closely with emotion. In their comprehensive overview of the contributions of psychology to language teaching, Williams and Burden (1997:44) argue that educational psychology shares much with humanistic approaches to language teaching, especially in the need to go beyond mere language instruction to a concern with 'making learning experiences meaningful and relevant to the individual, with developing and growing as a whole person. We would argue also that it has a moral purpose which must incorporate a sense of values'. And current work on the neurobiological base of learning, which will no doubt have increasingly important implications for language learning and teaching, emphasizes the centrality of our emotional reactions in the learning process. Schumann (1997 and this volume) relates recent developments in neurobiology to affect and language learning.

Cognition or affect? Cognition and affect!

Noted learning and cognition specialist Ernest Hilgard recognized the need for an integrative approach: 'purely cognitive theories of learning will be rejected unless a role is assigned to affectivity' (1963:267). Speaking of mega-trends for learning in the twenty-first century, Gross has stressed the importance of whole-brain learning, which recognizes the contribution that affect makes:

> Insights into the ways in which our brains function have

generated tremendous excitement in scientific and educational circles over the past decade. It is now apparent that learning can be enlivened and strengthened by activating more of the brain's potential. We can accelerate and enrich our learning, by engaging the senses, emotions, imagination. (Gross 1992:139)

In the remainder of this chapter we will consider some of the specific ways affect relates to second language acquisition. In an attempt to provide an organizational framework for such a broad subject, we will look at affectivity in second language learning from two perspectives: that which is concerned with the language learner as an individual and that which focuses on the learner as a participant in a socio-cultural situation, an individual who inevitably relates to others.

Individual factors

The first of these aspects has to do with internal factors that are part of the learner's personality. Although learning a language and using it are basically interactive activities that depend on varying types of relationships with others and with the culture as a whole, the second language acquisition process is strongly influenced by individual personality traits residing within the learner. The way we feel about ourselves and our capabilities can either facilitate or impede our learning; accordingly, the learner-intrinsic factors will have a basically positive or negative influence, though there can sometimes be a mixture of liabilities and assets for each. It should be noted, of course, that the various emotions affecting language learning are intertwined and interrelated in ways that make it impossible to isolate completely the influence of any one of them. We now turn to some of these factors that are of especial importance for second language learning.

Anxiety

Anxiety is quite possibly the affective factor that most pervasively obstructs the learning process. It is associated with negative feelings such as uneasiness, frustration, self-doubt, apprehension and tension. Heron (1989:33) makes reference to what he terms *existential anxiety*, which arises out of a group situation and has three interconnected components that are relevant to the language classroom: '*Acceptance anxiety.* Will I be accepted, liked, wanted? ... *Orientation anxiety.* Will I understand what is going on? ... *Performance anxiety.* Will I be able to do what I have come to learn?'

It is not always clear how foreign language anxiety comes into being. For some people it may be a case of having been ridiculed for a wrong answer in class; for others it may have to do with factors unconnected with the language class itself. In many cases, the roots may be found in what Heron (1989:33) terms *archaic anxiety*, which is 'repressed distress of the past – the personal hurt, particularly of childhood, that has been denied so that the individual can survive emotionally'. Thus unhealed past wounds may impinge on present situations with potentially threatening elements.

There are few, if any, disciplines in the curriculum which lay themselves open to anxiety production more than foreign or second language learning. There is a great deal of vulnerability involved in trying to express oneself before others in a shaky linguistic vehicle. It is possible in some cases that the methodology used can contribute to furthering anxiety. With the grammar-translation method one might assume a reduction of the possibility of anxiety, since the learners have relatively little of themselves invested in the activities required. However, with the advent of methods which focus on communication, and especially communication involving more personal aspects of one's being, such as feelings, if care is not taken to provide an emotionally safe atmosphere, the chance for the development of anxiety-provoking situations can increase greatly. This is particularly true if at the same time the stakes involved are very high, such as in academic settings, where the evaluation of the learner can conceivably have far-reaching consequences.

When anxiety is present in the classroom, there is a down-spiralling effect. Anxiety makes us nervous and afraid and thus contributes to poor performance; this in turn creates more anxiety and even worse performance. The feelings of fear and nervousness are intimately connected to the cognitive side of anxiety, which is worry. Worry wastes energy that should be used for memory and processing on a type of thinking which in no way facilitates the task at hand (Eysenck 1979). Although it is a major obstacle to language learning, anxiety can be reduced; suggestions for dealing with it can be found in Oxford (this volume), Horwitz and Young (1991) and Young (1991).

Inhibition

Making mistakes is implicit in language learning. We made them when we were children learning our first language, and we cannot help making them when we learn a second language as older children or adults. However, as young children, we were not inhibited and thus could participate freely in the learning adventure, taking risks as needed. When learning, we have to be able to 'gamble' a bit, to be willing to try out hunches about the language and to take a reasonable risk of being wrong. Inhibitions develop when small children gradually learn to identify a self that is distinct from others, and their affective traits begin to form. With greater awareness comes the need to protect a fragile ego, if necessary by avoiding whatever might threaten the self. Strong criticism and words of ridicule can greatly weaken the ego, and the weaker the ego, the higher the walls of inhibition.

Similar to Freud's idea of *body ego*, which refers to the child's conception of the limits of his or her physical self, is Guiora's use of the construct of *language ego* to explain the presence of language boundaries (Guiora, Brannon and Dull 1972). In the course of their development, the lexis, syntax, morphology and phonology of the individual's language acquire firm boundaries. During the early formative period the language barriers fluctuate, since learners are less aware of language forms and of making mistakes in using the forms, but once ego development is complete, the permeability of the boundaries is greatly reduced. (See Ehrman 1996 and this volume.) Thus it is that aspects of a second language may be rejected, as they do not fit into the patterns contained within the language ego boundaries. Post-puberty learners of a second language, for example, often report inhibitions when pronouncing the language or trying to use it for communicative purposes.

In the 70s and 80s studies were made on the effects of inhibition-reducing substances, such as alcohol and Valium, on pronunciation performance (Guiora, Beit-Hallami, Brannon, Dull and Scovel 1972; Guiora, Acton, Erard and Strickland 1980). The results were inconclusive, though there is strong intuitive support for the negative influence of inhibition on language learning. What was shown in one of the experiments was that the person administering the test made more of a difference on the scores than the tranquillizer. These results point to the encouraging hypothesis that human factors, rather than external chemical substances, can be most efficient in reducing inhibition.

Language teaching approaches in recent years have taken into special consideration the necessity of creating learning situations in which inhibition and ego barriers are lowered so that free communication can take place. Dufeu (1994:89–90) speaks of establishing an adequate affective framework so learners:

> feel comfortable as they take their first public steps in the strange world of a foreign language. To achieve this, one has to create a climate of acceptance that will stimulate self-confidence, and encourage participants to experiment and to dis-

cover the target language, allowing themselves to take risks without feeling embarrassed.

A closely-related area of concern is the question of errors. Mistakes can be viewed as both internal and external threats to our ego. Internally, our critical self and our performing self can be in conflict: when as learners we perform something 'wrong', we become critical of our own mistakes. Externally, we perceive others exercising their critical selves, even judging us as persons when we make an error in a second language. Therefore, language teachers should not ignore affective factors when establishing the most appropriate policy of error correction for their particular situation.

Extroversion-introversion

There is sometimes an erroneous connection established between inhibition and introversion. Extroverts are often stereotyped as being outgoing and talkative and, therefore, better language learners, since they are more likely to participate openly in the classroom and seek out opportunities to practise. Introverts, by implication, might be considered less apt language learners, since they seem to be too reserved, too self-restrained. North American classrooms, for example, tend to reward extroverted behaviour, and there the outspoken student may be considered a better speaker of the target language. Actually, extroversion has to do with the need for receiving ego enhancement, self-esteem and a sense of wholeness from other people, while introversion refers to the degree that individuals derive this sense from within themselves. Introverts can have a great inner strength of character and may show high degrees of empathy, both qualities being useful for language learning. Consequently, they do not necessarily have the higher ego barriers characteristic of inhibition.

The current state of research does not permit us to draw firm conclusions as to whether either extroversion or introversion is directly related to success in language learning. However, what is clear is that certain types of classroom activities are more appropriate for one or the other. For example, teachers must be sensitive to learners' reticence towards participating in tasks that require expansiveness and overt sociability, such as drama and role-play, and lead them towards these very useful activities in a suitable manner. Teachers should also take into account any cultural norms which may make an outsider confuse cultural patterns of correct behaviour with individual feelings of inhibition or introversion.

Self-esteem

Self-esteem has to do with the inevitable evaluations one makes about one's own worth. It is a basic requirement for successful cognitive and affective activity. We derive our notions of self-esteem from our inner experience and our relationship with the external world. The foundation for our concept of Self is laid in early childhood. As we incorporate beliefs, attitudes and memories, new experiences and ideas will be affected by the previously existing notion of who we are and by our need to protect this fragile Self. Ehrman (in press) points out that self-esteem 'begins with the approbation and reliable attachment of important others but is eventually internalized so that it can be maintained relatively independently of the outside world. Teachers can build on this phenomenon with students of any age'.

Canfield and Wells (1994:5) suggest that:

> the most important thing a teacher can do to help students emotionally and intellectually is to create an environment of mutual support and care. The crucial thing is the safety and encouragement students sense in the classroom ... Further, they must recognize that they are valued and will receive affection and support.

Like anxiety, self-esteem may be described on three progressively more specific levels: *global* or general self-esteem, *situational* self-esteem, which refers to one's appraisals of oneself in specific situations, such as education or work, and *task* self-esteem, which has to do with particular tasks in a specific situation. Heyde (1979) found that all three correlated positively with performance on an oral production task by students learning French.

Extensive research indicates conclusively that the cognitive aspects of learning are fostered in an atmosphere in which self-esteem is promoted (Waltz and Bleuer 1992). Self-esteem is especially significant in young children (see de Andrés, this volume) and has been shown to predict beginners' native-language reading ability better than IQ (Wattenberg and Clifford 1962). But learners never outgrow the need for a healthy self-concept. In what they call the 'poker chip theory of learning', in which poker chips represent learners' self-concept, Canfield and Wells (1994:6) conclude that:

> the student who has had a good deal of success in the past will be likely to risk success again; if he should fail, his self-concept can 'afford' it. A student with a history predominated by failures will be reluctant to risk failure again. His depleted self-

concept cannot afford it ... One obvious recommendation in this situation is to make each learning step small enough so that the student is asked to only risk one chip at a time instead of five. But even more obvious, in our eyes, is the need to build up the student's supply of poker chips so that he can begin to have a surplus of chips to risk.

Motivation

Second language acquisition theory leaves no doubt about the crucial importance of a further affective variable, motivation, which is actually a cluster of factors that '*energize* behaviour and give it *direction*' (Hilgard, Atkinson and Atkinson 1979:281). Chomsky (1988:181) points out the importance of activating learners' motivation: 'The truth of the matter is that about 99 percent of teaching is making the students feel interested in the material'. Motivation involves the learner's reasons for attempting to acquire the second language, but precisely what creates motivation is the crux of the matter. In the early work of Gardner and Lambert (1972), motivation was seen to be divided into two very general orientations: integrative and instrumental. The former refers to a desire to learn the language in order to relate to and even become part of the target language culture, and the latter has to do with practical reasons for language learning, such as getting a promotion. One type of motivation is not necessarily always more effective than the other; what is important is the degree of energizing and the firmness of the direction it provides, and that will also depend on other variables within the learner.

This basic social psychological model for language learning motivation has been elaborated further by Gardner (1985) and his associates and by other SLA researchers. In fact, the abundance of mature theorizing about the concept in recent years (Brown 1990; Crooks and Schmidt 1991; Dörnyei 1990 and 1994; Oxford and Shearin 1994; Tremblay and Gardner 1995, Williams and Burden 1997, among others) would seem to indicate that language learning motivation research is definitely coming of age. Several frameworks have been proposed to explain motivational aspects of language learning. At the present time we must still wait for empirical verification of many of their components and for further elaboration, clarification and discussion of the relationship among the components, as well as their unification in a definitive model. However, valuable implications for the L2 classroom are not wanting; Dörnyei (1994) Oxford and Shearin (1994) and Williams and Burden (1997) provide some useful practical suggestions for motivating L2 learners.

In their discussion of extending the motivational framework for SLA, Oxford and Shearin consider other contributions from general psychology, such as the concept formulated by Maslow (1970) of the 'hierarchy of needs', which range from fundamental physical necessities to higher needs of security, identity, self-esteem and self-actualization. Whereas FL learners might not register needs on the lowest levels, the SL learners' needs 'would be negotiated in the target language from the very lowest levels of the hierarchy; even physiological, physical safety, and physical security needs might not be assured without the use of the target language' (Oxford and Shearin 1994:21).

Extrinsic and intrinsic motivation

Extrinsic motivation comes from the desire to get a reward or avoid punishment; the focus is on something external to the learning activity itself. With intrinsic motivation the learning experience is its own reward: 'Intrinsic motivation is in evidence whenever students' natural curiosity and interest energize their learning' (Deci and Ryan 1985:245). Discussing the optimal conditions for the development of intrinsic motivation, Deci (1992:60) highlights 'autonomy support, competence-promoting feedback and interpersonal involvement'. Research indicates that, while extrinsic motivation can also be beneficial, learning is most favourably influenced by intrinsic orientations, especially for long-term retention. Studies have shown that adding extrinsic rewards can actually reduce motivation. In experimental situations subjects have been shown to exhibit reduced efficiency and pleasure in an intrinsically interesting task when an extrinsic reward was introduced (Kohn 1990).

With their emphasis on teacher-directed classrooms, grades, tests and competitiveness, most schools encourage only extrinsic motivation. This has the effect of leading students to work to please teachers or authorities, rather than of developing a love of knowledge in independent minds. Bruner (1962) speaks of 'the autonomy of self-reward', affirming that one of the most effective ways to help children think and learn is to 'free' them from the control of rewards and punishments. It is reasonable to assume that our language learners will generally have a better chance of success with the development of intrinsic forms of motivation in which they learn for their own personal reasons of achieving competence and autonomy, although feedback leading to increased feelings of competence and self-determination is one extrinsic reward shown to further intrinsic motivation (Brown 1994b:39). In any event, what matters is how learners internalize the external aspects, making personal sense of them (Williams and Burden 1997).

Some suggestions for stimulating the growth of intrinsic motivation in the L2 classroom would be: (1) help learners develop autonomy by learning to set personal goals and to use learning strategies, (2) rather than over-rewarding them, encourage learners to find self-satisfaction in a task well done, (3) facilitate learner participation in determining some aspects of the programme and give opportunities for cooperative learning, (4) involve students in content-based activities related to their interests which focus their attention on meanings and purposes rather than on verbs and prepositions, and (5) design tests which allow for some student input and which are face-valid in the eyes of students; provide comments as well as a letter or numerical evaluation (H. D. Brown 1994b:43–44).

Very closely related to intrinsic motivation is the concept of *flow*, developed by University of Chicago psychologist Mihaly Csikszentmihalyi. Flow, or optimal experience, is a state of effortless movement of psychic energy. Goleman (1995:90) underlines its connection with affect: 'flow represents perhaps the ultimate in harnessing the emotions in the service of performance and learning. In flow the emotions are not just contained and channeled, but positive, energized and aligned with the task at hand'. It is so relevant because it is the ideal state for effective learning: 'Because flow feels so good, it is intrinsically rewarding. It is a state in which people become utterly absorbed in what they are doing, paying undivided attention to the task, their awareness merged with their actions' (Goleman 1995:91).

In language learning, as in many other activities, this pure enjoyment may not be present in the intitial stages when some of the more elementary processes have to be made automatic (McLeod and McLaughlin 1986; McLaughlin 1990) in order to free energy for higher level learning, which can be more engrossing. At the beginning, then, teachers may need to be concerned with ways to encourage students to make the necessary effort. At this point external incentives (grades, possible job qualifications) may be useful. But learners should move beyond the extrinsic. Echoing Dewey's thinking, Csikszentmihalyi (1990:69) affirms that 'if experience is intrinsically rewarding, life is justified in the present, instead of being held hostage to a hypothetical future gain'.

For an activity to enter the flow channel, it must be neither so easy that it produces boredom nor so challenging that it leads to anxiety. Extensive studies (Csikszentmihalyi and Csikszentmihalyi 1988) have outlined the major components of flow. Flow can occur with a task if we have a reasonable chance of completing it and if we are able to concentrate on it. The task should have clear goals and provide immediate feedback. A deep but effortless involvement keeps everyday worries at bay. There is a sense of control over one's actions, and concern for the self disappears, paradoxically actually strengthening the self. Finally, the sense of time is often altered.

These components readily suggest important implications for language learning, and, although we have been looking at intrinsic motivation and flow from the point of view of the language learner, the concepts are no less relevant for language teachers. Teachers for whom their work is a source of flow, who themselves are motivated by the pleasure of participating in the learning experience, are highly motivating models for learners.

Cognitive theories of motivation

Dörnyei (1994) refers to cognitive theories in educational psychology in which motivation is seen to be a function of a person's thought processes; these formulations, however, provide a clear example of the difficulty of isolating the cognitive, for at many points affect inevitably enters the picture. He mentions three major conceptual systems described by Weiner (1992) which are related to motivation: *attribution theory, learned helplessness* and *self-efficacy.*

Attribution theory states that what we see as the causes for our past successes or failures will affect our expectations and, through them, our performance. Failure attributed to lack of ability is much more limiting than failure attributed to bad luck or other non-stable factors. As Weiner (1985:560) explains:

> success and failure perceived as due to internal causes such as personality, ability or effort respectively raises or lowers self-esteem or self-worth, whereas external attributions for positive or negative outcomes do not influence feelings about the self.

It is a question of shifting the causal dimension. Language learners can be encouraged to attribute failures to causes which can be remedied and which do not lead to a devaluation of the self.

With *learned helplessness* (Seligman 1991) learners are convinced through past failures that attempting to change the situation is useless and thus have 'learnt' not to try. They are submerged in a helpless state that engulfs them and they feel that they cannot possibly achieve their goals, no matter what they do. They should be taught to formulate realistic goals which are within their grasp so that success in achieving them will bring them greater self-confidence.

Self-efficacy has to do with learners' opinions about their ability to carry out a task. Within the educational setting, Ehrman (1996:137) defines it as 'the degree to which the student thinks he or she has the capacity to cope with the learning challenge'. Oxford and Shearin (1994:21) point out that learners must believe they have some control over the outcomes of the learning process and they must feel a 'sense of effectiveness within themselves' if they are to make the effort necessary to learn the new language. They suggest that teachers can encourage self-efficacy 'by providing meaningful tasks at which students can succeed and over which students can have a feeling of control ... [and] by giving students a degree of choice in classroom activities ...'.

In all three cases motivation could be increased by encouraging learners to use positive self-talk, which can help to replace feelings of limitation by those of empowerment. Many learners, especially low-achievers, have been strongly affected by years of negative self-talk, much of it on a semi-unconscious level: 'I'll never get this', 'I'm always making mistakes', and so forth. They can be taught to tell themselves 'I did that well', 'I can learn this' or 'I can do better next time' in order to reinforce their beliefs about their ability to learn. Revell and Norman (1997) describe a strategy for dealing with negative self-talk in which students imagine telling themselves the negative message in a variety of silly voices which keep them from taking the message seriously.

The above theories not only have to do with *learner* beliefs; it goes without saying that the outcome of the learning process can also be strongly influenced by *teacher* beliefs. Claxton (1989:111) lists some of the limiting beliefs that can 'block the expression and the development of the personal qualities that teachers need'; the list is long but the core notion is that the feeling of ' "It can't be done" is likely to be buttressed by either or both of two personal beliefs "I can't do anything" and "I don't know what to do" '. These negative beliefs are sizeable obstacles to successful teaching.

Learner styles

We only have to glance for a moment at any classroom to realize the number of different ways in which students are learning (see Reid this volume and 1995). Among the cognitive learning styles are Field-Independent/Field-Dependent and Global/Analytic styles. Learning styles research has made a significant contribution to language teaching by increasing our awareness of the need to take individual learner variations into consideration and to diversify classroom activities in order to reach a wider variety of learners. What is suitable for a learner who functions well in the visual mode, for example, may not address the needs of someone else who learns best with auditory or kinaesthetic activities.

One categorization that has been dealt with in second language acquisition research (Ehrman 1996) is the Myers-Briggs Type Indicator, an inventory based on Jung's theory of psychological types. Jung (1923) said that people are different in fundamental ways and that an individual has preferences for 'functioning' in ways that are typical for that particular individual. The Myers-Briggs test includes four poles of functioning: introversion-extroversion; sensing-intuition; thinking-feeling; judging-perceiving. These lead to sixteen personality profiles which have been described by Keirsey and Bates (1984). Ehrman and Oxford (1990) and Ehrman (1996) have applied these concepts to language teaching. Learning styles research is especially useful in small group situations in which there is more opportunity to give individual attention to each learner, but in any case it can sensitize educational facilitators to the importance of learner differences.

Ehrman (1996:129) notes that it may be enough just to let learners know you recognize their special needs. One can:

> gradually build in an increased array of options for classroom work and homework assignments. Guidance to students in structuring their own homework along lines that begin in their comfort zones and gradually stretch them out of the comfort zones is generally well received.

Relational factors

In nearly all language teaching situations, not only are we dealing with the language and with learners and their particular cognitive and affective characteristics; we must also take into account the relational aspects of learning a new language. Language learning and use is a transactional process. Transaction is the act of reaching out beyond the self to others, and, as such, it is intimately connected with the learner's emotional being. A good part of who we consider we are is formed by our social identity, 'that part of an individual's self-concept which derives from his [or her] knowledge of his [or her] membership in a social group (or groups), together with the value and emotional significance attached to that membership' (Tajfeld 1978:63).

When we bring a social focus to language acquisition studies, we become aware that learners are not anchored in a fixed state but rather are conditioned by forces in the social context affecting them. The extent to which the social structures within the second language situation affect one's identity has not yet been researched thoroughly. Peirce (1995:12) laments that 'SLA theorists have not developed a comprehensive theory of social identity that integrates the language learner and the language learning context'.

The others we relate to in transactions in the target language may be those we coincide with in time and space as we participate in the language learning adventure taking place in one specific classroom, or they may be part of what is for us at least partially an anonymous new linguistic and cultural community. What seems to be true is that for any intergroup behaviour to be understood, 'both cognitive and affective factors must be incorporated' (Gudykunst and Ting-Toomey 1988:217).

Empathy

Spanning both of these types of transaction is the variable of empathy. In everyday language, empathy is the process of 'putting yourself into someone else's shoes'. One need not abandon one's own way of feeling or understanding, nor even agree with the position of the other. It is simply an appreciation, possibly in a detached manner, of the identity of another individual or culture. Empathy is a factor, perhaps the most important one, in the harmonious coexistence of individuals in society. It is closely related to cultural relativity, which frees us from our conditioning and helps us to recognize that our way is not the only way and possibly not even the best way.

For empathy to flourish there must be an identification with another person, but before this can exist, there must also be an awareness and knowledge of one's own feelings (Hogan 1969). As teachers move into closer contact with their own feelings, they will be better able to model empathetic behaviour in their dealings with students and to lead them to greater cross-cultural empathy.

The jury is still out on the question of the degree of correlation between empathy and success in language learning; however, there is strong intuitive support for its existence, and there are interesting questions to be considered regarding teaching methodology and research. For example, what type of classroom activities could be used to encourage empathy in the learners? Are certain teaching approaches more conducive to the development of empathy than others?

Classroom transactions

Francis Bailey (1996:261) refers to the social structure of the classroom as 'a kind of "culture" which is created out of the communal interactions among course participants'. In this special society established within the classroom, the affective dimension of the relationships among the learner, the teacher and the other learners can greatly influence the direction and outcome of the experience. As Angi Malderez points out, the importance of affect for what occurs in the classroom can be seen in the shift in the dominant metaphor for the teaching/learning process from transmission to dialogue; dialogue involves people – thinking *and* feeling, spiritual and physical human beings – in negotiation of meaning. What is important in the end is not that words have meanings but rather that people have meanings they use words to convey (personal communication).

The role of facilitation in education and other group processes has become increasingly important since the 1970s, when it referred basically to non-directive vs. directive forms of interaction. This polarity has been elaborated on since then, with John Heron's (1989:16–17) distinction between the three modes of facilitation being particularly useful, as it provides the means for avoiding or at least mitigating the frustration on both sides when teachers offer learners more responsibility than they are prepared for in the beginning. In the *hierarchical mode*, as the facilitator, you are still in charge of all major decisions in the learning process; in the *cooperative mode* you share some power and decision-making with the group and guide them towards becoming more self-directing; in the *autonomous mode* you let them do things on their own, without intervening. Heron (1989:17) points out that the latter mode 'does not mean the abdication of responsibility'. The facilitator will make use of all three modes at some point, moving from one to another as needed.

Facilitation involves encouragement and assisting rather than pouring something into the learner's mind, and it is in consonance with the notion, grounded in experience and research, that one thing is teaching and often quite another is learning. As we cannot be sure that what we think we are teaching is what is being learnt, we are well-advised to equip our learners to learn. In this vision of the learning process, 'teaching is no longer seen as imparting and doing things to the student, but is redefined as *facilitation of self-directed learning*' (Heron 1989:12). One of the benefits of this type of approach is that it enables students to keep on learning after they leave our classrooms. Gross (1992:141) points out how a lifelong-learning model offers educational institutions 'the opportunity to shift to a new paradigm ... and take seriously the mission they have always claimed to have: teaching students *how* to learn rather than merely "covering" a fixed curriculum'.

Intimately related to facilitation is group dynamics. Facilitators are at all times sensitive to the characteristics of the group they are working with and aware of the processes developing there. Group dynamics can be seen as 'the combined configuration of mental, emotional and physical energy in the group at any given time; and the way this configuration undergoes change' (Heron 1989:26). It can be extremely significant in determining the success or failure of a learning experience because, as Heron notes, 'the group dynamic ... could also be called the emotional dynamic: it is grounded in the life of feeling – which is at the core of the group's state of being' (1989:94). Much of the work done by the facilitator with group dynamics will be managing emotional states – encouraging positive ones and finding ways to overcome the negative ones and, ideally, utilizing both for growth. Cooperative language learning experiences are examples of particularly effective exploitations of classroom dynamics (see Crandall this volume).

Cross-cultural processes

The contrasts between second and foreign language learning have often been discussed, but it is important not to take them for granted. Teachers in each case need to develop special skills to deal with aspects specific to the situation. Second language learning often involves particular emotional difficulties produced by the confrontation between two cultures. In a second language situation the learner is not only faced with the target language but – except in the case of what Kachru (1992) calls 'World Languages', like English in India – also with the target culture. 'Culture' is a mental construct, a conceptual network that evolves within a group to provide a manageable organization of reality. It will involve ideas, beliefs, customs, skills, arts, and so forth; and it fills definite biological and psychological needs and establishes for the individual a context of cognitive and affective behaviour. It is bound inextricably to language.

In his influential work *Cultures and Organizations*, Geert Hofstede (1991) refers to culture as the 'software of the mind', a sort of mental programming of the members of a social group which conditions their behaviour. Generally, for successful second language learning to occur, learners 'must be both able and willing to adopt various aspects of behaviour, including verbal behaviour, which characterizes members of the other linguistic-cultural group' (Lambert 1967:102). Schumann defines acculturation as 'the social and psychological integration of the learner with the target language (TL) group' (1986:379) and suggests that this combination of social and affective factors is a significant causal variable in SLA, since learners will learn the language to the degree that they acculturate.

When individuals come into contact with another culture and in some way must incorporate at least part of it into their way of thinking and being and of experiencing reality, there may often be major emotional disruptions. Stengal (1939) described *language shock* as the situation when adult learners fear that their words in the target language do not reflect their ideas adequately, perhaps making them appear ridiculous or infantile. Not controlling the language properly, they lose a source of narcissistic gratification which they might otherwise receive when using their own language.

Language acquisition may also be inhibited by *culture shock*, which can be defined as anxiety resulting from the disorientation encountered upon entering a new culture. In their classic study of culture shock, Larson and Smalley (1972:41) point out how great amounts of energy are used up dealing with culture shock: 'New climate, the new foods, the new people all mean that the alien must muster up every bit of available energy and put it to use in new ways'.

The symptoms present may be fairly serious in some cases:

> Culture shock refers to phenomena ranging from mild irritability to deep psychological panic and crisis. Culture shock is associated with feelings in the learner of estrangement, anger, hostility, indecision, frustration, unhappiness, sadness, loneliness, homesickness, and even physical illness. Persons undergoing culture shock view their new world out of resentment and alternate between being angry at others for not understanding them and being filled with self-pity. (Brown 1994a:170)

While severe culture shock may not last long, more subtle problems may persist, producing what Larson and Smalley (1972) call *culture stress*, which has to do with questions of identity. The individual has no fixed reference group to relate to, no longer being a part of the native culture, and not yet belonging to the target one. Feeling incapable of adapting to the new country and learning the language, learners may begin to reject themselves and their own culture. At this point, they may experience *anomie*, where one has no strong, supportive ties to either the native culture or the SL culture.

It is perhaps useful to think of acculturation in terms of four stages. The first is a state of excitement about the new culture. The second stage would be culture shock, which appears as cultural differences intrude into images of self and security. The third stage, culture stress, is a tentative move towards recovery. Some problems persist but slow progress is made, as the individual begins to accept more aspects of the new culture. Stage four represents assimilation or adaptation to the new culture and acceptance of the self within it (Brown 1994a:171).

As cross-cultural learning experiences may produce considerable blocks and inhibitions in the learner, second language teachers need to be particularly sensitive to the difficulties that may arise. First of all, it is helpful to discuss them with learners. Listening on the part of teachers can lead to significant changes in attitude among learners who are thus able to give expression – give voice – to their problems in a second language situation. Van Lier (1996:185) affirms that poverty of expression in our learners may be due in part to the fact that they 'are not encouraged to find sources of speaking, their own voice, within themselves, and with each other'. In a discussion of working with Freire's concept of problem posing in a methods course, Francis Bailey (1996) points out the importance of developing the voice of all class members to enable them, through dialogue, to find possible solutions to their problems. Some of the stress may be eliminated when they realize that they are going through a normal process and that they are not alone in their feelings of isolation and incapacity. It is helpful to discuss cultural differences and explain aspects of the target culture which may be problematic for foreign learners. However, Scarcella and Oxford (1992) also indicate the importance of emphasizing common ground.

Language learning activities can focus on working through affective problems encountered in the process of adapting to the new culture and language. Donahue and Parsons (1982) propose the use of role-play to overcome 'cultural fatigue', which is the physical and emotional exhaustion coming from the stress involved in adjusting to a new cultural environment. With role-play, learners have the opportunity to express their feelings of negativity, to act out difficult situations and to search for solutions in an emotionally safer atmosphere. Written expression can also be useful. Diverse written tasks, such as journal writing, can be given to encourage reflection and work on emotional aspects of the learning process. Individuals who are reticent about expressing their feelings directly might be asked to write about fictional characters in situations similar to their own.

Through means like these, teachers can help learners in a second language situation to understand the source of any anger, frustration, anxiety or isolation felt, to express those feelings and then to move beyond them to acquire the new language at the same time as they also become proficient in the new culture.

Conclusion

Heron (1992) has developed a model he calls multi-modal learning, which refers to four modes of learning from experience: action, conceptual, imaginal, emotional. If we adapt this to language learning in particular, at the top of the pyramid would be the action mode, 'learning through doing', or developing the basic skills. Next, the conceptual mode would involve learning 'about' the language. The imaginal mode would take in the imagination and the intuitive understanding of the scheme of the language as a whole. At the bottom, the emotional mode would deal with the awareness of the different ways our feelings influence our language learning. What is especially important to note about Heron's pyramid is that the top three modes of learning all rest upon the broad affective base. Heron (1990) has pointed out that the higher do not control and rule over the lower, but rather the higher branch and flower out of the lower.

As language teachers, we already have many areas of competence to attend to. Yet adding one more, rather than increasing teachers' burdens, might make attending to the other areas an easier task. At the same time, it might lead to a more holistic development of our students as individuals and as responsible participants in a healthy society. We suggest that positive waves will spread in many directions from a greater commitment in language teaching to the growth of emotional competence.

Part B   Exploring the learner's space

In examining the terrain of affective language learning, the starting point is, of course, the learner. In the first place, very little can be accomplished if the learner is not at least minimally willing or motivated. Williams and Burden (1997:205) caution that 'whatever language input is provided, we cannot predict what each individual will learn or how the learner's language system will develop'. They point to the necessity, then, of focusing on the learner: 'Individuals will tend to learn what they think is worth learning ... Unless teachers have a sound grasp of what their learners see as important and meaningful, they will not possess all the information they need to make their courses truly motivational'.

In the second place, learning is a goal; teaching is but a tool. It is healthy to approach language teaching with a focus on the learners; after all, as teachers, we should make their progress our main concern. Among others, Gattegno (1976) insisted on the importance of concentrating on learning more than teaching. Likewise, Penny Ur has said, 'learning may take place without conscious teaching; but teaching, as I understand it, is intended to result in personal learning for students, and is worthless if it does not do so' (Ur 1996:4).

In a constructivist theory of learning what the individual does is construct personal meaning. Diametrically opposed to static views of the learner as a passive element in the process, constructivism applied to language learning would consider learners as 'actively involved in making their own sense of the language input that surrounds them as well as the tasks presented to them' (Williams and Burden 1997:23). In this model emotions must 'be considered as an integral part of learning, as also must the particular life contexts of those who are involved in the teaching-learning process' (*op.cit.*:28).

An obvious fact about language learners is that they achieve quite different degrees of success. Much of the theorizing and research that has been done in the field in the past twenty years has been prompted by one intriguing question: Why do some language learners learn better than others? Stevick's answer was that 'success depends less on materials, techniques, and linguistic analysis, and more on what goes on inside and between the people in the classroom' (1980:4). In this section we will be focusing on some of the affective aspects of the 'inside' of language learners; referring to the role these aspects have in promoting success, Stern commented that 'the affective component contributes at least as much and often more to language learning than the cognitive skills ...' (1983:386).

In Chapter 2, working within a motivational framework, John Schumann presents a neurobiological perspective on stimulus appraisal and its role in variable success in SLA. Between our perception of an event and our response to it, a system of emotional appraisal or evaluation of the event is activated in the brain. Schumann shows how the language learning situation may be appraised positively without being appraised as pleasant. He also argues that each learner's appraisal system is different and that accommodation to this variation is a major challenge in teaching. Finally, he contends that there can be no best method for teaching a foreign language because individual brains respond to instruction in different ways.

Earl Stevick explores in Chapter 3 the affective side of language learning as it relates to a key element, memory. He explains how, contrary to popular belief, the processing of new information takes place as a two-way interaction between long-term memory and working memory, rather than as a unidirectional flow from the senses through 'short-term memory' and thence into long-term memory. He describes five ways in which affect can influence memory and the learning process. Stevick provides a very useful point of view for this volume in that he wants to make it clear that concern with affect will not solve all learning problems. This then frees us to investigate in exactly which ways it can promote better language learning.

In Chapter 4, Rebecca Oxford investigates anxiety as a negatively conditioning factor in language learning. She discusses the relationship between language anxiety and a number of other factors. After explaining how anxiety may be identified in the classroom, she includes a synthesis of the latest research-based recommendations for reducing language learning anxiety and shows how learners may not always have to resign themselves to suffering from anxiety in the language learning situation.

In Chapter 5, Madeline Ehrman looks at the effects of certain personality variables on language learning, specifically tolerance of ambiguity and the underlying concepts of ego boundaries and regression in the service of the ego. These constructs are related to the ability to cope with changes in personal identity structure which may accompany language learning. Awareness of individual differences in ego boundaries and tolerance of ambiguity can also contribute to better understanding of learner motivation, anxiety and defensive behaviour. Familiarity with these psychological mechanisms increases our understanding both of learner difficulties and of learner successes.

The emotional configurations in language learning may be of a highly positive nature. In the last chapter in this section, Verónica de Andrés eloquently presents her case for the enhancement of self-esteem in the second language classroom as a means of improving social skills as well as academic performance. Bringing in both theory and her classroom research on self-esteem in primary school EFL classes, de Andrés provides a detailed example of the process involved in carrying out an action research project about a very significant area of affect.

2 A neurobiological perspective on affect and methodology in second language learning

John H. Schumann

The neural basis for stimulus appraisal[1]

The findings of research on the brain in the last part of the twentieth century have brought rapid advances in our understanding of mental processes. Research on the neural substrate has been aided tremendously by the use of imaging techniques such as Positron Emission Tomography (PET) and Magnetic Resonance Imaging (MRI). The brain is, of course, the site of language acquisition, and thus a better understanding of the brain can shed light on how the language learning process functions. The neurosciences, which are concerned with the workings of the nervous system, are providing us with an ever increasing body of data on the brain mechanisms underlying language acquisition. Neurobiology, including neuroanatomy, neurochemistry and neurophysiology, deals with the nervous system and how it interacts with the environment. It informs several areas of interest for language acquisition studies, for example, plasticity, affect, memory and learning. (Further discussion of basic neurobiological information relating to language acquisition can be found in Jacobs and Schumann 1992 and Schumann 1997.)

For the past several years I have been working on a model of learning that attempts to link the neurobiology and psychology of stimulus appraisal with variable success in second language acquisition. The brain evaluates the stimuli it receives via the senses from the language learning situation, either in the target language environment or in the classroom, and this appraisal leads to an emotional response. In the first

---

[1] The first section of this chapter is based on a presentation I made at the Colloquium on Classroom Applications of Motivation Assessment at the 31st Annual TESOL Convention held in Orlando, Florida, March 15, 1997. A more detailed discussion of the issues in the first two sections of the chapter can be found in Schumann (1997). The last section is a revised version of an article published in *The Clarion: The Magazine of the European Second Language Association*, 3, 23–24, 1997; it is reprinted here with the permission of the publisher.

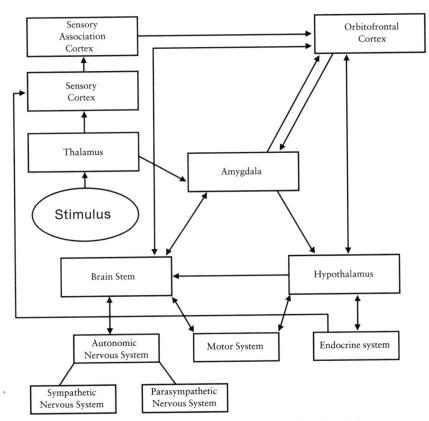

Figure 1 The neural mechanism for stimulus appraisal (based on Schumann 1997)

part of this chapter I want to examine how positive and negative appraisals of the second language learning situation are subserved by a neurobiological system that is involved in appraising the emotional relevance and motivational significance of stimuli.

The system (see Figures 1 and 2) consists of the amygdala in the temporal lobes, the orbitofrontal cortex in the prefrontal area of the brain, and parts of the peripheral nervous system located in the body proper (specifically the autonomic nervous system, the endocrine system and the musculoskeletal system). The amygdala and the orbitofrontal cortex are both connected to the peripheral nervous system and feedback to the brain from this system helps generate the appraisals. (See appendix on page 41 for further development of the neurobiological aspects of stimulus appraisal.)

Psychologists interested in emotion have identified several dimensions along which stimulus appraisals are made. They include novelty and familiarity, pleasantness, goal or need significance, coping potential and

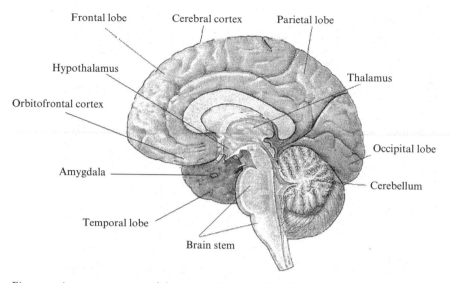

Figure 2 A representation of the internal aspect of the brain

self and social image (Scherer 1984). The novelty appraisal assesses whether internal or external stimulation contains unexpected or familiar patterns. Pleasantness determines whether an agent, an action or an object is appealing and thus fosters approach or whether it is unappealing and promotes avoidance. The goal/need evaluation assesses the degree to which the stimulus event is conducive to satisfying the individual's needs or achieving his or her goals. The coping potential check determines the individual's ability to cope with the event. Finally, the norm/self compatibility check assesses (a) the compatibility of the event with social or cultural norms, or with the expectations of significant others, and (b) the compatibility of the event with the individual's self-concept or ideal self (Scherer 1984).

Researchers in second language acquisition have investigated motivation for language learning using questionnaires that elicit stimulus appraisals along at least four of the five dimensions. It is reasonable to consider that motivation consists of various permutations and patterns of these stimulus appraisal dimensions and, in fact, if one does an item by item analysis of motivation questionnaires, the items can quite readily be classified according to the appraisal categories (Schumann 1997). This is illustrated in Table 1 with items taken from the motivation research by Gardner (1985), Schmidt and Savage (1992), Schmidt, Boraie and Kassabgy (1996) and Clément, Dörnyei and Noels (1994).

TABLE 1: APPRAISALS AS THE BASIS FOR MOTIVATION

Gardner's (1985) Attitude and Motivation Test Battery

Pleasantness
If the opportunity arose and I knew enough   Appealingness of an activity (goal)
French, I would watch French TV programs:
a) sometimes
b) as often as possible
c) never

French Canadians are very sociable,   Appealingness of agents
warm-hearted and creative people.

The French Canadian heritage is an   Appealingness of an object
important part of our Canadian
identity.

Goal Relevance
Studying French can be important to me
because it will allow me to meet and
converse with more varied people.

Coping Potential
I never feel quite sure of myself when I
am speaking in our French class.

Norm/self Compatibility
Studying French can be important for me
because other people will respect me more
if I have knowledge of a foreign language.

Schmidt and Savage's (1992) Experience Sampling Method Questionnaire

Pleasantness
Do you wish you had been doing   Appealingness of an activity (goal)
something else?

Goal Relevance
How important was this activity in relation
to your overall goals?

Coping Potential
Were you succeeding at what you were doing?

Norm/self Compatibility
Were you living up to your own expectations?   Self-compatibility
Were you living up to the expectations   Norm-compatibility
of others?

TABLE I *(contd)*

Schmidt, Boraie and Kassabgy's (1996) Motivation Questionnaire

Pleasantness

I enjoy learning English very much.	Appealingness of an activity
Americans are very friendly people.	Appealingness of agents

Goal Relevance

I plan to continue studying English for as
long as possible.

Coping Potential

If I don't do well in this class, it will be
because I don't have much ability for
learning English.

Norm/self Compatibility

Being able to speak English will add to my social status.	Norm compatibility
It is important to me to do better than the other students in my class.	Self compatibility

Clément, Dörnyei and Noels (1994): Item Loadings From Factor Analyses

Pleasantness

Attitudes toward the British	Appealingness of agents
Attitudes towards learning English	Appealingness of activity

Goal Relevance

Will help when traveling.

Coping Potential

Course difficulty

Norm/self Compatibility

It is expected of me.	Norm compatibility
Satisfaction with competence	Self compatibility

I would also argue, based on data from motivation studies, diary studies (Bailey 1991; Bailey and Ochsner 1983), and autobiographies (Schumann 1997) of second language learners, that *positive* appraisals of the language learning situation (the target language, its speakers and the culture in which it is used, the teacher, the syllabus and the text) along the five dimensions mentioned above enhance language learning and *negative* appraisals inhibit second language learning.

Now the question is: To what extent are the appraisal dimensions identified by the psychologists and elicited by SLA researchers (studying motivation) actually controlled by the biological appraisal system suggested by the neuroscientists. One way to answer this question is to examine the impairments in stimulus appraisal evidenced by individuals who have damage to parts of the neural appraisal mechanism. Another way to address the issue is to examine the research on animals who have had electrodes implanted in areas of the neural appraisal system, or who have had damage to the system.

Damasio (1994) reports the cases of two orbitofrontal patients who have severe deficits in making appraisals of goal relevance and self and social image. These patients have difficulty in deciding on a plan of action, and sticking with that plan until the task is completed. They get distracted and switch goals frequently. On the other hand they sometimes execute a project with detail and attention far beyond what is needed to accomplish the task. Therefore, the patients have difficulty selecting goals, maintaining them, and abandoning them when the task is completed or when the effort ceases to be rewarding. Clearly they have difficulty appraising stimuli in terms of goal relevance.

These patients, because of their impaired judgment, make disastrous personal and social decisions. They fail in marriage, business and social relations. Their lives unravel; they frequently become impoverished. Nevertheless, they do not suffer. They are not shamed, depressed, embarrassed or frightened by their failures. It is as though the tragedy is happening to someone else. Orbitofrontal patients are also frequently characterized by socially inappropriate behavior. They become crude, use foul language such that they embarrass and offend others, but feel no shame themselves. Clearly they have difficulty appraising stimuli in terms of self and social image.

Damasio (1994) also reports the case of Patient *A* who was studied in the 1930s by Brickner (1936). Patient *A* bragged about his current business acumen on the stock exchange, but had not worked there since the brain damage. He boasted of his athletic ability but undertook no sports activity. He portrayed himself as sexually active outside of his marriage, but he had had no sex life with his wife or anyone else since the brain injury. Patient *A* demonstrates deficits in appraisals of both his coping potential and self and social image. Therefore, these examples show how orbitofrontal patients demonstrate difficulties in making appropriate appraisals along three of the five dimensions: goal/need relevance, coping ability, and self and social image.

What about appraisals of novelty/familiarity and pleasantness? On the basis of experiments with chronically implanted electrodes in the amygdalas of monkeys, Rolls (1995) reports that neurons in these areas respond to reward-related (hence pleasant) stimuli such as food and stimuli associated with food. These neurons also fire as the monkey explores novel items introduced into the experimental environment by the researchers. He suggests that these 'amygdala neurons ... operate as filters, providing an output if a stimulus is associated with a positive reinforcer or is positively reinforcing because of its relative novelty' (Rolls 1995:1098). Rolls also reports lesions of the amygdala lead to reduced neophobia in rats who then more readily accept unfamiliar foods. In monkeys, such lesions have been shown to foster indiscriminate sampling of positive, negative, novel, and familiar items. Gaffan (1992:475) reports that monkeys with amygdalectomies are unable, when sated, to recognize the 'yellow shape' of a banana as rewarding, palatable and therefore pleasant. Normal monkeys show great excitement when shown a banana, both when hungry and when sated.

One interpretation of the orbitofrontal patients' frequent inability to stay on task and their distraction by various extraneous stimuli in the environment may be that they are, in some ways, slaves of local appraisals of pleasantness, and are in some way, unable to control such appraisals. In neuropsychological tests, orbitofrontal patients continue to make responses that are not rewarding. Thus, to the extent that reward is pleasant (and for normal individuals it is), these patients appear to have difficulty in appraising the pleasantness of a situation. Research data like these suggest that both the amygdala and the orbitofrontal cortex participate in appraisals of novelty/familiarity and pleasantness.

There seems to be evidence that all the appraisal dimensions outlined by Scherer and elicited in motivation questionnaires are subserved by the neural mechanism consisting of the amygdala, orbitofrontal cortex and the body proper. However, the novelty dimension did not appear in the motivation questionnaires or in diary studies; it was also generally absent in the autobiographies of second language learners (but see the Rowlands Shrimpton autobiography in Schumann 1997 for a discussion of the issue). It may be too soon to discard novelty as an appraisal category. As we know from language learning and language teaching experiences, too much novelty in terms of pedagogical innovation can be threatening, but too much familiarity in terms of the repetition of pedagogical activities can be boring. Therefore novelty might emerge as an appraisal issue in SLA, but we may have to probe for it directly.

Because there is a neurobiological stimulus appraisal system that makes appraisals along the five dimensions identified by psychologists and used by SLA researchers to study motivation, do we have evidence that second language learners are guided by that neural appraisal system in their learning? Such evidence is not yet available because to date no one has demonstrated neural activity in the amygdala, orbitofrontal cortex and the body proper during second language learning. However, second language learners have brains, brains have appraisal systems, and as demonstrated by SLA motivation researchers, motivation is based on appraisal. Therefore, we can hypothesize with some degree of confidence that the amygdala, orbitofrontal cortex, body proper and related mechanisms subserve stimulus appraisal and motivation in second language learning.

Positive vs. pleasant in stimulus appraisal

In this section, I want to distinguish between appraisals that are made on the dimension of pleasantness and those that are made on the dimensions of goal conduciveness and self and social image. In doing so, I will refer to the case of a learner, Eva Hoffman, who wrote an autobiography called *Lost in Translation* (1989) which describes her acquisition of English. Eva immigrated to Canada from Poland in 1959 when she was 14 years old. From the beginning, her reaction to Canada is very negative. She criticizes the landscape, the houses – their design and furnishings, the appearance and behavior of her peers at school. She dislikes her peers' jokes, conversation and social activities. She finds Canadians boring, conformist and unadventurous. In general, we can say that on the dimension of pleasantness, Eva appraises Canadian people and culture negatively.

At the same time, Eva has high goals. She wants to learn English, but she wants to learn it well and in its refined and articulate form. In her early stages of acquiring English, she reports that she does not like expressions such as 'you're welcome' which she describes as gauche. However, she becomes fond of literary words such as 'enigmatic' and 'insolent'. She is determined to speak English well, and even though she currently lacks that ability, she has a good sense of what well-spoken English sounds like. She doesn't like the way Polish immigrants speak English and struggles to lose her accent. Her experience in Poland has taught her that correct speech confers status, and she is convinced that high proficiency in English is the key to success. She believes that the marginality of her immigrant status can only be overcome by mastering the language of the most articulate among the dominant group.

While Eva is motivated to acquire English as spoken by elite intellectual and artistic members of North American society, she is also motivated by the fear of failure. She knows her family depends on her; she worries about being poor. She labels this anxiety the 'Bowery'; she imagines that if she isn't successful, this is where she will end up. Eva is convinced that it is only by achieving academically that she can move from her tenuous immigrant status to the other place she wants to be – a place of security and respect. This combination of ambition and fear empowers her and motivates her not just to survive, but ultimately to thrive.

Eva is not only motivated by high goals but is also supported by high aptitude. She graduates valedictorian of her high school class, goes to Rice University as an undergraduate, and then to Harvard to pursue a Ph.D. in English. After completing two years of graduate study, she appraises her English in the following way:

> I've become obsessed with words ... I will not leave an image unworded, will not let anything cross my mind till I find the right phrase to pin the shadow down. (p. 216)

> The thought that there are parts of the language I'm missing can induce a small panic in me, as if such gaps were missing parts of the world or my mind – as if the totality of the world and mind were coeval with the totality of the language .... When I write, I want to use every word in the lexicon, to accumulate a gravity of things. I want to re-create, from the discrete particles of words, that wholeness of a childhood language that had no words. (p. 217)

The point to be made about Eva's case is that her positive appraisals were dominant along the goal and self and social image dimensions, but not necessarily on the dimension of pleasantness or appealingness. Eva seemed capable of dissociating local appraisals of the pleasantness of agents, events and objects from the value she placed on the goals she wanted to achieve. We might surmise that certain experiences that she found unpleasant may have been appraised positively because of the contribution they made to her long-term goal to speak excellent English and to achieve the status associated with that skill. Therefore, she seems to have been willing to endure events that she appraised as unpleasant because they were desirable as steps to the achievement of a long-term goal. Ortony, Clore and Collins (1988) point out that going to the dentist is frequently viewed negatively in terms of pleasantness, but nevertheless, is appraised positively in terms of maintaining dental health.

We must note that Eva was in North America for good; there was no going back to Poland. She could not stop learning English simply because she found certain aspects of the language, its speakers and its culture unpleasant. However, anglophone North Americans who generally have no need to learn a foreign language beyond very limited school requirements frequently find an unpleasant appraisal of the language learning situation sufficient reason to abandon the enterprise. It is for this reason that Gardner's (1985) Attitude and Motivation Test

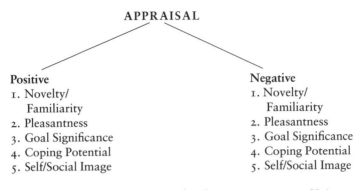

APPRAISAL

Positive	Negative
1. Novelty/ Familiarity	1. Novelty/ Familiarity
2. Pleasantness	2. Pleasantness
3. Goal Significance	3. Goal Significance
4. Coping Potential	4. Coping Potential
5. Self/Social Image	5. Self/Social Image

Figure 3 Positive appraisals along any of the five dimensions promote SLA; therefore, in terms of stimulus appraisal, positive does not necessarily mean pleasant

Battery, which is a questionnaire designed to examine the motivation for second language acquisition by anglophone North Americans, focuses on pleasantness. Approximately 70% of the items on the questionnaire elicit appraisals of pleasantness or appealingness of agents, activities or objects in the language learning situation. It may also be for this reason that our first inclination is to associate positive appraisal with pleasantness. But as illustrated in Figure 3, appraisals can be positive or negative on any of the five dimensions.[2] Thus, positive does not necessarily mean pleasant.

Beyond the need to know English, Eva had the goal of becoming a masterful user of the language. Her positive appraisals of the language learning situation in terms of her needs were sufficient to make her competent, and her appraisal in terms of her goals and self and social image eventually carried her to excellence. We should note that Eva was in no way impeded by lack of aptitude which would have interfered with positive appraisals on the goal dimension. (See Schumann 1997 for a discussion of appraisal/aptitude interactions.) She had the ability to achieve her goal. But aptitude cannot be the whole story. There are many people with Eva's language learning aptitude who do not receive a Ph.D. in English from Harvard and who have not been an editor of *The New York Times Book Review*.

What might be the implications of this neuropsychological perspective for language teaching? Zoltán Dörnyei (1996) offered ten suggestions, based on extensive research with teachers and learners, for how teachers might enhance their students' motivation. In addition, I would like to indicate four things teachers might want to avoid in order *not to*

---

[2] This is a variant of a figure developed by Rowlands Shrimpton for Schumann (1997).

diminish their students' motivation. Teachers should not do things which the students would appraise as unpleasant; they should not do things that interfere with the students' goals in language learning; they should not do things that are beyond or below the students' coping ability, and they should not do things that would diminish the students' self and social image.

This is a formidable challenge because the teacher has fifteen to thirty, or possibly many more, different appraisal systems to deal with in one classroom. In addition, teachers should not consistently do things that they find unpleasant or damaging to their language teaching goals, coping potential and self and social image. Therefore, it would appear that teachers should, in any way possible, negotiate their appraisals of the language learning situation with those of the students. The negotiation space may frequently be quite narrow, but it would appear that negotiation is the only alternative, and I suspect that teachers cease to be motivating when they stop negotiating.

Why there can be no best method for teaching a second language

Regarding classroom teaching, there has been much debate about which method is most effective; we might ask if there is neurobiological evidence on this matter. To address the issue, this section takes the position that there is a sensitive period for second language acquisition after which language learning is similar to recovering from brain damage. Evolution has designed the brain to acquire grammar and phonology by about four years of age through natural interaction with others. Some margin of heightened adaptability probably extends this learning period to the middle of the second decade of life. Once that period has passed, the brain can be viewed as 'damaged' with respect to the skill to be acquired, and it must use a more general form of plasticity (Jacobs 1988) to adapt.

Oliver Sacks (1995) in his book *An Anthropologist on Mars*, describes his adaptation to using his left hand after surgery on his right and then the gradual recovery of the use of his right hand.

> But recovery, in such circumstances, is by no means automatic, a simple process like tissue healing – it will involve a whole nexus of muscular and postural adjustments, a whole sequence of new procedures (and their synthesis), learning, finding, a new path to recovery. My surgeon, an understanding man who has had the same operation himself, said, 'There are *general* guidelines, restrictions, recommendations. But all the particulars you will have to find out for yourself.' Jay, my physiotherapist,

expressed himself similarly: 'Adaptation follows a different path in each person. The nervous system creates its own paths. You're the neurologist – you must see this all the time.' (p. xvi)

The reason the surgeon and the physiotherapist can only provide general guidelines is because each brain is different. At the level of microanatomical ramifications every brain is unique (Edelman 1992). Each brain has lifelong plasticity, but the degree and type varies within and across brains. In one person certain regions or networks may be well adapted to reacquire the skill lost in the brain damage; in another person the neural plasticity may not be as amenable to such reorganization and only partial recovery may be achieved.

It is for the same reason that no second language teaching method can be the single best one. Teachers can provide '*general* guidelines, restrictions, [and] recommendations', and each individual brain has to figure out the best way to adapt to the input, using brain regions and circuits that are not necessarily specialized for language acquisition. However, within an individual's brain, certain regions or networks may respond well to the acquisition of lexicon, others to the perception or production of sounds, others to the formal learning of grammar, and still others to learning through conversational interaction. A learner may be better at some of these skills than others, and the right method will be one which allows him to learn best, i.e. the method to which his brain most readily responds. A method which presents material in a way that fails to target efficiently a learner's neural circuits to subserve the skill being taught will not be the right method for that brain. It may, on the other hand, be perfectly appropriate for another individual's brain. Once again a teacher can provide general guidelines, but no guaranteed approach. Brains respond differently, and this phenomenon may be related to what psychologists have identified as differences in learning styles.

Another reason why there can be no right method is because post-sensitive period learning is also more dependent upon motivation. It is here that appraisals of the language learning situation (according to novelty, pleasantness, goal relevance, coping ability and self and social image) are crucial. In the same way that recovering from neural damage requires dedication to the therapeutic regimen, an adult second language learner has to find the instructional program that works for him, and he must stick to it for the lengthy period of time needed to become proficient. Of course, the learner's needs will change with time and therefore pedagogical needs will also change. The right method at one time may not be the right method at another because the learner's brain will have changed. An approach, method or technique that does not resonate with the learner's neural systems that subserve appraisal and learning will frustrate achievement and will demotivate. If the learner cannot find an alternative, learning is likely to be abandoned.

As mentioned earlier, evolution has designed the brain to acquire language through naturalistic interaction during the sensitive period. Thus there can be no single correct method for *teaching* a second language, even during the time of heightened adaptability before the close of the sensitive period. Language *instruction* during this time is equivalent to learning under conditions of environmental deprivation. An instructional environment, in comparison to an environment involving genuine language use, is deprived, and individual brains will respond to such conditions very differently. Under the artificial conditions of instructed learning during the sensitive period, some children's brains may have auditory systems that respond, and they may learn to distinguish some target language sounds. Other children with adept motor articulatory systems may learn to pronounce target language sounds. Others with good lexical memory systems may acquire a substantial target language vocabulary, and others may incorporate grammatical rules. Some children's brains may be adept at several of these components. But variation across learners will likely be considerable because each child's brain will have to adapt as best it can to the highly deprived linguistic environment. Thus no language teaching approach, method or set of techniques can substitute fully for genuine naturalistic interaction, which is the experience the neural system expects and requires in order to learn under the heightened plasticity of the sensitive period.

In a discussion of brain development, it has been recommended that foreign languages be taught in elementary schools because of the brain's receptability to language during those years (Nash 1997). This is a conclusion that is misleading. No language teaching method can provide an adequate alternative to the natural conversational interaction with others which the brain requires to learn a language during the sensitive period. Nevertheless, if a society is committed to having its children become bilingual, then providing an eight-year course of instruction in elementary school during the sensitive period and an additional eight years of instruction in high school and university after the close of the sensitive period is likely to have successful results. But it will be because sufficient instruction and motivation will have been provided to allow most brains to accommodate in one way or another.

In conclusion, from the neural perspective, post-sensitive period language acquisition involves learning with diminished biological resources. Instructed learning during the sensitive period constitutes learning in an impoverished environment. Some learners will achieve considerable proficiency under these conditions, but the proficiency level will depend on the adaptability of each individual's brain. There is no single language teaching method that can respond adequately to such variation.

Suggestions for further reading

Damasio, A. 1994. *Descartes' Error: Emotion, Reason, and the Human Brain*. New York: Avon.
LeDoux, J. E. 1996. *The Emotional Brain*. New York: Simon and Schuster.
Schumann, J. H. 1997. *The Neurobiology of Affect in Language*. Boston: Blackwell.

Appendix

When the brain's sensory systems perceive a stimulus situation, the amygdala and the orbitofrontal cortex, based on past experience with similar stimuli, automatically appraise the stimuli for their emotional relevance and motivational significance. Both the amygdala and the orbitofrontal cortex project to the brainstem and the hypothalamus. Nuclei in the brainstem control the autonomic nervous system, which has two components – the sympathetic nervous system (SNS) and the parasympathetic nervous system (PNS). The SNS prepares the body for activity by causing dilation of the pupils, as well as inhibition of salivation, digestion and genital function. It produces an increase in respiration, heart rate, and glucose, adrenaline and noradrenaline release. It also relaxes the bladder. The PNS calms the body and promotes its nourishment and growth. In achieving these effects the PNS causes the constriction of the pupils and stimulation of salivation, digestion and genital and gall bladder function. It also slows respiration and heart rate and contracts the bladder (Bernstein, Roy, Srull and Wikens 1991). Other nuclei in the brainstem influence body position, muscle control, facial expression and movement.

The hypothalamus controls endocrine function and influences glands such as the pituitary, thyroid, adrenal medulla, pancreas, ovaries and testes. These glands synthesize hormones and peptides which influence the body through secretion into the blood stream. The pituitary regulates growth and controls the other organs of the endocrine system. The thyroid gland controls metabolic rate; the adrenal medulla, which is located on the kidneys, controls adrenaline release; the pancreas regulates insulin and glycogen levels and sugar metabolism; the ovaries and testes influence physical development, the reproductive organs and sexual behaviour (Bernstein, Roy, Srull and Wikens 1991).

Based on the appraisal that the amygdala and orbitofrontal cortex make of the stimulus situation, a state is created in the body proper via the autonomic nervous system, the endocrine system and the musculo-skeletal system. This bodily state is an emotion which is communicated back to the brain as a feeling that helps the individual decide which mental or motor action to take with regard to the stimulus (Damasio 1994). The feeling may cause the individual to attend to the stimulus, to make an effort to comprehend and acquire information contained in the stimulus situation, and to revisit the stimulus in the future to learn more. Of course the appraisal-based feeling may also have the opposite effect. It should also be noted that stimulus situations which have been frequently associated with particular appraisals and bodily states may form representations in the brain itself and thus obviate the need for the generation of a bodily state (Damasio 1994; Brothers 1995).

3 Affect in learning and memory: from alchemy to chemistry[1]

Earl W. Stevick

An ancient quest

Medieval alchemists were known for trying to take what was available and cheap and ordinary, and transform it into something rare and special and lasting. Lead into gold was their best-known project, I believe. Similarly, we language teachers try to work miracles from old newspapers, or simple objects, or line drawings and the like. Moreover, and central to what I have to say in this chapter, the alchemists' great quest was for some quick and simple piece of equipment – the so-called philosopher's stone – that would make this transformation possible. And I'm afraid we do tend to be like them in this respect also.

Let me explain what I mean. When I was getting started as a language teacher back around 1948 or 1949, the philosopher's stone was thought to be the principle of minimal contrast. A few years later it was mimicry-memorization and overlearning of basic dialogues, or perhaps it was the double-track tape recorder which allowed learners to compare their versions of a sentence with a native speaker's version. More recent candidates for the status of philosopher's stone have been cognitive code learning, computers, communicativeness, and comprehensible input. I would like to emphasize that I'm not denying the value of any of these – not the value of contrast, or of comprehensible input, or of any of the others in between. The danger in all of these, I think, was not that they had no value, but that their proponents and their new converts tended to deny the value of anything else. 'Before us nothing was' has been a slogan taken up by more than one party. The second half of the same slogan is 'and after us nothing else need ever be'.

Of late, a possible candidate for philosopher's stone is exactly the topic that I propose to address in this chapter: 'affect' – the teacher's

[1] This chapter is a further development of a paper presented at the symposium on Humanistic Language Teaching at the University of Seville in November, 1995. I am grateful to Jane Arnold, organizer of the symposium, for numerous suggestions.

sensitive awareness of learner affect. If we can only – if we *will* only manage our teaching so as to take learner affect into account, then dead materials will come to life, and lead-headed students will produce golden achievements. The age-old quest of the language teaching profession will be consummated, and we can all live happily ever after. I hope readers will forgive the slightly sardonic tone of the last sentence. I intend it only as a reminder to them, and to myself as well, not to see affect as the philosopher's stone – not to join the chorus of 'Before us nothing was'!

Three basic terms

Affect

The word 'affect' has been used in a number of overlapping but slightly different ways in the literature. Here, I shall follow Dulay, Burt and Krashen (1982) in saying that one's 'affect' toward a particular thing or action or situation or experience is how that thing or that action or that situation or that experience fits in with one's needs or purposes, and its resulting effect on one's emotions. The inclusion of emotion along with needs and purposes is not surprising when we consider that emotions are commonly responses to how one's various needs and purposes are or are not being met.

For a nonlinguistic example, a few years ago a friend gave me a copy of a book titled *Do You Panic About Maths?* (Buxton 1981). For some people, just being faced with the need to add up a column of figures or multiply 18 × 263 puts them into a situation where their need to feel competent, and their need to appear competent to others, cannot be met, and this can produce emotions like anger and discouragement, as well as physical symptoms such as nausea or sweaty palms. Or, to give an example from language learning, I once had a student whose need for clearly structured activity was not being met by the open-ended methodology we were using at the time. He was too disciplined a person to object, however, so instead of protesting, he developed a stubborn psychosomatic reaction that required a week's hospitalization.

Learning

What, then, about learning? Most generally, *evidence of* 'learning' means showing some sort of change in how we react to what is going on around us. The first time I heard the Catalan language being spoken, which was in an airport in the United States, my reaction was 'Hmm!

44

Sounds like Spanish, but it's not. Could it be Portuguese?' If I were to learn Catalan, however, my reaction would be 'Ah! That's Catalan', and then I would react in some appropriate way to whatever was being said in that language at the moment. In a nonverbal example, my first step off a curb into the street in England in 1954 was almost my last, because I looked to my left instead of to my right.

And how I am likely to react to language, or to traffic patterns, or to whatever, depends on a vast and incredibly complex collection of resources that have built up over the years inside my brain. Damasio (1994:104) speaks of 'dispositional representations', which encompass both innate knowledge and knowledge acquired by experience. So learning itself – not just *evidence* of learning, but learning itself – means making some sort of change in those internal resources in my brain. And what we call 'teaching' is then simply helping someone else to make needed changes in his or her internal resources.

Memory

These internal resources, then, are lasting but changeable – they're changeable but lasting. Change is piecemeal: as the Swahili proverb puts it, *Haba na haba hujaza kibaba.* When we're thinking about the changeable aspect of these inner resources, we talk about 'learning'. When we're focusing on their lasting aspect, on the other hand, we use a different terminology, and we talk about 'memory', or more precisely we talk about 'long-term memory'. So I can say that my nearly disastrous experience stepping off the curb in London resulted from something that was 'in my long-term memory' at the time, and that has been altered by experience. The same is true for my relationship to some of the words and grammatical structures of the Spanish language.

I am, however, going to be using this word 'memory' a little differently from how it frequently gets used. We commonly think of 'memory' as somehow containing whole pictures and whole mechanical skills and bird calls and fragrances and words and rules and so on and so on. Then we talk about 'retrieving' an address or a face or a past subjunctive verb form 'from memory'. If we can't get the whole address or the whole verb form back from memory, we may say that part of the record is somehow missing, or that it has been damaged in storage.

In fact, however, research is showing more and more clearly that the data that come in through the senses are generally not stored as whole pictures or whole sentences or whole words or whatever. Rather – and from the point of view of common sense this is hard to believe, hard to understand, even hard to think about – the new experience is broken up into an incredibly large number of incredibly small, incredibly detailed items (Spolsky 1988:392). Or as Damasio (1994:102ff.) puts it colourfully: 'Aunt Maggie as a complete person does not exist in one single site of your brain. She is distributed all over it'. These items in memory represent the so-called 'five senses', of course, but they also include many other kinds of information, among them time, purpose and emotion. And all these items – all these *kinds* of items – are interconnected with one another in the brain so as to form networks, whose heterogeneous contents are described by Damasio (1994:132, 134), and subnetworks, and subsubnetworks and so on. Within these networks, the connections between pairs of items that have occurred together oftener in past experience are stronger. Each new experience strengthens or weakens connections among many pairs of items in these networks. So when we 'remember' something, we're not so much 'retrieving' whole images from an archive as we are 'reconstructing' new images from those networks. Damasio (1994:100) explicitly rejects the folk view:

> The brain does not file Polaroid pictures ... or audiotapes ... There seem to be no permanently held pictures of anything, even miniaturized, no microfiches or microfilms, no hard copies ... Whenever we recall a given object [or whatever], we [are getting] a newly reconstructed version of the original.

A detailed discussion of the contents and operation of memory and the relationship between learning and memory can be found in Stevick (1996).

Five roles for affect in learning and memory

Affective data

Within this general view, there are at least five ways in which affect can play a role in learning. The first can be seen in connection with the Swahili proverb, meaning 'Little and little fills the bucket', which I quoted earlier. I have on several occasions incorporated it into what I was saying to an audience, and then a few minutes later invited the listeners to try to write down as much of it as they could. Under those circumstances their recall is inevitably fragmentary, and represents several degrees of abstraction. Some of the things that get reported correctly are: individual syllables such as *ba;* an entire word *haba;* 'There are lots of *a*-sounds'; the rhythm pattern; 'It rhymes'. There are of course also incorrect reports: 'The syllable *li* occurs several times'.

Next, I go on and ask my listeners how they felt about this surprise task. Replies typically range from 'It was fun' to 'It was annoying'. Finally, I ask how the task fitted in, or failed to fit in, with any of their needs and purposes. In this little informal exercise, we get a glimpse of the first of the five ways in which affect – ways in which purposes and emotions – can participate in the process of learning, in the process of changing what is in the lasting resources of the brain: namely, that affective data are themselves stored *along with* all other kinds of data, including visual or verbal, auditory or olfactory data. Hamilton (1983:77) affirms that affect is encoded to various degrees in the cognitive schemata of memory. What makes this even more interesting is that some researchers think these same items of purpose and emotion are not merely just some more parts of the networks of memory: they may actually be the parts that those networks are *organized around* (Stevick:1996). Damasio remarks that:

> because the brain is the captive audience of the body, feelings are winners among equals. And since what comes first constitutes a frame of reference for what comes after, feelings have a say on how the rest of the brain and cognition go about their business. Their influence is immense. (1994:159–160)

Affect as a source of clutter

A second role for affect is found in the processing of new information. When new data come in through the senses, what happens is apparently something like this:

1 The new data somehow *activate* corresponding items in the networks of long-term memory.
2 This activation *spreads* through the networks (Anderson 1984), and as it spreads, it produces various pictures or words or other mental images; Damasio (1994:136) writes of both *verbal* and *nonverbal* mental *images*. This spreading of activation, and the processes by which the mental images are formed are swift, they are automatic, and they are *inaccessible to our conscious observation or manipulation.*
3 The images that have been produced in this way then enter a special state. In this new state, they *are accessible to conscious observation and deliberate manipulation.* The name of this state is 'working memory' – metaphorically, 'the Worktable'. This Worktable has very limited capacity.

An example may help here. When I talked on this subject to an audience in Andalusia, I presented them with a sequence of six letters: S E V I L L. I asked my listeners what this sequence threw onto their Worktables. Most of them came up with a final A, and thus with the whole word SEVILLA. The fact that my networks supplied a final E was a simple reminder of how the operation of these networks is shaped by previous experience. Damasio (1994:181–182) refers to dispositional representations which reflect the contingencies of the real-life experiences of individuals.

But we also noticed something else. We found that those six letters produced more than just a seventh letter, or more than just a completed word. That word went on and produced for each of us a host of pictures and remembered experiences, *and* memories of how those experiences related to our several needs or purposes, *and* some appropriate emotions. That is to say, the cognitive side of input (in this example, the six letters) was placing on the Worktable not only additional cognitive material, but affective material as well.

4 Items that come to the Worktable may remain available there for a short period of time, something like 20 seconds. This means that in working memory we *hold onto* things without trying. In an everyday example, if someone tells us a phone number while we are busy addressing an envelope, we can often go ahead and finish writing the address, and then 'play back' the spoken telephone number in our heads without difficulty. The same ability is being used whenever a language student repeats a word or a sentence that someone else has said a few seconds earlier. In terminology familiar to computer users, it's as though the information were being stored in some kind of buffer that had limited capacity and limited duration.

5 All these things, once they're out on the Worktable, can be *shuffled and compared and recombined* in a wide variety of ways. For example, if Spanish *pan* and its Portuguese equivalent *pão* are on the Worktable together, a learner might compare them and notice both the similarities and the differences.

6 And what has been done on the Worktable, even though it did not come in through the senses from some outside source, can then act on long-term memory, and be stored in long-term memory, *just like the data that did come in from outside*. According to Damasio (1994:97), 'Images of what has not yet happened and may not in fact ever come to pass are no different in nature from the ones you hold of something that has already happened'. To continue the same example, the learner who had compared *pan* and *pão* might draw on this new addition to his or her internal resources in order to predict or to understand Portuguese *vão* or *tão*. This means that there is a *constant two-way traffic between the inner resources of long-term memory, and the Worktable.* (See Figure 1.)

Working memory ('the Worktable')

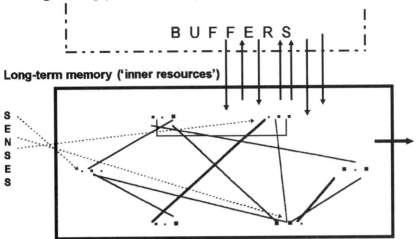

Figure 1 A contemporary view of memory

Hamilton (1983:52) is among those who have noted a two-way relation between memory and perception. Damasio (1994:196) points out the necessity that the images over which we reason be sustained for a certain interval of time. He then goes on to describe what I have been referring to as *two-way traffic*:

> What dominates the mind landscape once you are faced with a decision is the rich, broad display of knowledge about the situation that is being generated by its consideration. Images corresponding to myriad options for action and myriad possible outcomes are activated and keep being brought into focus.

These processes draw on and depend on the 'vast store of factual knowledge' represented by what in this chapter I have been calling *long-term memory.*

7 All of this applies not only to vowels and consonants and visual images and meanings like *bread* and *they go* and *such*. It applies also to affect, and it is true on a large scale as well as for small-scale items like the ones I have just mentioned. The two-way traffic between long-term memory and the Worktable may result in a connection, not just between simple forms such as *-an* and *-ão*, but also between the French language or the Korean language on the one hand, and feelings of elation and enjoyment, or of frustration, defeat and humiliation on the other hand (see MacIntyre and Gardner 1989).

49

And these feelings may in turn bring back with them all sorts of pictures and personalities and assorted tricks for defending oneself, which Hamilton (1983) calls *cognitive by-products* of affective stimuli, and all of these new elements may act as *clutter* on the Worktable so that there is less room – less capacity – for sorting out Spanish *van* and Portuguese *vão* and the like. Another, more physical kind of 'clutter' is suggested by Goleman's report that:

> [t]he prefrontal cortex is the brain region responsible for working memory. But circuits from the limbic brain to the prefrontal lobes mean that the signals of strong emotion ... can create neural static, sabotaging the ability of the prefrontal lobe to maintain working memory. (Goleman 1995:27)

Thus affect participates in the process of learning in this second way by *interfering* with it. Ehrman (1996) brings to bear her training both as language educator and as psychotherapist as she illuminates some of the ins and outs of this function of affect.

I've recently observed two other examples of negative affect interfering with intake. In these examples, however, the negative stimuli have come not from a teacher, but from the materials themselves. During the past three or four years, I've been trying to refurbish the university German that I learned back in the early 1940s. Two obvious sources of readily-available comprehensible input are the German translation of my book *Teaching and Learning Languages*, and a modern German translation of the New Testament that came into my hands about 1990. I've tried to use both of them for improving my German, but without success. The reasons are different, but they both have to do with affect. With my own book, I immediately become anxious about the content: 'Would I still say this?' 'Should I have organized things differently here?' and the like. With the New Testament, here again I'm very familiar with the content, and I take it very seriously, but my comparisons of the German text with other translations and with the Greek interlinear version have all too often shown that the German translators seem to have slanted or distorted the original, possibly to get across their own ideas of what it *ought* to say. So I find I simply can't stay focused on either one of these otherwise ideal sources for more than a minute or two.

Affect and feedback from one's own use of the language

The third way in which affect enters the learning process is in the constant reshaping of the networks of long-term memory in the learner's brain. We know that the change or the stability of those networks depends on what feedback the learner receives. In talking about feedback, however, we need to make three two-way distinctions[2]: (1) Feedback may be either *cognitive* or *affective*. Cognitive feedback answers questions like 'How satisfactorily did I get my message across?' Affective feedback, on the other hand, answers questions like 'What kind of feeling did I come away with?' (2) The source of feedback may be either *external* (from other people) or *internal* (from how one sounds to oneself). (3) Feedback may be either *positive* or *negative*. These three two-way distinctions give us $2 \times 2 \times 2 = 8$ varieties of feedback. Let us consider them one at a time.

External cognitive feedback derives its effectiveness from the learner's desire to transmit and receive ideas. When the learner perceives that communication has been full and accurate, then external cognitive feedback will be positive. When part of the message seems to have been lost or garbled, then external cognitive feedback will be negative. The function of this kind of feedback is to shape whatever features of linguistic form are message-bearing (e.g., the difference between the pronunciations of English *seat* and *sheet*; the use or omission of English plural *-s*; or the choice between the verbs *hear* and *understand*). Oliver (1995) reports a study showing how external cognitive feedback from native-speaking peers is usable and used by children learning a second language.

External affective feedback derives its effectiveness from a quite different source: from the learner's desire to identify with a particular group of people, or possibly to dissociate from some group. If the other person – that is, the person the learner is talking with – seems to be attentive, interested and enjoying the exchange, then external affective feedback will be positive. To the extent that the other person seems indifferent, bored, critical or annoyed, external affective feedback will be negative. External affective feedback influences a learner's willingness to keep on trying to communicate in spite of occasional negative feedback of the external cognitive variety.

Internal cognitive feedback is made possible by the two-way traffic between the Worktable and long-term memory, and particularly by the comparisons that take place on the Worktable. Suppose, for example, that a learner has in mind a *picture* that fully competent speakers might verbalize as 'on the desk'. Suppose further that that picture elicits from this particular learner's long-term memory at this particular time, and

---

[2] This set of distinctions is an elaboration of ideas suggested by Vigil and Oller (1976). Pulvermüller and Schumann (1994) have interesting things to say about the neurobiological basis.

places on the Worktable, the linguistic *form* 'in the desk'. That linguistic form, while it is still on the Worktable, in turn elicits from long-term memory *a second picture*[3] – a picture that corresponds to what you and I would verbalize as 'in the desk'. With these two pictures on the Worktable at the same time, the learner compares them, and notes the discrepancy. This is an example of negative internal cognitive feedback. Having noted the discrepancy, the learner may then modify the linguistic form so that the before and after pictures agree with each other. Now internal cognitive feedback becomes positive. Internal cognitive feedback, like its external counterpart, shapes only the message-bearing features of the learner's developing language.

Internal affective feedback, like internal cognitive feedback, depends on two-way traffic between the Worktable and long-term memory. The mechanism is essentially the same. The difference lies in what is being compared. In internal affective feedback, the learner is asking, 'Do I sound like a member of the community?' The criteria again include message-bearing features, but they also include non-message-bearing features: minor points of pronunciation, or of word-choice, or of idiom: (e.g., precise placement of tongue tip somewhere near the teeth; use or omission of English third-person singular present tense -*s*; choice between *do a mistake* and *make a mistake*).

Each of these types of feedback may, of course, be positive or negative, making the eight varieties, and all types are found in a number of different combinations, depending on circumstances. For example:

1 Learning one's native language. A child learning its first language in a homogeneous surrounding community receives mixed external cognitive feedback, which is to say that sometimes the child is completely understood, but often is not. This shapes the message-carrying features of the child's developing language in the direction of the message-carrying features found in the surrounding community. The same child receives overwhelmingly positive external affective feedback, which is to say that parents and others act delighted at the child's attempts to communicate, even when those attempts are not linguistically perfect. Such reaction ensures that the child will continue to try to interact through language. This continued interaction provides the raw material for increasingly reliable internal cognitive feedback, which makes it possible for the child to plan and self-correct what it is going to say. This leads to an upward spiral. The internal affective feedback that this child receives is, however, mixed

---

[3] A learner's inner resources for comprehension and for production are in constant interaction with each other, but they are not derived from a common source (Straight 1993). The former are commonly more complete and more subtle than the latter (Ard 1989:249).

– an awareness of sometimes sounding like others in the community, and sometimes not. This helps to bring the *non*-message-bearing features into conformity with the surrounding community. The end result is a new native speaker.

2 Learning in an accuracy-oriented course. A student learning a new language in an accuracy-oriented course also receives external cognitive feedback that is mixed, and this shapes the message-carrying features of the student's language in the direction of the message-carrying features found in the teacher's use of the language. But unlike the native child, the student-learner frequently receives external affective feedback that is negative: correction, mechanical tasks, evident impatience and the like. This reduces the learner's readiness to engage in any unnecessary further interaction. This reduced frequency and degree of interaction in turn inevitably mean a relatively slow-growing basis for internal cognitive feedback. The result of that is poorer performance, which in turn becomes the occasion for negative cognitive and affective external feedback from the teacher. This leads into a downward spiral.

The internal affective feedback that such a student receives is based largely on the norms of a peer group made up of other non-natives, which leaves any non-message-bearing features that had not been dwelt on by the teacher largely untouched. The end result is a graduate who controls many, or even all, of the message-bearing features of the new language, but who speaks neither idiomatically, nor comfortably, nor fluently.

3 Learning in a communication-oriented course. In a course that places most of its emphasis on communication and little or no emphasis on accuracy, a student again receives mixed external cognitive feedback, which shapes the message-carrying features in the direction of those found in the surrounding community. External affective feedback is overwhelmingly positive, and so it ensures that interaction will continue. Continuing interaction provides a basis for increasingly reliable internal cognitive feedback, which helps the learner to plan and self-correct the message-bearing features of utterances.

But internal affective feedback is again based largely on the norms of a peer group made up of other non-natives, and this leaves any unfamiliar non-message-bearing features largely untouched. The end result is a graduate who controls many, even all, of the message-bearing features of the new language, and who speaks comfortably and fluently but not natively, with residual errors of grammar, pronunciation and so on. The shorthand term for this is 'fossilization'.

Affect and playback from others' use of the language

Many people find that from time to time bits of language get played over in their minds. This phenomenon may be either voluntary or involuntary. A clear example of voluntary playback is found in Murphey's account of a Japanese woman (Murphey 1995). This woman's English was so good that Murphey asked her how many years she had spent abroad. She replied that she had never been abroad at all, but had simply exposed herself to the language at every opportunity, *and replayed it in her mind* between exposures. 'You may not control the external environment as much as you would like,' she told Murphey, 'but you are in control of the internal one. You can tune your own brain in to any channel you want, at any time.' Murphey summarized her account by saying she was 'English-hungry'.

This story is probably an example of the powerful fourth role played by affect – by purpose and emotion – in the process of learning a language. Apparently any activity, external or internal, that fed this woman's extraordinary 'English-hunger' was rewarded by positive emotions, and by awareness of having partially realized a driving purpose. Of course, we still can only guess why her 'English-hunger' was so much stronger than most people's.

Internal playback of language fragments may also be involuntary. In its auditory form, this has been called the 'din in the head' (Barber 1980). We are not clear either about the conditions under which this kind of playback takes place in general, but affect certainly will help to determine what one does with 'dinned' material once it has reached the Worktable.

Affect and the use of what one knows

The fifth effect of affect in language study is dramatically illustrated in one of the most consistently effective workshops I have ever conducted. This workshop is built around a simple three-centimetre green cuisenaire rod. I start by placing the rod in the center of an empty table-top. Then I call for two volunteers, one at a time, and I do the same thing with them but in contrasting ways. I ask each to visualize the rod as some sort of building, and to tell me about it. With the first volunteer I play the role of an interested conversation partner; with the second I am a polite but no-nonsense elicitor and evaluator of his or her linguistic output. Without exception, the first volunteer talks more fluently, talks longer, and comes up with a richer, more interesting, more personal image.

After each volunteer, I first invite the volunteer her- or himself to comment on the experience. Then I invite the audience to venture their guesses as to how the experience seemed to the volunteer, and to let the volunteer confirm or deny their guesses. The results are always the same. The first volunteer consistently reports that the experience was enjoyable, while the second consistently reports feelings of confusion, embarrassment, frustration, even anger. The final effect of affect in language learning is that it can interfere with one's ability to *draw on* the resources that are already well established in long-term memory, even in one's native language. Nor is this just a chance outcome of that particular workshop. The same effect on production by native speakers has also been documented by conventional research (Höweler 1972; Blubaugh 1969). Possibly of relevance here from a neurological point of view is Damasio's statement that 'along with negative body states, the generation of images is slow, their diversity small, and reasoning inefficient; along with positive body states the generation of images is rapid, their diversity wide, and reasoning may be fast though not necessarily efficient' (1994:147). Body states are of course influenced by one's inner, partially endocrine, reactions to the external reactions of other people.

Summary

Affect in learning and memory

In summary, then, affect is a term that refers to the purposive and emotional sides of a person's reactions to what is going on. Affect plays a very important role in learning – that is, in the process of changing a learner's inner resources so that they will become more useful. It does so in five ways: (1) Affective data are *stored* in the same memory networks with other kinds of data, and may even be the kinds of data around which those networks are organized. (2) Affective data may call up from long-term memory certain other kinds of data, and these extra data may act as *clutter* on the Worktable, using up processing capacity and keeping the kinds of data we're interested in from being processed efficiently. (3) The affective side of feedback influences the *shaping and reshaping* of the networks of long-term memory. (4) Affect is important in initiating *voluntary playback* of language, and plays a part in response to *involuntary playback*. (5) Even after data have been well stored in long-term memory, affect may still interfere with one's ability to *draw on* them.

What I have not said

Just to put my discussion into perspective, let me list three ways in which what I have said in this chapter differs from much that is sometimes said about second language acquisition:

- I have not used the expression 'short-term memory'. My reason is that when people talk about 'short-term memory', they generally seem to have in mind some sort of *stage* through which incoming data pass in a *unidirectional* flow from the senses, through short-term memory, and toward possible retention in long-term memory. By contrast, the Worktable is a *state* in which information can be, and there is *two-way* traffic between this state and long-term memory (see Stevick 1996).
- I have not used the term 'language acquisition device'. As far as I can understand, that is a cover term for whatever combination of assorted and variously interconnected features of the human nervous system enables humans and no one else to produce and understand – to control – what we call 'language'. I have not needed such a cover term in this chapter.
- I have not used the expression 'affective filter'. That metaphor apparently refers to the second of the five ways I've listed in which affect can affect learning (the 'clutter'). Unfortunately, however, the metaphor gives the impression that the effect of affect is concentrated at one particular point along the unidirectional line of flow that I just mentioned.

Implications

What, then, does this chapter suggest about affect in language teaching?

- When the subject of affectively appropriate teaching comes up, the first thing that pops into people's minds is probably a friendly, cheerful, reassuring teacher who keeps students relaxed and amused. I agree that this is certainly part of it: the feeling side.
- A second part, however, is keeping in contact with the students' needs, whether their need for a certain range of vocabulary, or for knowing what they're supposed to be doing at the moment or how they're doing in general, or for whatever. Without this needs part, the feeling part is mere sentimental manipulation. On the other hand, the needs part without the feeling part is mere mechanical manipulation.
- But to the extent we can manage both parts at the same time – the feelings and the purposes – something both beautiful and effective can emerge. This will still not be the philosopher's stone of the

alchemists, but it may enable some wonderful chemistry among the people in the classroom.

A practical postscript

The central role of affect in learning suggests that perhaps we should:

- Plan units of various sizes so that they will build toward and culminate in the learners actually using the language.
- Be sure this use is interesting, entertaining, practical or otherwise meaningful to the learners.
- Design and justify all other parts of the unit (observations of how established speakers use the language, mechanical drills, or whatever) only on the basis of the contributions they make toward the culminating activity.[4]

Suggestions for further reading

Damasio, A. 1994. *Descartes' Error: Emotion, Reason, and the Human Brain.* New York: Avon.

Ehrman, M. E. 1996. *Understanding Second Language Learning Difficulties.* Thousand Oaks, CA: Sage.

Goleman, D. 1995. *Emotional Intelligence.* New York: Bantam.

Stevick, E. W. 1996. *Memory, Meaning and Method: A View of Language Teaching (revised edition).* Boston: Heinle and Heinle.

[4] This format is derived from Widdowson (1978). It is discussed more fully in Chapter 10 of Stevick (1996).

4 Anxiety and the language learner: new insights

Rebecca L. Oxford

Introduction

True story number 1

Ressa was enrolled in a graduate program in Russian at a famous university. She did not have a strong background in speaking Russian or in understanding spoken Russian, although her reading and writing were passable in the language. Ressa had expected that her graduate program would give her the strength that she lacked in speaking and listening. However, she discovered that the Russian graduate program was taught completely in English with an emphasis on literary analysis, except for the linguistics classes on Old Church Slavonic, which had very little to do with the modern Russian language. Ressa learned that at the end of the first two years of the graduate program, without once having used the Russian language in the classroom, each graduate student was required to stand up in front of a large group of professors and peers and present in flawless Russian a one-hour lecture on some aspect of Russian literature or linguistics. If a student failed in this task, he or she would be thrown out of the program. Ressa's worry began when she found out about that requirement. She did not want to make a fool of herself in front of a mass of professors, nor did she want to face the greatest humiliation: being involuntarily released from the program. Her anxiety turned to terror; she started having nightmares about the lecture she was required to give. She gained weight and started feeling depressed as well as anxious. What she called her 'terror quotient' became so high that she quit the Russian program. She never told the professors why, and they never asked. By dropping out, she gave up possibilities of using Russian for a career.

True story number 2

Maurice studied French in high school and made a botch of it, earning failing grades in French although he was an honors student in all his other classes. He believed he was a total language failure. He did not know at the time that he had auditory processing problems. Later, Maurice needed to learn a foreign language to graduate from college. Because of his very painful experiences earlier in high school French and a new understanding of his auditory difficulties, he knew he could not learn through conventional means in the usual language classroom. His only hope, he thought, was some kind of nontraditional immersion program. Therefore, he went to Guatemala to study Spanish at a well-reputed language institute. His main goal was to learn to speak Spanish well enough to pass a proficiency test at the university back home. The stakes were high: If he did not pass ordinary classes or the language test, he could not graduate. He was already anxious when he arrived. As a visually-oriented learner who needed to see things written down, Maurice became increasingly fearful when he was placed in a mostly-auditory class in Guatemala. Halfway through the class he panicked, deciding that he needed outside help. He quickly hired two Guatemalan tutors to assist him. Maurice's anxiety finally diminished, because he was able to get the tutors to write everything down for him. With their help, he finally learned Spanish well enough to pass the examination. If he had not acted in a positive way when he recognized his growing anxiety, Maurice would have failed the crucial examination.

These are two real-life examples of language anxiety. In the first story, Ressa's anxiety caused her to drop out of the program and lose a prospective career in Russian. In the second story, Maurice recognized his anxiety and did something positive about it. Unfortunately, when learners experience language anxiety, Ressa's reaction – giving up – is more frequent than Maurice's response.

Language anxiety is fear or apprehension occurring when a learner is expected to perform in the second or foreign language (Gardner and MacIntyre 1993). This anxiety is linked directly to performing in the target language, so it is not just a general performance anxiety (Gardner and MacIntyre 1993; Horwitz, Horwitz and Cope 1986). Language anxiety ranks high among factors influencing language learning, regardless of whether the setting is informal (learning language 'on the streets') or formal (in the language classroom).

The importance of anxiety in language learning has led to significant research and discussion on the topic (Horwitz and Young 1991; Young in press; H. D. Brown 1994a; Gardner 1985; Oxford 1990a, 1990b; Reid 1995). The purpose of the current chapter is twofold: to present an updated review of the research on language anxiety and to offer classroom implications based on research findings.

Research review

This section reviews research concerning whether language anxiety is a short-term state or a lasting trait, whether it is harmful or helpful, which factors correlate with language anxiety, and how anxiety can be identified in the language classroom.

State or trait

Anxiety sometimes arises in response to a particular situation or event (*situational or state anxiety*), but it can be a major character trait. Language anxiety can start as transitory episodes of fear in a situation in which the student has to perform in the language; at this time, anxiety is simply a passing state. Ideally, language anxiety diminishes over time, as shown in studies of students learning French (e.g., Desrochers and Gardner 1981). However, language anxiety does not decrease over time for all students. If repeated occurrences cause students to associate anxiety with language performance, anxiety becomes a trait rather than a state (Gardner and MacIntyre 1993). Once language anxiety has evolved into a lasting trait, it can have pervasive effects on language learning and language performance.

Harmful anxiety

Though some language researchers assert that a positive mode of anxiety exists, most language research shows a negative relationship between anxiety and performance. The negative kind of anxiety is sometimes called 'debilitating anxiety', because it harms learners' performance in many ways, both indirectly through worry and self-doubt and directly by reducing participation and creating overt avoidance of the language. Harmful anxiety can be related to plummeting motivation, negative attitudes and beliefs, and language performance difficulties.

Gardner and MacIntyre stated that the strongest (negative) correlate of language achievement is anxiety (1993). Studies show the *negative* correlation of anxiety with the following:

- grades in language courses (Aida 1994; Horwitz 1986; Trylong 1987);
- proficiency test performance (Ganschow, Sparks, Anderson, Javorsky, Skinner and Patton 1994; Gardner, Lalonde, Moorcroft and Evers 1987);
- performance in speaking and writing tasks (Trylong 1987; Young 1986);
- self-confidence in language learning (MacIntyre and Gardner 1991; Gardner and MacIntyre 1993);
- self-esteem, i.e., the judgment of one's own worth (Horwitz, Horwitz and Cope 1986; Price 1991; Scarcella and Oxford 1992).

The relationship between language anxiety and language performance is not simple. Young (1991) explained that sometimes language anxiety is negatively related to one skill and not another. Ganschow, Sparks, Anderson, Javorsky, Skiller and Patton (1994) suggested that high anxiety might be a *result* of language learning problems rather than the *cause*.

Helpful anxiety

Some research suggested that language anxiety was actually 'helpful' or 'facilitating' in some ways, such as keeping students alert (Scovel 1978). Helpful anxiety has been shown in a few studies to be related to:

- high language proficiency and self-confidence among a hand-picked group of excellent language learners (Ehrman and Oxford 1995);
- oral production of difficult English structures among native Arabic-speakers and Spanish-speakers (Kleinmann 1977);
- good grades in language classes for students in regular French, German, and Spanish classes but not for students in audiolingual classes (Chastain 1975).

Language researchers hold different views about the existence or significance of helpful anxiety. Horwitz (1990) stated that anxiety is only helpful for very simple learning tasks, but not with more complicated learning such as language learning. Young (1992) interviewed language learning experts Rardin, Omaggio Hadley, Terrell and Krashen about their views on the helpfulness of language anxiety. Rardin responded that a positive aspect of anxiety operates all the time, but we only notice when a negative imbalance occurs. Omaggio Hadley suggested that a certain amount of tension might be useful for language learning, but she refused to term this tension 'anxiety'. Likewise, Terrell preferred to call such tension 'attention' rather than 'anxiety'. Krashen contended that there is no helpful aspect to anxiety in language acquisition, which almost by definition requires that anxiety be zero, but that helpful anxiety might exist for language tasks in formal language learning situations. Clearly, the jury is still out concerning the existence of helpful anxiety.

Correlates of language anxiety

Correlates of language anxiety range from highly personal (such as self-esteem) to procedural (such as classroom activities and methods).

Self-esteem

Self-esteem is a self-judgment of worth or value, based on feelings of efficacy, a sense of interacting effectively with one's own environment. Efficacy implies that some degree of control exists within oneself. Unsuccessful language learners often have lower self-esteem than successful language learners (Price 1991). Whether this affects their overall self-esteem or only their situational self-esteem partly depends on how important language learning is to the individuals involved. Self-esteem is vulnerable when the learner perceives himself or herself as very competent in the native language and totally inadequate or limited in the target language (Price 1991). Horwitz, Horwitz and Cope (1986) noted that foreign language learning can cause a threat to self-esteem by depriving learners of their normal means of communication, their freedom to make errors, and their ability to behave like normal people. Among highly anxious language students, those with high self-esteem might handle their anxiety better than those with low self-esteem, resulting in better performance. Like anxiety, self-esteem can be a trait (an inherent personality characteristic) or a state (related to a particular situation). A person can feel good about himself or herself globally or generally, yet at the same time experience low self-esteem in a particular situation or environment (Scarcella and Oxford 1992).

Tolerance of ambiguity

Tolerance of ambiguity is the acceptance of confusing situations. Second language learning has a great deal of ambiguity about meanings, referents and pronunciation, and this can often raise language anxiety. Therefore, a degree of ambiguity-tolerance is essential for language learners. Students who are able to tolerate moderate levels of confusion are likely to persist longer in language learning than students who are overly frightened by the ambiguities inherent in learning a new language (Chapelle and Roberts 1986).

Risk-taking

Students who are highly anxious about the frequent ambiguities of language learning often suffer reduced risk-taking ability. It is more useful for language learners to take moderate but intelligent risks, such as guessing meanings based on background knowledge and speaking up despite the possibility of making occasional mistakes, rather than taking no risks at all or taking extreme, uninformed risks (Oxford 1990a, 1990b; H. D. Brown 1994a). Language students who fear ambiguity or whose self-esteem is low, frequently 'freeze up', allowing their inhibitions to take over completely (Beebe 1983). Decreases in risk-taking frequently occur when students feel extreme discomfort in the language classroom (Ely 1986). Students who avoid risks are stalled by actual or anticipated criticism from others or by self-criticism that they themselves supply. When they do not have enough practice, their language development becomes seriously stunted.

Competitiveness

Using diary studies of language learners, Bailey (1983) asserted that competitiveness can lead to language anxiety. This happens when language learners compare themselves to others or to an idealized self-image, which they can rarely attain. Scarcella and Oxford (1992) agreed that competitiveness can relate to language anxiety but suggested that this link does not occur in all students. Some students, particularly those in competitive cultures, thrive on competition. The emotional import of competitiveness for a given individual depends on the learning style preferences of the student, the precise nature of the competition, and the demands and rewards of the environment.

Social anxiety

Social anxiety can include speech anxiety, shyness, stage fright, embarrassment, social-evaluative anxiety and communication apprehension (Leary 1983). Social anxiety occurs along with the prospect or actual presence of interpersonal evaluation. People who are highly concerned about others' evaluations of them – and we might assume these to be people with shaky self-esteem and/or strong external locus of control (the learner's belief that his or own performance is controlled by external factors) – tend to act in ways that minimize the likelihood of negative assessments. These people are more likely to avoid or withdraw from social situations in which others might view them negatively. When they relate to others, they often fail to take the initiative or participate only minimally in conversations (Aida 1994). In the language classroom, this is observable in behaviors such as keeping silent, responding only when necessary, being passive, and avoiding class entirely. Communication apprehension is defined as a person's level of anxiety associated with either real or anticipated communication with another person or persons (McCroskey 1984). People who suffer from communication apprehension are more reluctant to converse or interact with others; therefore, they tend to avoid communication or withdraw from it as soon as possible. McCroskey, Fayer and Richmond (1985) and Foss and Reitzel (1988) observed communication apprehension in ESL/EFL classrooms.

Test anxiety

Test anxiety can be part of social anxiety, particularly in an evaluative situation where the student is asked to communicate in the target language. However, test anxiety can occur in noncommunicative situations, too. Test anxiety is 'the tendency to become alarmed about the consequences of inadequate performance on a test or other evaluation' (Sarason 1984), regardless of whether the fears are realistic. Students with test anxiety frequently experience cognitive interference (Sarason 1984) and have a difficult time focusing on the task at hand (Aida 1994).

Identity and culture shock

Identification with a language group or target culture implies that the learner is an insider, a member of the 'club' of French, Spanish, German or Chinese speakers. Young (1992) suggested that anxiety is lower (that is, the affective filter is reduced) if a student feels such identification, and anxiety is higher if the student does not identify with the language group. Paradoxically, for other learners anxiety can arise because of over-identification with the language group and the concurrent feeling of loss of personal identity. This idea is similar to Guiora's (1972) theory of language ego and Clarke's (1976) theory of clash of consciousness.

Anxiety about losing one's own identity can be part of culture shock. Culture shock is defined as 'a form of anxiety that results from the loss of commonly perceived and understood signs and symbols of social intercourse' (Adler 1987:25). Culture shock can involve some or all of these symptoms: emotional regression, physical illness, panic, anger, hopelessness, self-pity, lack of confidence, indecision, sadness, alienation, a sense of deception, a perception of 'reduced personality', and glorification of one's own native culture. However, if handled effectively, culture shock can become a cross-cultural learning opportunity involving increased cultural awareness, increased self-awareness and reintegration of personality (Adler 1987).

Beliefs

Research suggests that the beliefs of both learners and instructors are linked to language anxiety (and possibly to learner performance through instructors' classroom procedures and students' responses to those procedures, discussed later). Foreign language learners in Horwitz's (1988) study believed that they should be able to speak with great accuracy and an excellent accent, language learning consists mainly of translation from English, two years is long enough to become fluent, and some people could learn languages more easily than others. Some of these beliefs were extremely unrealistic and led to language anxiety. Many language teachers maintain the belief that they should be directive, authoritarian and even intimidating and that they must correct every error. However, these behaviors can lead to language anxiety (Young 1991).

Classroom activities and methods

Koch and Terrell (1991) found that more than half of their subjects reported oral skits and oral presentations in front of the class as the most anxiety-producing activities and that oral quizzes and being called on to respond orally were also anxiety-producing. Similar results were found by Horwitz and Young (1991) and Young (in press). Yet speaking tasks are not the only anxiety triggers. For some language students, writing, reading or listening can also create fear, depending on the student (see Horwitz and Young 1991; Scarcella and Oxford 1992). Some teaching methods, such as Community Language Learning, can reduce language anxiety for many learners (Samimy and Rardin 1994).

Instructor-learner interactions

Many researchers relate language anxiety to instructor–learner interactions (Horwitz, Horwitz and Cope 1986; Koch and Terrell 1991; Price 1991; Scarcella and Oxford 1992; Young 1990). Harsh error correction, ridicule and the uncomfortable handling of mistakes in front of a class are among the most important instructor–learner interaction issues related to language anxiety. An important aspect of instructor–learner interaction has frequently been overlooked: style conflicts between teachers and students. Teacher–student learning style conflicts have been shown to relate to lower grades for students and to contribute to stress in the classroom (Oxford, Ehrman, and Lavine 1991).

Ways to identify language anxiety

Teachers and researchers might sometimes be able to infer language anxiety through tests of general anxiety. However, this practice is not recommended (Gardner and MacIntyre 1993) because researchers view language anxiety as a specific phenomenon that is better assessed directly. A number of instruments exist, the best known of which is the 'Foreign Language Classroom Anxiety Scale' or FLCAS, by Horwitz (1986). The FLCAS was developed to capture the specific anxiety reaction of a student to a foreign language situation. This instrument integrates three related anxieties – communication apprehension, test anxiety, and fear of negative evaluation – but is more than the sum of these parts (Aida 1994; Horwitz, Horwitz, and Cope 1986). Language anxiety is often readily observable even without an instrument like the FLCAS. However, behaviors vary across cultures, and what might seem like anxious behavior in one culture might be normal behavior in another culture. The following are likely signs of language anxiety.

- General avoidance: 'Forgetting' the answer, showing carelessness, cutting class, coming late, arriving unprepared, low levels of verbal production, lack of volunteering in class, seeming inability to answer even the simplest questions.
- Physical actions: Squirming, fidgeting, playing with hair or clothing, nervously touching objects, stuttering or stammering, displaying jittery behavior, being unable to reproduce the sounds or intonation of the target language even after repeated practice.
- Physical symptoms: Complaining about a headache, experiencing tight muscles, feeling unexplained pain or tension in any part of the body.
- Other signs which might reflect language anxiety, depending on the culture: overstudying, perfectionism, social avoidance, conversational withdrawal, lack of eye contact, hostility, monosyllabic or noncommittal responses, image protection or masking behaviors (exaggerated smiling, laughing, nodding, joking), failing to interrupt when it would be natural to do so, excessive competitiveness, excessive self-effacement and self-criticism ('I am so stupid').

Classroom implications

After diagnosing anxious behavior, language teachers can act to reduce anxiety, depending on students' needs and cultural background. Teachers can use any or all of the following suggestions for diminishing language anxiety.

- Help students understand that language anxiety episodes can be transient and do not inevitably develop into a lasting problem.
- Boost the self-esteem and self-confidence of students for whom language anxiety has already become a long-term trait by providing multiple opportunities for classroom success in the language.
- Encourage moderate risk-taking and tolerance of ambiguity in a comfortable, non-threatening environment.
- Reduce the competition present in the classroom.
- Be very clear about classroom goals and help students develop strategies to meet those goals.
- Give students permission to use the language with less than perfect performance.
- Encourage students to relax through music, laughter or games.
- Use fair tests with unambiguous, familiar item types.
- Help students realistically assess their performance.
- Give rewards that are meaningful to students and that help support language use.
- Provide activities that address varied learning styles and strategies in the classroom.
- Enable students to recognize symptoms of anxiety and identify anxiety-maintaining beliefs.
- Help students practice positive self-talk (self-encouragement) and cognitive 'reframing' of negative or irrational ideas.

Using suggestions such as these, teachers can enable students to deal more effectively with language anxiety. When teachers help their students reduce language anxiety, situations such as Ressa's and Maurice's can be halted before becoming full-blown disasters. Students like Ressa and Maurice – and many others – can be spared the pain of severe language anxiety and can experience what it means to succeed in the language classroom.

5 Ego boundaries and tolerance of ambiguity in second language learning

Madeline Ehrman

Two kinds of student

When they begin their intensive language training at the Foreign Service Institute (FSI), students receive a consultation about their language learning styles. In the course of these interviews, I have noticed two approaches to learning pronunciation. Many, even most, students rely heavily on explanations of articulatory phonetics and extensive drilling to achieve an approximation of native pronunciation and feel deprived when their language programs lack sufficient conscious emphasis on improving pronunciation often and early. A smaller number of other students are rather easygoing about pronunciation and expect it to take care of itself without much direct attention. For most of them, this expectation is fulfilled.[1]

This distinction between student types fairly consistently reflects a fundamental personality difference that affects nearly all of their learning. It relates to thickness or thinness of the student's *ego boundaries*, a concept which, while coming from psychoanalytic theory (Hartmann 1991), is also characteristic of people in general. I define it operationally as the *degree to which individuals tend to compartmentalize their experience*. The need to compartmentalize experience can affect internal conceptual categories, such as thought vs. feeling or receptivity to intuitive insights. It also affects *receptivity to outside influences*, such as new languages and cultures. Thickness of ego boundaries has effects on students' ability to learn by osmosis, to make use of teachers or other native speakers as models with which to identify, to permit development of a target language persona, and above all to tolerate ambiguity.

---

[1] FSI is the training bureau of the US Department of State, like the foreign ministry in many countries; it offers full-time intensive training in roughly 60 languages to members of the US foreign affairs community. Programs do not aim to produce native-like speakers but rather speakers who are professionally functional in the language and culture of the country to which they are assigned.

The student who ignores pronunciation drilling in favor of letting pronunciation take care of itself is likely to have relatively thin ego boundaries and to rely on strategies of receptivity to outside influence. The other student is more likely to have thick boundaries, reject 'osmosis' learning, and rely on such conscious processes as analysis, formal explanations and drilling. (Some 'thin boundary' types also call for pronunciation drills because they do not trust their less conscious processes which, after all, are seldom validated in academic settings.)

My formal research (Ehrman 1993, 1994; Ehrman and Oxford 1995) has found that thin boundary students tend to perform somewhat better on the FSI end-of-training oral interview, which tests oral production, interactive comprehension and reading ability through an interaction with a testing team, at least one member of which is a native speaker interlocutor. However, though thin boundary students have some statistical advantage, many thick boundary students do very well, and quite a few thin boundary students have a very difficult time with both training and testing. In fact, on the Hartmann Boundary Questionnaire (HBQ, Hartmann 1991), a self-report instrument which I use to assess ego boundary thickness, FSI students average considerably 'thicker' than Hartmann's more generally representative sample, and yet they achieve notable amounts of language learning in rather short periods of time, so preference for clear compartmentalization of experience alone is not particularly predictive of learning difficulty, nor is receptivity alone a guarantee of success.

What aspects of this model, then, account for learning success, and how can the concept of ego boundaries help us enhance the learning of all our students? I believe it is the relationship between flexibility of ego boundaries and tolerance of ambiguity.

What do we mean by thick and thin ego boundaries?

Ego and ego boundaries

As a result of his work with people who suffer from nightmares, Ernest Hartmann (1991) proposed a bipolar scale based on the degree to which one keeps aspects of one's personal experience separate; he used the psychoanalytic term 'ego boundary' to represent this construct. By 'ego' is meant a system of mental operations, cognitive and affective, that constitute an individual's sense of self, rather than a perceivable object. Gardner Murphy says:

> ... we can quite conveniently ... use the term 'ego' to describe the processes by which [one's] picture of the self is magnified,

> inflated, protected by socially active dynamic functions. Ego
> mediates between drives and environment; it *uses* the environ-
> ment. (1968:32, emphasis in original)

In order to 'mediate' between internal drives (unconscious wishes,
needs, fantasies) and the external environment, the ego is to some
degree apart from both and at the same time is influenced by both. The
separation is maintained by boundaries that delineate 'me' from 'not
me', thinking from feeling, fantasy from reality and so on. The ego is at
the same time influenced both by unconscious processes such as wishes,
unconscious construals of life events, and intuitions and by such
external phenomena as personal relationships, education (formal and
informal) and life experiences. The degree to which one's conscious ego
is amenable to such influences is part of the ego boundary construct.
Boundaries help maintain the ego's autonomy from both internal drives
and the environment (Rapaport 1958). Rapaport points out, however,
these two types of autonomy are always relative to each other and
therefore never reach the logical extremes of complete autonomy from
'instinctual' drives or environment.

Ego boundaries relate to amount of fluidity in mental categories,
especially those that relate to one's identity, one's relation with other
people and other ways of perceiving the world. Too much such fluidity
can be pathological; some psychological disorders involve an inability
to maintain a stable sense of identity, for instance. However, very thin
ego boundaries can also be associated with great sensitivity and
creativity (Levin 1990; Hartmann 1991). Among individuals within one
or two standard deviations above Hartmann's general population
means, Ehrman (1993, 1996; Ehrman and Oxford 1995) has found
certain advantages for communicative second language acquisition, as
long as the student has the means to impose cognitive structure on his
or her experience. Contrariwise, too much stability of identity and
compartmentalization can result in very constricted lives with little
adaptive flexibility, including dealing with new languages and cultures.
Most people vary within a range of normal function, and that is what
we are describing here.

Individuals can have a variety of sub-personalities that are related to
different roles they play. Most have some amount of consistency across
roles and a set of stable 'selves' based on firm beliefs, attitudes and
values. However, in certain social situations, they might well undertake
sharply differing approaches and have a variety of transient 'selves'
(Schein 1986) or repertoire of social identities. Peirce (1995), for
example, describes the importance of different situations for senses of
the self (social identities) and for motivation to interact in a foreign

language. She emphasizes the effects of differential power between interlocutors.

What are people at the ends of Hartmann's ego boundary continuum like?

At one extreme of Hartmann's continuum are *thick ego boundaries*, characterized by tendencies to make clear separations among internal states (such as states of wakefulness) and to make clear delineations among categories in daily life. People who have generally thick boundaries tend to be relatively meticulous and orderly, and they are often relatively unreceptive to new information. In Hartmann's sample of people with a range of ego boundary thickness, the prototypes for thick boundary people were naval officers (Hartmann 1991). This is not to say that people with 'thick' boundaries lack the ability to adapt. In fact, many people who tune out much of the world's ambiguity lead well adapted, successful lives: many of them are the businessmen, lawyers, and other bricklayers of our society. These people, however, are likely to feel some resistance to learning material that requires them to tolerate ambiguity, suspend identity boundaries or 'regress in the service of the ego' (e.g., through role playing and the like).

In contrast, people whose style falls at the *thin boundary* end of the continuum tend to make few distinctions among internal states, so that, for instance, thinking and feeling are not necessarily always distinct processes. Such people are often open to their own intuition and trust it; they may profess to have had extrasensory perception experiences. Some thin boundary people accept almost all aspects of their experience in the world – almost as if they had no skin – and can become overwhelmed by it all. They are often active in the arts or other forms of creativity. Hartmann's prototypes are art students and psychotherapists. People with thin ego boundaries are not necessarily more functional than those with thick boundaries, though they may not only tolerate but embrace ambiguity. Unless they accompany their flexibility with some element of internal structure, they can seem 'flaky' and out of touch. Though they may 'play' comfortably with the subject matter they are learning or engage readily with others, they may have difficulty focusing on problems and thus not use analytic strategies or appropriate forethought. In their own way, they can be as rigid as their opposites, insisting that there are no blacks and whites, only shades of grey.

Both types contribute to society, thick boundary people through such occupations as engineering, certain branches of medicine, law enforcement and business, for instance, and thin boundary people particularly in the arts, helping professions like social work, or the teaching of literature, for instance. Hartmann (1991) found younger people and females to have somewhat thinner boundaries than older people and males.

Ego boundary preference as a learning style

As a personality disposition, thickness or thinness of ego boundaries is a kind of personal style: an enduring preference and predilection for processing one's experience in consistent ways. Many teachers are now familiar with learning styles (see Reid 1995 and this volume) like sequential vs. random processing, extraversion-introversion, auditory-kinesthetic-visual intake, or the various approaches to learning that are referred to as 'multiple intelligences' (Gardner 1983). Learning styles are not ordinarily the same as abilities, though 'multiple intelligences' and field independence (Witkin and Goodenough 1981) are linked in theory with specific abilities. For most individuals, preferred processing styles are *comfort zones* which suggest probabilities of a certain kind of behavior. Behavior and strategies associated with a stylistic preference can be adapted to accommodate circumstances (Ehrman 1995, 1996).

It seems useful to view the ego boundary construct as a kind of personality-based learning style that is fairly fundamental to the individual's personality structure. For example, thick boundaries correlate moderately with sensing, thinking and judging on the Myers-Briggs Type Indicator (Myers and McCaulley 1985), another personality model; thin boundaries correlate with intuition, feeling, and perceiving.

With thick ego boundaries, the student is likely to want a clearly structured curriculum, seek conscious approaches to learning, display some discomfort with role-playing and similar suspensions of everyday identity and reject ambiguity. On the other hand, adults, particularly those who have achieved educational and professional success, have usually learned to adopt a variety of coping strategies. Successful thick boundary students can 'thin down' their boundaries temporarily through a phenomenon called 'regression in the service of the ego', addressed below.

Students with thin boundaries tend to enjoy content-based learning where the focus is on what is being said more than how it is said. They often like to have everything available at once so they can get a sense of how everything relates. Many of them prefer non-linear ('random') approaches to learning and enjoy unexpected learning events. They also have to learn coping strategies to prevent what they take in from becoming a kind of amorphous ocean of experience. Successful thin boundary students can impose structure and hierarchy on what they take in through a process that Piaget (1967, 1973) called 'accommodation'.

Two students

To give an idea of what thick- and thin-boundary students might be like in a classroom, we can look at Keith and Jenny, who are typical of adult thick and thin boundary students. Both perform at a roughly average level on a test of language learning aptitude, but both are having trouble in their language class (these two cases are adapted from Ehrman 1993, 1996).

> **Keith** (thick ego boundaries) wants to know the grammar first, do exercises and be well prepared before he engages in the more communicative activities his language class requires. He wants his tasks clearly defined. He is spending many, many hours on his studies and feels guilty when he takes time off, because he feels strongly that he should do perfect work. His difficulty comes especially in the constant unstructured class activities like debates or round-robin story-telling, where it is certain that language he hasn't learned will come up. He majored in engineering, and this is his first language learning attempt. (Ehrman 1996:109)

> **Jenny** (thin ego boundaries) really likes learning through content-based materials. She had some previous exposure to another language abroad and enjoyed learning it 'by the seat of her pants'. She finds it disruptive when the flow of content is stopped by unfamiliar structure or vocabulary. She wants everything she is to learn to be out on the table at once, so that she can try to integrate it. Her difficulty can be summarized as 'things just mush', and she gets overloaded quickly. She was a literature major. (Ehrman 1996:109)

Hartmann himself suggested that thinner boundaries might be helpful when an individual needs to make shifts of mental set or try new ways of thinking. He specified philosophy, theoretical mathematics and learning foreign languages 'as native speakers do' (Hartmann 1991 221). As mentioned above, my research findings confirm Hartmann's hypothesis in a general way for performance on an oral interview and for professional reading. Why, then, is Jenny having trouble? The difficulty is that she lacks skills related to making discriminations, chunking down information and organizing what she takes in. Thin boundaries help one get information in and make it easier to tolerate the contradictions that are likely to occur in large masses of information. Keith runs into trouble because he tends not to let much enter his mental systems in the first place if it is likely to upset his schema of the world.

Assessing ego boundary thickness

When I work with students, I make use of the Hartmann Boundary Questionnaire (HBQ, Hartmann 1991). It has twelve subscales and a total score. The subscales relate to boundaries (1) between states of wakefulness, (2) between thinking and feeling, (3) among memories of earlier ages, as well as to (4) experiences of ESP, (5) sensitivity to slights, (6) interpersonal receptivity, (7) need for neat surroundings, (8) preference for sharp or fuzzy lines in visual images, (9) opinions about various age groups, (10) lines of authority, (11) ethnic groups, and (12) abstractions like beauty or truth. Subscales 1–4 relate to boundaries among states of mind (*internal*); subscales 7–12 represent boundaries between the individual and the outside world (*external*).

The statistics suggest that the subscales that are most predictive of communicative language learning success are high (thin) scores on 7 (tolerance of messiness in surroundings – I call it the 'messy desk' subscale) and 8 (preference of loose, even flowing clothing and visual images with somewhat blurred delineations). A pattern of thin external boundaries and average to thick internal boundaries usually suggests a learner who does well, at least in FSI classrooms, with a minimum of anxiety. I would anticipate that such a learner would also be likely to do well at non-classroom learning. Thick external boundaries and thin internal ones sometimes suggest students who are in fact quite vulnerable to anxiety but use rejection of outside influence to defend themselves from it. This kind of student may well reject almost all linguistic and cultural influence beyond rules, drills and use of language limited to task objectives.

What do we mean by 'tolerance of ambiguity'?

> Language learning for real communicative use, especially in situations which demand structural and lexical precision, is an extremely demanding whole-person engagement. It requires the learner to cope with information gaps, unexpected language and situations, new cultural norms, and substantial uncertainty. It is highly interpersonal, which is in itself fraught with ambiguities and unpredictabilities. Language is composed of symbols, which are abstract and often hard to pin down. Concepts and expressions in any two languages do not relate one-to-one. (Ehrman 1996:119)

Given these complexities, it makes sense that tolerance of ambiguity is crucial to success in language learning aimed at real communicative use. Students like Keith who lack ambiguity tolerance tend to have a great deal of trouble in language learning, both formal and informal.

Tolerance of ambiguity can be viewed as made up of three levels of function. The first level is to permit information to enter one's conceptual schema in the first place. Thick ego boundaries, especially external ones, can interfere at this level, so that a learner like Keith fails to become aware of the new information, or receives it only superficially, without linking it to other knowledge. In Ehrman (1993, 1996) I called this level *intake*.

What most people think of as tolerance of ambiguity constitutes the second level; I call it *tolerance of ambiguity proper* (Ehrman 1993, 1996). At this level, intake has been successfully accomplished, necessitating that the learner deal with contradictions and incomplete information or incomplete constructs. This is often very difficult for thick-boundary learners. When thin-boundary people reach this point, they may become overwhelmed with all the information and treat it all as equally valid or as if it were all at an equal level of abstraction or concreteness.

At the third level the learner makes discriminations, sets priorities among competing concepts, and develops hierarchies of information in terms of level of abstraction. These activities usually entail integration of the new information with existing schemata to change the latter and make something new, that did not exist before. Borrowing from Piaget (1967), I call this level *accommodation*.

Piaget contrasts accommodation, alteration of schemata to account for experience, with *assimilation*, in which perception of the new information is changed so that it is consistent with existing mental constructs. Inasmuch as learners also may make changes in the concepts they have taken in, there is always some assimilation as well as accommodation. However, assimilation can also serve as a way to defend oneself from ambiguity and new learning, through claiming that the new is really like the old.

The three levels of tolerance of ambiguity can be summarized as follows:

> *Intake*: letting it in; *Tolerance of ambiguity proper*: accepting contradictions and incomplete information; *Accommodation*: making distinctions, setting priorities, restructuring cognitive schemata.

John's behavior in the classroom illustrates difficulties at the intake level:

> When the curriculum follows the textbook closely, John works steadily and systematically. He readily performs the drills and exercises that fill the text. When asked to participate in more free-form activities like story-telling or role-plays, John grumbles and stumbles. He becomes upset when too much new vocabulary is introduced in the course of an hour's activities, and he regularly mistranslates because he assumes that every English word will have a close equivalent in the new language. He takes almost no conversational risks in the target language (Ehrman 1996:120).

Kelly seems to run into trouble with tolerance of ambiguity proper in listening comprehension. She lets the information in, but then she cannot retain it.

> I review words in the book or from my flashcards first before I listen to the tapes. For grammar, I do the same kind of thing: I look at the patterns in the book, then I do oral drills. Listening comprehension in class is hard, especially when there is no visual support. I can't keep all the different things I hear in my mind. If you just gave me a list, that would be OK, I could remember that, but when it's ideas and they don't hang together, then I start feeling that it's all a kind of mess and I lose interest in the task. (Ehrman 1996:121).

As for Jenny, her skills at the middle level (tolerating contradictions and incomplete information) are well developed. Her difficulty is at the level of accommodation. She finds it difficult to decide what to focus on, to extract data out from her internal ocean of concepts, to organize her knowledge, and successfully reconstruct her cognitions.

What is the relationship of ego boundaries to tolerance of ambiguity?

Flexible ego boundaries are related to disinhibition and potentially to openness to unconscious processes; they tend to promote empathy and the ability to take in another language and culture. Individuals vary in the amount of such openness. Rigidity in mental categories is clearly related to tolerance of ambiguity: if mental categories must be kept apart, there is likely to be little room for overlapping or apparently contradictory concepts in one place. In contrast, those who tolerate ambiguity are likely to have much less difficulty with experiencing themselves in a variety of ways and seeing the world through the eyes of other people (Ehrman 1993, 1996; Hartmann 1991).

What are regression and regression in the service of the ego?

When a small child is faced with a new sibling and experiences envy of the attention the newcomer receives, it often happens that the older child evinces behaviors that the parents had thought he or she had outgrown, such as thumb sucking, lap-seeking, or tantrums. This kind of behavior is called 'regression'. It can occur at any age. Regression often entails the loss of some of the structures and controls we develop to meet the demands of our social settings; it is thus often a form of disinhibition and may be expressed in emotional reactions and displays of temper. Regression can also be cognitive, as in the case of a student who blanks out in class. Regressive experiences can be linked with boundary disturbances: Lofgren (1975) states, 'Encountering a complex and perplexing situation probably involves a temptation to regression. ... regression means a move in the direction of malfunctioning [inter-personal] boundaries ...' (1975:186).

   Most of us experience some form of 'regression' in response to intense stress, and we usually find it embarrassing. However, creative endeavor can often be enhanced by a reduction in our socialized inhibitions, as can certain kinds of empathy. Much creative endeavor benefits from increased expression of unconscious processes, whether in the arts or in the sciences or in everyday life. For instance, poetry represents verbal expression of symbolic content full of the kinds of metaphor common in unconscious processes; scientific insight often is the result of extensive unconscious processing that may come to mind in the form of an image (see Arnold this volume); and solutions to workaday problems some-times come to us because of an association with something that seems at first completely unrelated. Unconscious material may reach conscious-ness accompanied by other impulse-related material that is socially uncomfortable. However, the process serves mature and constructive goals, which are hypothesized to be under ego control. For this reason, this phenomenon is called 'regression in the service of the ego' (Kris 1952).

   Communicative language learning is another activity in which a certain amount of reduction in psychic controls and disinhibition can be helpful. As mentioned above, investigation of personality dimensions of language learning has suggested a certain advantage for flexible psychic ('ego') boundaries between individuals and the world they live in. Such flexibility may be expressed in tolerance of less-than-neat surroundings or loose lines of authority. It can also appear in an ability to act and feel temporarily as if one were someone else who experiences the world in a very different way, a kind of cross-cultural empathy (Ehrman 1993,

1996). Relaxation of strict control over thoughts and feelings, the ability to make associations between phenomena, and relaxation of one's identity boundaries are all related to lower inhibition and constructive regression. I therefore suggest that *what thin boundary learners bring to the language learning process is a ready ability to tap regression in the service of the ego.*

One important application of regression in the service of the ego is second language social identity formation. Berger and Luckmann (1966) suggest that social interactions disrupt existing schemata for individuals and thus require cognitive and affective adaptation. This process leads to some amount of reconstruction of the self. Foster (1992) points out the difficulties entailed by established identity rooted in a first language for interaction in a second language. Use of a second language as a medium of social interaction occasions reconstruction of the self to incorporate a new identity in terms of the second language and its culture. In fact, Peirce (1995) addresses the necessity for multiple social identities in a second language for people living in a new culture. To accept such a challenge to one's pre-established concepts of self necessitates letting oneself be 'someone else' at least on a temporary basis, a lifting of adult reality testing, and a form of regression. To the degree that such regressive acceptance of a kind of fantasy of being someone else is adaptive – that is, it contributes to language learning and new ways of interaction with others – it is regression in the service of the ego, and not simply regression in defense against anxiety.

What is the relationship among accommodation, tolerance of ambiguity and language learning?

The most effective and mature levels of accommodation entail substantial tolerance of ambiguity and the ability to cope with strong feelings engendered by what individuals may experience as assaults on their construals of the world and of self. Mandler (1982) suggests that being forced to accommodate in the face of too much new information or contradiction may lead to strong affective reactions, positive or negative depending on the success of the accommodation.

A particularly relevant form of such accommodation is what Guiora (1981, 1984) calls language ego development; he is especially aware of the affective dimension and its effect on one's ability to accommodate one's schemata. He describes the process as follows:

> The task of learning a new language is a profoundly unsettling psychological proposition ... What is required of the learner is

not only a cognitive shift in terms of vocabulary, grammar, and syntax, but something much more formidable: the necessity to recategorize information ... that inevitably must lead to a demand to ... [re]conceptualize, and ultimately experience, events in and around us ... It is here that *individual* differences in the psychological defense systems and flexibilities will be reflected in a capacity (or willingness) to attempt the shifting ... without fear of losing the grip on the psychological integrity for which native language serves as such a powerful anchor. (Guiora 1984:8, emphasis in original)

Guiora relates this emotionally charged accommodation process to tolerance of ambiguity when he writes, 'The capacity to tolerate ambiguities and uncertainties is ... essential to the understanding of the other. The capacity to entertain an alternate hypothesis is the mark of the successful blend of cognitive and affective templates that can lead to new discoveries' (1981:171).

What is the role of the affective domain?

Disruptions of existing mental constructs, particularly those relating to oneself, often entail strong feelings. Simply the necessity of acknowledging ignorance and imperfection, let alone the fear that one will be inadequate to fill the gaps, are sufficient reasons to feel distress (Bernstein 1989; Curran 1972; Stevick 1980; Sussman 1989). Interpersonally, learners face the risk of shame before others (and self) for perceived inadequacy (Elson 1989; Morrison 1989). Cohler (1989) suggests that lasting effects of relationships within one's family of origin can bring about anxiety about competition and the envy of classmates, and in response to this anxiety, some students may limit their cognitive capacity or set up barriers to new input. In fact, such barriers may be possibly an affective source of certain thick boundary behavior. For that matter, simply the threat entailed by new input may be sufficient to bring about defensive behavior, either through thick boundaries that let in little or nothing, or through thin ones that let everything in, all of it equally important or unimportant, thus making potentially painful choices unnecessary.

Second language learning need not be only a threat to identity and other internal constructs. Greenson suggests that 'A new language offers an opportunity for the establishment of a new self-portrait' (1978a:38), particularly when the old self-image is laden with negative feelings. In this article, Greenson describes a patient who used her learning of

English as a way to set aside painful old experiences from her native language and incorporate new and more positive experiences of other people. Regression in the service of the ego can also be the source of gratification: Greenson, after reviewing psychoanalytic writing to date on creativity, states, 'I have the impression that the ego in creative people not only tolerates, but even enjoys or needs regressing ...' (1978b:346).

In my work with the thick-thin ego boundary model, there appears to be no relationship between self-report of anxiety and thin external boundaries. However, students who report thin internal ego boundaries often acknowledge substantial conscious anxiety. Such students are often thin on subscale 5 (interpersonal sensitivity or 'thin skin') as well. Self-report of thicker internal boundaries usually accompanies defenses from *unconscious* anxiety such as intellectualization, attempts to remove affect from one's cognitions, strong task focus and, of course, rejection of new information that may upset existing schemas. Thick boundary students are often unaware of possible unconscious anxiety.

How can I apply these concepts in my classroom?

This question is answered first by addressing how to recognize ego boundary tendencies, especially as related to tolerance of ambiguity. I then suggest some steps the teacher can take to make use of these observations.

'Diagnosis'

Most teachers are unlikely to have either access to the HBQ or the time or authorization to administer it. (See Appendix on page 84.) The model can still be useful if you use it to make inferences from student behavior and interests. What is the student interested in? What is the main area of academic interest? (Business, law, hard science, security professions, hands-on vocations tend to attract thick boundary people; literature, the arts, psychology, social service, and the like frequently attract thin boundary students.) How does the student react to unstructured activity? (Thick boundary students seldom like it; thin boundary students who do not have effective accommodation skills also find it unhelpful without considerable 'scaffolding'.) Does the student have a strong need to have a place for everything and everything in its place, both physically and conceptually? How strong is the student's need for clear lines of authority? Does the student seem to have some difficulties with ethnocentrism? What kinds of difficulties cause the student the most trouble: For instance, are they related to a need for excessive clarity? Or does the student work best when everything is in context and have a hard time with target language out of context (grammar rules, drills)? All of these observations can combine to help the teacher make a working hypothesis about the student's ego boundary preferences and tolerance of ambiguity.

Students need not be having difficulties to display differences along the ego boundary continuum. For example, Ellis and Miriam (cases adapted from Ehrman 1996:111–112) are very similar on a number of individual difference dimensions: Both are visual and kinesthetic learners, and they have the same psychological type – introverted intuitive thinking perceiver – on the Myers-Briggs Type Indicator (Myers and McCaulley 1985). On the other hand, they are quite different on the ego boundaries dimension: Ellis reports thick boundaries, and Miriam reports relatively thin ones. As you read the cases, look for the differences and how they relate to thick and thin boundaries.

> Ellis is a military officer and former physics major. He learned some of a Western European language in high school and in informal experiences with native speakers of that language. Although he describes his vocabulary as very limited, he uses what he knows to get his points across, though he understands better than he can speak. He says, 'grammar is not a problem for me'. He describes language learning as easy for him, though he experiences little desire to integrate with the society of the people whose language he is studying. He is motivated by task and by the fun of learning. Ellis has experienced little anxiety in language class since the first few days. He recognizes the value of direct communicative use of the language, activities outside the classroom, and open-ended activities, where he is forced to use everything he knows and cope with much he does not know. He rejects rote learning, perfectionistic correction by the teacher, group study, and mechanical drilling. He also expresses discomfort with overt attention in classroom activities to student feelings.

> Miriam, an organizational psychologist with a BA in linguistics, is an experienced learner of both Western and non-Western languages who finds language study very exciting. She has never met a foreign language she didn't like. She learns best when she can operate in a largely non-linear fashion, where she develops her own practice in interactive contexts with native speakers (teachers and non-teachers). She enlists non-teacher native speakers as informal teachers. Miriam wants to assimilate into

the culture and society of the people whose language she is studying to the degree possible for a foreigner. She sometimes becomes anxious if she thinks she has transgressed socially. She is outspoken about considering rote learning, mechanical drilling, and meaning-free activities a waste of time for her but enjoys context-free grammar analysis, though she may find it sterile if not turned into real language use. Miriam expresses a strong preference for open-ended language use activities, the more open-ended the better. She appreciates recognition of feelings in the classroom, as long as it does not interfere with the learning task.

In general, both of these learners are well equipped for contemporary language classrooms and unlikely to have much learning trouble.

Characteristic of successful thick boundary students, Ellis has ready access to analytic strategies to work with language out of context, and he has learned that he needs to work with ambiguous 'authentic' material in order to reach the proficiency he needs. However, open-ended activities are less comfortable for him than those he can predict and control, and he needs to make an effort to overcome his preference for clear categories and 'everything in its place'. He is flexible enough to manage the challenge and to work successfully at the intake, tolerance of ambiguity, and accommodation levels, though intake feels excessive to him sooner than it does for Miriam.

Miriam makes deliberate use of her ability to 'regress in the service of the ego' when she lets herself identify with target language people and attempts to assimilate into the culture. She has developed a very high level of ability to 'accommodate' and to cognitively restructure her large amount of intake. When appropriate, she can work sequentially as well as non-linearly. She thus functions comfortably at all three levels of the tolerance for ambiguity model. Miriam experiences more conscious anxiety than Ellis and is more comfortable with acknowledgment of feelings in general.

Helping students learn

Most students, like Ellis and Miriam, can operate outside their styles when they need to do so. The goal for them is to help them maximize their strengths and minimize wasted time. There are greater difficulties when the students are rigid in their approach. Many of the learners I work with on learning difficulties are affected by mismatches between the prevailing curriculum (usually adapted to students like Ellis and Miriam who tolerate ambiguity and have good accommodation skills) and the students' approach to learning, especially deep-seated personality dispositions that the ego boundaries model accounts for well.

The ego boundaries model not only helps me understand and prescribe for difficulties in tolerance of ambiguity, it also suggests how the students' motivational systems are likely to work. Thick boundary students are likely to be motivated by task accomplishment and achievement of control, whether of their time use or of learned material. They usually seek a sense of order and can find too much open-endedness disruptive to their sense of security. Thin boundary students tend to be motivated by establishing relationships – with people, with a new culture or among concepts. They like the freedom to make a wide range of associations between concepts and experiences, even if some of the associations may seem strange to their thicker boundary classmates.

When dealing with such students and their teachers, I usually suggest that the students begin working with what is difficult for them in small increments and with tasks on which nothing important depends. I describe this approach as getting into swimming at the shallow end of the swimming pool and describe it as if it were weight training, in which one begins with light weights and works up to real power lifting. A student like Keith needs to practice working with material that is over his head without knowing every word. He can benefit from small attempts at regression in service of the ego through light role-playing or techniques that come from methodologies like Total Physical Response, Community Language Learning or Suggestopedia. Suggestopedia is particularly useful in the extensive use it makes of regression in the service of the ego through controlled induction of dissociative stages and blurring of identity boundaries.

Jenny and students like her can do the same kind of 'weight training' to learn to make discriminations between different grammatical forms and among ways to express their ideas and feelings. They can attempt to achieve increased precision of grammar and vocabulary, a little at a time. Ideally, such activities will include an element of playfulness and open-endedness, to permit the regression in service of the ego that such students value. Thin boundary students who have difficulties with accommodation and cognitive restructuring often appreciate external structure in the curriculum, though for different reasons from their thick boundary classmates, but both types need to be helped to learn increasingly independently of external structure (see Aoki this volume). They may not achieve the extreme independence of a Miriam, but they can become more like Ellis. Community Language Learning and its underlying philosophy of Counseling Learning (Curran 1972) also call attention to the need to understand the student's security system. Activities that overtly address the security needs of students through too rapid establishment of intimacy can repel students like Keith. Students like this are more likely to respond to maintenance of a friendly distance and an early sense of success at the learning task. Thin boundary students like Jenny are more likely to respond to community-building efforts, but they, too, can be seriously affected by a sense of shame and need early success experiences. Students who are affected by anxiety are likely to benefit from activities like those in Oxford (this volume).

Most programs benefit from a balance of activities, some of which require conscious mediation that tends to appeal to the thick boundary student and some of which work through unconscious, 'acquisitional' processes, which tend to advantage thin boundary students. Students can work with those activities that fit in with their motivational systems in order to build a base of knowledge and self-efficacy and use the other, more challenging ones to round out their learning experience. Part of the art of teaching is to help students find which activities belong in which category for them and make use of them appropriately.

Appendix: the HBQ and Assessing Tolerance of Ambiguity

There are few formal ways to assess tolerance of ambiguity. The pointer to tolerance of ambiguity that I prefer is the Hartmann Boundary Questionnaire (HBQ, Hartmann 1991), described in the body of this chapter. The second language research literature also reports use of two other instruments, the MAT50 (Norton 1975) and the Tolerance of Ambiguity Scale (Ely 1989).

The HBQ instrument is found in Hartmann (1991). There are twelve *a priori* categories; an illustrative item is provided for each (adapted from pp. 58–60).

- States of sleep/wake/dream: On waking up I am not sure for a few minutes whether I'm really awake.
- Unusual experiences: I have had *déjà vu* experiences.
- Thoughts/feelings/moods: My thoughts blend into each other.
- Memories of childhood, adolescence, adulthood: I am very close to my childhood memories.
- Interpersonal: When I get involved with someone, we sometimes get too close.
- Sensitivity: I am very sensitive to other people's feelings.
- Neatness and precision: I keep my desk or worktable neat and well-organized.
- Edges, lines, clothes: I like houses with flexible spaces where you can shift things around and make different uses of the same rooms.

- Opinions about children and others: I think a good teacher must remain in part a child.
- Opinions about organizations: In an organization, everyone should have a definite place and a specific role.
- Opinions about people, nations, groups: People of different nations are basically very much alike.
- Opinions about beauty, truth and other abstractions: Beauty is a very subjective thing. I know what I like but I wouldn't expect anyone else to agree.

If you intend to use the HBQ, you should take several steps first. (1) Read Hartmann's book carefully and review the material on the ego boundaries construct in this chapter. (2) Delete some of the items that were clinically valid for Hartmann but which may make students reject the questionnaire. (3) Explain why you are using the questionnnaire. I usually mention that it was designed for investigating nightmare frequency but that it has proved useful as a measure of tolerance of ambiguity, which is an important factor in language learning. I also emphasize that I never look at answers to specific items but only to responses on scales. I have worked up local norms so that students are compared only to other students and not to Hartmann's population. If the student expresses discomfort, I listen and respond non-defensively. This approach usually succeeds in disarming resistance, but if the student still objects, I do without the HBQ.

If you cannot get access to the HBQ or authorization to use it, you can take the steps described in the last part of the chapter to make inferences about student boundary preferences and tolerance of ambiguity. As mentioned there, student interests, particularly as expressed in choice of university studies and occupation, provide a good clue. Student reactions to unstructured (or overly structured) classroom activities, response to the teacher as an authority (or need for independent learning), degree of orderliness, tendency to ethnocentrism, need for clarity and so on can serve as the basis for some hypothesis building about student ability to cope with ambiguity. These hypotheses can be tested by use of a range of different activities and assignments.

Suggestions for further reading

Ehrman, M. E. 1993. Ego boundaries revisited: Toward a model of personality and learning. In J. E. Alatis (Ed.), *Strategic Interaction and Language Acquisition: Theory, Practice, and Research.* Washington, DC: Georgetown University.

Ehrman, M. E. 1996. *Understanding Second Language Learning Difficulties*. Thousand Oaks, CA: Sage Publications.
Hartmann, E. 1991. *Boundaries in the Mind: A New Psychology of Personality*. New York: Basic Books.
Stevick, E. W. 1980. *Teaching Languages: A Way and Ways*. Rowley, MA: Newbury House.

The contents of this chapter do not represent official policy of the U.S. Department of State; the opinions and observations are those of the author.

6 Self-esteem in the classroom or the metamorphosis of butterflies

Verónica de Andrés

> All the flowers of tomorrow are in the seeds of today.
>
> Ancient Chinese Proverb

Why do children fail at school? What are the learning blocks that hinder achievement? What happens when a child feels 'I can't do it', 'I'm not good enough', 'I'll never learn this'? There is no doubt that these complex questions cannot have a single, simple answer. They open up a multifold spectrum of delicate matters, but most of these problems seem to have the same root: a poor self-image, a deep fear of failure, a feeling of inadequacy. In other words, low self-esteem. Psychologist Nathaniel Branden (1987) claims that all problems, except those that have a biological origin, are related to low self-esteem.

The question of what makes the difference between a child that can easily grasp concepts, words, meaning in a second language and one that can hardly understand or utter a word often baffles language teachers. One answer can be found in research which has shown that children who suffer from low self-esteem are greatly incapacitated for reaching their learning potential (Purkey 1970; Gurney 1987). The strong link between self-esteem, social relationships, and academic performance can be witnessed in the everyday world of the classroom.

Theoretical background or 'the pioneers of a butterfly's flight'

Stanley Coopersmith, child psychologist from the University of California, was one of the pioneers in the field of research on self-esteem. In his book *The Antecedents of Self-Esteem* (Coopersmith 1967:4–5) he wrote:

> By self-esteem we refer to the evaluation which the individual makes and customarily maintains with regard to himself; it

expresses an attitude of approval or disapproval, and indicates the extent to which an individual believes himself to be capable, significant, successful and worthy. In short, self-esteem is a personal judgement of worthiness that is expressed in the attitudes that the individual holds towards himself.

As an outcome of his research, Coopersmith (1967) developed a list of 'warning signals' considered as indicators of low self-esteem. Some children with low self-esteem may be excessively fearful and timid, unable to make decisions, expecting failure and reluctant to express opinions; others may be bullying and bragging. Coopersmith pointed out that children's self-esteem largely depends on the experiences, positive or negative, that they have in their environment, on how they are viewed by the 'significant others' and how they see themselves. The significant others are the people the child sees as worthy: parents in the first place, teachers next and peers later on. Their repeated responses serve as mirrors through which children see and judge their image. If a positive image is reflected, children will feel worthy of love and valued. On the contrary, if the image is negative, children will believe that they are rejected, unloved and unwanted, and they will act accordingly. Indeed, this description of the development of a child's self-image has a powerful implication for us as teachers: being one of the most important mirrors through which children discover who they are, we are in a very strong position to create conditions that can be conducive or detrimental to their self-esteem. It has been said that parents hold the key to children's self-esteem, but teachers hold a spare one.

Robert Reasoner (1982), former superintendent of Moreland School District in California, claimed that it is essential to acknowledge the uniqueness of each student and to protect his or her rights and feelings in order to develop the five key components of self-esteem: a sense of security, a sense of identity, a sense of belonging, a sense of purpose and a sense of personal competence. In his hierarchy of needs, Maslow highlighted the importance of security, concluding that 'only a child who feels safe dares to grow forward healthily. His safety needs must be gratified' (Maslow 1968:49). He stated that the apex of his famous Pyramid, the need for self-actualisation, can only be reached if all other needs – security, belonging and self-esteem – are fulfilled first. Similarly, Carl Rogers (1961) pointed out the importance of giving satisfaction to both the inborn needs (food, shelter) and the social needs in order to develop a psychologically healthy personality. In Rogers' view the most important social need is the one for a *positive regard*, which he considered the main socialising force behind behaviour.

In summary, human beings – children and adults – need to be liked, valued and appreciated. This need appears to be especially crucial for young school children as they are still building their self-image from the significant people that surround them. Unfortunately, many children, unintentionally or not, are humiliated in the classroom in the so-called 'pursuit' of high standards, achievement and controlled behaviour. The findings of a study in 1982 with one hundred children reported by Jack Canfield (in De Porter 1995) showed that on average children receive 460 negative or critical comments a day and merely 75 positive ones. As Bobbi De Porter (1995:24–26) said:

> This continuous feedback is deadly. After a few years of school, an actual 'learning shutdown' occurs, and children block their learning experiences involuntarily. By the end of elementary school, the very word *learning* can make a lot of students feel tense and overwhelmed.

This point is considered to be highly significant for language teachers, as success in language learning is inextricably linked to the way in which learners experience the classroom: as a place where their weaknesses will be revealed or as a space for growth and development. Can the classroom be an environment where values, positive attitudes and a 'can-do-spirit' are promoted? Which practical activities could be implemented to help children approach learning with confidence and joy? In 1993, while participating in a conference of SEAL (Society for Effective Affective Learning), I met Murray White, leader of the self-esteem movement in the UK; his pioneering work in the field of self-esteem in schools inspired me to seek out the answer to these questions in the implementation of two small scale research projects.

Classroom research or 'on the wings of self-esteem'

If a child's self-esteem can be enhanced in the foreign language classroom, will any consequences be observed in social relationships and academic performance? This question spurred two qualitative classroom research projects called 'I'm Glad I'm Me' conducted in 1993 and 1996 by the writer in co-operation with three EFL teachers working in two privately-owned Argentine primary schools. In the light of the nature of our research, ultimately aimed at attacking the 'I can't-do-it-feeling' with practical solutions, it seemed particularly appropriate to choose action-research as the methodological frame to bring together theory and classroom practice. As Kemmis and McTaggart (1982:5) put it, 'action-research provides a way of working which links theory and practice into one whole: ideas-in-action'.

The subjects of both studies were Spanish-speaking Argentine children, ranging from six to nine years old, who were learning English as a foreign language through intensive instruction given by their language teachers in the school's afternoon shift. The children had had two years of English instruction previously. The first study (de Andrés 1993) was conducted and implemented in Grade 3 by the writer with the assistance of the language teacher, while the second one (de Andrés 1996) was implemented in Grades 1 and 2 by language teachers themselves under the guidance of the researcher. Cohen and Manion's eight-stage model was chosen as a flexible framework for both studies. Cohen and Manion (1994) define 'collaborative action research' as an on-the-spot procedure, pursued by a group of teachers working alongside a researcher in a sustained relationship, designed to deal with concrete problems located in an immediate situation, with an emphasis on obtaining knowledge for a particular situation and purpose.

Procedures

In a nutshell, the procedures for both studies were the following:

The first stage involved identification, formulation and evaluation of the problem. The main concerns were the need to set a pilot study to determine the feasibility and usefulness of implementing self-esteem activities in the language classroom; the need to find positive ways to deal with behaviour in the school; and, above all, the need to enhance children's self-confidence and thus improve their academic performance, given that some children seemed to have problems that appeared to be related to their self-image.

The second stage embraced discussion, negotiation and formulation of purposes and assumptions. Several meetings were held in order to discuss the above issues with school authorities and the teachers who volunteered to participate in the studies.

The third stage involved a review of the research literature. Latest findings on the topic were discussed in several meetings and workshops.

In the fourth stage, as an outcome of the previous work, a set of objectives were projected, namely:

1 To develop children's understanding of themselves: to learn about their uniqueness; to enhance their ability to express feelings; to encourage them to think positively about themselves.
2 To develop understanding of others: to be respectful of others, tolerant and cooperative; to increase awareness of and skills in friendship-making; to encourage children to think and express themselves positively towards others.

3 To communicate more effectively: to listen while others are speaking; to wait for their turn; to improve language skills. To achieve these objectives, the following concepts were to be explored: Uniqueness, Growth and Change, Feelings, Talents and Abilities, Cooperation, Friendship, Communication. These concepts would be taught through a mixture of: (1) Brainstorming, (2) Feelings circles, (3) Activity-sheets, (4) Arts and crafts, (5) Reading and writing, and (6) Singing.

The fifth stage was concerned with the selection of research tools. In order to ensure triangulation, we decided to incorporate a variety of procedures, making use of both qualitative and quantitative tools: discussions with the teachers, questionnaires to students and parents, interviews with the teachers, classroom observations, field notes and teachers' diaries. In addition, some children with indications of low self-esteem would be selected in order to construct case studies. Data collection for these would be provided by the researcher's and teachers' diaries, field notes, classroom observations and projective tests.

The sixth stage was devoted to choice of evaluation procedures; it was decided that evaluation would be continuous. Evaluation of case studies would analyze whether there had been improvement of children's social relationships (attitude towards peers and adults) and enhancement of their self-image. It was expected that the latter would be reflected in academic achievement: since the teachers involved in the projects were language teachers, children's performance and attitude towards language learning were considered relevant.

The seventh stage encompassed the implementation of the projects. The time limit set for each study was ten weeks. The first was conducted in 1993 in two forty-minute sessions a week. In 1996 the second was carried out in forty-minute sessions three times a week.

The last stage involved the interpretation of data: inferences to be drawn and overall evaluation of the project would be carried out by the teachers and the researcher.

Some of the techniques used in this project are presented below; for an overview of the content and language areas, see the planning webs in the Appendix on pages 101 and 102. In addition, a case study is provided as evidence of the transformation that took place with individual children during the project.

Classroom techniques or 'unfolding our wings'

The activities used were aimed at enhancing children's sense of security, identity and belonging, which, according to Reasoner (1982), are three major components of self-esteem.

Most of the activities were based on the work of Murray White (1992), Michele Borba (1989) and Michele and Craig Borba (1978, 1982), pioneers in the area of self-esteem in schools. One of the major problems encountered was adapting these activities – originally designed for English speaking children – to the context of our EFL learners. To meet that challenge we decided to build a 'Whole Language Environment' where language was kept whole and the four skills were integrated. In practical terms this meant that literature had a leading role: the use of the best available literature for children was essential. It also meant opening up significant spaces in the classroom: a writing corner where children could write messages to each other, a poetry corner that could evoke creative responses, an art corner to show the transformation of those stimuli into words, drawings and colours. It was considered that the activities would work best with children at about third grade level, so it was necessary to implement a programme with concrete tasks and examples and to allow the students to use the mother tongue as much as they needed, especially at the beginning when they lacked the vocabulary to communicate their feelings and ideas in English.

The activities

John Holt said that a good teacher makes children glad it's Monday. Is it feasible to create a classroom where children feel 'this is a happy place to grow, to learn, to be'? The techniques described in this section aim to demonstrate that it is not only possible, it is our pleasant duty to build such an environment, where learning will be, in Krashen's words, inevitable.

Literature

The use of literature covered two main purposes. One was to build vocabulary and develop language, a fundamental need of these young children for whom English was a foreign language. The other one was to encourage self-acceptance and self-understanding, as the subjects discussed in these stories dealt with children's most common difficulties: anger, isolation, lies and rejection. The children were able to identify with some of the characters in the stories, and group discussions helped them to feel that their fears and concerns were shared by many others in the class. Moreover, these books were read to trigger off discussions of the topics that would be woven into Circle Time later on. Some of the books used in the classroom were:

- *Do You Want to be my Friend?* by Eric Carle (Friendship)
- *The Very Hungry Caterpillar* by Eric Carle (Growth and change)
- *Ernie's Little Lie* by Elliot Dam (Lies)
- *Nobody Cares About Me* by Sara Roberts (Isolation)
- *Where the Butterflies Grow* by J. Ryder (Growth and change)
- *Where the Wild Things Are* by M. Sendak (Anger)

Circle Time (White 1992)

Circle Time was a group activity aimed at helping children understand themselves, express their individuality and listen to others. It contributed to enhancing communication skills as the rules were: talk only when it is your turn; behave in a friendly way when other people are speaking; find your own words to avoid repeating what others have said; you can say 'I pass' if you want. Children sat on the floor in a circle, the teacher said an incomplete sentence and gave an example to finish it off, the child next to her repeated the phrase and put his/her own ending and so on. Children could pass if they wished and were allowed to use their mother tongue if necessary. As children said their thoughts (mostly in Spanish at the beginning) the teacher translated what they had said into English and registered their comments on a mind-map which was permanently on display in order to build a vocabulary bank. Some of the topics discussed during Circle Time were: 'I feel sad when ...', 'I'm good at ...', 'I feel angry when ...', 'When I grow up I ...', 'A friend is ...', 'I feel hurt when ...'.

At times the children found it difficult to talk openly about certain matters such as 'I feel jealous when ...' or 'I feel silly ...' so we introduced a variation to the game: 'Secrets'. The 'secret thoughts' were written on a slip of paper and were put inside a box. The children took turns to draw out the papers at random and read out the secrets; if the authors wanted to disclose their identity, they raised their hands.

For further development of writing skills, at the end of each Circle Time, children were invited to write their thoughts on a 'Circle Time Sheet', making use of the words that were shown in the mind-maps. Circle Time was also an invaluable tool for the development of speaking and listening skills: from our observations it was noted that listening to each other gradually became part of the normal attitude and speech was significantly improved. Towards the end of the ten-week programme most children were expressing themselves in English, with little use of the mother tongue.

From the language learning perspective, the linguistic gains were remarkable; this could be attributed to the 'magical' nature of this activity, often referred to as Magic Circles because of the transformational effect they produce on the participants (White 1994). Firstly, the circle, the shape of harmony and wholeness, gave children a feeling of security and belonging; secondly, the translation of children's *own* comments displayed on the walls made up an ideal resource bank of meaningful words to communicate in English and, thirdly, the rules of the activity encouraged students to listen and be listened to by others and gave participants the freedom to speak when they really wanted to do so. As White (1992) says, Circle Time is an excellent forum for shy children to express themselves and be heard. Even in a foreign language!

Special Day (White 1992)

Special Day was another significant activity used to promote a sense of security, identity and belonging. It was aimed at helping children learn to listen to each other, to wait for their turn and to develop language skills. Above all, it encouraged them to praise others. According to White (1994), this is one of the most effective ways of enhancing children's self-esteem; making positive remarks about others makes children think positively about themselves too.

The procedure was the following: one child's name was selected at random from a 'magic' box; all children knew they would get a turn sometime during the school term. He or she was invited to leave the room, while the others brainstormed positive comments about this classmate which were registered by the teacher on a Special Day Certificate. The child was invited to come to the classroom and sit in the middle of the circle and was given a badge that read 'I'm special!' and the Certificate. The other children took turns paying compliments such as: 'I think you are a good friend', 'I believe you are a good football-player', 'I think you are strong, capable, talented ...' These remarks were prefaced with the statements 'I think' or 'I believe' to indicate that it was the speaker's opinion, and thus it stopped the child receiving the compliment from rejecting it.

The positive statements that children could use were displayed on the leaves of a 'giving tree' that was used as a reminder of language 'acquired' from the songs, story-books and poems throughout the project. Words such as *capable, dependable, intelligent, responsible, punctual, tolerant, talented*, became part of the everyday vocabulary of these young students. Moreover, this 'lexical core' created a new possibility for the children to relate to each other in a more positive way. As indicated by Fontana (1988), if teachers encourage students to use language to express their feelings, both their linguistic abilities and their emotional development are greatly enhanced.

At the end of each Special Day, the child was given another sheet that said 'The reasons my friends like me are ...' where he or she was asked to 'copy' the compliments from the Certificate. Many times we found that the children wanted to do so immediately; they just could not wait to do this 'homework'. One mother said that her child had put the Special Day Certificate on the refrigerator door so everyone could see it. Among the many activities used in the project, Special Day proved to be the most popular; as one child said 'I loved Special Day because we could express our feelings, we said nice things to each other and ... we learned English!'.

The Paper Chain (Borba and Borba 1982)

This activity consisted of the children's writing the name of a person who made a positive comment or did a friendly deed on one side of a coloured strip of paper and sticking the ends together to form a link. The next strip was passed through the link forming a chain. Children were encouraged to write not only the name of the person but a short explanation of the caring gesture observed. Statements such as: 'Thank you for helping me!', 'You are a special friend', 'I liked the way you played with me!' were kept inside a box labelled 'Magic Thoughts' to be used by the children as models of comments to write. The paper chain was displayed at a height easily accessible to the children. As the chain grew, the students had tangible evidence of all the positive attitudes that they were developing throughout the project. It was interesting to observe that, although at the beginning there were just a few names used, towards the end all the names were on the chain. Perhaps even more important was to see that the children did not compete among themselves. They did not compare which names had more links; instead they counted the number of links that were on the chain to value the progress of the whole class.

The Car Wash (Canfield and Wells 1976)

The Car Wash was a popular self-esteem exercise aimed at helping children express affection both verbally and physically. The children were asked to form two rows facing each other. A child volunteered to go through the car wash, while the others stroked, touched, hugged him or her or said something friendly as he or she moved slowly through the lines. It was extremely encouraging to see how all children, without exceptions, came out glowing and smiling at the end of the line. As the children came out, the teacher hugged them too. From the very first day this exercise proved to be very effective for strengthening the feeling of belonging in the group. Touch is extremely important. White (1992) observes that many children (and adults) do not get the amount of touch that is necessary for growth, and this is a simple but powerful way to remedy that situation. After a car wash children smiled, looked more relaxed and were ready to learn.

Sparkle Bags Centre (Borba 1989)

Sparkle Bags Centre was used to provide opportunities for children to write and read positive comments to their classmates and to practise receiving positive statements from others. The children decorated their own paper bags which were pinned on a Sparkle Centre Board at their eye level. Suggestions for writing were displayed on a large chart with the teacher's and the children's own ideas. Every day the children wrote a 'Sparkle Message' to others which they put inside the appropriate bags. This activity was found to be particularly helpful for the development of reading aloud skills. There was a special moment when children looked inside their bags and read out the messages they had received. As some had difficulties with reading, the teacher encouraged the ones that could read 'more' to help the others. The recipients of messages were invited to respond with verbal thanks. It was moving to see how these young learners, who were at an early stage of literacy in their mother tongue, were willing and able to read simple but meaningful sentences in English.

The Mail Box

The Mail Box was another way to motivate children's thoughtful gestures towards others. In this place children could create special notes or letters for their classmates and other people who were important to them. The teacher introduced the Mail Box by sending one letter to each child. They discussed the meaning of the words and the purpose of sending letters or notes to each other. Suggestions for letter writing were displayed on the walls and were also kept inside a box near the activity centre. Ideas included thank you letters, get well notes, congratulations and birthday cards. Some children did not use this 'vocabulary bank', writing their letters spontaneously and thus making many mistakes. These were not corrected but instead were used to help the teacher to discover the children's most common difficulties and to create language charts with high frequency words they needed to communicate their feelings and ideas in writing.

At the beginning some children did not receive letters, but as the project progressed, this situation changed radically. The teacher herself received many letters and notes with the same expression of happiness that the children showed when they received theirs. It was observed that this routine nurtured the self-esteem, not only of the children but also of the teacher. The Mail Box contributed to building a bond of love and acceptance and a highly positive environment where the children and the teacher looked forward to working together.

Arts and crafts

In view of the age of the students, concrete tasks and hands-on activities were essential to help them see their progress. Some of the most relevant activities were the following:

1 *Sunflowers* (Borba and Borba 1982). With a circle of construction paper, the children made a flower face with no petals. They added a long green stem and a green leaf where they wrote their names. The flowers were pinned on a display board. An assortment of pre-cut petals was stocked in a box near the board. When someone did a thoughtful act, the children gave recognition to that classmate by adding a petal with a written comment to his or her sunflower.
2 *Fingerprints* (Borba and Borba 1978). To discover their uniqueness the children observed their own fingerprints and looked at them with a magnifying glass. They compared them to those of others and noticed differences and similarities. This activity generated a lot of excitement and led to learning vocabulary items such as: thumb, index, middle, ring and little fingers.
3 *Butterflies*. To explore the concept of growth and change the children prepared a small science project on butterflies. Working in groups they illustrated the life-cycle of butterflies using the vocabulary items related to the project. Then they built a butterfly-mobile: with pre-cut shapes each child decorated his or her own butterfly. When they were all displayed, one child said: 'They are all different, but they are all beautiful, like our fingerprints!'
4 *Big books*. Grade 1 made an oversized book, illustrating the story 'Do you want to be my friend?', and Grade 2 made one titled the '"I Can" Book', with descriptions and illustrations of their own talents and abilities.

Case study: Nathaniel

One of the case studies done dealt with a six-year-old boy from Grade 1 who showed the following indicators of low self-esteem: daydreaming, avoiding work, remaining on the fringe of the group, hesitating in new situations and being reluctant to express opinions (Coopersmith 1967). His attitude towards learning English seemed to be conditioned by his fear of making mistakes. He did not like to talk about his feelings. The class teacher found it very difficult to work with him because he was afraid of expressing his doubts and did not ask for or accept help.

When the project began, the children were asked to draw a picture of themselves and write a comment about themselves in English. Although Nathaniel drew a nice picture of himself with a smiling face, when asked to make the comment about himself he said: 'I am good but I am ugly'. The intention was not to analyze in depth the implications of the drawing, but it could be observed that, although all essential features of a child were present (legs, arms, head and torso), the figure was not well-proportioned, as the torso was excessively large. The figure was not fully grounded and was quite rigid. The face and hands were fully shaded.

No change was noticed until the fourth week of the programme. That week Nathaniel showed great interest when the teacher read out the story *Where the Wild Things Are*. During Circle Time he said 'I feel angry when my parents send me to bed'. That day for the first time he was able to finish his activities at almost the same time as the rest of the class. The turning point seemed to be a compliment he received from one of his classmates who told him: 'You are a talented artist'. Nathaniel looked absolutely surprised and fascinated. According to the teacher's diary, from that day on his attitude towards learning changed remarkably. Significant improvement was evidenced in his reading and oral skills and in his involvement in the activities.

An analysis of all data gathered showed that Nathaniel's learning blocks were related to his lack of confidence in himself. His lack of confidence was translated into a lack of ability to accept his own mistakes and those of others, which hindered the development of learning skills and integration in the group.

During the last week of the project children were asked to make a picture of themselves and a picture of the group. Compared with his earlier drawing, Nathaniel's figure showed much more flexibility, the lines were less rigid and the proportions of the figure were much better.

The class teacher pointed out that the project produced highly positive results in Nathaniel, both in his academic performance and social relationships. His parents commented the following: 'Nathaniel has improved in many areas: his use of English, his ability to listen to others, to wait for his turn and to respect others. We believe that with time other areas will be improved too, as Nathaniel still has difficulties with sharing his feelings. We are highly satisfied with this project'.

Perhaps the most significant comment was the one made by Nathaniel himself: 'I liked the project because we said lovely things to each other'. In short, the most remarkable progress was Nathaniel's shift in his attitude towards his abilities and towards facing mistakes, undoubtedly an important change.

The proverb at the beginning of this chapter spoke of planting the seeds of today for the flowers of tomorrow. Clearly, Nathaniel exemplifies how the seeds of affective teaching help effective learning to blossom; in the same spirit we could state that the most valuable lesson that we have learned from him is that *for teaching to be effective, attention to affect is crucial.*

Knowledge claims or 'unfolding our talents and helping others do the same'

Should schools devote time to helping students learn to feel better about themselves? The intrinsic value of teaching self-esteem has been subject to controversy. Some research (Kohn 1994) questions the desirability of focusing on this issue on the grounds that to focus children's attention on themselves could encourage self-absorption or narcissism. This would not seem to be necessarily true, but in any event, Reasoner claims that if we limit the concept to 'happy feelings', 'feeling good' or 'confidence boosting', we are missing the depth of the issue. In his words:

> Programs and efforts limited to making students feel good are apt to have little lasting effects, because they fail to strengthen the internal sources of self-esteem related to: integrity, responsibility and achievement. Only by addressing these areas can one effectively build self-esteem. (Reasoner 1992:24)

Perhaps the value of developing self-esteem in the classroom could be best evaluated quoting the children's own comments. To the question 'What did you learn in this project?', they answered: 'I learned that reading makes me grow', 'I learned that I'm glad I'm me', 'I learned that love is very important', 'I learned that I don't have to hit, I can talk', 'I learned that I know a lot of English' ... What did the children develop? Love and support for others, deep insights about themselves, a space for others to grow and an enriched language to express their feelings and communicate their ideas.

What did I learn as researcher? I learned that, as has been said, 'Children don't care how much we know until they know how much we care'. I discovered how important it is to discuss concepts of growth, change, uniqueness and friendship in the classroom. I learned how powerful it is, both socially and linguistically, to work with children's needs and feelings on a systematic basis. I learned that all classrooms should be places built on care, respect and mutual support. In such a place self-esteem is enhanced, social relationships are improved and the acquisition of the second language is inevitable. In such a place children's fears about themselves are transformed. In such a place children can grow up, be beautiful and unfold their talents. They can become butterflies. With a gentle flap of their wings they can tap into the reality of their potential . . . and fly high, very high.

Suggestions for further reading

Borba, M. and C. Borba. 1978. *Self-Esteem: A Classroom Affair: 101 Ways to Help Children Like Themselves*. Vol 1. San Francisco, CA: HarperCollins.

    1982. *Self-Esteem: A Classroom Affair: More Ways to Help Children Like Themselves*. Vol. 2. San Francisco, CA: HarperCollins.

Borba, M. 1989. *Esteem Builders*. Rolling Hills Estates, CA: Jalmar Press.

Canfield, J. and H. Wells. 1976. *One Hundred Ways to Enhance Self-Concept in the Classroom: A Handbook for Teachers and Parents*. Englewood Cliffs, NJ: Prentice Hall.

Coopersmith, S. 1967. *Antecedents of Self-Esteem*. San Francisco: Freeman & Co.

Reasoner, R. 1982. *Building Self-Esteem: A Comprehensive Program for Schools*. Palo Alto: Consulting Psychologists Press, Inc.

White, M. 1992. *Self-Esteem: Its Meaning and Value in Schools*. Sets A and B. Dunetable: Folens.

Appendix

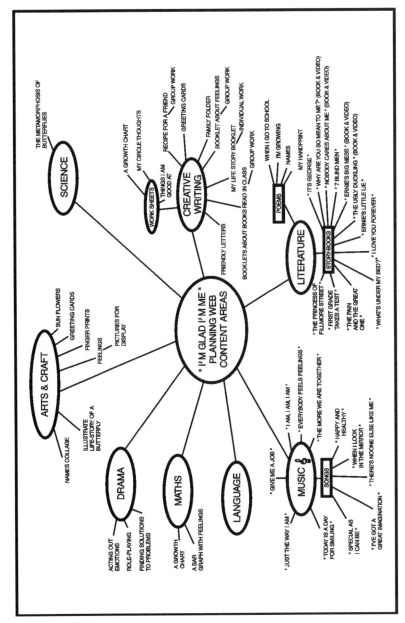

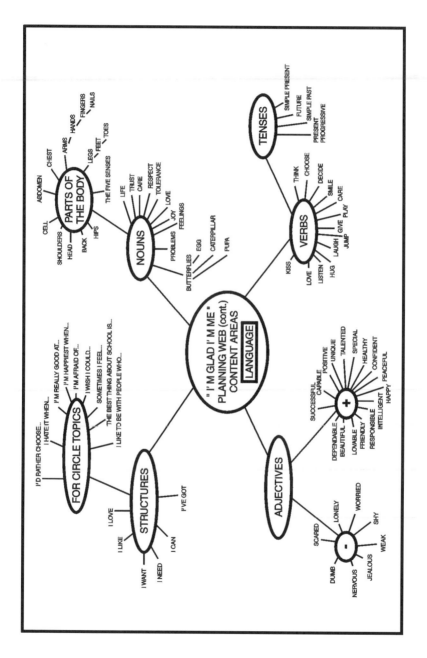

Part B: Questions and tasks

1 In Chapter 2 Schumann discusses language learning from a neuro-biological perspective. How might this information relate to language teaching methods and techniques you have used or studied?

2 Discuss which of the stimulus appraisal dimensions have been most significant for you in your own experiences with language learning.

3 Schumann suggests that when teachers stop negotiating, they may no longer be motivating. What are some of the implications for language teaching of this statement?

4 How many language teaching techniques – traditional or non traditional – do you know for getting new words or new structures into a student's 'holding memory'? In your experience, how effective is each in pushing new material towards 'permanent memory'?

5 In your classroom, how do you use affect to enhance remembering? What else might you do?

6 What relation do you think exists between anxiety and error correction? List possible ways to correct errors and discuss which ways of dealing with errors might be least anxiety-provoking.

7 Make a list of the main activities you would use to teach a unit. Divide them into two groups, depending on whether they are high or low risk for students. How many of the high risk activities are actually indispensable? What could you do to reduce the possibilities of learner anxiety when doing them?

8 Based on the descriptions in Chapter 5, would you describe yourself as tending more to thick or thin boundaries? Has your previous language learning experience been consistent with these preferences? What would help you learn better in the future?

10 Think about a few of your students or language learners you know. Where do they fall on the ego boundary continuum? What is your evidence for your placement of them? Do these students have difficulty with tolerance of ambiguity? If so, at what level (intake, tolerance of ambiguity proper, accommodation)?

11 In the light of the ego boundary and tolerance of ambiguity

constructs, what do you think you might do differently in your teaching?

12 Arrange to observe a class and analyze the type of atmosphere created by the teacher's interaction with the learners. Did the teacher's talk contribute to a positive or negative climate? In what ways? Discuss the implications for learners' self-esteem of creating a positive verbal environment in the classroom.

13 In Chapter 6 de Andrés presents a number of self-esteem activities. How could some of them be adapted to your teaching situation and the needs of your students?

14 In pairs choose one of the following topics and prepare a joint comment for the rest of the class.

'Self-esteem cannot be taught, it can be learned.'

'The duty of language teachers is to teach language, not self-esteem.'

'Self-esteem activities might promote bragging and self-centred attitudes in students.'

'Self-esteem can "make or break" the language learning experience.'

Part C   Exploring the teacher's space

Of unquestionable importance for language learning has been the development in recent years of learner-centred models of education. These models, however, do not deny the importance of the teacher, nor imply that there is no role for the teacher in a learner-centred classroom. Quite the contrary. There is a new, more evolved role which can be, if in some ways more challenging, also more exciting and fulfilling. Similarly, learner autonomy is a welcome goal for education, but it doesn't mean the absence of the teacher in the learning process. As Stevick (1980), Lozanov (Lozanov and Gateva 1988), Heron (1989), Aoki (this volume) and others have pointed out, learners must be prepared for autonomy gradually, and their expectations and felt needs, which at times may be for non-autonomous structures, must be considered.

Salzberger-Wittenberg notes that 'many children come to school with a notion that the teacher ought to have an encyclopaedic mind which pours out facts and information, rather than someone who is concerned to help children to learn and acquire ways of finding out about the world'; she emphasizes that if not given what they expect, at first students may 'feel angry and cheated as if one was withholding something they feel entitled to and could possess if only the teacher would be more willing to share' (Salzberger-Wittenberg, Henry and Osborne 1983:25–26). In this light, an important task is preparing learners to modify their ideas about what teachers should do, pacing in a careful and sensitive manner any changes from traditional expectations. One must not forget the primary need of language learners – and anyone else – for security; Curran (1972; 1976) stressed repeatedly that emotional security was necessary for learning to occur.

There are clear signs today that the importance of the teacher's role in the language learning process has not diminished. This can be seen in the proliferation of publications on teacher development (Richards and Freeman 1996; and Woods 1996 are good examples). A related sign is the emphasis in current second language acquisition studies on qualitative research in which teachers are active participants or initiators.

Feuerstein's notion of mediation gives a very empowering role to the teacher. Mediation refers to the intervention of others – in a classroom setting, especially the teacher – in the learning processs through the selection of learning experiences and the interaction with learners (Feuerstein, Klein and Tannenbaum 1991). In mediation, 'cognitive, social and emotional development are seen as inextricably linked, and the establishment of an appropriate climate in the home or classroom within which this can be effectively fostered is as important as the content of what is conveyed' (Williams and Burden 1997:67). Given the necessity of establishing meaningfulness for learning to occur, in mediation a particularly important facet of the teacher's work is 'helping individuals to see the significance to them of what it is they are required to do', including 'aims of a more life-long nature' and 'a more holistic attitude to learning involving the development of the whole person' (*op.cit.* 205).

According to Vygotsky, efficient teaching *'awakens and rouses to life those functions which are in a stage of maturing, which lie in the zone of proximal development'* (Vygotsky 1956: 278; quoted in Wertsch and Stone 1985, emphasis in the original). In other words, in the area just beyond the learners' current stage of competence, the teacher provides them with assistance so that they may become progressively more autonomous and in control. In neo-Vygotskian theory one of the principal means of providing this assistance to learners is modelling, defined as 'the process of offering behavior for imitation' (Tharp and Gallimore 1988:47). Physical skills are often developed this way; for example, the complex series of movements in tai-chi are mastered by many hours of modelling. In education, modelling is generally applied in a cognitive context, but it is no less effective on the affective plane. Teachers, even in non-teacher fronted classes, are the focus of learners' attention and they inevitably provide models – positive ones to be followed or negative ones to be rejected. Cognitively, we are good models when we provide examples of appropriate use of the language to be learned in a way which can be assimilated well. As such, we fulfil what is often assumed to be our function. Nevertheless, this volume embodies a second assumption: since we provide affective models at the same time, and even more so in the case of young and adolescent learners, it is important that these models also be 'appropriate'. Bernard Dufeu warns that 'the teacher who doesn't take the affective life of the group into account may unconsciously contribute to the development of affective factors that inhibit learning' (personal communication). So just as we strive to pass on to our learners linguistic knowledge which is useful and empowering, we should also be concerned to provide a model that leads to increasing their affective competence. Christison

(1997:3) states that 'L2 educators need to model the emotional intelligences they are trying to teach through caring, respectful, and honest interactions with students and colleagues'.

Waters (1998: 11) concedes that teachers obviously cannot control all the factors in their situation, but he suggests that they can bring about improvements by developing aspects of themselves. Teachers need to nourish and sustain themselves as a first step towards more effective teaching. A teacher who, for example, lacks self-esteem will hardly be able to contribute to raising the self-esteem of learners. Indeed, as teachers, we need to be concerned with learners' emotional IQ, but no less with our own. The latter may be the key that opens – or closes – the door to language learning: 'Pupils feel the personal emotional structure of the teacher long before they feel the impact of the intellectual content offered by that teacher' (Pine and Boy 1977:3).

Vital for both personal and professional growth is the practice of reflection, which is explored by Claire Stanley in Chapter 7. Reflection is being highlighted with increasing frequency in a broad variety of learning situations (see Richards and Lockhard 1994). As teachers are indeed learners themselves, real progress in their development is linked to the use of reflective skills. Stanley presents reflection as a tool that not only involves thinking but feeling. She underlines the affective dimension of reflection and the inhibiting or stimulating role that emotions can play in the reflective process. The connection is drawn between teaching students to reflect and learning to reflect on one's teaching. Discussion includes the principles behind reflection, tools for implementing it and the voices of teachers as they strive to become reflective practitioners.

Basic to a more effective affective learning environment is the change of roles of the educator from teacher to facilitator. In Chapter 8 Adrian Underhill first acquaints the reader with the concept of Facilitator by contrasting it with those of Lecturer and Teacher. The chapter then provides a series of thought-provoking questions which are a teacher-friendly guide along the path towards facilitation. Underhill (this volume) touches on a key theme of this book when he notes that what makes a facilitative approach to teaching 'so exciting and so revitalising is that I find that I can help my students' learning through my own learning . . .'.

The notion of facilitation is closely related to the next two chapters in this section: a facilitative attitude on the part of the teacher will lead directly to the development of some degree of learner autonomy and will necessarily include a concern with the dynamics of the group established in the classroom.

Learner autonomy might seem at first to belong to the learner's space;

however, it is, more often than not, an outcome of a conscious decision on the part of the teacher to share power and enable the learner to become more self-directing. Heron (1989:17) refers to the 'subtle art of creating conditions within which people can exercise full self-determination in their learning'. His wording makes it clear that such autonomy is a *creation* of the facilitator. The chapter by Naoko Aoki looks at learner autonomy as a political issue, showing how 'being affective can also be political'. She stresses the importance for learner autonomy of the teachers' role, which, to use Voller's (1997) terminology, may be that of facilitator, counsellor or resource. Her conclusions are supported by the voices of her students in a Japanese teacher preparation programme, all the more interesting coming, as they do, from a tradition that is widely believed not to have emphasized autonomous learning.

The last chapter in this section, by Zoltán Dörnyei and Angi Malderez, stresses the importance of group processes in determining the effectiveness of the learning environment; the role of the group leader, here the teacher, is the key to the successful establishment and maintenance of a well-functioning group. The functioning of the group and of the activity it is involved in can be greatly improved when the teacher is familiar with the key issues in group dynamics. In this chapter a number of relevant matters ranging from group formation and the stages of group life to the main characteristics of groups are discussed. Practical suggestions are given for exploiting the principles of group dynamics in the L2 classroom.

7 Learning to think, feel and teach reflectively

Claire Stanley

Imagine that it is the end of a teaching day and you've just finished a class that didn't go well. As you leave the school and head home, you think about this class. What runs through your mind? How do you reflect on what happened? Gloria,[1] an experienced EFL teacher in La Paz, Bolivia thought about her unsuccessful lesson this way:

> I didn't feel nervous but somehow I didn't know where I was heading. And I should have taken that sentence and written it on the blackboard and started from there. But I don't know why I left it. I didn't take advantage of that sentence. Instead I kept on talking ... Well, starting from there everything, well I think it was a mess although I tried to sort of organize things later. But again, somehow I felt it was not working.

Do similar thoughts run through your mind? Do you reflect on your teaching as Gloria does by recalling the situation, thinking of what you should have done instead ('I should have taken that sentence ... and started from there'), and then evaluating it globally ('I think it was a mess')?

As teachers who are concerned about the affective dimensions of our students' learning experiences, we are probably quite concerned when a class does not go well. In an effort to reflect on our teaching so that we improve it and thereby enhance our students' learning experiences, we may actually be doing ourselves a disservice. If the tone of our inner dialogue is judgmental or regretful and our reflections are characterized by sweeping generalizations, such as Gloria's were, we may not have reflected in a way that actually helps us develop and grow as teachers and as learners of teaching.

---

[1] All of the teachers in this chapter are real people whose names have been changed for the purposes of publication.

What does it mean to reflect on one's teaching?

In the first part of the twentieth century, John Dewey recognized the fact that most people and most teachers do not know how to use reflection as a tool for changing their classrooms, their lives and our societies. Thus, he devoted a major part of his life work to establishing what he knew reflection to be (*How We Think* 1933), and in creating teacher education programs which developed teachers who could not only look back at what had happened in their classrooms in detail, but could also analyze why certain events took place and what next steps needed to be taken. Dewey's work and more recently that of Donald Schön (1983, 1987, 1991) have presented the purposeful process of reflection as having the following sequence:

- *think* back,
- try to *remember* as much detail of the events as possible,
- *investigate* reasons for the events,
- *re-frame* events in light of several theoretical frameworks,
- *generate* multiple understandings,
- *decide* on what needs to be done next in relation to the analysis of what has already happened.[2]

In remembering what Gloria and many of us do very naturally and spontaneously when we try to reflect on our teaching and then in comparing that with what Dewey and Schön describe, I began to ask myself the following questions: 'What prevents Gloria or any of us from implementing a purposeful process of reflection?' 'How are the ways that practicing teachers reflect similar to or different from what Dewey and Schön have described?' and finally, 'How do the theory and the practice of reflection unite in an integrated and meaningful way?'

These questions shaped several qualitative research projects I have conducted over the past six years in an attempt to understand what it means to reflect on one's teaching. The research findings presented in this chapter are the result of two of these projects. The first was conducted in the summer of 1992 and the second was a longitudinal study conducted between 1990 and 1994. The participants in the studies were graduate students in the Master of Arts in Teaching program at the School for International Training in Vermont in the United States. The dummrt program is designed for experienced teachers from around the world who come for a period of intensive coursework in Vermont and then return to their current teaching

---

[2] Dewey (1933) and Schön (1983) give extensive descriptions of the reflective process. I have condensed their work in the sequence presented here.

position, which is used as a teaching practicum over a ten-month period. After the practicum, they return to Vermont for further intensive study and then prepare a Master's thesis. I sought out these experienced EFL, ESL and FL teachers in an attempt to comprehend not the abstract conceptualization of reflection, but rather the concrete lived experience of language teachers who tried to learn the purposeful or formal process of reflection as outlined by Dewey and Schön.

In the analysis of the data gathered from extensive interviews, correspondence, and in many cases the reading of teachers' reflective journals, I was able to discover some very important answers to my questions. First of all, emotions play an important role: they either prevent the implementation of a formal process of reflection or they actually stimulate the process. Secondly, teachers reflect in a number of different ways using a variety of techniques, tools and styles, some of which are consistent with Dewey and Schön and some of which are divergent. And finally, it became clear that more than simply an abstract conceptualization, reflection is a complex cognitive and affective process which takes time and practice to develop and integrate into one's mind, heart and life.

The affective dimension of reflection

The role of emotions proved to be influential in the teachers' ability to reflect on their teaching. In all cases the teachers were interested in learning to reflect on their teaching, but when faced with the actual task of doing it, some found that fear, judgment and resistance kept them from actually engaging with the analytical process of reflection. Others found that negative emotional situations in their classes led them to want to reflect and investigate the reasons for these situations. Still others were propelled by a strong desire and willingness to follow the entire process of reflection on their teaching and found the experience creative and rewarding. Emotions played distinct parts: as inhibitors, as catalysts, and as part of the fabric of reflection.

Emotions as inhibitors

Five of the twelve teachers I studied found it difficult and sometimes impossible to engage with the process of reflection. While they had a basic interest in learning to reflect, they resisted sitting down and writing a reflective journal entry, listening to a cassette recording of a lesson or watching a videotape of a class. This reaction seemed to stem from a climate of inner dialogue in which self-judgment and negative criticism were predominant. Their thinking was similar to that of Gloria, cited at the beginning of the chapter. When they made an effort to remember events in a class, they would focus exclusively on a part of the lesson that they felt had not gone well and while they dwelt on what they should have done, there was also a strong emotion of blame and often anger. The three teachers described in this section corroborate the findings of a study done by Hargreaves and Tucker (1991), which focuses on the relationship between teaching and guilt.

Janet, who was teaching English in a Japanese language institute at the time of the study, described how she would 'tear [her]self down' when she began writing in her journal about a class because she would begin to see how she was 'screwing the students up'. This would lead to her getting angry at herself for not 'doing it right'. Another teacher, Lenore, who teaches adult refugees and immigrants in the US, resisted keeping a journal for a long time because she said, 'My tendency has always been to fault myself [and to say] there's something wrong with me, I'm lacking in something'.

Looking at videos of a class was particularly difficult for some of the teachers. The most experienced of the twelve teachers was Cecilia who teaches at a university in Italy. In the midst of teaching a lesson that was videotaped, she felt that her 'responsibility as a teacher hadn't been met and [she] had blocked [the students'] learning'. Because of this, she could not look at the videotape for two weeks. When she finally did sit down and watch the tape, she was surprised to 'see how blinded' she had become by her expectations of perfection in her teaching. In viewing the video, she was able to see that one small segment of the lesson had not gone well, but that the rest of it had been fine. The memory of that small segment had triggered fear, dread and self-blame, blocking her ability to engage with the process of reflection. Wagner (1987) found that many teachers frame what they do and do not do in classrooms using either admonitions to themselves or the word *must*. Their concept of teaching holds a perfectionist quality to it and does not allow them to make mistakes, learn from them and subsequently grow as teachers. While Cecilia held many of the beliefs Wagner describes, her viewing of the videotape seemed to help her, temporarily at least, to accept mistakes as part of the reflective process.

Therefore, certain emotions are inhibitors to the process of reflection. Teachers may be fearful of reflecting on their teaching if they experience blame, guilt or anger at themselves for not having taught well or for having adversely affected the students' learning. Nevertheless, while emotions can block the process of reflection, they can also stimulate it.

Emotions as catalysts

Four of the twelve teachers used emotions as catalysts in the process of reflection. They found that they were most interested in fully reflecting on their teaching when a negative emotional situation had occurred in their class. The situation piqued their interest and spurred them on either to write in their journals, talk with another person about the situation, or in some instances, talk with the students in order to understand the situation better and come to a mutual resolution.

In focusing on those who used negative emotional situations in class to engage with the process of reflection, I will present stories from two of the four teachers' experience with reflection. Gloria, the teacher from La Paz, Bolivia, started learning how to reflect on her teaching; her ability to remember details and to investigate reasons became much stronger. As a result, she was able to see how the authoritarian stance she took in her classroom sometimes created discomfort and fear in her students. In remembering details, she could describe the look in students' eyes, and in several instances, see their brows sweating or hands trembling.

Tuning into these detailed reactions in her students and analyzing them as the result of negative emotions such as fear, anxiety or shame, Gloria began to question her stance in the classroom and to contemplate the kind of relationship she wanted to establish with her students. Simultaneously, Krashen's concept of the affective filter led her to re-frame her understanding of the students' learning experience. She there-fore decided to experiment with some aspects of the Community Language Learning approach and with a particular technique called the Human Computer in which the teacher stands behind the student.

During the class where she experimented with the Human Computer, Gloria paid close attention to what was happening and was later able to reflect in a way that gave her new understandings of her role as a teacher and her relationship to her students:

> What I noticed [was] that the affective filter of the student lowers down nearly to the bottom because I am behind him; I'm not mad at him and I'm helping him. And at the same time, I feel myself okay too, because I'm kind of controlling myself and I'm seeing that nothing – I will not get anything if I shout or if I get mad at students. Instead I think I get much more from them if I am nice and kind and help them. And yesterday I felt the energy when I was close to this student. He was okay. Whereas, I don't know if it was on Monday or Wednesday that I was close to one student – Fabiola – and she was shaking.

These insights would be the basis for introducing other new techniques into her classroom which created a positive learning environment for Gloria and her students.

The second teacher who used negative emotional experiences in his classroom to trigger reflection was Howard, a New Zealander who teaches at a university in Japan. Before formally undertaking the practice of reflection, Howard had gotten very angry in one of his classes and this had disturbed him. Because he and his Japanese wife had been trained in active listening as part of a parent effectiveness training course they had taken together, he was able to ask his wife to sit down with him and let him talk through the situation in an effort to investigate the reasons for his anger.

> And through this I began to see that what was really happening was a racial thing and that was right at the bottom of it. [I]t was that these guys because they were Japanese in a Japanese university they were not really taking their academics seriously. They were not serious academics. And the other side is I really felt that these guys were my intellectual inferiors and I was taking this judgmental stance towards them as a result.

Howard's reflections unearth personal attitudes and values based on race and class. These are extremely difficult attitudes to discover in oneself and can trigger other layers of emotional reaction. Luckily, Howard welcomed a deepening of self-awareness through the process of reflection. His experience connects with what Kemmis (1985), Smyth (1989) and Zeichner (1993) call critical reflection; when teachers reflect critically on their teaching, they use a race, class and gender analysis to understand their experience and to promote social justice in their classrooms and in the greater context of society.

Howard's realizations were part of 'a very painful learning experience' for him, but they also served as background for another situation which occurred later. In a class a number of months after the situation described above, another negative emotional situation arose. Howard had announced to the class that it was not acceptable to fall asleep in class because the course was a conversation class and all of the students needed to be present and participating in the conversation. Nonetheless, one of the students kept falling asleep and for several weeks Howard's tactic had been to walk by the student's desk and 'wake him up for a bit'. But then one day Howard found himself once again getting extremely angry.

This time, several things were different. First of all, he became aware of his anger before he expressed it, no doubt due to the previous experience. Secondly, he had begun using some of the techniques of the process of reflection, and was able to stop himself, set the class on an independent task, and then return to his desk to begin writing his feelings down in a teaching journal. By writing down the details of the situation, he was able to let his anger subside without expressing it to the student or the class. At that point he was able to take the student in question aside and talk with him about the situation openly.

The student told him how he could sleep in his engineering professor's class, which gave Howard a new understanding of the culture of many universities in Japan. But then Howard was able to affirm to the student that in New Zealand 'sleeping like that is seen as an insult'. He urged the student to leave the class if he was really tired, but that if he wanted to stay, he needed to be awake and participating. The student complied and Howard felt a tremendous sense of relief, knowing that he could approach the student in an effort to understand the cultural differences between them, and then he could clearly state his expectations for class behavior without the edge of anger. By formally reflecting, then investigating and re-framing the events, Howard and his student were able to understand one another and change a difficult situation.

From Howard's and Gloria's stories we can say that emotions sometimes serve as a catalyst for reflection and even change. In fact, all four of the teachers whose experience of reflection fell into this category spoke of a situation where their students had either directly or indirectly shown that they were not happy or involved in the class or with learning the language. The teachers' initial emotional reactions were ones of anger, frustration or fear, but as they investigated the reasons for their students' feelings, they were able to transform the situation, which had been seen as a problem, into a source of new creativity and insight into the teaching-learning process. Emotions not only serve as catalysts, but can also permeate the reflective process.

Emotions as part of the fabric of reflection

Three additional teachers, Fran, Eric and Sabina, helped me to understand further what it means to reflect on one's teaching. They experienced emotions as part of the fabric of reflection. Sometimes they were anxious about examining their teaching, and sometimes they were compelled by negative emotional situations. Overall, they had a keen interest in investigating both positive and negative aspects of their teaching, in using a variety of frameworks for analysis, and in generating multiple understandings and next steps. Two of the three teachers described how they did this.

Fran, who teaches at a college in California, talked about how she worked with reflection. She recalled a day when she walked out of a class thinking that it had been a 'disaster'.

> I remember I immediately sat down and I started to journal and I saw there were some things that actually worked during the class and I could see what they were. And then I looked at all the things that didn't work and started writing down why it was ... [then] I just got hold of it again and was able to go on and plan the next day and get back on the road again.

Fran said that she kept two journals – one which dealt with personal and emotional material and another that connected to her classes and teaching. Writing in the teaching journal 'became a very ingrained habit and I began to go directly from reflection to planning'.

For Eric, who was teaching at a language institute in Paris at the time, an important turning point in his ability to reflect happened when he began to look more closely at his students' learning as the focus of reflection.

> [And] another thing that really changed for me was I felt free to make mistakes and to have classes that didn't go so well and whereas before I might have felt intimidated by that (I mean it never feels good to teach a class where you don't feel comfortable), [but] I would sometimes find myself in situations where I would say, 'Gee, that didn't work. That's really interesting.' And think about why it didn't work. Because I had had classes that hadn't worked before but I didn't really reflect on them so much.

Both Eric and Fran were able to look at their classes and their teaching with interest and a degree of detachment. For Fran, keeping a reflective teaching journal was a way of 'mining for gold'. She could sift through everything that had happened and find the golden nuggets which would give her insight and become a vehicle for planning her next classes. Eric, who didn't mention using a journal, commented that he could reflect easily by using several theoretical frameworks, such as Community Language Learning and the Communicative approach to teaching second languages, as lenses through which he could examine his teaching. He was also aware of the influence of curricular and cultural issues on his students' learning.

The third teacher who reflected with relative ease was Sabina who teaches adult refugees and immigrants in San Francisco. Her impetus for reflecting came from the implementation of a new teaching-learning strategy which required her students to use their inductive reasoning powers. As a result, she began watching her students very carefully, attempting to track their ability to work inductively and to learn English in a new way. The experiment proved successful and Sabina experienced 'a lot of personal gratification in drawing as much under-standing from the students as possible [and in sensing] an excitement from the students for this way of learning'.

Fran, Eric and Sabina show us that emotions are part of the fabric of reflection. If negative emotions arise, they work with them and move through to a new place of understanding. These teachers know how to 'get back on the road again', as Fran put it. If positive emotions such as happiness, enjoyment, connectedness and caring emerge, these teachers recognize them, enjoy them, and continue their process of reflection.

In summary, the affective dimension of reflection is a strong influen-cing factor in teachers' willingness and ability to reflect on their teaching. Some teachers may be blocked by their emotional responses to their teaching and thereby not be able to use the reflective process as a way to help them learn and grow. For other teachers, emotions may be a compelling focus of their reflections as they try to understand why certain situations took place in their classrooms. And for others, emotions are part of the fabric of reflection, and are accepted as integral to the process of reflection. However, as a result of their reflections, they feel more positive about and connected to their teaching and their students.

The research findings give an indication of the techniques and tools that were beneficial for the participants in the study when learning to use a more formal process of reflection.

Ways and means of reflecting

It is interesting to note that even among a small group of twelve, most of the teachers reflected in different ways and used a variety of means to do so. The ways in which teachers reflected differently had to do with the places, times and tools they used for reflection. The means they used involved focusing points for reflection and two divergent styles of reflection, which I have called microscopic and wide-angle, multidimensional.

Places and times for reflection

Several of the teachers talked about sitting down at their desk at home or at school as a place to reflect. While reflecting at school might seem to some teachers an unlikely possibility, several teachers were able to do so. They found that by writing as closely after a class had taken place as possible, they could remember more of the details of the class and discover numerous reasons why certain events took place.

The two working mothers in the group talked about reflecting while doing other things. They needed to seize moments of relative quiet when they were alone in order to recall the events of a class or a day's teaching. For Jean, a Canadian woman who was teaching in a business corporation in Japan at the time, her early morning jogging routine became the best time and place for her to reflect. Being out in nature and listening to the rhythm of her feet and breath allowed her to focus on her teaching and to see events in a new light. Isabelle, a French woman who taught French in a private preparatory school in New England at the time, was able to reflect while driving back and forth to work in her car. It was the best time in the day for her to clear her head and begin to recall her teaching.

Thus, reflection can take place immediately after a lesson, at the end of a teaching day, or later, perhaps on the following morning before teaching once again. For several of the teachers, reflection was only possible once a week, usually on the weekend when they planned the overall direction of their classes and their teaching for the next week. In certain circumstances, when a teacher's reaction to a situation was emotionally charged, it might take several weeks to get enough distance in order to reflect on the situation.

Tools for reflection

The most common tools used for the implementation of reflection on one's teaching are the reflective teaching journal, a cassette or video recording of a lesson, and dialogue with another person. These tools are particularly useful in helping teachers to remember the details of the events in their classes and in creating some distance between teachers and their work. Recalling details of an activity or class through writing in a journal is one way of establishing a sense of objectivity in relation to those events. Listening to a cassette recording or watching a video of the class can also help teachers step back and see many of the details of a lesson that were not apparent while they were in the midst of teaching. Undertaking the discipline of observing and recording what happens in one's classes can move some teachers away from a level of primary identification with their work towards a place of seeing their work as one part of their lives and not identifying with their successes and failures so closely.

Using a journal, a cassette or video to record one's teaching can put negative emotional reactions in check since the task of remembering or reviewing details on paper or tape often forces a more factual and even neutral stance towards the events. Spontaneous inner reflections which do not have a form or purpose are usually not factual or neutral. In

Gloria's inner dialogue about the class that didn't go well from the beginning of this chapter, a characteristic of her thinking was a sweeping evaluation of the class: '. . . well I think it was a mess although I tried to sort of organize things later. But again, somehow I felt it was not working'.

In contrast, Fran's story tells of how she walked out of her class thinking it was a 'disaster', but then by sitting down and writing out everything, she could also remember what went well. Whatever didn't go well, she was able to slip into an analysis of the lesson and subsequently 'go on and plan the next day'. Without using a tool for recalling detail, it is too easy to keep replaying the parts of the lesson that one thinks went wrong, which in turn triggers evaluations like 'it was a mess or a disaster' and heightens negative emotional reactions.

Another way of externalizing reflection is by talking with another person. Howard asked his wife to use the technique of active listening with him to help him sort out what had happened in his class. Four other women in the study mentioned talking to their husbands as a way of reflecting on their teaching. Since all of the participants in the research project were graduate students in an MAT program, they also mentioned conversations with other graduate students in courses and conversations with their teaching practicum advisors. Finally, colleagues from their school were also cited as a source of dialogue and reflection on one's teaching. In many cases, a reflective and investigative dialogue with another person who listened well and asked important questions helped teachers to re-shape the quality of their own inner dialogues.

Styles of reflection

Two distinctive styles of reflection emerged from the findings of the research: a microscopic, close-up style and a multidimensional, wide-angle style; these terms were chosen to indicate the quality of enhanced vision possible with reflection. Most of the teachers, once they had been introduced to the idea and sequence of reflection as a formal practice, were able to sharpen their skills in observation and recall details of the events in their classroom. Their attention to detail became more microscopic on both the recall and analysis of teaching-learning situations through the use of the above-mentioned tools.

The following text is an example of microscopic reflection. It was written by Gina, a Chinese-American teacher of Chinese immigrants at a community college in San Francisco. The text is an excerpt from a paper she wrote during her teaching practicum after looking at a videotape of her class.

Review of vocabulary: This section [of the lesson] was intended as a quick review, but ongoing student feedback told me that half of them didn't really know the words. The class was dragging and I wanted to see if they all understood the vocabulary. Having individual students come up [to the blackboard] to point and others to say it got the class more involved – also, I could confirm if their lack of oral response was because they didn't know it. At this point the class energy picked up – they were helping each other, more actively participating individually and as a whole group in reading and pronouncing. Students in front were listening and pointing.

Sometimes I find it hard to read the 'no response' mode – sometimes it's because they are just plain tired, other times bored, other times they don't know the material. This review section was not very challenging to the more advanced students, [and] I felt although it was quite teacher-directed, I tried to rely more on the students, make it more student-directed by having them come up and point and other students ask/tell. I was also trying to get the more advanced students to use more difficult words to challenge them while the slower ones were up front.

On the tape I see how much I interfered and repeated, when I thought I was giving them a chance to do more of the work. Maybe rather than approach [the class] from a traditional teacher to students way, [I could] give them more opportunities to work with the language among themselves.

Gina captures the microscopic style of her reflective thinking process quite clearly in this text.

First of all, we can see how she recalls many of the details of this segment of the lesson, greatly aided by having watched the video. She is able to note what the students were doing, and to assess that their lack of response is because half of them do not 'know the words'. Therefore she moves on to a different kind of activity in the class in order to check and see if her assessment is correct. She then generates several understandings for the 'no response' mode in the second paragraph. The framework through which she is examining her lesson is the concept of what she calls 'teacher-directed' and 'student-directed' activities. At the end of the text, she returns to this concept and generates a next step for a subsequent class which is to give the students 'more opportunities to work with the language among themselves'.

This example can help us to see what a microscopic style of reflection looks like and sounds like in a teacher's actual words. It is important to note that Gina began her 10-month teaching practicum by reflecting with a tone of blame, self-judgment and anger. The above text came from a paper at the end of her practicum and represented months of practice and feedback from her practicum advisor on how to engage with a more formal process of reflection. With time and practice, Gina was able to learn how to reflect in a microscopic way. This was true for most of the teachers in the study.

A few of the teachers, however, particularly those for whom blame and self-judgment were issues, began to reflect in a multidimensional way which allowed them to gain a wide-angle but focused view of an issue in their teaching. It did not involve a close examination of the teacher or the students. The following story will illustrate the case of a teacher who preferred to use a multidimensional style of reflection.

The least experienced teacher among the participants in the study was Maya, a woman who had raised her family and had begun a new career. Three years prior to her participation in my research project she had started teaching ESL in a public middle school in California. Listening to cassettes of her teaching or watching videos precipitated much self-judgment and criticism to the point that the cassette or video, which work at a microscopic level of reflection, were self-defeating. Maya was able, however, to use a topic as a way of reflecting on her teaching in a multidimensional way. She was most interested in the issue of classroom management. She had large classes of predominantly Hispanic early adolescent students who were the children of migrant farm workers, and her middle-class Anglo-Saxon approach to discipline and behavior problems was proving frustrating for her and for her students. Among other things, Maya discovered race and class issues embedded in her approach to classroom management. Her Hispanic students were accustomed to both a polychronic style of communication for discussions and to more direct, confrontational modes of discipline and pedagogy. (See Delpit 1988 for a further discussion of these issues.)

For the following three years Maya examined issues of classroom management in a multidimensional way: she tried to remember techniques that worked for the students and for her, she talked extensively with Hispanic colleagues and administrators in her school and with clergy who worked with the families in the community, she took workshops on classroom management and used the techniques suggested. Finally, she also investigated the political dimension of her situation, discovered that she had too many students in her class according to her working contract, and filed a grievance with the teachers' union at her school to reduce her class size to be in accordance with her contract. After these changes were made, she told me that her classes seemed to go much better for her and for her students.

Maya's story illustrates another way of reflecting which is more accessible for some teachers and therefore successful for them. Taking a particular topic or issue and following it for an extended period of time, getting input from many sources, and then implementing change in the classroom based on both the broad examination and the input seems to be an equally viable style of reflection.

Focusing points of reflection

Throughout the teachers' stories of their experience with reflection they mention focusing points they used which helped them to get a more sharply defined image of their teaching. I have used the word *purposeful* at different times throughout the chapter and the teachers' choice of a focusing point helped to make the reflection purposeful.

In the example given of Gina's reflective text, the focusing point was taking a small segment of a lesson and putting it under the microscope, using a video recording and writing as tools to do so. The purpose of using this focusing point was to train Gina's ability to observe and recall detail so that she could move closer to becoming student-centered as a long-term goal and to reducing the percentage of teacher talk in ratio to student talk as a short-term goal.

The focusing point for Fran, who enjoyed and profited from writing in her teaching journal, was a series of four short questions: what went well? why? what didn't go well? and why? Fran used these questions as a focusing point for her reflection because she wanted to develop a broad sense of her strengths and weaknesses as a teacher. Her goal was to learn how to build on what was successful and to find a way to process the emotional impact of events that didn't go well in her classes.

For Eric, the teacher from Paris, the focusing of his reflection was his students' learning. He became fascinated with the times when he could actually see learning happening and wanted to adjust his teaching so that the students had a maximum of learning opportunities. In a slightly different way, Sabina implemented a plan for creating activities which required her students to use inductive reasoning powers and used reflection as a way to examine when and how her students could work successfully with and learn from these activities.

While a focusing point guides teachers in knowing what to look for and sharpens their observation and reflection skills, it can also activate teachers' interest in reflection by engendering a quality of experimentation. I may have a specific point to investigate. For example, if I decide that I want to examine the relationship between anxiety and language learning that Rebecca Oxford writes about in Chapter 4, I can use her ideas as a focusing point for my reflections with the purpose of seeing how my experimentation with those ideas or activities is influencing me and my students. On the other hand, my purpose may simply be to understand my students better and to observe how the decisions I make in my teaching do or do not help them to learn the target language.

In summarizing what the teachers describe about their ways and means of reflecting, we can see the amount of time at one's disposal and the nature of one's personal life may affect the what, where, when, how and with whom aspects of reflection. Teachers with extremely busy lives may be able to use a window of quiet time in their day when they can think back, investigate and analyze their teaching. Some may want to train themselves to approach reflection from a detailed, close-up and microscopic perspective, while others may prefer a more global, wide-angle and multidimensional perspective. Those with more time and a preference for working alone may choose writing in a journal, or using cassette or video recordings to review, re-frame and generate next steps for their classes. Finally, for those who have the time, a combination of some form of recording plus conversations with a listening partner may help teachers integrate both the ideas and the feelings that the process of reflection engenders.

Conclusion

Just as the diverse perspectives of the chapters in this volume show that affective factors are essential for language learning, my experience as a language teacher, teacher educator and researcher indicates that the affective dimension is integral to reflective thinking and teaching. For most of the teachers in the study, it took at least eight months to develop a purposeful reflective teaching practice which integrated their emotions and their thinking, and which took into account the abstract concept of purposeful reflection as well as the reality of their personal and professional lives. Some took more time and a few took less time, but all of the teachers needed to accept three basic principles in order to forge ahead in the development of a reflective teaching practice.

The first principle is that *teachers tend to have emotional reactions during teaching-learning situations.* This is a fact for all teachers, although it is often ignored or misrepresented in the professional literature on teacher reflection. Therefore, teachers need to develop skill in: first becoming aware that their emotions have been activated at some point during or after a class; then recognizing the nature of the emotions; and finally, identifying a way, be it journal writing or talking with another person, that is comfortable to process the emotions. By developing processes for working with the affective dimension of their own learning, teachers are more prepared and skillful in helping their students with the same issues.

The second principle is that *teachers are the agents of their reflective processes*. As such, they have choices about the ways and means of implementing reflection. The examples in the previous section illustrate only a few of the options regarding styles and directions available to practicing teachers. When teachers connect with the source of creativity they use to nourish their students' learning and realize that they can use that same creativity for their own teacher learning, they reflect on their teaching with more ease and enthusiasm.

The third principle is that *teachers learn reflection through relationship*. Relationship means that teachers develop a relationship with themselves, through the initiation of inner dialogues about conscious and unconscious aspects of their teaching. In developing a relationship with themselves, teachers can integrate the affective and cognitive dimensions of their work. Relationship also means that teachers begin to see their teaching in relationship to the students' learning and to the entire context in which they are teaching. Finally, relationship means that teachers can learn to support one another by developing reflective relationships in which they dialogue about their work, their hopes and fears, and their desires for continuing growth and development.

As teachers encounter topics of interest from the fields of second language acquisition, linguistics, sociolinguistics, psychology and pedagogy, they need a vehicle for exploring those topics so that they may continually grow and develop, both personally and professionally. Although it takes a substantial amount of time and practice to learn how to integrate all of the aspects of a reflective process, it is a form of personalized professional development that can last a lifetime. Learning how to think, feel and teach reflectively gives teachers direct access to the integration of theory and practice in their everyday working lives.

Suggestions for further reading

Dewey, J. 1933. *How We Think*. Chicago: Henry Regnery and Co.
Richards, J. and C. Lockhart. 1994. *Reflective Teaching in Second Language Classrooms*. New York: Cambridge University Press.
Schön, D. A. 1983. *The Reflective Practitioner*. New York: Basic Books.
Zeichner, K. and D. Liston. 1996. *Reflective Teaching: An Introduction*. Mahwah, NJ: Lawrence Erlbaum Associates.

8 Facilitation in language teaching

Adrian Underhill

In this chapter we will focus on the ideas and practices of Facilitation from two points of view. First we will look at the gradual emergence of Facilitation in language teaching as something different and distinct from Lecturing and Teaching, and then we will look at some practical steps you can take if you wish to explore a more Facilitative approach in your own teaching.

Lecturing, Teaching and Facilitating

Throughout this chapter I use the three terms Lecturer, Teacher and Facilitator (spelt with capital letters) in a specific way to refer to three different kinds of teacher. Clarifying these three special definitions, which cut across conventional use, is what the first half of this chapter is about, and though I may tend to make things sound clearer than they are in reality, I do not suggest that this conceptual framework applies to everyone. There are all sorts of exceptions. I simply propose the following as a useful thinking tool for the time being.

By Lecturer I mean a teacher in any educational context (primary, secondary, tertiary, private, state, general, specialist) who has a knowledge of the topic taught but no special skill or interest in the techniques and methodology of teaching it. The main qualification of the Lecturer is knowledge of the topic, but the procedures and techniques the Lecturer employs to assist learning are not deeply questioned, studied or even valued, nor do they form part of the qualification to be a Lecturer.

By Teacher I mean a teacher in any educational setting who has a knowledge of the topic and is also familiar with a range of methods and procedures for teaching it. This dual focus on topic and method is probably embodied in the teacher preparation and qualification. However the development of significant personal and interpersonal classroom skills and the systematic intention to develop learner self-direction and self-evaluation are not seriously investigated, nor are they a part of the qualification to be a Teacher.

By Facilitator I mean a teacher in any educational setting who understands the topic, is skilled in the use of current teaching methods and techniques, and who actively studies and pays attention to the psychological learning atmosphere and the inner processes of learning on a moment by moment basis, with the aim of enabling learners to take as much responsibility for their learning as they can. This last is what differentiates the Facilitator from the Teacher. The qualification of the Facilitator is having knowledge and practical expertise in all three of these areas (topic, method and inner processes).

Thus the Teacher adds to the Lecturer repertoire the practical skills and knowledge for working with teaching activities. Similarly the Facilitator adds to the Teacher repertoire the practical skills and sensitivities for managing the intra- and inter-personal experiencing of the group. The Teacher can also do what is expected of a Lecturer, but in a more informed and flexible way, and the Facilitator can also do what is expected of a Lecturer or a Teacher, but in a more informed and flexible way.

It is important to remember that my special terms – Lecturer, Teacher, Facilitator – do not necessarily correspond with the normal use of these terms. It is possible that someone whose job is lecturer, or teacher, may according to my definition be an excellent Facilitator. Conversely, someone who describes themselves as a facilitator, may according to my definition be closer to Teacher or Lecturer. It is also important to bear in mind that each of the three types of teaching that I call Lecturing, or Teaching, or Facilitating is suited to different learning contexts and, moreover, that each can be practised well or badly. Someone who teaches mainly by giving lectures may have an outstanding ability to initiate vivid and successful learning, and someone who calls themselves a facilitator may fail to create an inspiring learning atmosphere.

The change in teaching style from Lecturer to Teacher or Teacher to Facilitator can come about within the development of a single person's teaching career, or more slowly over several generations, or not at all. I can identify with each of the three types (as you probably can too) and I shall therefore write in the first person while I develop these distinctions.

Lecturer

As a Lecturer my main area of expertise is my knowledge of the topic, and this is also my main qualification for teaching. The study of teaching methods has not been part of my preparation, so I rely on a relatively small range of individual and intuitive techniques that may reflect how I myself was taught. You can infer from the way I teach my underlying assumption that learning is a matter of exposure to the topic, which you will see me providing by transmission, explanation, information, assignments and so on. I may perhaps have an inspiring and imaginative style, but I do not pay much attention to my students' personal involvement; indeed I have no methodology for doing that. I may be aware that there is a field such as methodology, but it does not seem important to me to investigate. So I do not feel I am missing out on anything, nor do I make a connection between the lack of flexibility in my teaching technique and some of the difficulties that arise in my students' learning.

This lack of flexibility makes it difficult for me to respond creatively to my students' own learning needs and styles, and therefore my presentation of the topic, however effective I may feel it to be, may not correspond to the ways my learners need to learn. I don't have a systematic way of checking learning, getting feedback and diagnosing learning difficulties, nor a conceptual framework that encourages me to develop such strategies. However, I don't see this as a problem, nor perhaps do my students, because in my environment no one expects anything different. The 'successful' students in my class are those who are able to find within themselves, or from elsewhere, what they do not get from me.

My professional development consists mostly of extending my knowledge of the topic I teach. This does not of itself improve my ability to teach, though the enthusiasm it generates in me may help my learners; however, it can also cause me to lose touch with my students if I get carried away with my own enthusiasm at the expense of their interests. Such development can be called *horizontal* in that it does not challenge my underlying values and assumptions about how learning takes place nor about how my teaching can affect my students' learning. Being horizontal also implies that such development is somehow an extension of what I already know, and, in a sense, more of the same.

Over a period of time I may be struck by the observation that sometimes my lessons seem to 'go better' and that sometimes I seem more in touch with my students' learning. I may get used to this and assume that the variables governing this fluctuation are 'out there' (i.e. not 'in here') and that this is an unchangeable fact of teaching. On the other hand, my resulting creative dissatisfaction with my teaching, and my curiosity about what else could be possible, may lead me to see that how I teach is itself a field worthy of investigation. I may begin to investigate the field of methodology, if it is accessible to me; and if it isn't, then I may begin to 'invent' methodology and class management skills by myself or with others who share my interest. If this gains enough momentum, then we have the beginning of a local body of shared methodology, which will contribute to and benefit from other groups elsewhere with similiar questions and interests.

Such development can be called *vertical* in that it represents a kind of quantum jump into a new area of interest rather than an extension of a previous one. In the case of the move from Lecturer to Teacher this vertical development consists of a shift in my underlying values and assumptions towards a greater valuation of the process of learning itself. This is shown by my interest in a more methodical approach to the way I divide up, sequence, present, and provide practice of the topic, and in the way I manage classroom activities and monitor learning. Those who value and systematically pay attention to both the topic they teach and also the methods they use for teaching are, according to my terminology, Teachers.

Teacher

As a Teacher my twin areas of expertise are my knowledge of the subject matter and my skill with the methods and techniques I use to help my students to learn. My preparation probably reflects this double interest, though colleagues in some countries still qualify as Lecturer first and then 'upgrade' to Teacher through in-service work on methodology. Being able to employ a variety of teaching techniques and having a range of class management skills provides me with greater contact with my learners and their learning processes than was available to me as Lecturer. My Lecturer skills are still available to me, though I now have additional options. I have a conceptual framework that opens me to the different choices of activities my learners can do, and to the different consequences that flow from these choices. My methodology comes not only from workshops and training courses but from exchange with colleagues, from teacher methodology books and articles, from my own experience and experiments. I 're-invent' what I get from others to suit my own situation and my preferences of style.

My professional development as a Teacher consists of further exploration of both the topic and the methodology as it relates to my own teaching situation. I may take an interest in the cascade of methodological materials that come on the market. Such development is *horizontal* in that it does not usually require me to extend my underlying values and assumptions beyond the Teacher paradigm. Being horizontal, this development is somehow more of the same, even if it is a refinement. However, although methodology has helped me as Teacher to make progress with some of the problems that I faced as Lecturer, it has also brought me closer to other problems that were invisible to me as Lecturer but which now become visible.

Some of these new problems are to do with the subjective experiencings of learners and teachers in relation to themselves, to each other, and to their learning, and with processes such as engagement in what we do and having access to making the decisions that matter. For example: 'Good' lessons are still elusive and unpredictable, and even when they do occur, they seem not to be repeatable. They cannot be caught and released again later. Compared with myself as Lecturer, I have a sharper sense of what constitutes a 'good' lesson for me, and a corresponding sharper disappointment when such lessons don't happen. I become aware that the psychological atmosphere of my class does not have the quality of relationship that I want and that I recognise as 'happening' in my 'good' lessons. Lessons planned well don't always turn out well, and unplanned lessons are sometimes the highlight of the week. The cause and effect of good teaching seems both beckoning and elusive. I am frustrated by my apparent inability to affect the motivation of some of my students, among whom there is resistance and boredom that I cannot fathom. I begin to value rapport but do not really understand how to create it. Teaching has brought me closer to all these questions than did Lecturing, and the questions disturb me more. For a long time I may seek answers through the horizontal development of new course books and techniques, but methodology that enabled me to move from Lecturer to Teacher and whetted my thirst for what might be possible in learning does not have answers to these new sets of questions.

I come to realise that the way I am has as much effect on the class as the methods I use, and that patience, relationship, spontaneity, empathy, respect and so forth, are qualities that are of the utmost importance, yet cannot be put in place by more methodology or a different course book. At this point in my development I may do what many Teachers do, that is to freeze myself into this state of affairs by convincing myself that good teachers are born and not made. On the other hand, I may conclude that good teachers can make themselves if they have the will to find out how, and this brings me up against a second quantum shift in values and assumptions that can allow me to take my search in a new direction, and to find a new ally. This is the *vertical* development for the Teacher, since it leads out of the Teacher paradigm by questioning the values and assumptions that drive my work.

If my creative dissatisfaction is sufficient, I will invent or gain access to a significant, systematic and workable way of affecting these important variables that are bubbling away below the surface of my class and whose energy I have so far been unable to tap. The Teacher who becomes a serious student of this new field can be called a Facilitator; but, though Facilitation can be talked about in a way that was not possible twenty (even ten) years ago, it is still not a generally accepted part of pre-service teacher preparation or in-service training. Therefore Facilitators in language teaching are still pioneers working alone or through networks without 'official blessing'.

Facilitator

As a Facilitator my triple area of expertise consists of my knowledge of the subject matter, my skilful use of teaching methods, and my developing capacity to generate a psychological climate conducive to high quality learning. My enlarged equation connecting people and learning embraces the psychological learning atmosphere itself, which in turn contains all the work we do on language and all the learning techniques we use. This new equation includes the relationships in and between people in the group, the degree of security felt by individuals, the sensitivity of the trainer to undercurrents, the quality of listening and acceptance, the possibility for nonjudgemental interaction, the way the needs for self-esteem are met, and so on. It also includes the issue of power, that is who makes the decisions, how, and about what and who carries them out.

Things are by no means easier, but as there is a wider field of vision, there is a greater chance of recognising problems which are to do with personal and interpersonal skills and linking them to their causes. Some of the 'people processes' that were invisible to me as Teacher become visible to me as Facilitator, just as some of the 'methodological processes' that were invisible to me as Lecturer became visible to me as Teacher. My *horizontal* development as Facilitator consists in my study of some of the approaches to Facilitation that are increasingly available these days, mostly imported from outside mainstream ELT and outside general school education. However, ELT interest groups and networks are re-inventing this imported material, restructuring it for ELT contexts and making it ever more available to Teachers as indicated by the increase in books, articles and courses. These initiatives are characteristically individual, local, and 'bottom up' (i.e. not officially initiated), and, like methodology, may in the future become institutionalised as part of official qualifications.

At this transitional stage, writers and practitioners typically view the Facilitator landscape through the filtering lens of Teacher or even

Lecturer attitudes, values and experiences. (Just as the movements of new planets were first tracked and explained by observers who believed Earth was at the centre of the solar system.) One example of this is the contemporary attempt to move towards greater learner autonomy, which is sometimes implemented with values and attitudes regarding the use and sharing of power that belong to the Teacher rather than the Facilitator paradigm. The method is driven by the wrong attitude and the initiative hits difficulties. To put it another way, what should be a vertical development (involving the development of new attitudes to drive new behaviours, both belonging to the Facilitator paradigm) is reduced to a horizontal development (the new behaviours from the Facilitator paradigm are seen as being on the same level as behaviours from the Teacher paradigm, therefore capable of being driven by Teacher attitudes) and so the initiative, starved of the attitudes and values that nourish it, fades away.

Though the superficial copying of techniques that belong to the next level doesn't work, it is nevertheless widespread and probably inevitable. In the last two decades Facilitative techniques have, perhaps because of their exotic nature or the promise of something different, been written about, demonstrated and copied, but often without the attitudes that are necessary to make them work. The effect of this has been to reduce the new to the old, to reduce a vertical development to a horizontal development, to copy the technique and miss the insight.

Here are a couple of examples of Teacher copying a Facilitative technique: (1) The Teacher uses an activity that requires a degree of self-disclosure by the participants, but the atmosphere is not sufficiently supportive nor is the level of trust sufficiently high to enable the activity to run. The activity either grinds to a halt or redirects itself along a safer path that may lead nowhere. (2) The Teacher forces the students to decide for themselves (Humanistic tyranny!), or leaves them to self-direct when they aren't ready to (Abdication).

To complete the picture here are a couple of examples of Lecturer copying a Teaching technique: (1) The Lecturer, in his attempt not to Lecture or 'tell', over-compensates and tries to elicit what isn't there, missing the opportunity to give just what is needed. (2) The Lecturer sabotages her own attempts to set up group work by her unconscious conviction that it would be much better if she simply told them, and by her reluctance to leave centre-stage.

The point of all this is that new techniques with old attitudes may amount to no change, while new attitudes even with old techniques can lead to significant change. From the outside Teaching and Facilitating appear to be driven by different techniques, but from the inside they are driven by different attitudes, intentions and experiences.

Individuals are always pioneering the thresholds between Lecturer and Teacher and between Teacher and Facilitator and they face all the difficulties that pioneers usually face. But the quantum jump to a wider acceptability occurs only when a critical mass of teachers, researchers, authors, etc. put the new area firmly on the map on behalf of the profession. This has happened and is happening in many places for methodology at the Teacher level, but has not happened yet at the Facilitator level of people processes. However, I foresee a considerable increase in this area of activity over the next couple of decades.

There are aspects of this Lecturer – Teacher – Facilitator framework that need to be questioned; nevertheless I propose it as a useful thinking tool, and I offer it for discussion and for improvement. Within the framework of the main issue, which does not in fact depend on the validity of the framework itself, is the view I have proposed of the Facilitator, and in the remainder of the chapter we will focus on a few practical aspects of Facilitation.

Practical steps towards Facilitation

Facilitation is holistic. This means that everything counts: all aspects of the Facilitator's presence including feelings, attitudes, thoughts, physical presence, movements, quality of attention, degree of openness and so on, have an effect on the learning atmosphere and on what possibilities within each group member are opened or closed at any moment. What follows are some invitations to experiment and explore these areas in simple and subtle ways in order to help you get to know some current and typical ways of working at the Facilitator level. I have found them helpful.

If you decide you'd like to work with them, here are a few suggestions:

- Approach these questions with the open spirit of an adventurer and explorer and try to greet discoveries with delight and curiosity.
- Choose a single question or experiment and try it out during your usual class teaching. Observe or witness yourself while teaching, perhaps by building reminders into your lesson plan.
- Try a question for a few days but leave it before it loses its freshness, and try another, then return to a previous experiment and so on.
- Though the questions look simple, you'll find as you work with them that they gradually deepen and reveal more and more about how you interact with yourself and with your students.
- Discussion with a colleague who is trying the same thing may help

clarify your experience, and recording your observations may help you discern your patterns.

- Reflection and discussion which is not based on concrete self-observation in the heat of the moment will leave the questions cold and incapable of catalysing insight. In other words be wary of too much theory talk.
- At all times be especially interested in the discrepancies you will certainly find between the effect you think you have and the effect you actually have.
- The process of becoming conscious of previously habitual ways of doing things can feel strange initially, but it is the first step in turning habits into choices, which seems to me an excellent approach to teacher development.

1 The way you listen

1.1 From time to time during lessons try to catch yourself in the act of listening to a student, and notice *how* you listen. Don't change your listening, just notice what you do and how you do it. What else takes your attention apart from the person speaking? What else goes on in you that distracts your attention away from the person you are listening to?

1.2 Can you, while listening to a student, very simply deepen the attention you pay, in a supportive and respectful way? Nothing need look different on the outside, the movement being entirely within. What is that movement? And what is necessary for it to take place? To pay attention in this way does not require agreeing with the person, it simply means listening accurately both to the words and to the person behind the words.

1.3 As you get a little accustomed to 'noticing the quality of your own listening', can you sometimes notice small judgements, or irritations or impatiences that seem to creep in from nowhere? For example, finding yourself silently disapproving of his pronunciation, or of her not having done her homework, or of his getting the answer wrong, or wishing she would hurry up and be correct. Can you catch yourself (very subtly) wishing a student was a bit different from the way he is?

1.4 Do you notice occasions when you feel you listen well? How do you know that? Do you notice that the quality of your listening can sometimes affect the quality of the speaker's speaking? What makes this possible? Maybe outer conditions (such as the location, noise, time of day) contribute, but you can also listen well when outer conditions are not so favourable.

2 *The way you speak*

2.1   Having made a provisional study of the way you listen to students, can you begin to notice more about the way you speak to your class? (I find this a more difficult and more advanced exercise of attention.) Start by noticing your words. Do you say more than you need? Do you repeat yourself? Can you be succinct? Try to notice this at the moment you do it, not just in retrospect. Never mind all that is said about teacher talking time, we are referring here to teacher talking quality.

2.2   For a few days notice features of your speech other than your words. For example, observe the tone of your voice, including intonation, timbre, softness, harshness. Notice the volume at which you speak, and also how fast you typically speak. What causes this? How do the tone, volume and speed compare with the way you speak in the staffroom? And with your family? And with your friends?

2.3   And what do you tend to do with silences? Fill them? Avoid them? Enjoy them? Worry that the class will get out of control during them? I find it helpful to look on silences and pauses as part of the words, rather than as something separate. In general, what other messages are carried by the *way* you speak?

2.4   I find it useful to distinguish between my first voice (my choice of words) and my second voice (everything else including my volume, tone, speed, body language, gesture, transmission of feelings). Then I can ask myself helpfully provocative questions such as 'Do my first voice and second voice say the same thing?' and 'If not, what is the effect on my students?' 'Which is the one I really mean, and which is the one they really listen to?' Can you try to monitor both your first and second voice? If you can, try to notice when they say the same thing, and when they give different messages.

2.5   From time to time during the day, when giving explanations or instructions in your class, make some subtle changes just to confirm to yourself that you have choices in addition to your habits. You could experiment with any of these: Be a bit more succinct, then stop and listen. Notice if you get carried away with the delightful sound of your own voice! Leave a few short pauses during which you listen and observe. Deliberately lengthen your existing pauses by just a second or so. Be behind your voice so that you speak with the force and warmth of your full presence. Speak just a little more softly than usual. These are just examples, but better still, experiment with small changes of your own.

Do you have the typical 'teacher's intonation' (just as priests, politicians and others have theirs) which maintains distance between you and the class? Just for an experiment you could try changing it, not so that it sounds different to others, but so that it feels different to you. Perhaps speak with one degree less anxiety, and one degree more intimacy. Again, make your own experiments.

3   Your use of power and authority

This is about the politics of the classroom, and particularly about *your* classroom politics, as manifested through the way you share or don't share power and authority with your students. Your political system is part of your overall classroom atmosphere which your students are immersed in for the whole of every lesson. There are two aspects to the political question. The first is 'To what extent are you aware of all the decisions that you are taking before and during your lessons?' And the second, which can only be answered after working on the first, is 'To what extent do you share power and decision-making wherever it is appropriate and possible?'

In other words, do you essentially trust or mistrust your students' capacity to become more self-evaluating, self-directing and autonomous? Or do you trust it with your first voice and mistrust it with your second? And if you feel you do have this basic trust, then are there perhaps opportunities for them to take more responsibility for their self-direction which you are missing?

3.1   Over several days keep a note of the decisions you take that affect either what your students learn or how they learn. This is not as easy as it seems because many decisions are taken habitually rather than consciously, simply as part of being a teacher. Some of the areas my decisions cover seem to be: the planning of what is to be done; deciding how it is to be done; deciding how decisions are to be made; how learners make sense of their learning; how a valuing and supportive atmosphere is maintained; how group difficulties and individual feelings are recognised and worked with; making class rules and contracts; dealing with their infringement; maintaining engagement and joy.

3.2   When you have identified a number of individual decisions divide them into those which are entirely non-negotiable (e.g. the lesson starts at 10.30; the syllabus is determined by the ministry; the book is already chosen; school is compulsory), and those which you could in theory negotiate with your students (e.g. how we start the lesson, which exercise we leave out, whether we have a dictation and how we go about it ...). Now discard those decisions that you have marked as non-negotiable, and divide the negotiable ones into those you feel would be a high risk to negotiate with your students, and those which would be a low risk.

3.3 Build some of the low risk decisions into the appropriate parts of your lesson, and invite your class to participate in making the decision. (Examples might include: 'Would you like to do the exercise this way or that way ... or do you have another suggestion ... ?' 'What would be useful and enjoyable homework to follow on from what we've done today ... ?' 'What shall we do with the mistakes from the dictation ... ?'.) If they have become unused to making decisions, they may be reluctant to participate at first, but that's quite acceptable, since you only ask learners to do what they are ready for, and you do this gradually, perhaps at first going with their initial preference for the teacher to provide the guidelines. To impose self-direction on a learner who is not ready for it is just another form of teacher-centred tyranny. The important thing is that you make the invitation, because that in itself educates.

3.4 Is there room for negotiation in the way you give instructions for an activity? After giving the instruction, can you consult the students to see if anyone has any variation or other suggestion for how the activity might be done? (When I was eleven, if my Latin teacher had asked me for suggestions on how we could make our learning more interesting, I could have given him many, but he never asked.)

3.5 And after finishing an activity, you probably review the learning content with your students. But can you also review the process of doing it? ('What did you enjoy about doing this ... ? What was not so enjoyable? How could we change it so that you would learn more from it ... ?')

There are many non-negotiable constraints on the students (syllabuses, exams, teacher, other learners, parental choice, school facilities, class size and mix) which impose directions they do not choose, and which are not optional. The Facilitator helps learners to deal with the impositions where they have no choice, and also to exploit the choices that are still open to them.

4 Your attention to the processes in the group

4.1 This is an exercise of attention. Can you from time to time in a lesson deliberately broaden your attention to take account of more of what is going on in the group? The aim is to notice along a wider waveband, to empathise, to put yourself in the place of others to get an idea of how the lesson looks and feels from their point of view. This requires not only mental attention, it is also helped by openness of feeling and lack of physical tension. Who in the group is struggling? Who is dominating? What are the contribution rates? What is the misunderstanding? Who is engaged and who seems not to be? Can you 'see' the learning going on in some of them? What is silently bubbling away just below the surface?

4.2 Inviting feedback at the end of lessons is a way of drawing everyone's attention to the processes in the group. Do you ask for feedback? And do you ask for it in such a way that students feel able to speak honestly? (The opposite, which I know in myself, is a kind of defensiveness and reluctance to have feedback which is carried by my second voice while my first voice apparently requests feedback. The resulting crossed message makes it difficult for my students to speak sincerely.) Next time you ask for feedback try to notice your choice of words and your voice tone, and indeed your real underlying intention. If students are not used to being taken into account and to having their views valued, they may at first find it difficult to give feedback. But again the fact of doing it at all is in itself educational.

4.3 Feelings are part of the powerhouse of the group process. Your students' feelings about themselves and each other, about what they are learning and how, all affect the quality of their learning. Your feelings too have a great effect on the group. There is no choice in this, the only choice is whether you pay attention to it or not. So, when it seems appropriate, perhaps when inviting feedback or having a review session, can you invite group members to say how they feel about being in the group and about what they are doing? And when there are disagreements or conflicts, which every group has, can you allow opportunities for them to be voiced? As Facilitator, you don't have to 'solve the problem' or 'make the feelings go away', simply respect, listen and understand. What they say is a fact, and facts are friendly to the consciously developing group.

4.4 Notice how you typically behave in non-classroom groups of which you are a member. What are your ways of making a group safe for yourself? Being silent, or careful, or outspoken, or funny, or confidential, or reckless, or foolish, or responsible, or sensitive, or insensitive or indispensible? How do your preferred roles change in an established group, a new group, a small group, a big group, a group of colleagues, or strangers, a group you've invested in, a group you haven't invested in, a group you value, a group you don't? What does your particular repertoire of group behaviours tell you about your behaviours in the classes you teach? What kinds of student behaviour do you admire or disapprove of? Are those similar to or different from some of your own behaviours in groups?

4.5 To what extent is your preferred teacher role one of distance on the one hand, or intimacy on the other? How much are you able to be yourself as well as the teacher? As the group gains its momentum, are you able to be a group member youself, learning alongside the others, not necessarily learning the same thing – after all you already know the topic – but perhaps learning about their learning through your watchfulness, learning about your capacity to see the options and then to make the right intervention at the right time? Are you able to be somehow 'on the same side of the learning fence'?

5 Noticing your own attitudes and beliefs

5.1 What do you really believe, according to your inner thoughts and deepest convictions, about learning and teaching? Is this embodied in the way you behave and relate in the classroom? What discrepancies are there between your beliefs, your intentions and your behaviours?

5.2 And what discrepancies can you notice between what you think you do and what you actually do, and what you'd like to do? How can you explore this more, and through conscious realisation, turn these discrepancies to advantage?

5.3 What is it like to be taught by you? How might an observant and sensitive student in your class describe your unique psychological signature, the atmosphere you create by the way you are? I have heard it said that 'we teach what we are', and I am aware that while the topic I teach may be the cognitive focus for the class, my students are immersed all the time in the manifestation of my attitudes towards, for example, authority, gender, time, mistakes, correctness, money, other people, individual differences, speed and slowness, and, not least of all, my attitudes towards myself. Can you catch the way your attitudes leak into the class atmosphere?

5.4 What habits do you have in the way you teach? I'm thinking of things like: your first words on entering the class; catch phrases; the pile of stuff you take into the class; how you begin a lesson; remarks you always make to a certain student; fossilised jokes; talking to one side of the class; giving the same examples, and so on. Identify a typical teaching habit of yours and try to do the opposite for a day – not because it's better that way, but as an experiment in working consciously rather than compulsively.

6   *Redefining problems. Seeing things differently*

6.1   Take a problem that you have at the moment in one of your groups (a learner who is difficult for you, lack of materials or equipment, a conflict in the group ...). Which components of the problem are 'out there' and which are 'in here'? And which can you change in some way, and which can you not change?

6.2   Of the aspects of the problem that you cannot change, can you find a different outlook, another viewpoint from which the problem looks different? This is an important skill to cultivate, not just for your own health, but because your students' view of problems is influenced by yours. Do you sometimes find a creative side to a difficulty? Can you turn a problem to advantage?

7   *Your own inner state*

This is the biggest question and the closest to home. Your inner state determines your outer behaviour, and speaks eloquently through your second voice. It affects the intelligence and warmth you can bring to situations as well as the anxiety or pleasure you get from them. It also affects the amount of energy you expend.

7.1   Your energy. On what do you spend your energy while at school? What exhausts you in a day of teaching? How does that differ from a day spent at home? Or the weekend? Or a day on holiday? Why the difference? And what is the difference between a good day and a bad day? What classroom events in particular consume your personal energy? And from what events do you derive energy? How much energy do you use on being impatient in the classroom? Is it possible next time to experiment with different and less costly responses to the same situation? Can you change the situation by changing your response to it?

7.2   Centering yourself. It may help you (as it does me) to think of this in two stages. The first has to do with letting go of the tensions that steal your energy and the second has to do with freeing up more attention to pay to the present moment. So the first step means letting go of unnecesary tensions in the body, in the feelings and in the mind. In the body by relaxing the muscles that are not actually needed for the job in hand (standing, sitting, speaking, writing on the board); in the feelings by letting go of emotional tensions like anxiety, impatience, disapproval, regret about the last lesson or apprehension about the next. And in the mind by slowing down the flow of associative, chattering thoughts, or at least allowing a bit more space between them.

This first step of relaxation frees up energy which is then available for the second step, which is increased alertness to the actions and interactions of the present moment. When the body is relaxed, and the feelings are open, and the mind is ready, I am more able to participate in and be present to what is happening here and now. I am actually more present, less absent. You can call this state 'relaxed alertness'. 'Relaxed' refers to letting go of tensions as far as possible, and 'alertness' refers to spending the energy thus saved on increased attention.

There are many ways of centering yourself, and you may have your own, but most will contain these two steps in one form or another. Experiment with your own ways of doing what I have described above, and take great interest in what you find out about yourself while looking for the results. A sustained and gentle search in this direction will lead to subtle and significant changes in your classroom.

Conclusion

Facilitation is a rigorous practice since more is at stake. It pays attention to a broader spectrum of human moves than does either Lecturing or Teaching. The move from Lecturer to Teacher to Facilitator is characterised by a progressive reduction in the psychological distance between teacher and student, and by an attempt to take more account of the learner's own agenda, even to be guided by it. Control becomes more decentralised, democratic, even autonomous, and what the Facilitator saves on controlling is spent on fostering communication, curiosity, insight and relationship in the group. This necessitates the development of a range of Facilitative skills and awarenesses, some of which have been referred to in the questions above.

Facilitation does not allow me just to work on my students 'out there'; it also requires me to work on myself 'in here'. The way I am becomes part of the learning equation, and from the humanistic point of view the way I am is not fixed but capable of development throughout my life. What makes this approach so exciting and so revitalising is that I find I can help my students' learning through my own learning, and my own learning is not just something I do before and after the lesson, what really counts is the learning I do during the lesson. My students' learning may be about the topic, but my learning is about the group and its members including myself, now, moment by moment. This is what keeps me and my students on the same side of the learning fence. Perhaps I even set a limit on the learning my students can do during a lesson by the amount of learning I am doing alongside them and at the same time.

Suggestions for further reading

Brandes, D. and P. Ginnis. 1986. *A Guide to Student-Centered Learning*. Oxford: Basil Blackwell.

Gattegno, C. 1972. *Teaching Foreign Languages in Schools*. Reading: Educational Explorers.

Hadfield, J. 1992. *Classroom Dynamics*. Oxford: Oxford University Press.

Head, K. and P. Taylor. 1997. *Readings in Teacher Development*. Oxford: Heinemann.

Jersild, D. 1955. *When Teachers Face Themselves*. New York: Columbia University Press.

Rogers, C. 1994. *Freedom to Learn*. New York: Merrill.

Stevick, E. W. 1980. *Teaching Languages: A Way and Ways*. Rowley, Mass: Newbury House.

Stevick, E. W. 1990. *Humanism in Language Teaching*. Oxford: Oxford University Press.

9 Affect and the role of teachers in the development of learner autonomy

Naoko Aoki

> I have realised that learning by trying and thinking for ourselves with the teacher's assistance is fun. I have also learned that learners can learn a lot from each other... I have also got used to talking in a small group and to the whole class. I give myself an A, because I was able to feel I had learned all these things.
>
> (Yuko, at the end of the course)

Introduction

The gist of learner autonomy is that a learner develops 'the ability to take charge of his or her own learning' (Holec 1981:3). The concept of autonomy has evolved over time, but it was in the 1970s when Henri Holec introduced the term to the field of second language pedagogy as a conceptual tool to discuss alternatives to the established language teaching tradition in the context of adult language learning. As Gremmo and Riley (1995) have pointed out, the work by Holec and his associates was a response to the political milieu in France in the late 1960s and shared its ideological stance with contemporary critics of the traditional educational system, such as Ivan Illich (1970), Paulo Freire (1972) and Carl Rogers (1961, 1969). The concept of autonomy has since found a place in mainstream education. Many national curricula in Europe, for example, state learner autonomy as an objective. An increasing number of self-access centres in Asian tertiary institutions have also stimulated significant work in learner autonomy. North American researchers have taken up the idea and integrated it in the tradition of research about the good language learner.

In the course of this rather rapid spread of the concept, the term *autonomy* has acquired many different shades of meaning, which have sometimes caused confusion about what learner autonomy might entail. Among the issues is whether learner autonomy is a matter of learners' psychology or if it involves socio-political factors surrounding the learners (P. Benson 1996). Focusing on the cognitive side of psychology, Little (1996a) affirms that the argument concerning how learner autonomy can be developed in pedagogical practice assumes psychological dimensions, but that it is also inescapably political because 'the psychological argument challenges traditional educational structures and power relationships' (1996a:8). In this chapter I shall elaborate my interpretation of learner autonomy and how it might develop, and show that being affective[1] can also be political.

Reconceiving autonomy

The concept of autonomy has traditionally been associated with individualism. This is not surprising because autonomy, as known to many in present day Western and non-Western societies, was born in the rationalistic tradition of eighteenth-century Europe. Claims have been made, however, that autonomy should not necessarily imply total independence. Little (1991, 1996b) shows that second language learner autonomy presupposes interdependence because language development requires interaction. From a communitarian point of view, Benson (1996) argues that the individualistic view of autonomy leads to social atomism, which disempowers individuals; he emphasizes the importance of collective effort in the exercise of autonomy.

In addition to these two arguments, I shall add yet another justification for not equating autonomy with complete independence. In her effort to reconceive autonomy in the field of political and legal theory from a feminist perspective, Nedelsky (1989) states that feminists, while valuing the human capacity for determining one's own life and self, take a view that people develop their identity in social and political relations. She recognizes the inherent tensions in 'the idea of autonomy as both originating in oneself *and* being conditioned and shaped by one's social context' (1989:11, emphasis in the original), and claims that the objective in reconceiving autonomy involves not only recognizing that the tension between the two forces leads to trade-offs but also moving beyond a conception of human beings as separate individuals. Furthermore, Nedelsky notes that the capacity for autonomy is unlikely to exist without a feeling of being autonomous and claims that this feeling is the

---

[1] Affect is commonly defined as the area covering feelings, emotions, mood and temperament (Chaplin 1975). I shall, however, use the terms affect, emotions and feelings almost interchangeably, because the writers I shall quote do not generally use these terms with explicitly distinctive definitions; and, for the purpose of the present chapter, it is not necessary to distinguish in a rigorous manner the concepts related to these terms in theoretical work in psychology.

best guide to understand the structure of those relationships which make autonomy possible. She also contends that focusing on the feelings of autonomy gives authority to the voices of those whose autonomy is at issue. Based on these arguments, Nedelsky sees autonomy as 'a capacity that exists only in the context of social relations that support it and only in conjunction with the internal sense of being autonomous' (1989:25). It is in this understanding that I shall develop my arguments in this chapter.

Autonomy as a capacity

Synthesizing existing literature (Holec 1981, 1985; Little 1991; Bergen 1990 cited in Dam 1995; Benson 1996), I define learner autonomy as a capacity to take control of one's own learning in the service of one's perceived needs and aspirations. I take the view that the core of learner autonomy is a psychological construct, but I think what this construct is put to use for is as important because this can greatly influence the feeling of autonomy. In concrete terms, learner autonomy as a capacity refers to the domain-specific knowledge and skills necessary (1) to make choices concerning what, why and how to learn, (2) to implement the plan and (3) to evaluate the outcome of learning. I limit the scope of autonomy to one domain because, as has been pointed out (Little 1991:4), 'the learner who displays a high degree of autonomy in one area may be non-autonomous in another'.

In the case of second language learning developing the capacity for autonomy entails considering areas such as the following:

– What benefits and drawbacks learning a second language could have in general.
– What benefits and drawbacks learning a particular language could have.
– What the nature of language and language learning is.
– What are the language elements, if any, that need to be learned regardless of one's purpose, and to what degree.
– For the purpose of one's study, what elements of the language need to be learned and to what degree.
– In what order these elements could be learned.
– How these elements could be learned.
– How much time it would normally take to learn a particular element.
– How objectives can be set and study plans made.
– What the necessary resources are and where they are available.
– What kind of language learner one is and how one learns.

– How the learning of a particular item can be evaluated as one learns and after one has learned.

In the case of present-day second language learning, learners can provide themselves with necessary information from libraries, the World Wide Web and self-access centres, as well as from other people's experiences, which have always supported everyday cognition (Lave and Wenger 1991; Rogoff 1995). As long as the learners know that information will be accessible when needed and that it will be transparent, or understandable, to their eyes, their feeling of autonomy will not necessarily be impaired if they do not have everything they need to know right at their fingertips. On the other hand, learners with a lot of knowledge and skills may still feel helpless if they are allowed no choice. The amount of knowledge and skills learners have and the degree of their feeling of autonomy do not necessarily correlate. Therefore, both factors need to be considered in order to develop learner autonomy more fully.

Development through practice

It has been shown in the studies of everyday cognition (Lave and Wenger 1991; Rogoff 1995) that learning comes about through participation in practice, although all types of participation are not necessarily empowering. In my understanding the characteristics of empowering participation are (1) novices are recognized as legitimate members of a relevant community of practice who share or are supposed to share the community's values, beliefs, customs and so forth, as well as knowledge and skills directly related to the practice, (2) novices work with expert practitioners, more experienced apprentices and their peers and carry out a role, secondary as it may be, in the process of the practice with a view to become a full practitioner in the future and (3) support to accomplish tasks assigned to novices is provided by making observation of others' work possible, by providing easily manageable tools, and by sharing experiences. If we substitute *decision-making* for *practice* in the above sentence, we come up with a description of how learner autonomy might develop. Learners are recognized as legitimate members of a decision-making body of an educational programme and work with teachers (plus head teachers, principals and curriculum developers, if the situation allows) with an expectation of everyone involved that learners will sooner or later take over all decision-making responsibilities. Learners do not have to make major decisions from the start, and a range of support is provided to enable them to make any decision they choose to make. This model seems to be compatible with Nedelsky's (1989) view of autonomy. Learners exercise the partial autonomy that they can handle with social support from the environment and thus develop their feeling of autonomy. The expectation that they will be fully autonomous in the future will further enhance the feeling.

One example of such a practice in second language education is Dam (1995). Dam starts her class with eleven-year-old Danish learners of English by asking them to bring some 'English' to the class. A cap bearing an English sentence, a tourist brochure, an advertisement, an old newspaper and a joke made by a learner all become 'Our Own Material'. Then learners write a paragraph of self-introduction by filling in a skeleton discourse with key words: My name is ... I live in ... My birthday is on ... etc. Learners can ask Dam or look up the words they need in a picture dictionary. There is also an activity of copying in their diaries words from the picture dictionary which learners find 'funny', 'exciting' or 'useful'. All of these activities involve making choices on the part of the learners. Dam also has brainstorming sessions as to what learners could do to learn English at home and in the classroom. After three weeks of two 90-minute lessons a week learners are able to choose an activity and do it in groups in the classroom. It is true that Dam works in a context where teachers have a fairly large amount of control over what to teach and how. In this particular situation learning English is supported by the social environment of Denmark, where a large part of the population speaks English and the significance of learning English is probably very obvious to the learners.

This does not mean, however, that practice of learner autonomy is only possible in an ideal situation. Teachers working under a national curriculum with an assigned standard textbook still have to make a series of decisions just to teach one lesson. A teacher can open the door to the practice of learner autonomy by sharing whatever control she has with her students.

If we are to follow the argument that autonomy develops through practice, we must trust that our learners have some knowledge and skills and that they can start developing their autonomy with whatever capacity they have. In fact, the importance of trust in learners has been pointed out by many practitioners interested in promoting learner autonomy and self-direction. Rogers (1980:117) maintains that 'there is in every organism, at whatever level, an underlying flow of movement toward constructive fulfillment of its inherent possibilities'. Brookfield (1993:1) contends that 'emphasizing people's right to self-direction also invests a certain trust in ... their capacity to make wise choices and take wise actions' and justifies this claim by stating 'if people had a chance to give voice to what most moves and hurts them, they would soon show that they were only too well aware of the real nature of their problems and of ways to deal with these'. The question, then, boils down to how we can support this flow of movement or provide opportunities for learners' voices to be heard. In other words, what are the social relations supportive of practice of learner autonomy?

The nature of supporting social relations

The role of teachers in the development of learner autonomy is generally considered to be that of facilitator, counsellor or resource (Voller 1997). According to Voller, both facilitators and counsellors provide psycho-social and technical supports, the difference between the two being that the former mostly work with groups and the latter in one-to-one situations. Psycho-social support refers to caring and to motivating learners, as well as to raising learners' awareness. Technical support refers to helping learners to plan and carry out their learning, to evaluate themselves, and to acquire the skills and knowledge needed to plan, implement and evaluate their learning.

The idea of teachers as resource is not as straightforward. In one sense a teacher can be seen as 'a talking encyclopedia or a talking catalogue' (Voller 1997:105). In another, the idea could, Voller warns, imply that teachers are the knowers or the experts and be used as a way of maintaining unequal power relations between teachers and learners.

Room for negotiation

In this section I shall share some of my students' comments, taken from their diaries and feedback to me. They all have an experience of being involved in decision-making concerning their learning, and I feel their view offers us valuable hints as to what might be the teacher's optimal role in building social relations supportive of practice of learner autonomy. After all, it is their autonomy that is at issue. The students I shall quote are all Japanese-speaking and enrolled in a Japanese as a second language (JSL) teacher preparation programme. I have translated all comments, which were originally written in Japanese.

The ultimate purpose of promoting learner autonomy is, I believe, for a learner to come to see him or herself as a 'producer of his [or her] society' (Janne 1977, cited in Holec 1981:1). Although dropping out and silent resistance may be considered forms of exercising one's autonomy (Breen and Mann 1997; Pennycook 1997), they are not likely to be the most constructive ways of doing so. If autonomy is to develop, there must be an opportunity to act upon the environment and change it through negotiation, in a way that is favourable to oneself. Dewey points out two aspects of experience:

> The nature of experience can be understood only by noting that it includes an active and a passive element peculiarly combined. On the active hand, experience is *trying* ... On the passive, it is *undergoing*. When we experience something we act upon it, we do something with it; then we suffer or undergo the consequences .... The connection of these two phases of experience measures the fruitfulness or value of the experience. Mere activity does not constitute experience. (Dewey 1916:139, emphasis in the original)

Working in a situation where learners can do anything they want would probably not produce salient experiences of changing the environment. In the following comment a student reflects on a brainstorming session and on her experience in a one-week intensive workshop which operated on the rights the students claimed during that brainstorming session:

> Rights need to be exercised as well as claimed, don't they? Perhaps we thought rights were something teachers gave us ... I felt our 'learners' rights' were very much respected in this course, but I've realized it was made possible by you. I feel frustrated with myself. I was no good ...

Her frustration seems to reflect her perception that she did not have a changing-the-environment experience in the course because of my 'generosity'. She was only undergoing. Not trying. This student's feeling validates Pennycook's (1997:46) concern that autonomy should not be seen as just a matter of handing over power. The lesson I have learned from this student's comment is that simply being a nice progressive teacher may not help much. On the other hand, I feel it is crucial that teachers are open to negotiations, not only because learners need the *undergoing* phase of experience, but also because the act of negotiation conveys the important message that a teacher-learner relationship does not necessarily have to be the one of the controller and the controlled.

One student points out how at first a more autonomous learning situation can lead to some confusion:

> It was a form of class I'd never experienced. I didn't trust you in the beginning. I kept wondering 'Is it really OK to do this?', 'Is she really going to be true to her words?'. Now I understand

this way of learning has a lot of merits, but it's so different from the teacher-learner relationship we know. I often didn't know what to do . . .

The only way I could think of to convince a student like her that a teacher-learner relationship can be different is to make myself open to negotiations and make sure that the outcome of the negotiation is implemented. Practice of autonomy in a classroom should not be confined to the freedom to learn within a framework the teacher has set.

Institutions also need to be prepared to be flexible if they claim learner autonomy as their goal. In this respect Jones' (1995) description of the physical design of a self-access centre in Cambodia and the students' involvement in the designing process seems to be a very good example of support to practice learner autonomy. Jones gave up his own image of what a self-access centre should be like and made way for students' ideas to be implemented. This must have had an immense influence on the students' inner feeling of autonomy. Jones reports that 'with enthusiasm [of the Self-access Advisory Committee which consists of student volunteers] came a sense of pride in and responsibility for the self-access centre which, we believe, other students are beginning to share' (Jones 1995:232).

A psychologically secure environment

Participation in decision-making involves voice, which is not, however, something that automatically comes with a teacher's decision to ask the students about their preferences. In fact the concept of voice is not unproblematic, as Ellsworth (1992:105) shows in her analysis of critical pedagogy. She claims that 'what they/we say, to whom, in what context, depending on the energy they/we have for the struggle on a particular day, is the result of conscious and unconscious assessments of the power relations and safety of the situation' and emphasizes the importance of 'issues of trust, risk, and the operations of fear and desire around such issues of identity and politics in the classroom'.

The following comment by a student, written at the beginning of a school year, seems to have far-reaching implications concerning what a language teacher could do to create an environment where students can comfortably speak up:

I'm not good at talking. I wouldn't take this course if the classroom had rigid rows of desks and the teacher had us go in front near the podium to be seen by everyone. There's one course that I sense is going to be like that and I'm so scared . . .

What this student is saying is that exposure to others is a threat, and that the teacher has the power to force learners into such threatening situations. And she notices that the arrangement of classroom furniture is a device to create such situations. If we want this type of learner to exercise their autonomy freely in the classroom, we would need to create an alternative physical environment, make reduced teacher power visible, and turn threatening others into caring classmates.

After a game played in a circle to learn everyone's name, another student who had had a similar feeling of anxiety wrote:

> I didn't know any of the people in the class and worried what kind of people my classmates would be, but the name game relaxed me a lot. My self-consciousness and anxiety about being looked at turned into a will to look.

Here is a dramatic transformation of a person from an object of other people's gaze to a subject who looks. Although she does not articulate what exactly triggered this change, it is suspected that the arrangement of the chairs, together with the personal nature of the game, might have contributed to bringing it about. Students often refer to the arrangement of chairs in a horse shoe or in a circle as a factor which facilitates participation.

I have also found verbal and nonverbal ice-breaking activities (e.g. Maley and Duff 1982; Klippel 1984; Hadfield 1992) are an extremely helpful way to start a course. The sense of groupness developed initially, however, needs to be nurtured if it is to last for the rest of the course and even beyond (Hammond and Collins 1991:42).

One student points out a further potential problem:

> The atmosphere of the group was good. If I could change anything, it would have been better if we had milled around in a more unstructured way. Students enrolled in the same pro-gramme tended to stick together, and juniors and seniors tended to be separate. But I assume some felt safer that way. So I guess it was alright.

Besides this tendency of learners to stay in previously existing comfort zone groups, gender and the first language are often limiting factors. And there is always a possibility that a power relationship exists not only between the teacher and the students, but also among the students. Although students often come to value one another through working together in groups and sharing reflections, and some-times even through conflicts with each other, it seems crucial to me that a teacher should gently but persistently insist that everyone's wish be heard and that everyone's contribution be acknowledged. As Rogers

(1980:300) claims, the teacher's attitude towards each learner seems to be infectious.

In terms of making reduced teacher power visible, a factor that might be worth considering is teachers' paralinguistic and nonverbal behaviours. The process of negotiation can have that function, but verbal negotiation is extremely difficult if the students decide not to talk. And talking to silent students will not change the landscape. Students, however, seem to be sensitive to teachers' paralinguistic and nonverbal behaviours and to respond to different behaviours in different ways. A junior high school teacher of English once told me that she had managed to have an interaction with a very quiet thirteen-year-old Japanese student by whispering questions to her. One of my students commented that in a group formation activity teachers should stay away from the front of the class to make the talking easier. This comment mirrors Hooks's (1994:138) reflection on the difference in her feeling of power when she is and is not behind the podium. Another student writes:

> You talked to us in the same posture as ours. I guess you were trying to erase the boundary between the teacher and the students by keeping your eyes on the same level as ours ...

Kelly (1996:96) points out that helpers in language counselling at a self-access centre need to acquire a set of nonverbal behaviours as well as verbal skills of counselling. Kelly's examples include orienting your body to them, turning your face to them, maintaining comfortable eye contact, pausing and being silent so that the other can speak, nodding, and smiling. I suspect that these factors might also play an important role in encouraging students' voice in a classroom.

When learners need a teacher

Learners in the process of becoming autonomous need a teacher for a variety of reasons. I shall, however, focus only on the issue of teachers as resource here. As Brookfield (1993) contends, exercising autonomy requires access to resources. A well stocked self-access centre with all materials nicely catalogued might to a large extent release teachers from playing the role of resource, but teachers would have to be prepared to be used by learners as a resource when a self-access centre is an unobtainable luxury. However, teachers need to be flexible in determining what exactly they should or could do in fulfilling this role, because it all depends on where each learner is along the path of becoming autonomous. Compare the following two comments:

> Your advice was very effective when we got stuck or needed some inspiration. But you were sometimes not in the room when we needed your help in putting things together and furthering our discussion.

> When we got stuck in our thinking we thought about going to look for you, but we didn't. Instead we examined the problem from a different angle and we almost solved it. If you had been there, we wouldn't have experienced the satisfaction of almost solving the problem.

Both refer to the teacher's absence. One student feels that the teacher's unavailability was a negative factor, while the other takes it as an opportunity to exercise her and her peers' capacity. Judging who needs what is actually a matter of moment by moment decision-making on the part of the teacher. On one occasion when I was working with a group of JSL learners, one of them wanted to say 'Among the pitchers, which one do you like best?', but only had in his repertoire 'Which pitcher do you like best?' He knew that it did not fit in the discourse which he and his peers had developed, and he looked at me. Whispering the sentence that he needed to the student on the spot would probably not have damaged his autonomy, but I missed the timing and the group carried on with the conversation.

To be a useful but not interfering resource requires teachers to always 'be' with the students, although this does not necessarily mean that teachers need to be physically present. Some learners prefer to have explicit error corrections in learning pronunciation. Learners' decisions to ask for a correction should be respected. In order to respond to the request, and not to correct when not requested or when learners should be able to correct themselves, teachers need to know exactly where each learner is in interacting with them, which requires specialized knowledge and skills. Somewhat paradoxically, teachers need greater expertise to level the power imbalance between the teacher and the learner than to hold all the power themselves.

Self-evaluation

In the case of university students, there is, of course, pressure to accumulate credits for the successful completion of their degree. Asked if teacher evaluation is necessary, many students express a view that teachers cannot have knowledge of all aspects of the process they are going through; therefore, truly accurate evaluation of learning by a teacher is not possible. But students still need credits. So I normally just ask them to evaluate themselves with whatever criteria they have and to tell me about the grade they give to themselves and why. This seems to have an extremely empowering effect. A student writes:

> I appreciate this way of evaluation very much because our effort is recognized. I couldn't think of any better way for me. I think everyone in this group has a clear conscience about this. I believe this evaluation satisfactorily represents our achievement.

What she is referring to here is the Kantian concept of autonomy: giving law to oneself. She is saying loud and clear that she and her colleagues are autonomous. Of course there are some who are unsure about the level of knowledge they have acquired. Others show concern that they might evaluate themselves higher than those who really deserve a higher grade. A few complain that it is difficult. But even those students tend to take self-evaluation as an opportunity for reflection. The teacher's role here is evidently not to evaluate. She or he should rather help students to clarify what they feel are appropriate criteria for evaluating their own learning.

One thing that is particularly important to mention in the context of affective language learning is the fact that students often refer to the feelings and emotions that they have experienced in learning as criteria for their self-evaluation: a sense of self-value arising out of the perception that one is an indispensable member of a group, frustration with a project that came to a halt, confidence about future academic work, satisfaction with and pride in one's achievement, fun ... The need to give emotions a legitimate place in education is increasingly clear. Self-evaluation seems to be able to contribute to that purpose by allowing students' 'natural' criteria of evaluation to have power.

By way of conclusion: how being affective can be political

At the beginning of this chapter I referred to Little (1996a), who claims that considering the cognitive side of learner autonomy is inevitably political and states that being affective could also be political. Rogers (1980:294) summarized a different meaning of the word 'politics':

> ... I believe that the word 'politics' has to do with power of control in interpersonal relationships, and the extent to which persons strive to gain such power – or to relinquish it. It has to do with the way decisions are made. Who makes them? Where is the locus, or center, of decision-making power? 'Politics' concerns the effects of such power-oriented actions on individuals or on systems.

Understood in this way, considering the roles affect might play in the development and practice of learner autonomy becomes no less political than considering its cognitive side. I have been exploring what roles affect might play in the development and practice of learner autonomy, and for several reasons this is also inevitably political. First, this position claims that it should be the students' feeling of autonomy that decides whether they are autonomous or not, thus giving an authority to their feeling. Second, it takes a view that learner autonomy only develops through practice, which leads to a recognition of the students as legitimate members of a decision-making body concerning their learning. Third, it presupposes negotiation between the students and the teachers, which requires a new teacher-learner relationship. Fourth, it acknowledges the influence of power distribution pattern in the classroom situation on students' voice and feeling of autonomy. Fifth, it claims that teachers and institutions are responsible for supporting practice of learner autonomy. And finally, because of all these features, if we regard the classroom as a society, it involves social change. This version of autonomy, however, reflects 'the level of engagement' (Benson 1997:32) that both my students and I feel we can handle. It will be insufficiently political for some, and too political for others. Our practice of autonomy in Japan has also been supported, perhaps unwittingly, by the Japanese tertiary education system, where the pressure on teachers for accountability is still minimal and where they enjoy a high degree of independence in their teaching. What I have claimed in this chapter should by no means be taken to be equally useful in all situations. I do believe, however, that teachers and learners working together creatively in the spirit of co-conspirators can find ways to practice their autonomy in almost any situation.

Suggestions for further reading

Benson, P. and P. Voller (Eds.) 1997. *Autonomy and Independence in Language Learning*. New York: Addison Wesley Longman.

Dam, L. 1995. *Learner Autonomy 3: From Theory to Classroom Practice*. Dublin: Authentik.

Little, D. 1991. *Learner Autonomy 1: Definitions, Issues and Problems*. Dublin: Authentik.

Pemberton, R., E. S. L. Li, W. W. F. Or, and H. D. Pierson (Eds.) 1996. *Taking Control: Autonomy in Language Learning*. Hong Kong: Hong Kong University Press.

Riley, P. (Ed.) 1985. *Discourse and Learning*. New York: Longman.

10 The role of group dynamics in foreign language learning and teaching[1]

Zoltán Dörnyei and Angi Malderez

> [In a language course] success depends less on materials, techniques and linguistic analyses, and more on what goes on inside and between the people in the classroom.
>
> (Stevick 1980:4)

In our quest to discover the nature of effective teaching and learning, we have come to agree more and more with Earl Stevick's statement (quoted above) concerning success in language learning. Consideration of the 'between people' factors led us to ask the following questions:

– What does, in fact, go on between people in a classroom?
– How does this affect the learning process?
– Will an understanding of the 'between people' factors provide clues to why some of our groups are easy and comfortable to work with and others more difficult?
– What can we, as teachers, do to influence positively what goes on between people in a classroom?

In this chapter we attempt to address these questions from the perspective of group dynamics, which, as we will argue, is potentially very fruitful for the language teaching profession. The basic assumption underlying the chapter is that group processes are a fundamental factor in most learning contexts and can make all the difference when it comes to successful learning experiences and outcomes. As teachers, we have all experienced occasions when something 'went wrong' with the class and the L2 course became a nightmare where teaching was hard, if not impossible. As Tiberius (1990:v) states in the introduction of his unique trouble-shooting guide to small group teaching, 'Unless teachers are singularly fortunate or exceptionally oblivious, they become aware of problems in their teaching from time to time. For example, a class is

---

[1] Work by the first author and Madeline Ehrman on a book on group dynamics (Ehrman and Dörnyei 1998) has generated many ideas which have been influential in this chapter as well.

bored, hostile, uncomprehending, or simply not learning'. On the other hand, the L2 classroom can also turn out to be such a pleasant and inspiring environment that the time spent there is a constant source of success and satisfaction for teachers and learners alike. What is happening in these classes?

Our past experience and a consensus in the research literature indicate that group events are greatly responsible for:

- the participants' attitudes toward and affective perception of the learning process (Ehrman and Dörnyei 1988);
- the quantity and quality of interaction between group members (Levine and Moreland 1990);
- the extent of co-operation between students and the degree of individual involvement (Johnson and Johnson 1995);
- the order and discipline in the classroom (Jones and Jones 1995);
- students' relationships with their peers and the teacher (Ehrman and Dörnyei 1998);
- a significant proportion of the student's motivation to learn the L2 (Dörnyei in press);
- student and teacher confidence and satisfaction (Dörnyei and Malderez 1997).

Thus, we see group-related issues as being very much at the heart of the affective dimension of the L2 learning process. Regardless of whether or not the group leader – that is, the language teacher – pays attention to them, learning is strongly influenced by such group properties as structure, composition, cohesiveness, climate, norms, roles and interaction patterns, to name a few. Knowledge of these will allow the teacher to interpret group events, to intervene at the right time and with a clear purpose, and thereby consciously facilitate the emergence of harmonic and organic learning groups. As Jones and Jones (1995:101) point out:

> it is important to realize that groups, like individuals, have needs that must be met before the group can function effectively. If the classroom group is to function in a supportive, goal-directive manner, teachers must initially set aside time for activities that enable students to know each other, develop a feeling of being included, and create diverse friendship patterns. Only after these feelings have been developed can a group of students proceed to respond optimally to the learning goals of the classroom.

In sum, a group-centred approach looks at what goes on 'between people' and, to a certain extent, how that affects what goes on 'inside' them. We see the L2 teacher as a juggler rushing to keep the various plates of 'skills', 'pace', 'variety', 'activities', 'competencies', etc. all spinning on their sticks. Yet this job is doomed to failure if the affective ground in which the sticks are planted is not firm. We would suggest that an awareness of classroom dynamics may help teachers establish firm footing; the time and effort invested in establishing a solid 'affective group ground' will pay off in the long run as it will lead to an experience that is rewarding interpersonally, linguistically, pedagogically and developmentally for teacher and students alike.

In this chapter after providing a brief overview of the discipline, our main focus will be on the *development* of groups. We will also touch upon the effects of various *leadership styles*. (For overviews of other significant related topics, see the works listed in the Suggestions for further reading on page 169.)

What is 'group dynamics'?

Although groups vary in size, purpose, composition, character, etc., there are two simple but basic facts that have led to the formation of a discipline within the social sciences – *group dynamics* – to study them:

1. A group has a 'life of its own', that is, individuals in groups behave differently than they would do outside the group.
2. Even the most different kinds of groups appear to share some fundamental common features, making it possible to study *the group* in general.

The systematic study of the dynamics of groups was initiated in the United States by the social psychologist Kurt Lewin and his associates in the 1940s, and group issues have been studied since then within many different branches of the social sciences – social, industrial, organizational and clinical psychology, psychiatry, sociology and social work – that is, in fields which involve groups of various kinds as focal points around which human relationships are organized. Interestingly, educational researchers and practitioners have been somewhat slow in realizing the relevance of group dynamics to teaching, even though most institutional instruction takes place within relatively small groups. This is partly due to the different research traditions: educationalists interested in the psychology of classroom events have tended to focus on a more static concept, describing the social psychological climate of the learning context, the *classroom environment* (cf. Fraser 1994; Fraser and Walberg 1991), which subsumes a number of variables also discussed in group dynamics-based approaches (e.g. cohesiveness, satisfaction, leadership styles, classroom organization).

A second reason for underutilizing the knowledge offered by group dynamics is that apart from certain special school types (e.g. private language schools where a student goes to only one class), class group boundaries lack the firmness necessary for autonomous group functioning and development, and group composition is often somewhat unstable (Ehrman and Dörnyei 1998). In most schools in the world, class group membership fluctuates continuously: the group is regularly split up into smaller independent units based on gender, competence or interest. Even with fairly steady class groups, at least one key member, the teacher, usually changes regularly, according to the subject matter.

In spite of the above, group theory has an important contribution to make to understanding what goes on in classrooms. Certain aspects of the classroom, such as the relationship patterns among students or the dynamic developmental progress of class groups, simply cannot be understood fully without a focus on classroom group processes. In the last two decades the growing popularity of *co-operative learning* (see Crandall, this volume; Dörnyei, in press) has also highlighted the relevance of group theory to education, since this instructional approach is entirely based on the understanding and positive exploitation of classroom dynamics.

The development of class groups

A great body of research suggests that groups move through similar stages during the course of development even in very diverse contexts (cf. McCollom 1990a; Wheelan and McKeage 1993). As Ehrman and Dörnyei (1998) contend:

> The development of groups ... has similarities from one group to the next that make it possible to describe a group's evolution in terms of phases, each of which has common patterns and themes. This generalizable change over time within groups has great practical implications for choosing appropriate interventions, whether by a therapist or by a teacher. It is therefore no wonder that group development is one of the most extensively studied issues in group research.

Ehrman and Dörnyei (1998) suggest that in educational contexts it is useful to distinguish four primary developmental stages: *group formation, transition, performing* and *dissolution*.

Group formation

Let us start our exploration of classroom dynamics at the very beginning: the first few lessons of a newly formed group. As a starting point, we must realize that the process of group formation is far from easy for the would-be members. In the first occasions participants meet, an element of tension is present in the interaction: people typically experience unpleasant feelings of anxiety, uncertainty and a lack of confidence (McCollom 1990b). They must deal with people they hardly know. They are uncertain about what membership in the group will involve, and whether they will be able to cope with the tasks. They observe each other and the leader suspiciously, trying to find their place in the new hierarchy. They are typically on guard, carefully monitoring their behaviour to avoid any embarrassing lapses of social poise.

The first few classes spent together, then, are of vital importance to the future functioning of the group. Development proceeds rapidly and much structuring and organization occurs in this period. Fairly quickly, the group establishes a social structure that will prevail for a long time. Aspects of this group formation process which are particularly relevant for L2 teachers are the promotion of the development of *intermember relations* and *group norms* and the clarification of *group goals*.

Intermember relations

When discussing peer relations, we must distinguish between initial *attraction* towards and *acceptance* of others. According to Shaw (1981), initial interpersonal attraction is a function of physical attractiveness, perceived ability of the other person, and perceived similarity in attitudes, personality and economic status. This type of relationship is very different from 'acceptance' – a term introduced by humanistic psychology, referring to a non-evaluative feeling that has nothing to do with likes and dislikes, but involves rather an 'unconditional positive regard' towards other individuals as complex human beings with all their values and imperfections. It is, in a way, the 'prizing of the learner as an imperfect human being with many feelings, many potentialities' (Rogers 1983:124). It could be compared to how we may feel toward a relative, for example an aunt or an uncle, whom we know well and who has his or her shortcomings but who is one of us.

A key concept in group dynamics is the understanding that group development can result in strong cohesiveness based on intermember acceptance *regardless* of the initial intermember attractions. This implies that even negative initial feelings may turn into understanding and affection during the course of the group's development, and that 'one may like group members at the same time as one dislikes them as individual persons' (Turner 1984:525)

How can we, teachers, promote acceptance in our classes? There are several factors that may enhance intermember relations and acceptance. By far the most crucial and general one is *learning about each other* as much as possible, which includes sharing genuine personal information. Acceptance is greatly furthered by knowing the other person well enough; enemy images or a lack of tolerance very often stem from insufficient information about the other party.

In addition to getting to know each other, there are some more concrete factors that can also enhance affiliation (cf. Dörnyei and Malderez 1997; Ehrman and Dörnyei 1998; Hadfield 1992; Johnson and Johnson 1995; Levine and Moreland 1990; Shaw 1981; Turner 1984):

- *Proximity*, that is, physical distance (e.g. sitting next to each other), which is a necessary condition for the formation of relationships.
- *Contact*, referring to situations where individuals can meet and communicate (e.g. outings and other extracurricular activities, as well as 'in class' opportunities).
- *Interaction*, referring to situations in which the behaviour of each person influences the others' (e.g. small group activities, project work).
- *Co-operation* between members for common goals (e.g. to accomplish group tasks). As Johnson, Johnson and Smith (1995:19) summarize, 'Striving for mutual benefit results in an emotional bonding with collaborators liking each other, wanting to help each other succeed, and being committed to each other's well-being'.
- *Successful completion of whole group tasks* and a sense of group achievement.
- *Intergroup competition* (e.g. games in which groups compete), which has been found to bring together members of the small groups.
- *Joint hardship* that group members have experienced (e.g. carrying out a difficult physical task together), which is a special case of group achievement.
- *Common threat*, which can involve, for example, the feeling of fellowship before a difficult exam.

Group norms

Teachers and students alike would agree that there need to be certain 'rules of conduct' in the classroom to make joint learning possible. Some of these behavioural standards, or *group norms*, are constructed by the learners themselves, often following influential peers, but in educational settings *institutional norms* which are imposed from without or mandated by the leader are also very common (e.g. special dressing and behavioural codes). The developing norm system has an immense significance: norms regulate every detail of classroom life, from the volume of speech to the extent of cooperation. Most importantly from an educational perspective, group norms regarding learning effort, efficiency and quality will considerably enhance or decrease the individual learners' academic achievement and work morale.

It is important to realize that institutional rules and regulations do not become real group norms unless they are accepted as right or proper by the majority of the members; ideally, members should internalize a norm so that it becomes a part of the group's total value system, as a self-evident precondition of group functioning (cf. Forsyth 1990; Levine and Moreland 1990). Therefore, it might be useful to include an explicit norm-building procedure early in the group's life by formulating potential norms, justifying their purpose, having them discussed by the group, and finally agreeing on a mutually accepted set of 'class rules'. The advantage of well-internalized norms is that when someone violates them, the group is likely to be able to cope with such deviations. This may happen through a range of group behaviours – from showing active support for the teacher's efforts to have the norms observed, to expressing indirectly disagreement with and dislike for deviant members, and even to criticizing them openly and putting them in 'social quarantine'. We should not underestimate the power of the group: it may bring significant pressures to bear and it can sanction – directly or indirectly – those who fail to conform to what is considered acceptable. Cohen (1994a) summarizes the significance of internalized norms well:

> Much of the work that teachers usually do is taken care of by the students themselves; the group makes sure that everyone understands what to do; the group helps to keep everyone on task; group members assist one another. Instead of the teacher having to control everyone's behaviour, the students take charge of themselves and others. (p. 60)

It must be emphasized that learners are very sensitive to the teacher's attitude towards the group norms. In a way the teacher, in the position of being the group leader, embodies 'group conscience'. If the members feel that you as the teacher do not pay enough attention to observing the established norms or having them observed, they are quick to take the message that you did not mean what you said, and consequently tend to ignore these norms.

Group goals

The extent to which the group is attuned to pursuing its goal (in our case, L2 learning) is referred to as *goal-orientedness*. As Hadfield (1992:134) emphasizes, 'It is fundamental to the successful working of a group to have a sense of direction and a common purpose. Defining and agreeing on aims is one of the hardest tasks that the group has to undertake together'.

Whereas in the 'real world' groups are often self-formed for a voluntarily chosen purpose, in school contexts the overwhelming majority of classes are formed for a purpose decided by outsiders – policy and curriculum-makers. Thus the 'official group goal' (mastering the course content) may well not be the only group goal and in extreme cases may not be a group goal at all; furthermore, members may not show the same degree of commitment to the group goal. Indeed, we have found that when participants of a new course shared openly their *own* personal goals, this has usually revealed considerable differences that lead to a negotiation process; this process, in itself, is a valuable form of self-disclosure that enhances intermember relations, and the successful completion of a set of 'group goals' is a good example of 'whole-group' achievement.

We find it particularly important, therefore, that the group agree on its goal by taking into account *individual goals* (which may range from having fun to passing the exam or to getting the minimum grade level required for survival) and *institutional constraints* ('you're here to learn the L2, this is the syllabus for this year!'), as well as the *success criteria*. Traditionally, these latter have been to do with exams and marks, but other communicative criteria can often be a better incentive, e.g. to be able to understand most of the word of the songs of a pop group, or other specific communicative objectives.

Further development of the group: transition, performing and dissolution

The development of a group is a continuous process; that is, after the ice has been broken and an initial group structure has been formed, the group enters into an ongoing process of change which carries on until the group ceases to exist. In fact, as Hadfield (1992:45) states, 'Forming a group is relatively easy: the initial stage of group life is usually harmonious as students get to know each other and begin to work together. Maintaining a cohesive group over a term or a year is far more difficult'.

The initial group formation phase is usually followed by a rugged *transition* period for the group to work through. As Schmuck and Schmuck (1988:42) state, 'It appears inevitable in classrooms that students will test their degree of influence with the teacher as well as with other students'. Indeed, at this stage of group development, differences and conflicts become common, stemming from disagreement and competition among members and between the group and the leader. These early struggles, however, are not necessarily detrimental to development; the turbulent processes usually elicit counter-processes involving more negotiation regarding goals, roles, rules and norms. Gradually a new awareness of standards and shared values emerges, and a finalized system of group norms is adopted with the explicit goal to eliminate tensions and increase productivity.

Stage 3, *performing*, involves the balanced, cohesive group in action, doing what it has been set up for. This is the work-phase, characterized by decreased emotionality and an increase in co-operation and task orientation: the group has reached a maturity, which enables it to perform as a unit in order to achieve desired goals. That is, the performing phase represents the point at which 'the group can mobilize the energy stored in its cohesiveness for productivity and goal achievement' (Ehrman and Dörnyei 1998). It should be emphasized that even during this stage group functioning is somewhat uneven: phases of *emotional closeness* (co-operation, intimacy) and *distance* (competitive impulses, status differentiation) recur in alternation. However, due to the group's increasing self-organization, the intensity of these phenomena decreases and affective energies are increasingly channelled into the tasks, as a result of which work output rises (Shambough 1978).

The last stage of a group's life is *dissolution*, which is an emotionally loaded period for most educational groups, demonstrated by the great number of reunion events often planned at the break-up of a group. This is the time to say goodbye and to process the feeling of loss, to summarize and evaluate what the group has achieved, pulling together loose ends, and to conclude any unfinished business. Learners may want to find ways of keeping in touch with each other, and they will also need guidelines and advice about how to maintain what they have learnt or how to carry on improving their L2 competence. Group endings, then, need to be managed as deftly as their beginnings.

Group cohesiveness

Group cohesiveness, the principal feature of a fully matured group, can be defined as 'the strength of the relationship linking the members to one another and to the group itself' (Forsyth 1990:10); that is, cohesiveness corresponds to the extent to which individuals feel a strong identification with their group. In a review of the literature, Mullen and Copper (1994) list three primary constituent components of cohesiveness: *interpersonal attraction, commitment to task* and *group pride*. Interpersonal attraction refers to the members' desire to belong to the group because they like their peers. Task commitment concerns the members' positive appraisal of the group's task-related goals in terms of their importance and relevance, that is, 'group feeling' is created by the binding force of the group's purpose. Group pride involves a cohesive force stemming from the attraction of membership due to the prestige of belonging to the group.

Cohesiveness has been seen as a prerequisite and predictor of increased *group productivity* (Evans and Dion 1991; Gully, Devine and Whitney 1995; Mullen and Copper 1994). This may be due to the fact that in a cohesive group there is an increased obligation to the group, members feel a moral responsibility to contribute to group success, and the group's goal-oriented norms have a strong influence on the individual. In cohesive groups, therefore, the likelihood of 'social loafing' and 'free-riding' (i.e. doing very little actual work while still reaping the benefits of the team's performance) decreases. Furthermore, Clément, Dörnyei and Noels (1994) also found that perceived group cohesiveness contributes significantly to the learners' L2 motivation, which again enhances learning success.

How can cohesiveness be achieved? The following factors have been found effective in promoting the development of a cohesive group (cf. Ehrman and Dörnyei 1998; Forsyth 1990; Hadfield 1992; Levine and Moreland, 1990):

- *Positive intermember relations*; this means that all the factors enhancing intermember relations (discussed earlier) will strengthen group cohesiveness as well.
- *Amount of time spent together* and *shared group history*: as part of their natural developmental process, groups with a longer life-span tend to develop stronger intermember ties.
- *The rewarding nature of group experience* for the individual; rewards may involve the joy of the activities, approval of the goals, success in goal attainment and personal instrumental benefits.
- *Group legends*: as Hadfield (1992) points out, successful groups often create a kind of 'group mythology', which include giving the group a name and inventing special group characteristics (e.g. features of dress) in order to enhance the feeling of 'groupness'.
- *Investing in the group*: people tend to become more favourable

toward their group – and thus cohesiveness increases – if they 'invest' in it, that is, spend time and effort contributing to the group goals.

- *Public commitment* to the group also strengthens belongingness.
- *Defining the group against another*: emphasizing the discrimination between 'us' and 'them' is a powerful but obviously dangerous aspect of cohesiveness.
- *Leader's behaviour*: the way leaders live out their role and encourage feelings of warmth and acceptance can also enhance group cohesiveness. Kellerman (1981:16) argues that a prerequisite for any group with a high level of cohesiveness is a leader whose presence is continuously and strongly felt: 'highly cohesive groups are those in which the leader symbolizes group concerns and identity and is personally visible to the membership'. Indeed, one of the surest ways of undermining the cohesiveness of a group is for the leader to be absent, either physically or psychologically.

The role of the teacher as group leader

Although there are a number of factors that contribute to successful outcomes for groups, according to N. W. Brown (1994), none is more important than the group leader. In educational contexts the designated leaders are usually the teachers, and the way they carry out leadership roles has a significant influence on the classroom climate and the group processes. Stevick (1996) expresses this very clearly:

> On the chessboard of academic-style education, the most powerful single piece is the teacher. Society invests him or her with authority, which is the right to exercise power. The personal style with which she or he wields that authority is a principal determinant of the power structure of the class. (p. 180).

The teacher affects every facet of classroom life (see Ehrman and Dörnyei 1998; Wright 1987). However, we will restrict our discussion here to one aspect of leadership which has a direct impact on group development, *leadership style*.

In a classic study, Lewin, Lippitt and White (1939) compared the effects of three leadership styles – *autocratic* (or 'authoritarian'), *democratic*, and *laissez-faire*. The autocratic leader maintains complete control over the group; the democratic leader tries to share some of the leadership functions with the members by involving them in decision-making about their own functioning; a laissez-faire teacher performs very little leadership behaviour at all. Lewin and his colleagues found that of the three leadership types the laissez-faire style produced the least desirable outcomes: the psychological absence of the leader retarded the process of forming a group structure, consequently the children under this condition were disorganized and frustrated, experienced the most stress, and produced very little work. Autocratic groups were found to be more productive (i.e. spent more time on work) than democratic groups, but the quality of the products in the democratic groups were judged superior. In addition, it was also observed that whenever the leader left the room, the autocratic groups stopped working whereas the democratic groups carried on.

From a group-perspective, the most interesting results of the study concerned the comparison of interpersonal relations and group climate in the democratic and autocratic groups. In these respects democratic groups exceeded autocratic groups: they were characterized by friendlier communication, more group-orientedness, and better member-leader relationships, whereas the level of hostility observed in the autocratic groups was thirty times as great as in democratic groups and aggressiveness was also eight times higher in them.

These pioneering results have been reproduced by a great number of studies over the past 50 years, and, based on these, we can say with some conviction that from a group developmental perspective a democratic leadership style is most effective. The authoritarian teaching style does not allow for the group to structure itself organically, nor for the members to share increasing responsibility, and thus it is an obstacle to group development. Consequently, as Schmuck and Schmuck (1988) argue, autocratic classes are often unable to 'work through' the stages of development and, as a result, frequently 'get stuck' and become stagnant: interpersonal relationships become formalized, distant and fragmented, dominated by cliques and subgroups rather than overall cohesiveness based on peer acceptance, and the group's learning goals and goal-oriented norms are not shared by the students.

An authoritarian role, together with highly structured tasks, however, does appear to many teachers as safer and more efficient than leaving the students, to a certain extent, to their own devices – and indeed the Lewin *et al.* (1939) study did point to the greater productivity of autocratic groups. Also, as Shaw (1981) points out, it is much *easier* to be a good autocratic leader than to be a good democratic leader: it is relatively simple and undemanding to be directive and issue orders, but rather difficult to utilize effectively the abilities of group members. All this means that, as in many cases in education, we have a conflict between short-term and long-term objectives: a tighter control over the students may result in a smoother immediate course and better instant results, whereas actively seeking student participation in all facets of their learning programme pays off in the long run.

Practical implications

In this last section we present ten practical suggestions which may be helpful in facilitating group development (the list is partly based on Dörnyei and Malderez 1997, which contains further ideas).

1 *Spend some time consciously on group processes.* This is likely to pay off both in terms of L2 learning efficiency and student/teacher satisfaction.

2 *Use 'ice-breakers' and 'warmers'.* Ice-breakers are activities used at the beginning of a new course to set members at ease, to get them to memorize each others' names, and to learn about each other. 'Warmers' are short introductory games and tasks used at the beginning of each class to allow members time to readjust to the particular group they are now with (reestablish relationships, implicitly be reminded of goals and norms, and at the same time 'switch' from the mother tongue into thinking in and articulating in the L2).

3 *Promote peer relations* by enhancing *classroom interaction* (using activities such as pair-work, small group work, role-play, 'mixer' classroom organization which not only allows, but encourages people to come into contact and interact with one another, as well as helping to prevent the emergence of rigid seating patterns) and by *personalizing the language tasks* (choosing, when possible, activities with a genuine potential for interpersonal awareness-raising to allow members to get to know each other).

4 *Promote group cohesiveness* by including small-group 'fun' *competitions* in the classes, by encouraging (and also organizing) *extracurricular activities*, and by promoting the creation of a *group legend* (establishing group rituals, bringing up and building on past group events, creating a semi-official group history, encouraging learners to prepare 'group objects' and symbols such as flags, coats of arms, creating appropriate group mottos/logos, etc.).

5 *Formulate group norms explicitly, and have them discussed and accepted by the learners.* Include a specific 'group rules' activity at the beginning of a group's life, perhaps as a negotiated pyramid discussion. Specify also the consequences for violation of any agreed 'rule'. It may be a good idea to put group rules (and the consequences for violating them) on display, and, as and when necessary,

re-negotiate them. Then, make sure that you observe the established norms consistently and never let any violations go unnoticed.

6 *Formulate explicit group goals* by having the students negotiate their individual goals, and draw attention from time to time to how particular activities help attain them. Keep the group goals 'achievable' by re-negotiating if necessary.

7 *Be prepared for the inevitable conflicts or low points in group life.* These are natural concomitants of group life which every healthy group undergoes, and you may welcome them as a sign of group development (much as L2 teachers welcome creative developmental language errors), rather than blaming yourself for your 'leniency' and resorting to traditional authoritarian procedures to 'get order'.

8 *Take the students' learning very seriously.* We must never forget that the commitment we demonstrate toward the L2 and the group, the interest we show in the students' achievement, and the effort we ourselves make will significantly shape the students' attitudes to their group and to L2 learning.

9 *Actively encourage student autonomy* by handing over as much as you can of the various leadership roles and functions to the group (e.g. giving students positions and tasks of genuine authority, inviting them to design and prepare activities themselves, encouraging peer-teaching, involving students in record-keeping, and allowing the group to make real decisions).

10 Prepare group members for the closing of the group. The adjourning or closing stage should not be simply about saying goodbye but also giving members some continuity and helping them to prepare for their new phase of learning after the course. This might include agreeing on a reunion, discussing long-term learning objectives, and checking whether anyone needs any support for taking the next steps.

Conclusion

We have found group dynamics a very 'useful' discipline with many practical instructional implications. One basic assumption underlying this chapter has been that a real 'group' is a desirable entity, one which will affect the learning outcomes for each group member in the short-term as well as the long term. It is desirable because a cohesive group:

- means established acceptive relationships between all members, which allows for unselfconscious, tolerant and 'safe' L2 practice;
- allows each member to feel comfortable in the sense of knowing the

rules of the game, which shifts the burden of 'discipline' from the teacher alone, to the group as a whole;
- encourages positive feelings as group goals and individual goals are simultaneously achieved and 'success' is experienced;
- acknowledges the resources each member brings, which can provide the 'content' for an infinite number of L2 practice activities of the information, opinion or perception-gap variety.

Valuing what everyone has to offer encourages all members (teacher included) to accept the challenges for their own learning that every group member's contribution can make. In other words, belonging to a cohesive learning group can help members take control of their own learning, as the teacher can neither know, nor 'control' the input from everyone. Learning, here, is viewed in a constructivist sense as 'concerned with how learners self-organise their own behaviour and experience to produce changes which they themselves value' (Thomas and Hari-Augstein 1985); in this sense groups are stepping stones, training grounds for autonomous continuous learning.

Our second assumption has been that as teachers it is valuable to learn more about the 'group', this powerful entity, which can have such an effect on the productivity, quality and impact of learning. By understanding how a group develops, and consciously striving to create and maintain one, we can make classroom events less threatening and more predictable. This is true both for ourselves and the students. In addition, we will develop more efficient methods of classroom management as well as learn from and with our students. Working on the group and with the group puts the excitement back into teaching.

Suggestions for further reading

Dörnyei, Z. and A. Malderez. 1997. Group dynamics and foreign language teaching. *System, 25, 65–81.*
Ehrman, M. and Z. Dörnyei. 1998. *Interpersonal Dynamics in Second Language Education: The Visible and Invisible Classroom.* Thousand Oaks, CA: Sage.
Forsyth, D. R. 1990. *Group Dynamics.* (2nd ed.) Pacific Grove, CA: Brooks/Cole Publishing Company.
Hadfield, J. 1992. *Classroom Dynamics.* Oxford: Oxford University Press.
Schmuck, R. A. and P. A. Schmuck 1994. *Group Processes in the Classroom.* (7th ed.) Madison, WI: Brown and Benchmark.

Part C: Questions and tasks

1 Think back on a class you taught recently. Try to recall a particular moment that seemed important to you at the time. Write a detailed description of that particular segment. After several hours, re-read it and underline what seem to be the most important points. Then ask the following questions: Why are these underlined pieces important and how do they connect to issues, concerns or goals I have in my teaching? What can I do in my classes to address what has been raised here in my reflective writing?

2 Make a list of four or five of the most important issues for you in your teaching right now. A few days later, come back to the list and identify one of the issues you would like to focus on for several weeks. Generate ways to address your issue. Keep journal entries about your findings and any sense of progress or change in your teaching as a result.

3 Why do you think that formal teacher education has at times tended to avoid the area of affect? In what ways do you think that this is changing? What benefits might teachers in training receive from practical courses in facilitation, interpersonal skills, group dynamics, values clarification and related work?

4 In what circumstances might it not be appropriate for a language teacher to take on a strongly facilitative role?

5 In Chapter 9 Aoki discusses the social relations supportive of the practice of learner autonomy. In the context of your work, how could you provide your students with this support?

6 Examine your own attitudes to autonomy. How comfortable do you feel working autonomously? Is there a relationship between these attitudes and your feelings about learner autonomy? Reflect on ways to increase your autonomy as a teacher and a person.

7 This volume has referred to the importance of educating students for lifelong learning. In what ways do you prepare your students to continue learning after they have finished your class? What else could you do?

8 Discuss the formation of groups you have participated in. What aspects helped the group to coalesce in its beginning stages? Were there obstacles present which hindered group development? How were they handled?

9 In Chapter 10 Dörnyei and Malderez stress the importance of closure for a group. Brainstorm ways to achieve successful closure for a group. Which of these would be useful in the groups you work with?

10 It is a well-known fact that there exist significant discrepancies between teachers' and students' perceptions of the reality of the classroom. In your experience, why do they exist? What can teachers do to reduce these discrepancies?

11 Teach yourself to apply the Lozanov mirror. First, use Assagioli's 'evocative words' technique to keep the unconscious mind working. Write 'The student is my mirror' on an attractively coloured and shaped piece of paper and stick it on the wall where you work. The conscious mind will cease to notice it but the unconscious will ponder it every time you work. Second, bring in the conscious mind: try to make a habit at the end of every class of reflecting on your interactions with learners that have taken place. Remember that the point is to avoid any kind of blaming or labelling of the learner. Over a period of time observe if there is a shift in your relationship with your learners.

Part D   Exploring the interactional space

Allwright (1983:196) sees the language lesson as a *'socially constructed event*, as something that is the product of the interactive work of all the people present'. In these chapters we will be concerned with that part of the learning space occupied by the resources available for facilitating interaction. We will be discussing aspects of the materials, exercises and activities used in the classroom and stressing the importance of incorporating the affective dimension. Referring to the whole language learner, Stevick (1980:197) has emphasized that the 'physical, emotional and cognitive aspects of the learner cannot in practice be isolated from one another: what is going on in one of these areas inexorably affects what is possible in the other areas'. Yet, traditionally many of the resources used in the interactional space do not reflect this holistic composition. All too often materials, for example, only take into account the cognitive side of the learner. We might do well to ask ourselves how to bring in the emotional and the physical as well, so that these aspects, with their special strengths, can support the cognitive processes. If we consider the three aspects (the thinking mind, the body and the heart), it is very likely that we will find that the resources we use frequently leave two of these aspects, the body and the heart, completely inactive.

There is growing evidence (Hannaford 1995; Diamond 1988) that learning is more efficient when the body and movement are incorporated. Learning styles studies have shown that certain people are specifically kinaesthetic learners and learn better when movement is involved; however, all learners benefit from increased attention to movement.

> The more closely we consider the elaborate interplay of brain and body, the more clearly one compelling theme emerges: movement is essential to learning. Movement wakens and activates many of our mental capacities. Movement integrates and anchors new information and experience into our neural networks. (Hannaford 1995:96)

In language learning there are many opportunities to use activities in which the body can be taken into account, providing support for the learning processes of the 'mind'. Speaking about using body rhythms and jazz chants which incorporate movement, Bell (1997) notes that these activities help to make changes in mental processes and to strengthen connections in memory; it is as if the mind part rides piggyback on the movement.

Likewise, this volume contends that the heart should be integrated into the resources we use for language teaching. In the interactional space a very basic way to deal with the emotional side of learners is to provide activities that raise their self-esteem. Another way would be to try to reduce anxiety in learning by using evaluative processes that are less anxiety-provoking (Kohonen, this volume; Rubio 1995).

Ehrman (this volume) has pointed out how regression in the service of the ego permits a healthy liberation of the unconscious and a necessary disinhibition which can lead to much greater creativity; she cites activities used in Suggestopedia as a means of bringing about this positive emotional disposition. In our classroom activities, whenever we use role-play that is personally meaningful for students, when we speak to learners' natural love of play and fun, when we stimulate their creative potential, when we bring in the aesthetic response – in all these cases we are working with the heart.

An important advantage to teacher development is that it opens up possibilities for organizing the interactional space in ways that respond more closely to students' likes and needs. And teachers' own likes and needs are also undoubtedly involved in the language learning process. Teachers can't be expected to produce satisfying results if they are tied to stale, unsatisfying resources they don't enjoy using any more than their learners do.

Stevick suggested five desiderata for materials for the whole learner. These can still serve as an effective affective guide for organizing the interactional space and are implicit in the type of activities suggested in this volume: the emotions should be dealt with as well as the intellect; students should have the opportunity to interact; they should draw on present realities; they should make self-committing choices; and activities should contribute to the student's sense of security (Stevick 1980:200–201).

In Chapter 11 Gertrude Moskowitz deals with the advantages of using humanistic activities in the foreign language classroom to develop learners' full potential. She provides a very insightful account of research which presents evidence of the value of using humanistic activities in language teaching. Data collected in several studies carried out by the author confirmed that humanistic activities have a positive effect on student attitudes towards themselves, others and the target language and on teachers' attitudes, as well.

Learner motivation is intimately related to the elements which make up the present moment in the classroom. In Chapter 12 Mario Rinvolucri presents very clearly the need to incorporate activities that engage the whole person and the present moment of the learning setting and points to ways to help learners experience real communication in the classroom. Distinctions are established between non-humanistic and humanistic exercises, and suggestions are given as to ways to implement humanistic language teaching concepts in the language classroom.

In Chapter 13 Grethe Hooper Hansen discusses the role played in the learning process by the emotions, including those which are often present in our unconscious life and which may stem from pre-natal influence. An exploration is made of the theories of Lozanov, which go beyond one specific method for language teaching to provide a connection with a possible new educational paradigm. Particular attention is given to the importance of the aesthetic in the language learning experience, both for its cathartic effect and its stimulation of the creative aspects of mind. Ways of creating a classroom environment that provides affective support for language learning are suggested.

In Chapter 14 Jodi Crandall discusses cooperative learning as a basis for classroom activities that have a positive impact on the affective nature of the language classroom. She presents research supporting the affective and cognitive benefits of cooperative learning for language acquisition and at the same time deals with ways to handle possible problems, such as cultural expectations of appropriate roles for learners and teachers, that may occur when implementing the framework.

Originally a model of human behaviour and communication, Neuro-Linguistic Programming has applications in many areas of experience, such as psychotherapy, health, business, creativity studies and education. In Chapter 15 Herbert Puchta presents NLP as the 'Psychology of Excellence', a system which uses the patterns of highly successful people as a model. NLP principles can help learners access affective states that are more efficient for learning. Following Robert Dilts' systemic approach, NLP speaks of the different logical levels of the brain, and Puchta shows how the proper alignment of these levels can lead to better performance in the second language.

In Chapter 16 Jane Arnold points out that imagery work deserves much more attention than it is usually given in education, since images, regardless of the sensory modality they originate in, are what thoughts are basically made of (Damasio 1994:107). While a vital part of cognitive processes, imaging is also intimately connected to the affective side of learning. For example, accessing images will often involve strong emotions, which mobilize or inhibit the mechanisms for learning. Also, visualization can help learners transform negative emotional states. Visualization has long been recognized by humanistic educators as an effective resource; this chapter looks at some of the specific ways imagery work can be used to promote language learning.

In the concluding chapter of the section Viljo Kohonen makes it clear that if affective language learning is to be part of new patterns of teaching, it will require new forms of evaluation. Evaluation is, of course, one of our resources for facilitating language learning; and one of the most basic signs of coherence in a learning programme is the compatibility of the goals, syllabus and activities with the system of evaluation. Evaluation takes on particular importance because of the 'backwash' effect, in which testing shapes teaching and curriculum development. Using data from experiences in Finland and elsewhere with affect-sensitive forms of evaluation, Kohonen makes clear the importance of developing and putting into practice new types of evaluation and of helping the language learner to participate in the evaluative process, thus moving towards greater autonomy.

11 Enhancing personal development: humanistic activities at work

Gertrude Moskowitz

Introduction

Teachers are powerful in ways we are not always aware of. And so is what they teach us. It is with this potential power in mind – the power our schooling has to affect our growth and learning – that the topic of this chapter is presented. Indeed, school is a place where we learn not only subject matter; it is a place where we learn about ourselves and also life.

Quite easily and unintentionally, teachers can affect the lives and personal growth of learners of any age by what transpires in the classroom. The infinite episodes, positive and negative, that students experience in the many hours spent in school, can greatly impact their lives. Unfortunately, in school, at home and everywhere else, a good many of us hear far more critical than encouraging remarks about ourselves and others too. The outcome is that our self-esteem suffers, which can cause us to feel unsure about trying new ventures, or can interfere with learning, relationships, succeeding and numerous other crucial things in life. And having negative feelings *about ourselves* can lead to having negative feelings *about others*. This results in not feeling that we can *be* ourselves and therefore in not being able to *know* ourselves, conditions which cause great unhappiness and impede our personal growth. Furthermore, what students study in school may seem meaningless and boring, with no application to their lives.

Ways growth takes place

Fortunately, teachers can help reverse the tide from content students find meaningless and boring to material that motivates, interests and contributes to their growth. Therefore, the theme I wish to address is how certain types of techniques in the second language class can have a very profound effect on the lives and personal growth of both students and teachers alike, due to the particular ingredients they contain. The techniques are referred to as humanistic, affective, awareness, confluent or personal growth activities. These exercises are derived from the field of humanistic education, which recognizes the intellectual *and* the emotional sides of people.

This area strives to help students develop their full potential and relate effectively with one another as they learn the subject matter. Therefore, the content is combined, at appropriate times, with the feelings, experiences and lives of the learners. So humanistic exercises deal with enhancing self-esteem, becoming aware of one's strengths, seeing the good in others, gaining insights into oneself, developing closer and more satisfying relationships, becoming conscious of one's feelings and values and having a positive outlook on life. All of these outcomes are highly relevant to learning, for the better students feel about themselves and others, the more likely they are to achieve. It should be noted that using humanistic activities is not to the *neglect* of the target language, but to the *enhancement* of it.

Why such themes are so compelling can be deduced from the work of psychologist Carl Rogers (1956:196), who revealed that the underlying problems that his clients faced were 'Who am I really?' and 'How can I become myself?' Consequently, discovering what you are really like and being that self are two highly motivating forces. Indeed, the most fascinating subject we can learn about and talk about is *ourselves*. And we learn about ourselves *through others*. So communication which satisfies these deep, innate needs develops from sharing about ourselves while others actively listen to us, showing understanding and accepting us as we are.

This suggests that the second language class is a natural setting for being able to communicate in highly appealing ways. That is, while conversing in the target language students can share their hopes and dreams and their ambitions; their experiences, memories, desires; their interests, values and insights; their feelings, strengths and much more. What results is that students can feel more positive about themselves and others, as they truly get to know and understand others and feel appreciated as well. It is in truly getting to *know* others that we are truly able to *like* them. In such ways, self-esteem flourishes and grows (see de Andrés, this volume).

Noted therapist and teacher Sidney M. Jourard (1971) conducted research on the effects of such sharing, known as 'self-disclosure', which, in his opinion, is the most important thing one can study. He maintained that the best way to learn about ourselves is through others and how they respond to us (Jourard 1964). That is why it is so crucial to be ourselves, so we can see how others respond to who we *actually are*. Barbou (1972) suggests that through self-disclosure, barriers in the group come down and cohesiveness grows.

If I were to list what I believe are deeply ingrained universal needs people have, topping my list would be being listened to, accepted, understood, cared about and having positive and rewarding relationships. Yet for most of us, these are not sufficiently met. So when classroom exercises serve to satisfy these universal human needs, learning becomes highly rewarding and enjoyable as well. In addition, sharing meaningful things about ourselves so others know us is healthier and more satisfying for our growth than being superficial or keeping to ourselves. It is important for the teacher to share too.

Research on the effects of humanistic activities

Through the years of working with humanistic exercises, I have discovered their numerous benefits in assisting the personal development, attitudes and outlook of people of all ages and stages in life. Throughout this time, I have gathered a substantial amount of evidence that supports their use. Some comes from personal experience in working with large numbers of teachers in courses, workshops and training programs. A good deal is also based on what enthusiastic teachers have written or reported to me after using the activities with their students. But in an area of education which advocates dealing with *emotions* and topics of a *personal nature*, it seems pertinent to have *tangible evidence* to confirm that these beliefs are not just personal impressions, but are indeed accurate *and* measurable.

For this reason, over a period of time, I conducted a series of five related studies. One of the principal aims of this chapter, then, is to present the key findings of this body of research which furnish evidence that strongly supports the use of humanistic activities in second language teaching and methodology.

An extensive search for relevant empirical research in second language teaching revealed only two studies by Beverly Galyean and my own work. However, because the findings of these studies are consistent and encouraging, it seems increasingly important to communicate an overview of all seven of these studies, which point to the value of humanistic techniques in the field of second languages. For the four earlier studies, fuller reporting with statistics can be found in the original references that will be noted. Statistical information on the three later studies is available in Moskowitz (in preparation). What is presented in this chapter then is a synopsis of the highlights of these different investigations, without the details of statistical tests and tables and research terminology.

Earlier studies: effects of humanistic activities on students

Galyean (1977a, 1977b) carried out her research in junior and senior high school French and Spanish classes, as well as in a college level 1 French course. Her results indicate that students at these grade levels, who were taught with confluent (humanistic) activities, scored significantly higher on oral and written tests than comparison groups not so taught. In addition, they showed greater gains in self-esteem, self-knowledge, relationships with classmates and positive attitudes toward the class than their counterparts.

In my earlier research (Moskowitz 1981), I carried out two studies because I had observed a number of positive occurrences and wanted to determine whether these changes could be measured and were significant. (The second study was a replication a year later of the first to see whether the findings were consistent.) There was a total of 461 students between the two studies. Their teachers took a methods course from me in which they were instructed experientially in how to incorporate humanistic activities in their teaching. I wanted to find out to what extent their students would be affected in a number of pertinent attitudes and feelings after experiencing awareness exercises. For example, could their feelings about studying the second language be improved? Could their self-concepts be enhanced? Could they actually learn to care more about their classmates, despite having already formed opinions of them? In summary, would the activities help promote the personal growth and development of students?

Therefore, the studies examined the effects of humanistic activities on the students' self-concept, feelings about classmates, and attitudes toward learning the target language. Appropriate questionnaires were developed and used to seek answers to such questions. These studies were conducted in 22 classes, ranging from grades 7 to 12, and included levels 1 to 4. Six languages were represented in these studies: ESOL, French, German, Hebrew, Italian and Spanish.

The teachers involved chose one class to be in the experiment. It was suggested that this be a class in which they would like to see improvement or which was a source of problems for them. Prior to introducing any of the personal growth activities, three questionnaires that I developed were given to the students: (1) The *Foreign Language Attitude Questionnaire* (FLAQ) examined the students' feelings about learning the foreign language, their attitudes toward the teacher and their emotions while in the class; (2) *My Class and Me* looked at the students' self-concepts and their perceptions of their classmates; (3) the third questionnaire consisted of sociometric questions which assessed discreetly who liked whom in the class to determine how accepted each student was. This was done by asking students to list classmates they would like to work with on certain forthcoming group tasks. How well each student is accepted, the number of choices one makes and receives, and the students who mutually choose each other can be discovered through such questions. To what extent males and females choose the opposite gender to be in a group can also be recorded.

As the methods course progressed during each of the two semesters involved, the teachers in both studies selected from a repertoire of personal growth activities those that they felt were appropriate for their students and for two months interspersed them in their ongoing curriculum. It should be noted that these studies took place during March and April when *attitudes are already well-established* in a class. The three questionnaires were administered once more to see whether any changes occurred over the two-month period.

In both studies, on all three questionnaires, there were numerous statistically significant changes in a positive direction. The following are some of the changes that took place after two months. The findings from FLAQ revealed an improvement in several interesting ways:

– The students were more positive about how they felt while in the second language class.
– The students were more positive about how they felt toward the teacher.
– Learning the language did not seem as hard to the students.
– Learning the language was seen as more enjoyable to the students.
– The students felt more relaxed while in the second language class.

The *My Class and Me* instrument indicated that many of the students' perceptions of themselves and their classmates improved, especially noteworthy being those dealing with an enhanced self-image. Examples of the latter items which increased greatly are:

– I have a lot of confidence in myself.
– I am the person I would like to be.
– I have a lot of good qualities and strong points about me.
– I like the way I look.

According to Bloom (1964:173), attitudes towards oneself are fairly stable and relatively difficult to change, so these improvements are particularly notable.

Closeness, acceptance, and belonging appear to have developed in these classes as evidenced by highly significant levels of probability for items such as these:

- The people in this class understand me.
- The people in this class like me.
- The people in this class know my good qualities and strong points.
- I like the students in this class a lot.
- I feel close to the members of this class.

The awareness activities served to help students get to know others better, and by their nature, evoked positive regard for one another. Students felt liked, understood and valued more. Since friendships and cliques form far earlier than March, when these studies began, these findings indicate that the students became better acquainted through the humanistic activities and that greater understanding, closeness and caring resulted.

Other goals of affective exercises are for students to get to know themselves better and to think more positively. That these were achieved can be seen in the significant gains in these items:

- I know myself quite well.
- I usually see the positive (good) side of things.

The sociometric data revealed that the students now chose significantly more classmates to work with in the task groups, and were chosen more often themselves by others to be in their groups. So the students became more accepting of their classmates and more accepted themselves. They now liked many more students well enough to want to work with them in groups.

All of the above gains indicate that the goals of humanistic education of enhancing personal growth were being fulfilled. The findings of this earlier research were encouraging, confirming that the teachers' perceptions of how awareness activities were affecting their students were indeed accurate.

Later studies: effects of humanistic activities on students

Given the inevitable sociocultural changes in a fifteen-year period, I considered it important to determine whether or not the results of the earlier studies would also hold true at the end of the 90s. Therefore, in a third study I replicated parts of my earlier work, while adding new dimensions to it. FLAQ and *My Class and Me* were used again, along with new instruments. The findings referred to for this study and for the two additional studies with teachers that are described later are all statistically significant, with a number of them reaching very high levels of probability.[1]

By chance, the teachers in the third study were all in their third year of teaching Spanish. Twelve classes participated with a total of 241 students who responded to the pre- and post-data questionnaires. Their data were coded so the students could be matched with themselves for statistical comparisons. The classes spread from elementary school to senior high school. The school settings were very diverse, ranging from a private school to two inner city schools.

In the two earlier studies, I had asked the teachers to use the humanistic exercises with a class that was difficult to teach. This time, the teachers were told to choose *two* classes, one that they felt good about, that they enjoyed teaching. This will be referred to later as the 'favoured' group. They were to choose another class in which they would very much like to see improvement, the one that was the most challenging for them to teach. This will be known as the 'unfavoured' group. Each teacher was to use awareness activities with both groups. For some of the teachers, it was their first year in that school, and many also felt they were in difficult, challenging situations. One of the teachers had given up on a class. She said she had no idea what to do with that class, as there were very antagonistic cliques in it that had formed before the class began.

FLAQ

Despite these circumstances, what happened after interspersing aware-ness activities in these classes for two months was very rewarding; the data collected with FLAQ revealed that these exercises fostered change and improvement in the students' attitudes toward the foreign language in the following ways:

- The students now felt that learning a language was not so hard as before.
- The students now felt the foreign language class was more enjoyable and fun.
- The students liked speaking in the foreign language more.

These changes suggest that student attitudes toward the target language can be enhanced even late in the school year.

---

[1] Appreciation is given to Joseph P. DuCette, Associate Dean of Academic Affairs, College of Education, Temple University, for programming and processing the data for the three later studies.

My Class and Me

Prior to the experiment, there were no differences between the favoured and unfavoured groups' attitudes toward their classmates and their feelings toward themselves, despite the different attitudes their teachers had towards the two groups. After experiencing personal growth activities for two months, both groups increased significantly in caring for the members of their class. Their attitudes became more positive, and they felt greater recognition from their peers. These are a few of the significant items on *My Class and Me* that revealed these changes in both groups:

- I know the students in this class better than those in my other classes.
- I feel close to the members of this class.
- I usually see the positive (good) side of things.
- The people in this class know what my good qualities and strong points are.

These results indicate that the students now felt they knew their classmates better, liked them more, and felt closer to them. They became more positive in their outlook on happenings around them, and they felt that their good qualities and strengths were now recognized more by their classmates. The differences in this study transcended the age of the learners, which is interesting, since some teachers believe these activities can only be effective with students of certain ages.

SAHT

A new questionnaire, the *Students' Attitude toward Humanistic Techniques*, SAHT, was developed for this study to obtain uniform information on students' reactions to the activities. Up to this point, only open-ended questions had been gathered from them. This 12-item questionnaire was administered at the conclusion of the study. The students checked along a 6-point scale the extent they agreed or disagreed with the items. The reactions of all of the students in the favoured and unfavoured classes were combined and scored together. It was apparent from the results that the students reacted favourably to the humanistic activities, having improved their feelings about the second language class and their classmates, too.

That the students responded more favourably toward the language class can be seen in the extent of agreement on items such as these:

- I want to continue humanistic techniques in our class. (86%)
- The period goes faster when we do humanistic techniques than without them. (83%)

- I look forward to classes when we do humanistic techniques. (79%)
- I feel like participating more with humanistic techniques. (78%)
- I like learning the language more since we have been using humanistic activities. (77%)
- If humanistic techniques were included in next year's class, I'd want to continue foreign language study more than I do now. (75%)
- I am more willing to speak the language when we are doing humanistic activities. (71%)

So students improved in their willingness to speak and participate in the language class and in their desire to continue the language, and they wanted humanistic techniques included as part of their class. Their outlook improved and their perception of class time was affected.

That they now knew their classmates better and cared more about them is reflected in these items:

- I know some of the students in this class better than I did before. (80%)
- I like some students in this class more since we have been working with humanistic activities. (68%)

They also felt the activities were of value to them and that they now knew themselves better, as well, as can be seen in these items:

- The humanistic activities we have done are relevant (meaningful) to me. (72%)
- I have learned more about myself as a result of the humanistic activities. (62%)

It should be recalled that all of these changes occurred in only eight weeks, after the classes were well-established in their structure, nature and social aspects. The teachers themselves had doubted whether anything could have a positive effect at that point in the school year. Despite these obstacles, the overall results of the third study were consistent with the findings of the two earlier studies.

Later studies: effects of humanistic activities on teachers

In addition, new and interesting results were revealed in these data that relate not just to the students in the third study, but to their teachers as well. As a result of verbal comments and written feedback I had previously received from teachers in my humanistic techniques courses, I also decided to measure some dimensions related to the *teachers*, not just their students. Since I had examined how the *students felt about their teachers and themselves* before and after experiencing humanistic exercises, I now wanted to see how the *teachers felt about their students and themselves* before and after teaching with and experiencing the activities. This also meant exploring whether the changes taking place *in the students* had any measurable effects *on the teachers*. And so as part of the third study described above, the teachers' attitudes were assessed prior to and after they taught with, as well as experienced, humanistic activities.

Two questionnaires were given to the teachers in this part of the third study: (1) The *Teachers' Attitude toward Class Questionnaire*, or TAC, which looks at how the teacher feels about the class and perceives the class, and how the teacher believes the class perceives him or her; and (2) The *Teachers' Self-Concept and Awareness Questionnaire*, or TSCA, which examines how the teachers feel about themselves and what they know about themselves. The 10 items on the latter were taken from the 20–item form *My Class and Me*, where they assessed the students' self-concept and self-awareness.

TAC

The teachers responded to TAC concerning their feelings and perceptions about their favoured and unfavoured classes, prior to and after introducing humanistic techniques to them for two months. The results of TAC were unusually interesting. Before the study began, the teachers had significantly more positive attitudes toward the favoured classes in all three areas: how they felt about the class, perceived the class and thought the class perceived them. Two months later, the teachers had significantly improved in their attitudes toward their *unfavoured* classes. *There were no longer any differences in how the teachers felt toward the two classes* when compared to each other. The teachers had developed much more positive feelings about their unfavoured group, feelings similar to those they had for their favoured group. These are some of the items which showed significant gains, reflecting the teachers' improved attitudes toward the unfavoured class:

– I know the students in this class quite well (know a lot about them).
– I can be myself with the students in this class.
– This class is one of my favourites.
– I get a great deal of satisfaction from teaching this class.
– The students in this class participate willingly and often.
– The students in this class seem to like me.

So the teachers' attitudes toward the unfavoured class improved, as well as the way the students conducted themselves. Unexpected changes such as these are certainly worth noting and reflecting on.

TSCA

At the start of the first day of the methods course on humanistic techniques, the teachers responded to the TSCA, using a secret code to conceal their identity. At the end of the last day, the teachers responded once more to this self-concept questionnaire now that they had experienced a number of humanistic activities themselves.

A look at the findings from the TSCA reveals that both the teachers' self-concept and self-awareness improved. Among the items indicating gains in their self-concepts were these:

– I have a lot of confidence in myself.
– I am the person I'd like to be.
– I have a lot of good qualities and strong points.

Increases in their self-awareness were seen in these items:

– I am usually aware of my feelings and can express them.
– I know and understand myself quite well.
– I am aware of my good qualities and strong points.

These results indicate that when the teachers experienced humanistic activities, their attitudes improved in similar ways to those of the students.

So far I have reviewed three of the five studies I conducted relevant to the effects of humanistic techniques. In the two additional studies, the focus was solely on the teachers in order to collect further data on the effects humanistic exercises have on them. Subsequently, the TSCA was administered in both of these additional studies, while the TAC could only be given in one of them. Since some of the teachers in the methods courses were not currently teaching, they could not respond to the TAC.

The findings from the TSCA in these two studies and the previous one were very consistent. There was significant improvement in both the teachers' self-concept and self-awareness after a semester of experiencing humanistic activities. Over the three semesters, a total of 60 teachers responded to this questionnaire anonymously.

Similarly, the results from the second study in which TAC was also administered indicate that the teachers once again formed more favourable attitudes toward the class in which they had introduced a number of humanistic activites. Between the two studies using the TAC, the teachers' attitudes significantly improved toward a total of 23 classes in which they previously had difficulty.

In this series of five related studies that I conducted, I purposely sought to replicate variables, as well as to add new ones to the research. The results of these studies were remarkably consistent, though carried out with different teachers, different students, different languages, different age groups, in different settings and in different time periods. The findings of these studies suggest that the personal growth of both students *and* teachers was enhanced by participating in awareness activities for a period of time and that the teachers' professional lives also improved when using them with their students. This research seems to illustrate that considerable benefits are derived by students when, over a period of time, they experience humanistic exercises in second language classes, and by teachers when they also experience the activities in methods courses and use them in teaching their own classes. It should be strongly emphasized that *only activities with a positive focus* were used by the teachers in these studies and in the methods courses.

Evidence from opened-ended responses

The findings from the research just reviewed lend strong support for including humanistic exercises in the second language class and in methods courses. They appear to contribute to more positive attitudes in students and their teachers and to enrich the personal growth of both.

Further evidence about the positive reactions of teachers and students to awareness activities comes from written feedback from them. These responses can be fascinating, surprising and moving to read. Here are some examples from students of the teachers in my methods course on humanistic techniques:

- This exercise was good because I talked to people I haven't spoken to all year.
- I feel more relaxed, more a part of the class, and more able to participate.
- In my 11 years of school, this is the first time I have looked forward to a class.

The voices of teachers who have implemented personal growth exercises also confirm the findings of the research:

- There are no put-downs any more. Everyone has learned to listen to others, self-concepts have improved, and the students have actually made new friends in my class.
- The difference in the students' attitudes is phenomenal. Motivation

was almost impossible because they had been labeled failures, but now there is a new atmosphere.

– These students now seem more mature and more sensitive to each other than those in my other classes.
– No more fighting with students to have them converse. The subject of the conversation has become relevant to them – themselves and their friends. They are now eager to share and participate.

The rationale for these activities is not merely that they are fun or interesting, since other exercises can make that claim too. Effective communication consists of listening and speaking. With humanistic activities, everyone has the chance not only to speak, but also to have everyone *want to listen*. And when students converse, the topics focus on the most meaningful and absorbing subject there is – *themselves*. In this way, they get to know one another less superficially – to see the inner being, not just the outer shell. Through this process, people can learn to care more about one another, which leads to feelings of acceptance and being understood. As this type of communication continues, warmth and a sense of belonging follow, and *the people and the place related to their language learning become attractive and special to them.*

I want to stress the importance of the types of topics used. There are many reasons why they should have a *positive* focus. Suffice it to say that we are already surrounded by so much negativity in the world that dealing with the positive is a much-needed and welcome change and a sound habit to form. When negative topics are introduced, the energy in the classroom can completely change. And areas that teachers may not be skilled in handling are much more likely to come up.

When initially using these exercises, start by choosing activities you feel are appropriate for your classes, non-threatening and highly involving. For classes that are quiet in nature, try an activity in which the total group gets up and moves around, asking questions of various partners. See that the questions used are non-threatening to answer. For large classes, where noise level and control are issues, start with an exercise where students work in pairs, followed by sharing with the total class. When people all participate at once, it produces an inviting sound of liveliness as a background, which serves to raise everyone's energy and enjoyment levels.

Each affective activity has its own particular goals and not any one of them alone captivates students or promotes growth. It is their collective use over time and their eventual effect on group members that foster the gains. Space permits only a few very brief descriptions of activities to illustrate their goals. Here is one intended to enhance self-esteem.

I like you, you're different[2]

Explain to students that sometimes people want to be like everyone else, and are concerned about their differences, yet these are the things that make us special and unique. For homework, ask the students to write on a card three things they feel good about that make them different from everyone else in the class. They should sign their names to their cards, which you will collect. The cards should be identical in size and appearance. Give them three examples from your life to illustrate. Be humorous and imaginative, if possible. Here are three of mine: (1) I was on a national quiz show once and won two prizes. (2) I took lessons on three musical instruments. (3) I wrote a poem when I was seven that was published in the school newspaper.

In conducting the activity, read each card aloud, one at a time, asking for three guesses as to whose card it is. It is important that these three students not reveal whether or not it is their card, nor give hints nonverbally. Trying to figure out the identity of the person and then voting on it is what makes the exercise fun. After the class votes on the three choices, ask the mystery person to stand to reveal to the class who was being described. The class then asks this student a few questions related to the card before you read the next one. Include a card for yourself, too, without making your identity obvious. The students learn new and unusual things about one another, with surprises and laughter following. There are many possible ways to follow up this activity.

Fortune cookies

This activity should be used when the students know one another to some extent. Place the students in groups of four, and ask them to write a fortune for the other three and themselves on separate slips of paper. The fortunes should be something they think would make each person happy. Each slip is then folded, with the person's name written on the outside of it, and placed in the center of the group. When all of the fortunes are completed, one at a time the group members pick up a slip with one of their own fortunes and read it aloud to the group, without having read it to themselves first. The focus person then comments or reacts to this prediction made for him or her. It is important that the students not read their fortunes ahead of time or to themselves before

---

[2] The three activities in this chapter are condensed from Gertrude Moskowitz, *Caring and Sharing in the Foreign Language Class: A Sourcebook on Humanistic Techniques*, 1978, with kind permission from Heinle & Heinle, Boston, MA.

reading them aloud as that spoils their spontaneous reactions that will be seen by the group. The fun and enjoyment come from the suspense of not knowing the fortune until it is read to the group. When all of the fortunes have been read aloud, the group can guess which ones were written by the individuals for themselves. After the groups finish, the students can each select one of their fortunes to read to the class. This activity usually evokes laughter and good feelings toward one another for these wishes of good fortune. It is especially enjoyed when the fortune is based on something the person has shared previously with the class.

How strong I am

The students should be well acquainted with one another for this activity. Place them into groups of four or five. On a sheet of paper, ask them to write down the names of the people in their group and to write two strengths they see in each person. They should include their own name on this sheet, and then list as many of their own strengths as they can think of. State the amount of time they have to do this, such as five minutes. When they are ready, tell them to focus on one student at a time, who will read his or her own list of strengths aloud. The others in the group will then share the strengths they see in the person, while the student to the right of the focus person writes them down. After everyone has been the focus person, the written summary is given to the owner to keep. The groups can then discuss such things as these: Did anyone say something that surprised you? Which strength mentioned means the most to you? What are your reactions to this activity? What did you learn? This activity builds closeness and self-esteem.

Conclusion

The intention of this chapter has been to provide a rationale for including humanistic exercises in the second language class and to present concrete research-based evidence that the benefits they purport to give are indeed worthy and achievable, even in difficult cases. Research has confirmed that these activities have a positive effect on students' attitudes toward the target language, themselves and their classmates. Teachers also benefit when using these techniques in teaching and when experiencing the activities for themselves. Not only can teachers achieve greater satisfaction and improvement in their teaching, but growth in their own self-concepts and self-awareness, too.

The last three studies reported here were carried out to determine whether the passage of time with its subsequent changes in schools and in students would alter the effects that earlier research indicated humanistic activities had on students. The findings of the earlier and the more recent studies were highly consistent. Clearly, time has not lessened the effectiveness of these growth activities for today's students. It appears that content which helps to satisfy the universal human needs of people serves to foster positive changes in their attitudes. *And those needs, which are critical and which people long to fulfill, transcend time*. It should be remembered, however, that this research is based on activities with a *positive focus*.

Through the years of working with these techniques, I have made a very rewarding discovery – that they also transcend cultures and work with all kinds of people. My experience with audiences from around the globe has taught me that we are *far more alike* than different, that our basic psychological needs are the same, regardless of what the group or culture dictates. As human beings, we all need to be listened to and to share, to have close relations with others, to understand ourselves better, and to be accepted as we are. I see implementing humanistic techniques as a *vaccine*, one that fights hatred, violence and antisocial behaviour, while promoting harmony, closeness and personal growth, certainly an ideal environment in which language learning can grow, develop and thrive.

Suggestions for further reading

Galyean, B. 1979. A confluent approach to curriculum design. *Foreign Language Annals*, 12, 4, 121–128.

Ittzes, K. 1988. Humanistic techniques – from aversion to conversion. *Practical English Teaching*, 8, 1, 42–46.

Moskowitz, G. 1978. *Caring and Sharing in the Foreign Language Class: A Sourcebook on Humanistic Techniques*. Boston, MA: Heinle & Heinle.

   1981. Effects of humanistic techniques on attitude, cohesiveness, and self-concept of foreign language students. *Modern Language Journal*, 65, 2, 149–157.

   1988–1989. Four articles in a series. *Practical English Teaching*. Who am I really? What am I like? 1988, 9, 2, 42–44; The greatest discovery is finding yourself. 1989, 9, 3, 46–48; Two negatives don't make a positive. 1989, 9, 4, 48–50; From giggles to growth. 1989, 10, 1, 48–46.

   1994. Humanistic imagination: *Soul* food for the language class. *Journal of the Imagination in Language Learning*, 2, 1, 8–17.

Richard-Amato, P. 1988. Affective activities. In *Making It Happen: Interaction in the Second Language Classroom: From Theory to Practice*. New York, Longman, 158–176.

Rinvolucri, M. 1984. *Grammar Games: Cognitive, Affective, and Drama Activities for ESL Students*. Cambridge: Cambridge University Press.

Rinvolucri, M. and P. Davis. 1995. *More Grammar Games: Cognitive, Affective and Movement Activities for ESL Students*. Cambridge: Cambridge University Press.

12 The humanistic exercise

Mario Rinvolucri

> You are all familiar with the .....-fill exercise of ..... this is a
> fairly typical example. As you read ..... lines, all over the
> world students are working their ..... through kilometres of
> gap-..... exercises, whether they be first-year ..... at Malaysian
> universities or candidates sitting the Cambridge exams any-
> where ..... the world.

The purpose of this extremely widespread activity, which gives many
learners and teachers a sense of authoritative security, is strictly
linguistic in its nature: it tests knowledge of vocabulary, collocation,
grammar and spelling. It sits comfortably within what Carl Rogers
(1983:20) describes as the traditional paradigm of education:

> Education has traditionally thought of learning as an orderly
> type of cognitive, left-brain activity. The left hemisphere of the
> brain tends to function in ways that are logical and linear. It
> goes step-by-step, in a straight line, emphasizing the parts, the
> details that make up the whole. It accepts only what is sure and
> clear. It deals in ideas and concepts. It is associated with the
> masculine aspects of life. This is the only kind of functioning
> that is acceptable to our schools and colleges.

'Strings-of-words' exercises

The gap-fill exercise calls on the student to work logically and linearly
and emphasises the parts that go to make up the whole. It is a clear
exemplification, at activity level, of what Rogers is saying about the
whole mindset of traditional education.

Various forms of translation activity belong to the same, no-nonsense,
male pedagogy of the type:

> *Please translate the following sentence first literally and then*

adequately from Latin into English: HIS REBUS FACTIS,
OPPIDUM GALLORUM CAESAR OPPUGNAVIT.

Grammar translation exercises of this type are an important element
in language classes round the globe, both in places where teachers have
heard of 'communicative methodology' and in places where they have
not, for example, among the more elderly of China's 400,000 secondary
teachers of English.

Another wide-spread type of exercise that focuses entirely on formal
aspects of language as its object is choral reading. In several classes in
South Korea I heard students reciting the lesson in slow unison with
their teacher. Choral reading can lead to memorising the text as a
whole, especially if the text is repeated often enough. This is certainly
one way to take a language on board; it is the way that Muslims round
the world come into possession of the Koran, which must always be in
Arabic. It was also the way Roman Catholics used to learn the Latin
liturgy until it was replaced by modern language versions in the mid-
sixties. I was brought up in this auditory learning tradition, and today
can effortlessly produce acres of church Latin. The problem is that if I
want to retrieve a sentence from the middle of a prayer I have to start
reciting it from the beginning. You may need to do the same if you
know the alphabet by heart as a sound sequence: which comes first, 'j' or
'h'?

Choral repetition is of course very different from gap-fill or the
typical translation exercise in that it is not at all analytical or logical.
The aim is to memorise the text as it stands and sometimes without the
meaning being clear to the learners. What the three exercises have in
common is that nobody is speaking or writing to anybody; no interpersonal communication is taking place and so it is arguable that the
learners are dealing with strings of words and not with language at all.

The semi-communicative exercise

When you fill in gaps in a text, when you translate a piece of text to
which you have no special relationship, when you read aloud/recite/
chant a textbook passage, you are not involved in one-to-one interaction with another person and so the social aspect of language is
missing. Some would say that this is as odd as thinking of music
without reference to sound. The simple hallmark of the communicative
exercise is that you are saying something to another person in the target
language. The most successful version of the communicative exercise is
when students are given a task and have to interact verbally to carry it

out. One example would be: Imagine two students sitting back to back. Each of them has a picture that the other student cannot see. The pictures are identical except that the second one has ten details missing. The students' task is to discover what the differences between the two pictures are. This sort of information gap exercise is somewhat interesting and has enough ludic appeal to create a mild level of energy in most students, but such exercises wear thin when over-used.

A less linguistically and psychologically successful communicative activity is one where students are asked to talk one-to-one about personal matters but in the context of artificial language work, often in the context of a coursebook unit. Let us take a typical unit on the family in a lower level coursebook. The unit starts with a genealogical tree of a fictitious family. Often no attempt has been made to characterise any of the people whose names appear on the tree. The students listen to a cassette about the names on the tree and then the teacher asks questions like: 'How many sisters does John have?' 'Is Mary John's aunt?' All of the above is psychologically contentless information and is clearly only there to somehow 'carry' the language exponents the unit is designed to teach. After half an hour of this humanly empty sort of activity, students are typically asked to work in pairs and ask each other about their real families. This should mean that they are now using the target language to speak about affectively important things but the shadow of the first half hour's psychological vacuity hangs over them. Often they will exchange what is potentially powerful information, like the number of sisters they have, but in a mood of relative communicational apathy. When the teacher comes round listening to the pair work, they have a shrewd idea she is not too interested in their families but is listening out for correct use of English personal adjectives. Though the information being exchanged at this 'transfer' stage in the lesson could be powerful and important in itself, it is emptied of meaning because the whole lesson is narrowly form-focused.

We have looked at task-orientated communicative exercises and ones that occur in the behaviouristically inspired coursebook following on from presentation and controlled practice in which the communicative stage is sometimes referred to as 'transfer to the student's own life'. We have seen how students may find it hard to change gear from vacuous language-like behaviour to energetic, motivated exchange of real, personal information.

A third type of communicative exercise is the rehearsal activity in which students try out the language they might need in future situations that may take place in the target language, such as ordering food in a restaurant, booking into a hotel or getting information in a railway station.

These exercises have high face value, especially if the student is shortly to go to a target language country and is likely to be in such situations. Extroverted students will sometimes fill such role-plays with energy and give the teacher the impression of a buzzing classroom. And yet such role-plays have a lot missing: they are dummy runs, they are the apprentice pilot on the simulator, not at the controls of a seven four seven; in fact they afford their players much less virtual reality than a simulator does. Lindstromberg (1990:xi) says of rehearsal activities:

> ... people learn a language better if their experience in it is as full of meaning and as rich in images as possible. Meaning and mental images come only when connection is made with the learners' own world of experience. The greater the connection, the better the learning ... Most classroom language learning activities are seriously lacking in this area. Take, for example, a role-play in which learners are expected to imagine they are in no particular train station speaking about departure times for imaginary trains going to arbitrary destinations. This is real and meaningful language use only in the sense that the picture of a flower is a flower.

While the entirely formal language-focused exercises like the gap-fill constitute the staple diet of the majority of the world's language learners from Hokkaido to Jakarta and from Alma Ata to Lima, the Anglo-North American sub-orthodoxy of communicative language teaching is to be found in secondary school text books across Europe, is implemented in private sector schools right round the world and is set before apprentice teachers in university training departments. Rivers of ink have flown in discussions of communicative language teaching, but meanwhile the grammar-translation teachers just quietly do their work and do not feel the need to enter into debates. They do the job the way it has been done, is done and will be done.

The humanistic exercise

So what is the difference between a semi-communicative exercise and a humanistic one?

The humanistic exercise is likely to be used in a classroom where the teacher has a strong awareness of group process and how this affects learning. This teacher will have started the course with activities that allow the students to get to know each other. This teacher will realise that the mood of the class has to be taken into account when imagining lesson plans and that the success of a certain set of activities can crucially depend on whether a group of fourteen-year-olds have just come from vaulting in the gym or working in maths in self-study mode or scribbling down geography with a note dictator.

The teacher will be the sort of person who is aware she is teaching forty individuals, not a great mass. She is likely to be a good observer and a good, empathetic listener. If the humanistic exercise is to be relevant and adequate to the task of offering students a new experience of themselves, then the teacher's attitude must be positive, her person skills good and her training adequate.

Properly used, humanistic exercises are not fillers for Friday afternoon (Thursday afternoon in the Arab world). Of course they do get used as fillers to liven up communicative work, but this use is trivial and, in the long run, uninteresting. When teachers use humanistic activities in this way, out of context and as Polyfilla, they often find them upsetting and irrelevant.

In contrast, let us now have a look at the reaction of a class of Austrian fourteen-year-olds to a fully integrated humanistic exercise aimed at offering learners fluency and self-expression practice (taken from Puchta and Schratz 1993:42–45).

The teacher laid a circle of rope (seven metres long) down on the floor in the centre of the classroom. He asked all 27 students to step inside it. As the teacher pulled the rope in tighter, a couple of students, without being asked, helped the teacher raise the rope so that it encircled the whole group at waist level. These were the instructions he gave: *Would you close your eyes now, please? Whatever you feel or notice, don't open your eyes. Just concentrate on your feelings.* Gradually the teacher drew the rope in so that all were tightly pressed together.

During the next stage of the activity the students filled the board with words that described their feelings. This dialogue then ensued:

> TEACHER *What about lovely? Who wrote that?*
> STUDENT 1 *I . . . I had a lovely feeling when we were all so . . .*
> TEACHER *. . . together, you mean?*
> STUDENT 1 *Yes.*
> TEACHER *Interesting. So you did not mind that. Did you all have positive feelings?*
> STUDENTS (some, hesitating) *Yes.*
> TEACHER *Could you describe your feelings a bit more. Tell me what was positive about them?*
> STUDENT 2 *I think we were all one big person, I think. We all were in the circle and the circle was so than a . . . than a, not a line, a wall round us and, I think, we all like to be in the class and so we are a big group.*
> TEACHER *Fantastic! And who wrote light?*

STUDENT 3 *I.*
TEACHER *What do you mean by that?*
STUDENT 3 *Er ... when I closed my eyes, I had no feeling of small. I*
was out, I was not in, I mean I was not in the middle of the circle.
TEACHER *So you didn't feel the pressure so much?*
STUDENT 3 *No.*

The conversation then went off into reflection on other tightly packed situations.

Puchta and Schratz comment: 'The students were thoroughly involved – not just cognitively but emotionally as well – and they had the opportunity to air both positive and negative feelings'. This activity provided a meaningful introduction to the next stage of the lesson, in which the students read a passage about the kids crushed during a pop concert in Melbourne.

The above extract illustrates at exercise level, at micro level, what Carl Rogers says in his overview of whole-person or humanistic teaching (Rogers 1983:20):

> To involve the whole person in learning means to set free and utilise the right brain. The right hemisphere functions in a quite different way from the left. It is intuitive. It grasps the essence before it understands the details. It takes in a whole gestalt, the total configuration. It operates in metaphors. It is aesthetic rather than logical. It makes creative leaps. It is the way of the artist, of the creative scientist. It is associated with the feminine qualities of life.

The Austrian teacher gave his fourteen-year-olds an experience which they will have processed in the ways that Rogers describes above and which then fed into and enriched the reading of the target language text. He put them in a position to make the external text their own and to experience it in the light of their own experience of being squashed together. The differences between the rope-to-reading exercise and the three semi-communicative exercises outlined above are striking:

– The heart of the humanistic exercise is a personal experience and a group experience in the here and now, which is where the language flows from. The students speak to the teacher because they have something to express, something that has welled up from their emotions. This is completely different from students rehearsing language for a future situation or producing personal information only because they are instructed to personalise previously practised language.
– In the humanistic exercise the quality of the students' language is

quite sophisticated. They are trying to say things they cannot yet express clearly in English and several of the teacher's interventions are genuinely to clarify meaning rather than to correct mistakes. In semi- communicative exercises it is rare for students to feel an internal emotional pressure such that they have to over-stretch themselves and grasp for language they do not yet have. In communicative exercises most of what is said is easily predictable and at or below their level of linguistic competence.

– In the rope exercise the fourteen-year-olds may well have learnt new things about each other in terms of physical reactions while being 'crushed', in terms of things said to the teacher in the target language, and in terms of after-class conversations in German with classmates and their families. Finding out interesting things about yourself and about others is a natural part of humanistic language work.

– In the humanistic exercise it is easy for the teacher to be genuinely interested in the students' replies to his questions. He has no way of knowing what they may come up with in reaction to the rope activity. How can he get bored with his job if he is bringing forth the unexpected, the spontaneous, the new?

– In the humanistic exercise there is acknowledgement that the students bring bodies to class. During the activity they leave their chairs, they stand and move, they crowd together and jostle, they go and write on the board. With teenagers and with some adults the need to get up and move comes near the bottom on a Maslowian pyramid of needs, which means it is very basic for them and so has high priority.

The way a good humanistic language exercise works is the same way many good primary school exercises work, and I have noticed that primary school teachers are often natural humanistic thinkers. You don't have to persuade them that children need to live through genuine experiences and that the best learning comes out of experience. You don't have to persuade them that children have brought their bodies to class and need movement. You don't have to persuade them that fun and novelty are central to fast, effective learning.

This might seem to suggest that humanistic teaching is just common sense, which sadly, is not the case. The attitudes and expectations of future teachers are moulded by the way the profession trains them, and once trained they can be very conservative. I recently received a letter from a Japanese teacher who, after six months' training in the UK, wants to introduce communicative exercises into his secondary class-room in Japan. He writes sadly that his students go through the motions of communicative exercises but that they are still entrenched in the earlier paradigm of language as a pure object of intellectual study. There is, in his mind, no question of introducing humanistic thinking into his classroom, and yet he has marvellous, deeply human rapport with his students when they meet in the school clubs and on the weekend trips which Japanese secondary teachers are expected to participate in.

Unfortunately, training in humanistic language teaching is still quite limited. In the UK it can be found mainly at International House and Pilgrims, and perhaps the only MA programme where students actually have space and time to study seriously the work of Gattegno, Curran, Rogers and other humanistic educators is that of the School for International Training in Brattleboro, Vermont.

Criticisms of the humanistic exercise

Let us divide the criticism of the humanistic exercise into two parts: criticism from within the humanistic belief system and criticism from outside.

A powerful internal critic is Bernard Dufeu who has worked unceasingly over the last twenty-five years to move humanistic thinking forward and whose book, *Teaching Myself* (1994) stands with Stevick's work at the centre of the humanistic movement in language teaching. In a recent survey of alternative approaches Dufeu warns of what he sees as lacking in current humanistic language work (which he calls the 'relational approach'):

> the relational approach has created some excellent but isolated techniques. It lacks an overall vision that would offer a progression for the learner based on relational and linguistic criteria and accompanied by a rich selection of exercises. Currently teachers only have isolated exercises that make up a very incomplete mosaic and very few of them are for complete beginners. There is no progression in the activities to allow a real entry into the target language and the first fifty hours are really problematic. (author's translation from Dufeu 1996:173)

I agree that the last twenty-five years have seen an explosion of creative exercises (for example, Maley and Duff 1982) and that less attention has been given to how to bring them into coherent sequences that help learners rather than confuse them. The problem here is that, outside the concrete reality of a given group of learners, it is hard to define what the 'relational and linguistic criteria' would be. If we are thinking of multinational classes, then we would have to add 'cultural criteria'. So there is work yet to be done.

As for criticisms of humanistic exercises from outside, some of the criticism is simply inaccurate and inappropriate and does not need to detain us. More interesting outside criticism comes from Legutke and Thomas. These two authors describe an exercise from Rinvolucri (1982) used with 11th, 12th and 13th grades in a German high school. In the exercise learners are each asked to choose half a dozen groupings they belong to or have belonged to. Each person then draws a shape for each of the collectives and marks with a cross their own relationship to and within the group. Students then explain their drawings to each other.

Here are some of the learner reactions that Legutke and Thomas (1991:57–8) report:

> Participants agreed with Rinvolucri that the exercise opened up an interesting and unusual perspective on their own personality and as a result could be quite motivating ... However, ... some participants repeatedly emphasized the point that when they drew their shapes they experienced in part strong emotions, and time and again quite surprising outlines emerged on the paper. Subconscious or semi-conscious contexts were uncovered in this way. In many cases, particularly with non-adult learners, this procedure has been accompanied variously by painful emotions because it exposed desires of group belonging or positions of being placed on the outside of the group. The inner dynamic of the exercise forced learners into momentary undesired public exposure.

The matters raised by these two authors are serious and well worth dealing with. However, for me they bring up the following questions about the groups where they had been used:

- Was this the students' first exposure to this kind of exercise?
- What did the teachers of the groups feel about using such exercises?
- What kind of relationship did each teacher have with his/her group?
- What had been done previously to promote an atmosphere of openness and trust?
- Were the classes aware that they were taking part in a sort of experimental situation?

Though I don't have answers to these questions, it is clear that since the activity caused distress to some of the students, it was not a good choice for this point in their group process. That learners should not leave the humanistic classroom in an unresolved state of upset goes without saying. This does not necessarily invalidate the use of an exercise, but it does point to the need to introduce it properly and take several factors into consideration.

The points brought up by Legutke and Thomas link back to Dufeu's worry about there being no adequate 'relational' framework that individual exercises can be fitted into. Dufeu (1996) suggests that the creation of a harmonious progression over days and weeks at the moment depends on the knowledge and skill of the teacher. Quite possibly it always will, and we are not likely to come up with a magic formula to obviate this reliance on teachers knowing their job.

Three areas of humanistic exercises

When teachers work with a class in a humanistic frame of mind they often find they have three main areas of focus:

– the task (in our case this is language learning);
– the mood of the group in the here and now;
– individual stuff that surfaces from the students' pasts.[1]

Humanistic exercises can generally be placed in one or more of these three categories.

Exercises for language learning (the task)

A humanistic exercise can have a very detailed and precise linguistic focus. For example:

Passing a word or phrase round the circle (pronunciation)

Ask the students to stand in a circle and tell them they are going to pass an object round the circle and this object will be a word or phrase. Cup your hands and mentally concentrate on the word you are going to pass to your neighbour in the circle. Get a feel of the word in your mind. Pass the word and say the word so that everybody can hear. Make sure you co-ordinate the passing with your hands and the saying so that they form one act of careful giving. In turn each student passes the word to their neighbour both verbally and manually. The linguistic focus of this exercise is on difficult sounds in the target language and on specific intonation patterns you feel the students need to get their minds round. If a student gets the sounds wrong, you quietly cross the circle and 'take' the word from the next person round the circle. You give the word back to a person in the circle upstream from where the mistake was made so that the person with the problem can hear the word a

---

[1] This framework was suggested in a workshop by Mike Eales.

couple of times more and then can have another go at it. This gentle, indirect form of correction is less likely to block the person with the pronunciation problem than direct correction would.

Comparing sub-routines (present simple first and third persons)

Ask each student to think of the last seven things they typically do before leaving their house or flat. Ask them to write these down, helping them with vocabulary when necessary. Now ask them to bring to mind a person they know well, a family member or a close friend. Ask them to write down the last seven things that they think this person does before leaving their house or flat.

The students now work in groups of three comparing the sub-routines. Sometimes they are struck by differences in sub-routine between themselves and the other person they have chosen. As they read out their sentences to each other they are practising very precise grammar points (first and third persons singular, present simple).

What I am stressing here is that a skilled teacher can use humanistic exercises to work on nitty-gritty aspects of the language. This teacher can be just as strictly 'on task' as her colleagues working with gap-fills or with communicative exercises. The difference lies in the human dimension. In the two exercises above, the students are relating to each other in a whole person way, in the first one very physically and in the second one more verbally. In the first exercise the symbolic aspect is very powerful, as the students are carefully giving and receiving nuggets of the target language.

Exercises that work on the here and now of the group

Since teachers working humanistically will have warmed-up students in their care, it makes sense to keep a close eye on the weather in the group. The teacher needs to know where they are and something of how they feel. Is this a honeymoon period in which everybody is getting on well with other people or are some people moving towards storm? Is the group in a post-storm period when some of the anger and frustration participants have experienced has blown itself out? I want to look at one exercise that helps the teacher gauge the mood people are in and another that modifies the way the group members are feeling.

Weather forecasting

Ask students to think of themselves as a weather system and to prepare to express their 'here-and-now' mood in a meteorological metaphor.

Also ask them to give a weather forecast for the rest of the day. One student might say: 'There is a mist everywhere this morning with patches of fog. It is cold and there is no wind. Later in the day there will be a breeze and the sun will come out'.

This short exercise gives the teacher a fair idea of how people feel at the moment and sometimes participants offer information about themselves in this type of metaphorical activity that takes on considerable significance later in a course. It goes without saying that the teacher's focus is on taking in the plethora of information the exercise throws up and on retaining at least some of it for possible use later in the course.

Breathing in rhythm

Everybody is seated in a circle so they can see each other. Ask one person to notice their breathing but not to change it. Ask this person to follow their own breathing by raising and lowering a hand. Ask everybody in the circle to raise and lower their own hand in rhythm with the first person. This person then looks at the person on their left who takes over the breathing leadership, raising and lowering their hand in rhythm with their own breathing. Everybody follows the second leader and so on round the group. (If you have more than 15–16 students, it is good to have two or more circles working simultaneously as it is hard work following the breathing of even ten other people.)

This exercise from Bernard Dufeu is a marvellous one to help create or to celebrate harmony in a group. If the group mood is not for harmony, the exercise is a useful catalyst for the start of a period of storming. If people are feeling angry, then a 'togetherness' activity of this depth brings them to a point where they need to interrupt 'task' and really speak about at least some of what is on their mind. (Since 'task' is language learning, the expression of their frustrations via the target language will be one of the most valuable language exercises on their course. There is no question of 'rehearsal' here.)

Exercises that work on things from people's pasts

Whenever a teacher walks into a class with 30 participants, she faces 30 'here-and-nows' and also 30 complex, walking histories. Frequently those histories will be conditioning what is really happening when the student and the teacher think they are on task. Let me offer a concrete and technical example. Sergei was a Baltic shipping agent whom I taught one-to-one. He told me that we had ten afternoons (over a fortnight) to try to solve his writing problem. As a speaker he was an able upper intermediate; as a writer he was a hesitant, foot-tapping, lower intermediate mess. As we worked, it became apparent to Sergei that he had a similar problem in his native Russian and that he could now link this with a mother tongue teacher he had had in middle school. She disliked him, put him down, punished him and gave him unfair marks. (He checked this out by copying a classmate's composition almost verbatim: she gave him a D and the classmate an A!) It was clear that Sergei's linguistic past was obstructing his present like a blood clot blocking an artery. The hurtful teacher had broken the little boy's confidence in himself in this area. She had efficiently created a problem where there had been none, and the problem had stayed with him. (Fortunately, Sergei left after that fortnight writing fluent faxes in English.)

Dealing with projections

This is an exercise that is useful near the beginning of a group's life to bring out things from the participants' past which can get in the way of their meeting each other effectively.

Bring a large soft ball to class and put it in the middle of the circle. Tell people to look around the group and see if anybody here reminds them of anybody they have known previously. When a person sees someone in the group who is like someone they already know, they pick up the ball, throw it to the person and say: 'you remind me of ... because ... and you are different from ... because ...'.

In a group of 20 people usually between six and ten people will have projections they feel able to share and these will tend to be positive ones. The exercise, if it is used early in the life of a group, will not be important in itself. Its importance lies in giving people permission to think and talk about projection. Often students become aware of much more powerful and serious projections days after this little exercise has been done in class. In one case, we did the exercise on the first Tuesday of a two-week course. On the Friday of that week Charlie told me that he had now finally disentangled me in his mind from a theatre director I reminded him of. This man was a person he both respected and loathed, and I looked like him, moved like him and spoke like him! Charlie felt a lot more comfortable in my class once he had really prised my image away from the other man's in his head. Sorting us out mentally turned a conceivably painful course into a good course for Charlie.

After strong experiences like this, when I meet a new group, I am acutely aware that I am meeting X number of 'here-and-nows' but also X number of walking histories. I ignore these latter at my peril.

Where do humanistic activities come from?

Opponents of the humanistic trend in language teaching will tell you
that a teacher goes on a couple of therapy weekends and brings some
dangerous techniques back to her class which she then uses recklessly
and fecklessly with her students. To support this point of view they will
tell you that some of the techniques by humanistic writers are taken
straight from therapy and could be very dangerous in the hands of an
unskilled person. (So, incidentally, could a breadknife.)

Actually, the sources of the humanistic exercise are many and varied.
Some activities come from a teacher looking with fresh eyes at an age-old
area, like, say, dictation. Some exercises come from identifiable feeder
fields, like drama training. Some are devised in response to a student
need that the teacher does not yet have a tool for in her kitbag. She forges
a new instrument to cope with the student need. Some activities arise
from ordinary life experiences in which the teacher suddenly sees the
beginning of a useful exercise. Let me start with this last category.

Exercises that come from life experience

Imagine a train going out of London: four seats, two and two, facing
each other. Seth and I took the two aisle seats. A young man with his
head shaved, smelly socks and a kitbag lay sprawled over the two seats
next to the window. It took him five minutes to move his dirty boot
over, away from my elbow. As the train swayed through the suburbs I
built up a truly ferocious mental caricature of this clearly undesirable
individual. All my stereotyping and racialist mental machinery was
working overtime. After about twenty minutes he straightened himself
up and very skilfully picked up on something I had said to Seth ten
minutes before. I liked his voice immediately, and very soon Seth and I
were in full conversation with him. My absurd, negative first impression
gurgled down the plug hole like bathwater. From this experience and
from discussion with colleagues comes this exercise that could be used
in the first five hours of a group coming together.

For this exercise the teacher tells the students of a time when she had
a very wrong first impression of someone, which could be positive or
negative. The students then think of a time when either they got a
wrong first impression of someone or someone got a wrong first
impression of them. They work on this in threes. The teacher then
rounds off the exercise by giving out a text on wrong first impressions.

Though apparently about the past of people in the learning group,
this activity is really focused on the here-and-now of the group, as
people try to sort out their first impressions of each other.

Exercises devised in response to student need

A good example of a whole set of exercises that was motivated by student need is *Letters* (Burbidge, Gray, Levy and Rinvolucri 1996). The authors of this book worked intensively with Japanese second and fourth year university students and found that these young women could express themselves much better on the page than they could orally. Writing letters to them, receiving letters from them and getting them to write letters to each other was a perfect way of getting them to use the English that they knew in the channel that felt most comfortable to them. Once their confidence had been built up this way, it was possible to help them to make the transition to meaningful oral communication. With these students it was certainly a case of their written fluency leading them later to oral fluency. Without the initial oral silence and relative written eloquence of those Gifu students, the useful exercises in *Letters* might never have been devised.

Exercises that come from feeder fields

Andrew Wright, Don Byrne, Alan Maley and Alan Duff were probably among the first EFL teachers to bring over ideas from other fields to enrich their language teaching. These pioneers, working in the 60s and 70s, launched the resource book genre in EFL, a category of book which has been the vehicle for the transmission of humanistic ideas and exercises for the last thirty years. There are many streams that feed the language teaching lake. Here are a few of them:

Drama

Alan Maley and Alan Duff, drawing heavily on Viola Spolin's work, brought a whole range of drama and actor training techniques into EFL. Their book, *Drama Techniques in Language Teaching* (1982), is an excellent source of humanistic activities.

Psychodrama

Bernard Dufeu has drawn on the work of Jacob Moreno and Willy Urbain to create a completely new approach to teaching beginners: Linguistic Psychodramaturgy. This is arguably the most complex and complete approach to teaching adult beginners yet conceived. It is packed with frames and activities that can be used in language teaching without necessarily buying the whole approach. Among the main techniques brought across from psychodrama and Gestalt are the ideas of role-reversal and doubling. In role-reversal, Person A takes on the role of Person B when playing out a scene, and, reciprocally Person B acts out the part of Person A. In doubling, Person A goes behind Person B and tries to speak on B's behalf, expressing things she thinks B might want to say but can't. These have now been used by many writers of humanistic language teaching exercises.

Graphology

In the same way that voice carries the primary expression of language, its oral form, handwriting carries its secondary expression, the written form. Some ideas culled from graphology have appeared in EFL magazines, but there is still much to be learnt and adapted from this largely French-dominated field.

Maths

The Silent Way and the whole of Gattegno's thinking about language springs directly from mathematical thinking. All the open-ended, semantically free sentence-manipulation exercises, which are so different from gap-fills, come from the area of mathematical creativity. (See Rinvolucri 1984, section 2.)

Neuro-Linguistic Programming

A growing body of EFL teachers have taken initial training courses in NLP and have turned some of its rich range of exercises to language teaching use. NLP is still a rapidly developing field and we have so far only seen the beginnings of its adaptation to language teaching ends.

The above listing of feeder areas is by no means exhaustive, but it shows some of the pastures in which adventurous language teachers have grazed. My hunch is that the borrowings and adaptations of the past twenty-five years have been so fruitful that many more feeder fields not yet approached will be pressed into EFL service over the first twenty years of the twenty-first century.

Exercises that come from a new look at an old area

In the 80s John Morgan and I stumbled on the fact that when we told stories to language students, some of them responded with a depth of feeling we did not at first understand. I remember an Italian business man who stopped me telling Little Red Ridinghood at the point where the little girl says 'What big teeth you've got!' 'Basta!' he shouted. He later explained that his three-year-old daughter stopped him at this point in wide-eyed anticipatory terror. For an instant he seemed to have become a copy of the little girl in a safe and linguistically useful regression. We were late comers to the age-old tradition of oral story-telling and the book we did (*Once Upon a Time*, Morgan and Rinvolucri 1983) has been useful to many language teachers who wanted to look at the old with new eyes, first ours and then theirs. The great thing about taking a new look at something very old and familiar is that new angles are genuinely surprising and exciting.

The future of humanistic language teaching

I have happily poured my professional life so far into active participation in the humanistic language teaching movement, a movement parallel to work in other fields such as community architecture and to the thinking of divorce lawyers who push their clients towards reconciliation rather than litigation. All these human-sensitive ventures participate in a new outlook that is evident in a growing number of areas. My own belief in the rightness of the humanistic approach to language learners grows firmer from year to year. And yet I know that the resource book genre, the main print carrier of these ideas, still only reaches a tiny minority of the language teaching professionals.

For me the big question is how to reach the great majority of language teachers out there beyond the relatively limited realm of the communicative approach. How do we also reach the choral readers, the gap-fillers and the grammar-translators in the huge countries of the East and the South?

Perhaps one way is to accept the methodology that is so normal in their societies that they do not remotely see it as a methodology, as a matter of choice, but rather as a given, a part of nature. If this hypothesis is correct, then a good way for humanistic methodologists to move at this point would be to set themselves the task of humanising whatever teaching is being done – grammar-translation, for example – so that it becomes more of a whole person activity. The humanistic frame of mind can inform any technology of language teaching, for it is, above all, a question of attitude, which can be embodied in many types of exercises that show concern for the whole learner. This might be an effective way to usher in a much greater predominance in the future of humanistic language teaching.

13 Learning by heart: a Lozanov perspective

Grethe Hooper Hansen

Friendship is ... an open hand,
Yourself in someone else's face,
Walking shoulder to shoulder,
Knowing there is someone you can trust,
Something that allows you to be yourself,
A shelter on a cold stormy night.
Friendship is but a glance ...
   ... you and me.

This appealing poem was written by a group of four people, not all native English speakers, in ten minutes. Although each person had worked alone at first, the result is highly unitary. Coincidence? No, empathy. The exercise is a simple one: make small groups, each of which decides on a title, for example, Happiness, Friendship, Night, Day, The Seasons; then each person, using four slips of paper, makes four short sentences either beginning with the chosen word or describing it. The group then chooses two from each person to make a composite poem, to be written out and read to the whole class. When done properly, this exercise reveals the astonishing power of group process as compared with solitary work: few individuals could do as well as this in the time. Furthermore, the product itself is less than the target benefit of bonding people together and of creating a feedback loop to reinforce the value of synergic activity. Many sectors of education are rethinking the nature of the classroom and incorporating activities like this. We will be examining some aspects of one direction in language teaching, though first we need to reach a better understanding of the emotional dimension of learning.

If you do the above exercise with a group that is not in synchrony, it doesn't work; the poem is a meaningless jumble, a mere disappointment and waste of time, which some 'humanistic' activities can be when they go wrong. This chapter is about creating emotional climates in the learning environment that might enable activities to work better. It takes the particular perspective of psychiatrist Georgi Lozanov, whose contributions to learning in general, and affective learning in particular, have been considerable, not only within the context of a particular method. Certain key ideas will be considered, which are basic to his multi-level learning approach, but which reach beyond a single effective system to point out significant general principles underlying the learning process.

The human mind is always full of emotion, much of it unconscious; emotion acts as an underlying cause for much of what we do. We only occasionally become aware of its influence, generally attributing our actions to 'reasons' thought up by the intellect, whose survival function it is to monitor our output and make sense of the environment. The physiology of the relationship between emotion and cognition has been described in fascinating detail by Antonio Damasio (1994) and the ideas applied to language acquisition by John Schumann (1994, 1997).

Humanism and Lozanov

Humanism brought a shift in education towards an internal frame of reference, considering capacity for learning in terms of motivational state conditioned by the individual's life experience and beliefs. This change in perspective led eventually to developments such as the theory of multiple intelligences and research on different learner styles. It also revealed the learner as subject to change, rather than in eternal possession of fixed qualities. Labels like 'intelligent' and 'aggressive' are now seen as indicators of conditions which are to a large extent a function of the quality of care the individual has received (though one must also acknowledge some genetic inheritance), resulting in a mindset which remains open to change.

Though rooted in humanistic philosophy, Lozanov's method rests on a paradigm which is very different in practical terms from that of Carl Rogers; the desired end is similar but the means are not. Criticism of his method often stems either from paradigm problems or unfamiliarity with the evolution of his ideas, poorly represented in the literature. For example, while his starting point was hypnotherapy, this served only to develop the understanding of unconscious process that brought him to the use of suggestion as a means to self-empowerment.

First, he noted the constant fluctuation of human belief states, given that our energy is in perpetual movement between the various 'modules' of mind, each of which carries its own particular informational set. (In his seminars Dr Lozanov demonstrates very effectively that the human mind is in a constantly changing state.) He then focused on how to invoke a useful state of mind for learning, setting up feedback loops to encourage its frequent reappearance and, over time, changing preference through a gradual bottom-up experiential process whereby the learner learns to select a more beneficial (neural) perspective. The immediate result was much more rapid learning (though in fact the individual achieves only the level that is appropriate to him/her) and sometimes dramatic personality change. How this happens is no longer the mystery it was when Lozanov wrote his first book; it is now explicable in scientific terms and well substantiated in the medical field, Lozanov's own professional starting point, as a way of achieving better health.

Herbert Benson, professor of medicine at Harvard University and author of the seminal *Relaxation Response* (1975), presents substantial research to support his hypothesis that human beings are 'wired for God' and can achieve optimal health as a direct result of their beliefs. According to his research, religious belief brings with it a better state of physical health (H. Benson 1996). What he shows to be the cause of this phenomenon is the influence of the believer's state of mind on the secretion of biochemicals in the brain that control the body state. William James documented the health benefits of spirituality in his *Varieties of Religious Experience*; neuroscience can now explain why this happens.

In Lozanov's paradigm, the learners' belief is in themselves and their capacity to learn. This is sufficient to produce a biochemical environment in which remarkable results can be achieved. Mind and body are locked into a biochemical circle whereby they both condition and are conditioned by their own deeper state. A very clear and detailed description of this situation is given by Rossi (1986) when he explains the physiological basis of hypnotherapy: carefully induced thoughts and emotions influence biochemical secretion so as to condition behaviour and thought.

Psychotherapy has proceeded on the assumption that emotional trauma must be consciously worked through, the crystallized pain 'unfrozen' by re-experience before it can relinquish its hold on the psyche. Thus, there is no healing without the reliving and recontextualising of pain. However, the work of hypnotherapists such as Milton Erickson demonstrates that it is possible to redirect the general stream of thought, in effect to bypass the trauma, creating new logical pathways in the mind by modifying memory. Starting from Erickson's work, Neuro-Linguistic Programming has begun to develop ways in which small influences can potentially spread throughout the vast complex of the human mind; the difficulty lies in ensuring that the spread is wide enough. Lozanov supports his top-down intervention with continuous bottom-up input: practice of the new behaviour in an appropriate environment.

Emotion and learning

The word *e-motion* implies movement and motivation. Its survival role is to provide a bias or colouring, which will influence the selection of future actions and trigger the appropriate biochemicals to set the internal scene in readiness for that action: the clearest example is fear, which orchestrates a massive physiological preparation for fight or flight. Negative emotions typically lead to defensive reactions, which include the passive (falling asleep, daydreaming, mental sluggishness – familiar in classrooms) as well as the aggressive. Positive emotions have the opposite effect, opening the mind – to learning, among other things. The pleasure principle is usually the dominant scale for incentive. Expression of emotion tends to reflect the context in which it occurs. Thus, in classrooms it may appear in intellectual form, as for example 'I don't understand', but Lozanov interprets this in terms of emotion, not of intellectual block. A psychological point of view does not take verbal messages literally, but evaluates them as manifestations of emotional process.

It is useful to think of the human mind as an iceberg, the tiny tip of which emerges into conscious awareness, while the far greater part remains below the surface, just as influential but in a different way. One area of this subaquatic life is the massive quantity of automated physiological process supporting action: I raise my arm to catch the ball hurtling towards me. This needs to remain outside awareness to be efficient; consciousness would make it too slow and clumsy to be useful (Dixon 1981:65–8). Although pre-conscious, it can be set down by the conscious mind: skills like bicycle riding or knowing multiplication tables shift from trial and rehearsal to automation, probably changing neural location as they do so. These processes have been discussed in the linguistic context by Barry McLaughlin (1990), who compares schizophrenia (breakdown of the mind's monitoring system) with the lack of automated implementation of the many complex tasks that is the substrate of language learning.

Another area of the iceberg is the ongoing battle for selection to consciousness, a continual vast competition between the armies of neurons underlying thought and action. This is the domain of dreams, hunches, impulses, thoughts not quite ready for expression, slips of the tongue, imminent poetry, myth, ecstasies and glooms. Its influence on conscious thought is enormous, though only a tiny stream will ever reveal itself.

Finally, down in the iceberg depths churn the emotional imperatives, carefully hidden from awareness. One of the functions of the conscious mind is to protect us from that which is too painful to think about – and which would probably waste our time and slow our responses – and yet is potentially all-powerful in determining our possibilities of thought and action, as psychotherapy reveals.

These selective processes, which result in exclusion from consciousness, are set up at different stages of our life: first genetic inheritance, then pre-natal life. The uterine environment exerts massive influence on the development of the fragile structures of the tiny foetal brain as it passes through the now identifiable critical periods of its growth. Work in this area is being done by Dr Michel Odent (1984, 1986) of the Primal Health Research Centre, London.

The next important input is birth itself. Birth complications, such as forceps delivery and separation from the mother can lead, among other things, to autism, schizophrenia, violent criminality and a host of learning difficulties – an astonishing revelation in a society that takes hospital delivery for granted. The current escalation of dyslexia and other learning impairments is almost certainly due to an increase in environmental stress factors, the consequences of which we have hardly considered (Odent 1986).

Since the primal adaptive system reaches maturity very early during the primal period, fears, expectations of the world and basic reactions to stress are set down at this stage. The child who does not receive sufficient physical nurture will feel more separate from its fellow humans, suspicious and hostile towards them, depending on the way it was treated. The survival terrors of early infancy (starvation, abandonment, displacement by a rival) are generalised into later life situations: am I receiving enough nourishment in the classroom? Will I be abandoned for x, y, or z behaviours?

There are universal patterns and idiosyncratic ones. Each family sets up its own 'culture'; its members shape their behaviour according to the reward system that prevails and speak the parental language. The culture in which early education is received will also leave its imprint. If the child is treated as an empty slate requiring didactic input, rather than an individual with an already formed and discerning mind, he or she will probably develop a need for informational filling up, and will be more likely to manifest low self-esteem and a lack of creativity in learning situations.

Given the infant damage endemic in our society, Lozanov set out to design a learning environment that precludes, as far as possible, the restimulation of predictable problems, and instead invokes an optimally responsive mindset. To give an example, from the above it would seem that the thing to avoid most in classrooms is producing fear, which may trigger the primitive panic reactions. Lynn Dhority (1984) states that extreme fear can direct neural energy into the lower survival areas of the brain so that there is not enough control in the neo-cortex to facilitate speech and the student becomes literally speechless. There would also be associated problems arising from individual cultures, each person's idiosyncratic negative reaction. (An exception is the student who has learnt to deflect attack by intellectual achievement; he or she may become the class star in a fear culture, but the stars will be few and the majority dim.) The opposite of fear is security and comfort, and this Lozanov endeavours to provide: each unit in his learning cycle begins with a long passive receptive period which learners are, however, at liberty to break; in language teaching translation is always available; pair work is avoided before there is enough competence to sustain it and so on.

A refinement on humanistic positions in education is his perception that autonomy must not be assumed but slowly created. Rather than expecting the learner to get on with it alone (as is sometimes the case in Rogers' work), Lozanov (Lozanov and Gateva 1988:26–7) first sets up a secure environment, waits until autonomous behaviour begins to manifest itself, and then gently nudges the learner into doing things alone. His overall dynamic is first teacher authority (to meet needs and establish confidence), then general co-operation, and finally learner autonomy, the same pattern that is followed in counselling practice, such as Heron's (1989) model of skilful facilitation.

Supporting procedures are non-directive teacher behaviour: minimal correction with assumption of teacher, not learner, error when things go wrong; and minimal command with instructions being, where possible, modelled and given only once so that students learn to pay attention better and to become more independent over the long term. Verbal praise, when overdone, can carry the implication of teacher superiority and norm learner incompetence, and so is strictly rationed, giving way to smiles and gestures which convey reward without the danger of negative suggestion. In addition, participation in activities is always optional. Learners can – and do – choose to sit and watch. Lozanov also restricts individual competition to demonstrably non-serious games, and otherwise encourages competition only between groups so that bonding precedes it.

Therapy and classrooms

Some humanistic practitioners questioned Lozanov's refusal, mentioned above, to 'work through pain'. As noted earlier, this is not part of his paradigm. Lozanov observed, in his early experimenting with different learning hypotheses with patients of his psychiatric institute, that for the duration of the learning course they lost their pathological symptoms. In place of hypnosis, he changes state of consciousness simply through the 'placebo effect' of suggestion, which suspends disbelief long enough for the more durable influence of feedback from genuinely accelerated learning to take effect. The placebo effect, much used by doctors in an attempt to activate the patient's own self-healing ability in preference to reliance on drugs, is known to have only a temporary influence: monitoring processes constantly scan the real state of the organism and adjust belief state accordingly. Hypnotherapy requires repetition to counteract this readjustment. Lozanov found that when there was conspicuous gain in learning speed, this would be fed back, to the point where suggestion, the placebo, was no longer necessary. Thus, his famous acceleration of learning was never an end in itself but a useful cogwheel towards the maintenance of belief in one's personal ability.

Lozanov does not deny pain, but simply finds it is counterproductive to deal with it in a learning situation since the mind becomes involved in material other than the subject in hand and also loses its buoyant expectation and openness. He does introduce cathartic procedures, as we shall see, to allow for the discharge of negative emotional blocks in a natural and inconspicuous way. However, his general approach to this issue is to move attention away from the 'sick place' towards a 'good place'. As the learner becomes emotionally healthier in a happy and supportive environment, the organism, in its natural growth towards health and perfection, allows ancient problems to rise to the surface of awareness so that they may be resolved. The monsters of the deep present themselves for transmutation, a process that may also occur naturally as we grow older. They can then be worked on as necessary – but outside the classroom.

Lozanov's aim and ambition, the psychiatrist's dream, was to create a system that produces optimal health, harmony and integrative social behaviour in the individual. His view is first and foremost that the organism will, if encouraged and enabled to do so, achieve its own healing and integration. He facilitates this by the gentle and gradual building of autonomy within the context of learning.

In his view, this precludes uninvited therapy by others. While the mind is obviously more open to new learning when relatively free from neuroses, psychotherapeutic interventions are very often counter productive in the hands of those who are not professionally trained to perform them, however good their intentions. Since the desire to help may well be an unconscious projection of one's own need to deal with one's own emotional problems, this is, in any case, dangerous territory. (Professional therapists remain in constant analysis themselves so as to try to retain awareness of their own emotional problems, which they know contaminate the work they do.)

Influence, as Lozanov has repeated through the years, is all around us, whether we like it or not; the environment exerts a massive determining influence on human thought and action. The extreme receptiveness of living organisms to minute changes in the environment is the pillar on which evolutionary science stands, from the Neural Darwinism of Gerald Edelman to the environmentalism of Richard Dawkins, in which, for example, he shows how bats develop a highly complex system for orientation ('batsight') through multitudinous minute but incremental changes in response to their environmental situation (Dawkins 1986:21–37).

The teacher, classroom and method cannot but influence the learner at many different levels below awareness; every teacher creates a potent environment, useful or not, albeit unknowingly. This is the basis of Lozanov's insistence that when learning fails, teachers must scrutinize their own practice rather than blaming the students. The teacher is always in control of the environment, whether he or she admits it or not, since environment includes methodological procedure; Lozanov teachers acknowledge and accept this responsibility. The therapeutic effect on the learner is bottom-up and self-reinforced, a result of practice or experience supported by feedback loops which mirror accurately the real progress made.

Much has been written about Lozanov's forages into the 'paranormal': visiting Vasiliev in Moscow, travelling in India, studying yoga and so forth. In fact, he observed these things from a scientist's viewpoint, and his method now succeeds in making the 'para' normal. H. Benson (1996) has shown clearly how the images fed into the brain change our biological structure and affect health and well being. Such phenomena have only recently become the domain of science, which has, through its exploration of the quantum dimension of reality, acknowledged the need to move beyond the boundaries of that which is perceived by the physical senses.

The aesthetic

With his combined focus on autonomy and environmental influence, Lozanov gravitated naturally towards his ultimate solution for drawing out the genius within: creative artistic self-expression fanned by aesthetic stimulation.

Given that the human brain is at all times involved in compulsive adaptive response to the environment, including the most subtle changes, and that the extent of our adaptive sensitivity is infinitely greater than we can be aware of, art and the aesthetic can influence us profoundly for better health and better thinking.

The ancient Greeks were the first to document this effect. They used art to provide 'catharsis', the discharge of negative emotion, and subsequently to re-integrate and harmonise the emotional complex. In Greek tragedy, for example, there is huge emotional involvement; the spectator's heart is wrung by one cataclysmic event after another, but by virtue of poetry, music and lofty sentiments, eventually purged and purified. This calming and re-integrating effect of art can be explained in neural terms. As a finely tuned adaptive instrument, the brain mirrors internally what it perceives. Perceived pain causes us to suffer and violence makes us more aggressive (according to whether we mirror the victimiser or the victim). And harmony harmonises.

This effect has now been explored and researched, especially in the area of music; there are a number of studies showing the predictable (replicable) influences of music, from harmonising the vegetative system of the body to increasing intelligence and accelerating the development of conceptual thinking in children. Researching Lozanov's work, Dieter Lehmann, a musicologist from Leipzig, noted the effect of catharsis produced by Lozanov's use of music of the Classical period. This is achieved because classical music, with its high emotional content, makes it possible to encode memories with emotion, to stimulate the need for communication (classical music includes dialogue, question and answer, as well as monologue, theme and variation), and to bring the emotional complex progressively towards integration. Baroque music, with its mathematical regularity and emphasis on symmetry, is particularly useful in harmonising the vegetative system, clearing the mind and bringing it to an optimally receptive state. Lehmann's research also shows that the emotional response will take place regardless of whether or not the listener is paying attention to the music (Lehmann 1988).

Among the many innovative musical research projects now underway in the US, perhaps the most relevant to Lozanov's work is the exploration of the physiology of emotional expression within music by Manfred Clynes, pianist and neuroscientist (Clynes 1982). Noting the many ways in which emotion is expressed through the body, Clynes tested the hypothesis that each emotion has a specific expressive signature of recognisable patterns, and that through these patterns the emotion will also be transmitted. Measuring micro-muscular movements, such as finger pressure, he found these movements to be at the base of emotional response across a wide range of cultures.

He went on to show that each composer has his or her own sentic form, a particular emotional pattern that is conveyed in the way that person habitually combines notes; this pattern is mirrored by the listener, albeit well below the threshold of conscious awareness. Beethoven, according to Clynes, typically expressed pain, and in the final movement would work through catharsis to resolution (Clynes 1991). While professional musicians have shown themselves to be acutely sensitive to the aptness of the 'correct' emotional gesture for a particular composer, non-musicians are also much more sensitive to tone and inflection than is normally imagined, as has been shown by popular use of Clynes' 'Super Conductor' computer program. This is an interactive computer program which allows the user to shape music to express emotion through pulse and phrase shaping. While professional musicians proved to be extremely sensitive to the emotional gestures 'demanded' by different composers, non-musicians were also surprisingly aware.

In fact, the human hearing system, adapted for babies to pick up the subtlest of signals from their parent and general environment, is highly discriminating of tone, intonation and timbre. We are all profoundly affected by music and all its subtleties. It is also quite likely that the music that has endured in popularity for centuries is that which has the most harmonising and healing effect on its listeners, which is one reason why Lozanov prefers the classics.

Ernst Chladni, a German physicist working in the early 19th century, demonstrated the formative power of music using fine particles such as sand or iron filings: music causes them to fall into pleasing patterns which, according to Lyall Watson, mirror fundamental organic form (Watson 1973). Hans Jenny, a Swiss scientist, pursued this work using his 'tomoscope' and 'stroboscope' to capture the symmetrical interactions of waves passing through liquid as music gradually imposed order on previously chaotic substances. At one level, the whole physical substance of the universe consists of particles in vibration, and clearly music is able to influence this dance of matter.

The effect of 'rhythm entrainment' seems to be a basic pattern of nature, observable in clusters of birds and animals all doing the same thing at the same intervals of time. There is a principle of economy of energy whereby periodic events which are close enough in frequency soon begin to occur in phase or step with one another (Bentov 1978:28). By extension, we can posit a principle of response by mirroring in which an observer is drawn into the state of mind or being of the object or person observed.

This is applied by Lozanov to the plastic arts (Lozanov 1979:162). Many readers will know the intense pleasure that can be gained from contemplating a painting. This is probably the result of multifarious minute responses integrated into one emotional whole, as the brain mirrors (to the extent of its own capacity at the time) the ecstatic perception of the artist conveyed brushstroke by brushstroke in, say, the multicoloured creation of a shadow. There may be catharsis, depending on the state of the observer: the painting may help the observer to transcend chaos in his or her mind through the influence of its own integration. This does not involve concept formation; its presence in conscious awareness will be no more than vague feeling, but a great deal of movement has taken place inside the iceberg.

In his text for teaching English (*The Return*), Lozanov reproduces classic English art as illustration. He also pins posters of good reproductions on the classroom walls. A similar effect can be achieved more simply through the use of photographs of landscapes, which also have a harmonising effect, and may invoke a wider response from the sensory cortex.

The reader is invited to try this now: close your eyes and picture in your mind a beach or another place you know and love. Extend the image to a wider picture and bring in more detail, then add sounds such as water and seabirds, and the taste of saltspray. Imagine yourself in the scene and the feeling of your body, perhaps the warmth of sun on your skin – and relax into the scene. When you open your eyes, you will almost certainly feel better, having activated different areas of the visual, auditory and motor cortex and secreted a whole range of new hormones!

Song and dance have similar therapeutic benefits and can easily be incorporated into the language classroom. Song can be highly cathartic, and one's own singing voice is generally therapeutic. We all have 'pain' songs which bring tears to our eyes, and these are a wonderful means of releasing unexpressed negative emotion; allowable classroom tears (sad songs, sad stories) can clear impediments to learning. Try singing 'My Bonnie lies over the Ocean' slowly and with attention to the words, and you may undergo a small catharsis.

Dance harmonises the body through rhythmic coordination and balance – and this stimulation of the motor cortex invokes a similar integrated state in the brain. It also triggers the secretion of hormones, notably endorphins, which are pain-inhibiting and by extension pleasure-enhancing. Oxytocin, the 'hormone of love', which is secreted in relational situations (sexual relationships, interaction between mother and child or horse and rider, eating with friends and so forth) intensifies bonding and dependency. Arguably, it might be in play to assist the matching of movement and holding of hands that are involved in circle dance; certainly dance has a softening effect on behaviour.

Poetry has its own characteristic form of influence. Rhythm and harmony, through their repetitive effect moderated by the brainstem, calm and harmonise. The wide sensory benefits of images and metaphors stimulate the brain very widely – the cortical and subcortical areas, right and left hemispheres and frontal lobes – requiring active search for meaning, rehearsal of memories and emotional involvement. Lozanov peppers his texts with poetry, symbol and paradox.

Thus, he uses the aesthetic in different ways to create an ideal learning state: the brain is integrated and harmonised, freed from emotional blocks by appropriate discharge, bathed in reassuring hormones and at the same time stimulated towards ever greater problem-solving activity.

Active expression

The above are all passive effects of art, passive in the sense that they are largely responsive, although that response may call for considerable internal activity. There is also the even more powerful effect of the learners' own artistic creativity. Consider this: the human brain is a compulsive pattern maker and problem solver; the more it exercises, the better it grows. Telling it information actually inhibits this activity, whereas making it work to discover the information itself, encourages it. The harder the brain works, and the more it is actively involved, the happier and thirstier it becomes. Artistic creativity is the ultimate expression of autonomy, combining the effects of passive and active response. It causes the brain to stretch itself to the limit and to remain as balanced as possible in the process.

Erich Fromm, as one of the German psychologists involved in the massive post-war study of the origins of violence, noted that the cause was most often frustration of expression, and consequent feeling of a life unlived. Creative expression is the quintessence of human activity, and as such a powerful source of strength and inspiration for learning.

The Lozanov teacher aims constantly at stimulating individual creativity, telling brief stories in order to provoke the students into telling theirs, watching for signs of individuals' readiness to contribute and drawing them out, encouraging and nudging gently into action. A similar approach was presented by Assagioli (1968) in a pamphlet on how to learn languages by stimulating the unconscious mind. This corresponds closely with Lozanov's thinking; indeed there is much common ground between Assagioli's Psychosynthesis and Suggestopedia.

Drama is another major tool that Lozanov uses to ease and encourage self-expression, to bring the learner into performance. First there is the ongoing role-play; each learner is invited (never forced) to create his or her own character in the target language and gradually build up a life story. There is also additional role-play of characters from the text. Within both frameworks, small groups constantly act, play and perform together.

The whole Lozanov course unfolds in the context of drama: the text is a play, the teacher an actor playing a role, the students all in their chosen, never assigned roles. Activities frequently draw on these, although triggered by the text. There is a great deal of learner performance, which is not focused on doing exercises but on drama, story-telling and creative activity. The rules for designing activities are that they must be seen to arise naturally from the text so as to keep the learners at all times involved in the content of the drama; they must always have an underlying didactic purpose – so that learners can relax in the knowledge that everything they are required to do is a necessary part of the learning process; and there must always be distraction of the conscious mind away from the target material so that learning occurs through peripheral perception, involving a different neuronal routing from conscious learning.

The roles provide a mask which shields the learner from error, from fear of exaggeration or excessive revelation, all the kinds of things that normally inhibit spontaneous expression. The learners, however timid, are unable to resist demonstrating to others the character they have created, and are lured into more and more risk taking. In addition, since the characters are personal constructions, they contain a large element of the autobiography of their creators, which involves considerable emotional investment. The mask also offers the opportunity to try out new ways of being and expressing, to launch into the process of change.

To give an example of the power of identification, a communicative activity to practise the present perfect tense might be to ask a partner to identify three things they have learnt in their life. The Lozanov approach would change this exercise in several ways: (1) it would arise from context; (2) the learner would have to consider the question with reference to his or her chosen role, which calls for immersion in the character and some reflection on what it deeply represents; (3) the learners would circulate, putting the question to many different people (since the whole 'family' has grown up together) and receiving many different answers; (4) the activity might also continue into the dramatic, with each person acting out one of his or her answers for the others to guess or remember.

All this would etch the memory deeper, given that we remember best the things we do. It also causes the learner to reflect on the most positive aspects of the role, and enjoy the sense of having achieved the wisdom he or she chose to express. Lozanov relies heavily on the subtle pervasive effects of mood, carefully selecting positive moods, to spin the mind upwards towards the peaks of what it might achieve rather than downwards into the trough of past mistakes.

Story-telling is a regular feature of classroom activity – but teacher stories are short to serve the major purpose of encouraging learners to tell theirs. Story has its own magic, galvanising bored learners to instant attention, perhaps because stories embody fundamental thinking patterns (problem, hypothesis, trial, resolution) and contain archetypal symbols, stimulating the imagination.

Conclusion

Given the dense planning of the Suggestopedic lesson, more teacher control is necessary than in some methods. Autonomy tends to develop gradually and emerge fully towards the end of the course, symbolised by the learners' creation and performance of the last lesson by themselves. In fact, learners often 'take over' before this point, reject the teacher's elaboration of the text and instead pursue their own. Lozanov's method is a model for autonomising rather than something to be used by the already autonomous learner.

Like all methodological approaches, it favours some learning styles over others and is probably best appreciated by those learners in the middle and to the right end of the brain dominance spectrum. However, it can be very useful to those with left bias because it introduces them in a dramatic way to other possibilities for learning, and helps them to achieve a better balance of right with left. Previously there may have been a bias towards the auditory, but the sensory balance has been corrected over the years.

The type of learning that stems from Lozanov's thinking represents a fascinating exercise in paradigm shift, and the research based on his work shows not only considerable acceleration in learning, but improvement in general emotional health. It incorporates useful resources for teachers themselves, particularly the application of Lozanov's mirror: the teacher takes full responsibility for learning breakdown, finding a solution by scrutinising his or her own practice as in a mirror and then making the necessary changes. This extends both the teachers' emotional understanding (admitting the possibility of their own error rather than assuming others are at fault) and their professional competence since they will have to continue to try new ways of doing things until they find one that works.

Recent scientific research has given support to Lozanov's method. It is a finely balanced complex of subtle effects, derived from medical and psychotherapeutic practice. As Thomas Kuhn (1973) noted, paradigm shift invariably comes from outside the field or from newcomers to the field.

His claims of success, once considered exaggerated because they were not replicated by other people, are at last understandable. Results depend on rigorous attention to detail and application of principles, meticulous preparation, and a high degree of emotional awareness and skill on the part of the teacher. The most remarkable learning gains reported probably reflected that level of teacher expertise at which intuition embodies principle; there comes a point at which the Lozanovian labour is superseded by spontaneous creativity.

Lozanov's approach to language teaching is admittedly not easy to apply in its entirety in all educational contexts. However, it is a pilot and model for future educational systems, which no doubt will apply brain theory in a systematic and scientific way and will recognise the need for training in emotional skills, the most sadly neglected area of the curriculum. When we understand that violence stems from pain, and classroom underachievement from learner inhibition and let ourselves be guided by this understanding, real progress can be made in the gentle facilitation of learning.

Suggestions for further reading

Dhority, L. 1991. *The ACT Approach*. New York: Gordon & Breach.

Jensen, E. 1995. *Brain-Based Learning and Teaching*. Del Mar, CA: Turning Point Publishing.

Neville, B. 1989. *Educating Psyche*. North Blackburn Victoria: Collins-Dove.

Woodhouse, M. B. 1996. *Paradigm Wars: Views for a New Age*. London: Frog Ltd.

14 Cooperative language learning and affective factors

JoAnn (Jodi) Crandall

Cooperative learning: an overview

Since the mid 80s, discussions of effective language instruction have shifted from an emphasis on teacher-centered to learner-centered class-rooms and from transmission-oriented to participatory or constructivist knowledge development. With that shift has come a renewed focus on small group or task-based learning which affords students the opportunity to develop a range of cognitive, metacognitive and social, as well as linguistic skills while interacting and negotiating in the classroom. Especially noteworthy, in this regard, has been the increased attention to and expanded use of cooperative learning in second and foreign language and bilingual and mainstream classrooms with students of all ages and language proficiency levels.

While many have suggested that cooperative learning is beneficial only for 'good students,' or conversely, that it only helps 'poor students', there is sufficient research to suggest that all students can benefit from being placed in the role of both tutor and tutee, of learning from and providing scaffolding for peers. The value of cooperative learning is likely to be understood by those from more cooperative or group-oriented societies, but its value can also be demonstrated to those living in more competitive societies, where it can help foster the development of social skills needed to interact and communicate equitably with diverse groups of people.

Some characteristics of cooperative learning

At its base, cooperative learning requires social interaction and negotiation of meaning among heterogeneous group members engaged in tasks in which all group members have both something to contribute to and learn from the other members. Cooperative learning is more than just small group activity. In a well-structured cooperative task, there is a genuine information gap, requiring learners to both listen to and contribute to the development of an oral, written or other product which represents the group's efforts, knowledge and perspectives.

There is a growing research base on the effects and effectiveness of cooperative language learning. A central theme of much of this research concerns the affective value of cooperative activities. Cooperative learning has been shown to encourage and support most of the affective factors which correlate positively with language learning: i.e. reducing (negative or debilitating) anxiety, increasing motivation, facilitating the development of positive attitudes toward learning and language learning, promoting self-esteem, as well as supporting different learning styles and encouraging perseverance in the difficult and confusing process of learning another language.

While there are differences among the models of cooperative learning, the three major models – those of Robert Slavin (1983b, 1990), Spencer Kagan (1989, 1994), and David W. Johnson and Roger T. Johnson (1989, 1994) – share the following essential characteristics, all of which have an impact on the affective nature of the language classroom:

1 Positive interdependence

In a cooperative group, the focus of interaction is on producing or completing together something such as a report, a newsletter, a poster, a lesson or a science project. Cooperative groups share a common goal; each learner has an essential role to play if that goal is to be achieved. Cooperation, in this regard, is more than just collaboration, where it is possible to complete a task or develop a product without the contributions of each of the members. The success (or failure) of a cooperative group is dependent on the efforts of all of its individual members.

2 Face-to-face, group interaction

Another feature of cooperative learning is the emphasis on small group interaction. While some cooperative structures use pairs (dyads), a more typical group consists of 3–6 students, small enough to encourage all members to participate, but large enough to benefit from multiple ideas and roles of the individual members. Groups of 4 or 6 can be particularly effective, since students can engage in both pair and group activities without having to change groups.

Cooperative groups are purposefully heterogeneous. Teachers form the groups to maximize each student's contributions to the group and to provide each student with opportunities to learn from other individuals in the group. For example, in an activity requiring individual roles, an extroverted or more self-confident student who likes to speak in class may be assigned the role of Reporter, while one who prefers to write may be named the Recorder. A quieter student who is a good reader might be assigned the role of Reader, while one who is more comfortable speaking and leading can be the Facilitator. There are even roles for students who have limited language proficiency, as Materials Person, Timekeeper or even Praiser, encouraging continued participation by the members. Although one student may be designated as Facilitator, the others in the group have an opportunity for leadership roles – Recording, Reporting, Reading or Praising – and all members of the group are expected to help the others to be equally prepared for large group activities such as a group discussion or quiz.

3 Individual (and group) accountability

Individual accountability is encouraged through the assignment of specific roles or tasks, and individuals are held accountable for the success of each of the other members. Accountability is also developed through activities which ask learners to engage in self-evaluation concerning their participation in the group, the value of their contributions and their attitudes and actions towards the other members. While all models encourage individual responsibility to the group, the degree to which students are evaluted in terms of their group participation varies in the different cooperative learning models.

4 Development of small group social skills

For cooperative groups to succeed, individual members need to develop not only linguistic but also social skills which facilitate teamwork, create trust and enhance communication, leadership, problem-solving and decision-making in group interaction. They need to learn how to work together as a team and how to help each other, assuming responsibility for their own and each others' learning. Needed are skills in negotiating (clarifying, seeking clarification, checking for comprehension, probing for more information) as well as group interaction skills in turn-taking, listening, encouraging, helping, disagreeing appropriately and accepting others' opinions and disagreements (Bennett, Rolheiser-Bennett and Stevahn 1991).

5 Group processing

Besides engaging in group tasks, learners also need to reflect upon their group's experiences, noting how group members interacted doing that task, the kind and number of contributions each made, and the difficulties that were encountered as different views were suggested or one member was noticeably silent or vocal. Through this processing, learners acquire or refine metacognitive and socio-affective strategies of monitoring, learning from others, and sharing ideas and turns. In that reflection they also engage in language use that is not typically available or fostered in traditional language classrooms or activities.

Some traditional cooperative activities and their application to language learning

A number of books have appeared in the last few years which provide hundreds of cooperative activities either designed for the language classroom or easily adapted for language learning. These include DeBolt (1994), High (1993), Kessler (1992), Sloan (1992), Bennett, Rolheiser-Bennett and Stevahn (1991), Andrini (1990), Coelho, Winer and Olsen (1989) Puttnam (1997) and Nunan (1992). What follows is a selection of cooperative activities which the author has used most effectively in language (as well as in teacher education) classrooms.

1 Think/pair/share

Perhaps the most basic cooperative activity or structure is think/pair/share, developed by Kagan (1994). In this activity, a question is posed or an issue is presented (by other learners or the teacher), and learners are given some time to reflect, take notes or engage in free writing before turning to another learner and sharing what they have just thought and written about. After sharing in pairs, the members of the pair share their ideas with the larger group. The focus of the sharing can be something as simple as thinking about all the things that one reads and writes in one day, or something as complex as the causes of homelessness, the qualities of a good teacher or the alternatives to burning wood for fuel.

Unlike the anxiety or terror that may overcome students when teachers pose questions to them without allowing time for thought or rehearsal, with a think/pair/share, learners have several opportunities to develop their ideas, rehearse their language and receive feedback on both language and content before having to commit to speaking in front of the entire class.

2 Jigsaw

Jigsaw, developed by Aaronson and colleagues (Aaronson 1978), is perhaps the most widely known cooperative language learning activity used to create a real 'information gap' in the classroom and encourage communication. In a Jigsaw activity, each member of the group has information which the others need in order to complete the puzzle and develop a report or complete a task. But before students are asked to share that information, they are given the opportunity to work in 'expert groups' with others researching the same topic or discussing the same text. When they feel sufficiently able to explain their portion to the rest of the group, they return to their 'home' group and serve as the expert on their contribution.

At the simplest level, Jigsaw can be used to divide the task for reading or listening to a text among members of a group (each reading a different section or listening for different information). In a language classroom it might also take the form of a country report, with expert groups focused on different aspects of that country (the political system, educational system, natural resources or population, for example); or the completion of a graphic organizer about the characters, setting and major events in several books by the same author. It is also possible to assign groups a different perspective on the same topic or issue to encourage development of higher order thinking skills in the target language. For example, students might read letters, manuals or texts written by factory workers, the Chamber of Commerce, the Department of Health and a farmers' cooperative about actions to take when a factory (major employer) is pouring pollutants into a river which is heavily fished by community members and is also the main source of irrigation and drinking water.

3 Roundtable/Roundrobin

Roundtable and Roundrobin are two activities from the Structural Approach of Kagan (1994). In both, students take turns giving answers, providing information or sharing ideas. In a Roundtable, students offer written contributions, sharing one piece of paper and a pencil and passing them so that each student provides a written contribution. In Roundrobin, the contributions are spoken. In both, turns continue until everyone has run out of ideas or time is called. Students 'pass' (yield their turn) when they have nothing they wish to contribute.

These activities are excellent for capturing ideas in brainstorming, for developing common background information, and for identifying possible directions for future activities. I have used them as part of a warm-up in a content-based lesson on the value of trees, in ESL writing classes for brainstorming possible topics for future writing assignments, and in ESL teacher education on ways that schools can involve parents and community members.

4 Numbered heads together

In this activity (Kagan 1994), members of a group count off. Then a question is posed for all of the group to discuss. When they have developed a team answer and are certain that each member knows that answer, a number is called and students with that number are expected to answer the question. Each member of the group is expected to help the others to understand and be able to answer appropriately.

Numbered heads together is particularly appropriate for reviewing grammatical structures, vocabulary or factual items from a reading or audio-visual text. For example, students may be given an infinitive and asked to form the past tense, or a word and expected to provide an appropriate definition (High 1993).

5 Group investigation

Developed by Sharan and Sharan (1992), Group investigation involves the distribution of tasks across a classroom so that different groups study different aspects of the same topic for an extended period of time. These groups are responsible for doing their own planning, carrying out the study, developing reporting mechanisms and presenting their find-ings to the class. As students plan, research, develop their reports and make their report to the class, they engage in a variety of socio-affective, cognitive and metacognitive strategies and also engage in academic language development that is more commonly reserved for the teacher. They also become increasingly responsible for their own learning, moving from dependence upon the teacher to more interdependence on each other, and from interdependence to independence (autonomy) as a language learner. Studies of this method show that teachers change their verbal behavior as well (Sharan and Hertz-Lazarowitz 1980; Hertz-Lazarowitz and Shachar 1990).

Other cooperative language learning activities

There are numerous other ways of incorporating cooperative activities which have been specifically developed to support language learning. These include:

1 Collaborative and cooperative writing and peer response

Process-based writing approaches (e.g. writers' workshop) involve peer interaction and conferencing, and there are numerous other ways of infusing cooperative learning into the writing classroom from initial pre-writing stages through the final product and publication (DeBolt 1994). Learners can brainstorm in small groups for appropriate topics, discuss possible vocabulary or directions for a first draft, or provide more detailed feedback (praise for effective passages; questions to elicit greater specificity or clarity; or suggestions for other directions the writer might take). They can also work in pairs or groups to edit or proofread each other's drafts.

Peer conferencing and written peer response help students develop both more finely-tuned negotiation skills and more socially appropriate ways of offering constructive criticism. In addition, students can work together to produce a group poem, story or even report. In several classes, I have had students focus their attention on only one sensory response to a special place, object or living thing, writing as much as possible about that and then sharing it with their group. Together, they produce a poem which captures their visual, aural, tactile and other responses. I have also used the language experience approach to have learners recount a group experience or write a thank-you letter to a guest speaker. And the Jigsaw approach, discussed above, can be a means of integrating different aspects or portions of a group report.

2 Paired classes

It is possible to structure cooperative activities across classes or groups, with students in each class equally responsible for a final product which represents the collective wisdom and efforts of all. Examples include the joint publication of a newsletter or report; joint collection and publication of proverbs, stories or ethnographic community profiles; on-line joint research and reporting through the internet or e-mail, and the like.

3 Cooperative cloze completion

Language teachers use both oral and written cloze activities in a number of ways: for example, asking students to complete a written cloze as a measure of recall or comprehension after reading a passage or to fill in the missing words of a song, dramatic piece or other text that is dictated. These activities can be done cooperatively in pairs or small groups. Roundtable is especially appropriate for the task, with each student having a turn trying to fill in one of the blanks with exact words or an acceptable equivalent.

A rationale for using cooperative learning in second and foreign language classrooms

Cooperative learning is gaining broad acceptance in a multitude of language learning classrooms, principally because of its contributions to improving the overall climate of the classroom and its potential for providing supportive and expanded opportunities for learners to use the language. Cooperative learning, like other group work, creates a more positive affective climate in the classroom, while it also individualizes instruction and raises student motivation (Long and Porter 1985). Some of the benefits of cooperative language learning are examined below.

1 Reducing anxiety

Fear of failing or appearing foolish is a constant threat to interaction in the language classroom, especially when teachers ask questions which only a few students can answer. However, this debilitating anxiety or fear is reduced when the possibility of providing a correct or acceptable answer is increased and when learners have had an opportunity to try out their contributions with each other before being asked to offer them to the entire class. Time to think, opportunities to rehearse and receive feedback, and the greater likelihood of success reduce anxiety and can result in increased participation and language learning.

According to Kagan (1994), if people are anxious, but allowed to affiliate, their anxiety level is reduced. Oxford and Ehrman (1993) include cooperative learning as a classroom procedure which can lower anxiety in the language classroom.

2 Promoting interaction

Cooperative learning places students in roles that are usually filled by teachers in traditional, teacher-centered classrooms (Holt 1994). In doing so, it also supports students who are not usually willing to take risks or suffer the frustration of not having adequate language to express their ideas or emotions. In cooperative classrooms, students learn to rely on each other and also have the security of knowing that they will have several opportunities to rehearse a contribution before they are asked to share it with the larger class.

3 Providing comprehensible input and output

Group interaction assists learners in negotiating for more comprehensible input (Krashen 1982) and in modifying their output to make it more comprehensible to others (Swain 1985; Swain and Lapkin 1989). In any cooperative activity, learners engage in tasks which require some tangible output: an oral report, a written summary or a completed form. Learners work together to develop that product, engaging in negotiation to accomplish the task (Long and Porter 1985; Pica and Doughty 1985). In effective cooperative groups, learners provide input modification for each other, asking for clarification, providing needed vocabulary or structures, explaining a key word or concept, reviewing directions or other procedures, and otherwise assisting learners in much the same way as an experienced and knowledgeable teacher tries to do with the whole class. In so doing, the groups also provide support for the risk-taking and ambiguity attendant in language learning.

4 Increasing self-confidence and self-esteem

By encouraging group interdependence, cooperative activities build greater learner confidence and self-esteem than is likely in a competitive environment, where self-validation is dependent upon a continuing need to demonstrate success (Slavin 1990). Edwards points out that 'competitiveness is really a deficit-motivated trait', and 'self-esteem is at stake' with each performance (1997:321).

With Cooperative Integrated Reading and Composition (CIRC) structures, which integrate oral language development with reading and writing in bilingual instruction, Calderon, Hertz-Lazarowitz and Tinajero (1991) found that bilingual students developed greater self-confidence in public speaking and in participating in classroom discussions, both situations where anxiety is likely to be the greatest and self-confidence most threatened for most language learners. An increase in self-confidence and self-esteem will lead to increased learner effort in language learning and a greater willingness to take risks or to continue attempting to make one's views understood.

5 Increasing motivation

Learner motivation in the language classroom can lead to more extensive use of the language and the development of greater language proficiency (see Gardner 1988; Oxford and Ehrman 1993 for further discussion). Peer support can be a powerful motivator for shy, insecure or even uninterested students. In cooperative groups, individuals know that they can get feedback and assistance in making their contributions as clear, relevant and appropriate as possible. This, in turn, can motivate them to continue to try, especially when peers encourage and support their contributions. Porter (1983) found that ESL students in the university provided much more support for each other than did native-speaker conversational partners, perhaps because of a shared sense of frustration in trying to communicate complex thoughts in less-developed linguistic systems. Long and Porter (1985) also found that group work increased student motivation. Cooperative learning involves task or reward structures which better ensure that all members of the group will participate and do so at their own level of proficiency. Resource, goal and reward interdependence contribute to motivation, and enjoyable activities encourage participation, as well.

Although there is widespread belief that competition is a better motivator than cooperation, a meta-analysis of 122 studies, completed by Johnson and his colleagues in 1981, revealed that cooperation promoted higher achievement than competition. Only 8 of the 122 studies favored competition; 65 favored cooperation; and in the other 36, no differences were found. Edwards (1997) concludes that 'competition is not much of a motivator' though that myth is 'deeply embedded' in many educational systems.

Additional benefits of cooperative language learning

It is not surprising that the characteristics of cooperative learning, which foster positive affective environments for language learning, can also lead to enhanced language learning. While not all attempts at incorporating cooperative language learning are effective, there is evidence that when done well, there are a number of important benefits.

1 Increased opportunities for learners to listen to and produce language

Numerous studies of cooperative or small group learning in second language classrooms have affirmed what would seem to be obvious to those who have observed, taught, or participated in these classes: that learners both listen to and produce a great deal more language than is possible in a classroom where individual students await the infrequent turn with the teacher (Slavin 1983a; Harel 1992; Chamot and O'Malley 1987; Long and Porter 1985). Teachers are estimated to talk between 60–75% of the time in a traditional class, with students usually talking one at a time during the rest (Flanders 1970; Goodlad 1984). In a cooperative structure, that distribution is almost reversed, with all students talking part of the time and the teacher's contributions reduced accordingly (Kagan 1994). Even when teacher talk remains high, the amount of learner talk is increased because more than one student talks at a time.

The safety of the small group encourages participation, and clearly-defined roles help ensure that the participation is equitably distributed so that more advanced, extroverted, self-confident, or articulate learners are less likely to dominate. Formerly shy language learners acquire the confidence to participate in small groups, where they can share ideas, receive feedback and rehearse potential contributions to the larger group. Students with more limited language proficiency also have been reported to speak more in cooperative contexts (Sharan and Shachar 1988).

This additional time, in turn, can result in increased language proficiency. Bejarano (1987) and Sharan, Bejarano, Kuissel and Peleg (1984) found that Israeli EFL junior high school students who partici-pated in cooperative structures scored higher on both an overall English proficiency test and a test of listening comprehension than did students in classes using large group instruction. Neves (1983) also found that task-related talk in Spanish and English contributed to development of English language proficiency. Cohen (1987) and Cohen and Intili (1981), found similar gains in oral proficiency in both Spanish and English, as well as language arts and reading, in their studies of *Finding Out/Descubrimiento* (De Avila, Duncan and Navarrete 1987), a Spanish-English bilingual elementary science program which uses co-operative tasks as the basis of instruction.

These results are consistent with the studies of the effect of small group work on academic achievement in general; it has been found that 'students in small groups within classrooms achieved significantly more than students not learning in small groups' (Lou, Abrami, Spence, Poulsen, Chambers and d'Apollonia 1996:439). Cohen (1994b) found that frequency of participation (talking and working together) is positively correlated with academic achievement in science and mathe-matics classrooms and that learners made substantial gains in English language proficiency because of the social, interactive nature of the cooperative classroom.

In mainstream classes in second language contexts, where those learning the language of instruction are mixed with students for whom that medium is the primary language, cooperative groups also provide the opportunity for more interaction with target-language speakers who can serve as models and provide linguistic (and other) feedback as language learners attempt to express their ideas in the new language.

2 An increased range of speech acts or language functions

Besides an increase in the quantity of student talk, the quality of student contributions also changes in group activities (Long and Porter 1985). In the shift from whole-class to cooperative Group Investigation, Sharan and Hertz-Lazarowitz (1980) found that students shifted from a focus on directives (asking questions, giving instructions, enforcing discipline) to more facilitative and encouraging discourse (praising, giving feedback, providing assistance and encouraging student initiative and communication).

The negotiation of meaning involves a number of speech acts which are not as evident in traditional question-response interactions. Moreover, since learners are filling roles formerly reserved for the teacher or the extroverted, self-confident learner, they also engage in a much wider range of language functions. For example, learners find themselves directing, clarifying, reminding, making suggestions, encouraging or praising, functions which dovetail nicely with a communicative syllabus but might not otherwise arise in the regular language classroom (Jacobs 1996; Coelho 1992; Gaies 1983; Long 1981).

3 Opportunities for learners to develop cross-cultural understanding, respect and friendships as well as positive social skills for respecting alternative opinions and achieving consensus

A number of reviews of cooperative learning in multicultural settings have shown significant positive effects on interracial relations (Sharan 1980, 1990; Sharan and Shachar 1988; Slavin 1990) and on prosocial behavior and conflict resolution. A particularly interesting example of this occurred when two teachers in Public School 124 in Chinatown in New York City decided to combine gifted, mainstream, special needs and ESL students in their third grade classes. While this 'untracking' experiment was initially begun to overcome 'bad chemistry' among the gifted students, the ESL students benefited as well. As Savitch and Serling (1995) describe it, 'From the start, children mingled socially and academically' in their classroom 'community'.

Even learners with a common language and culture have differences in experiences, opinions and world views. In cooperative groups, students are afforded the opportunity to develop skills in listening to divergent views, asking for greater support for ideas they find confusing or disagreeable, and providing for differences in opinion. These skills should help them to work more productively and harmoniously in groups outside of school as well (Bennett, Rolheiser-Bennet and Stevahn 1991).

Kagan (1986) believes that cooperative learning can help students learn to function in a democratic society. The growing racial, ethnic, linguistic and other diversity and the continuing racial, inter-ethnic and linguistic intolerance which characterizes so many parts of the world underscore the importance of providing educational structures which promote prosocial behavior (McGroarty 1989; Crandall and Tucker 1990).

It is also interesting to note that low-achieving students are liked more in cooperative than in competitive classrooms, even though they may provide limited contributions to the group (Johnson, Johnson and Scott 1978), perhaps because individuals in cooperative groups are perceived more multidimensionally, rather than valued only in terms of their academic abilities or achievements. Moreover, individual effort is valued and the opportunity of helping others provides satisfaction and its own type of reward (Johnson and Johnson 1989).

4 Greater learner-centeredness and learner direction in the classroom

Joyce and Weir (1986) place cooperative learning in the 'social family' in their classifications of models of teaching. 'Models in the *social family* capitalize on the energy and coordination of students working together in groups', with the primary aim of developing social interaction and problem-solving skills, along with the learning of academic content (Bennett, Rolheiser-Bennett and Stevahn 1991:8).

Comenius is reported to have said, 'He who teaches others, teaches himself' (Rodgers 1988:3). When working together on common tasks, peers provide the kind of support that is usually provided by the teacher. Both 'tutor' and 'tutee' benefit, and with students in small groups, the teacher is free to circulate, listening and assessing individual student learning, facilitating student interaction and offering individual help, and taking note of general problems to address to the large group. It is also possible, in these groups, to adapt the tasks, both in terms of the content and the level and type of reporting required for individual students.

This does not mean that the teacher abrogates all responsibility for instruction. To the contrary, as in any constructivist classroom, the teacher must provide the occasion for learning, the materials students will need to engage in the task, and guidance and support throughout the process. As Hertz-Lazarowitz and Shachar put it, 'instead of taking charge of teaching', teachers are now 'taking charge of learning' (1990:13). Nor is all class time devoted to cooperative activities. Lectures, large group discussions and teacher-student interaction are still likely to be a large part of instruction.

5 Increased opportunities for learners to develop academic language through content-rich tasks

Cooperative activities can be developed around any curricular content and involve language across the curriculum, leading to the development of both social and academic language, whether the locus is the content classroom or the language classroom (Crandall 1987; Crandall and Tucker 1990). Kessler (1992) reports on its value in developing academic language in the second language classroom; Freeman (1992), in the high school foreign language classroom; and Jacobs, Rottenberg, Patrick and Wheeler (1996) in the elementary social studies classroom.

6 Increased opportunities for learners to develop higher order and critical thinking skills

Language teachers using cooperative activities comment frequently about the amount of purposeful communication and development of metacognitive strategies which are encouraged through cooperative interaction. In working together to accomplish a task, group members need to plan, organize themselves for the activity, make decisions, defend positions and resolve differences of opinion, and solve problems, undertaking a number of higher order thinking skills and cognitive and metacognitive strategies which may be less available in whole group activities (Lotan and Becton 1990). To the benefit of language acquisition, these actions are undertaken through talk.

In cooperative activities, time to reflect, to think and to associate old and new ideas is built into the activity, as is time to discuss these with others in the group.

Because cooperative groups are heterogeneous, learners are able to function in a role more typically restricted to the teacher, providing 'scaffolding' to assist others in the group. Instead of one expert helping learners through the 'zone of proximal development' (Vygotsky 1978), there are several experts.

7 Increased support for language learners to move from interdependence to independence

Cooperative learning promotes self-determination among students, helping them to become more autonomous and self-controlled and less dependent upon outside authority (Boud 1981). Students 'learn greater autonomy gradually' (Edwards 1997:330), relying first on each other for direction and assistance, and over time, through leadership experiences in their groups, acquiring greater independence in their own learning (see Aoki this volume), actively choosing to use the resources of the teacher and other group members, rather than merely relying on them to get things done.

In carrying out various cooperative activities and tasks, learners engage in an increasing variety of procedures formerly limited to the teacher (for example, planning the task; monitoring its progress; identifying and obtaining needed resources). They also become much more responsible for the group's and their own learning. There is an axiom in cooperative learning, 'Ask three, then me', which is used by teachers as a way of weaning learners from their dependence upon the teacher to interdependence. The step to independence is one which gradually unfolds, as learners become increasingly autonomous.

Some problems in implementing cooperative language learning

Most teachers who have tried cooperative learning in their language classes have encountered resistance. Some of the problems in implementing cooperative language learning are reviewed below. (See Jacobs 1996; Jacobs and Hall 1994 for a fuller discussion.)

1 Cultural expectations of appropriate roles of teachers and learners

Many educational systems are based on the central role of the teacher in planning, directing and evaluating learning. Small group instruction, when it occurs, is usually relegated to practice of something that has been previously taught. To students who have grown up with traditional, teacher-centered, teacher-directed classes, the shift to learner-centered and learner-directed cooperative groups can be misunderstood as an abrogation of responsibility on the part of the teacher and an opportunity to engage in meaningless play. From the tightly controlled question-response-rejoinder structure of the teacher-fronted classroom, group interaction can appear to be (and even degenerate into) chaos, unless learners have had the opportunity of being socialized into the new structures and had time to reflect upon the process. Even with preparation, learners may need time to become comfortable with their new responsibilities and roles. Cooperative learning also represents a challenge to what are often very deeply held beliefs about the appropriateness of individual responsibility and competition in education.

2 Individual learning styles or preferences

In addition to cultural expectations about appropriate roles for learners and teachers, individual learners also have learning styles or preferences which affect the amount of time they wish to spend, for example, in individual experimentation or reflection, or group discussion and processing. Those preferences can be honored in the roles assigned in groups. However, over time, even those who prefer to try things out on their own before demonstrating them to another may learn to expand their learning repertoire.

3 Personality differences

While one goal of cooperative learning is to help students learn to get along with and work with all individuals in the class, there are sometimes personality differences which are so great that a member of the group may need to be re-assigned. If that student is unable to work with any other group, he or she may need to be given the opportunity to work alone during the group sessions. Over time, social isolation may provide sufficient motivation for renewed efforts at functioning within a group. Over time, as well, students who previously did not get along may come to develop respect or admiration for each other or even become friends through the cooperative learning process.

4 Over-reliance on the first language

In a heterogeneous class of learners from a number of linguistic backgrounds, it may be possible to form groups where students do not share a common language and thus need to interact and negotiate in the target language. When learners share a common language, however, as in many foreign language situations, any small group interaction can quickly shift to first language interaction. It may be unrealistic to expect learners to restrict themselves to the target language when they can express themselves more fully in a language that all can understand, but it is also important to find ways to encourage use of the target language.

Students can be encouraged to use the target language as much as possible both orally and in writing in their groups while acknowledging the reasonableness of using the first language occasionally for greater depth of expression. Tasks can also be structured to require use of the target language in reporting to the large group, either orally or in writing.

Overconcern with the use of the first language may be unwarranted.

In her study of an elementary Spanish-English bilingual classroom, Cohen (1994b) found that use of either the first or the second language in task-related talk in cooperative activities was positively correlated with second language learning. This would support the linguistic interdependence hypothesis of Cummins (1991), in which use of the first language and the accumulated conceptual knowledge stored through that language can lead to transfer of that knowledge to the developing second language.

Rather than viewing the use of the first language as a problem, McGroarty (1989:127) suggests that cooperative activities offer the possibility of developing or using the first language 'in ways that support cognitive development and increased second language skills'.

5 Exposure to imperfect language models and incorrect feedback

An additional concern voiced by both learners and teachers is with the imperfect nature of learner contributions in group discussions. They fear that learners provide poor models for each other and that inadequate knowledge of the language could result in either inappropriate or insufficient feedback. Such fears appear to be overblown or even unwarranted. Learners make no more errors in speaking with each other than they do with native speakers (Porter 1983) or with the teacher (Deen 1987 cited in McGroarty 1989). Possibilities of uncorrected or miscorrected student contributions are less important in the overall development of second language competence than opportunities for negotiation of meaning and interaction. Teachers need to help learners to understand that errors are natural when learners are focused on making themselves understood, and that there are appropriate and inappropriate times for and means of correcting each other.

Some strategies for facilitating cooperative learning for language learning

If cooperative language learning is to be successful, both teachers and learners need to be adequately prepared, and interesting, relevant topics and materials must be available. In addition, a number of strategies can be employed to facilitate cooperative language learning.

1 Preparing learners for cooperative tasks

Perhaps the greatest mistake teachers make in initiating cooperative learning is failing to prepare the learners for the new approach, especially in an educational context with teacher-fronted classrooms and a knowledge dissemination model of teaching. Children, especially, need to have explicit preparation and opportunities to practice and receive feedback on such skills as turn-taking, active listening, and positive feedback, before they can comfortably take on the responsibility of functioning in groups, and nearly all students, regardless of age, need help in learning how to provide constructive feedback on both oral and written contributions made by their peers.

2 Assigning learners to specific and meaningful tasks

The quality of the task is central to the success of cooperative activities. Topics must be genuinely interesting, in need of further research or discussion, and offer a number of different avenues for investigation or solution. Constructivist learning activities, such as developing a model country with its own constitution, investigating causes of hunger and organizing a food drive, interviewing family members to collect proverbs or folktales, developing a manual for new workers to use on the job, or studying water or soil samples for environmental health, are all likely to be motivating and result in meaningful interaction. Cooperative activities need to allow learners to use more of Gardner's (1993) 'multiple intelligences' – spatial, musical, kinesthetic, interpersonal and intrapersonal, as well as the more common linguistic and logical-mathematical – in their language learning, if they are to appeal to, support and provide opportunities to learn different learning styles and strategies.

3 Debriefing learners on their experiences with cooperative learning

To help students understand the social, cognitive and linguistic skills being developed through cooperative learning, it is important to plan some time for reflection and debriefing, not only on what was learned about language or content, but also on what was learned about social interaction and how it was learned, problems that arose, and ways that either the problems were addressed or could be addressed in the future. Students accustomed to competitive classrooms or more individualistic approaches to learning, especially, may need time to verbalize their frustrations with cooperative activities, especially those related to a fear that somehow they are not 'learning' or that others are unjustly relying on them and somehow 'cheating'.

Few researchers or teachers advocate full-time use of cooperative learning in any classroom; rather, they suggest regular and significant use of these activities. The learning of simple facts or the acquisition of simple skills may best be done individually, especially when a student's achievement is independent of other students (Johnson and Johnson 1994). But the cooperative activity may be the appropriate way to practice the skill, to review the facts that have been learned, or to apply what has been learned to a new context. Even when cooperative activities fill only a portion of the class time, it may still be appropriate to let students unhappy with group work do comparable classwork individually or to build in incentives such as competition between groups.

4 Involving learners in evaluating individual and group contributions

Involving learners in assessment and evaluation can lead to a sense of shared responsibility for the learning in the classroom, but it is a new experience for many students and may not be fully appreciated at first. Sometimes it helps if students are asked to evaluate themselves and the contributions to the group. They may also be asked to evaluate all the members of their group and the work of the group as a whole. It may be more effective to ask students to keep a portfolio of work from the academic term (see Kohonen, this volume) and to evaluate themselves on the portfolio. That work will have been produced through interaction in a number of different contexts (cooperative groups, individual work, etc.), providing a profile of each student's growth during that term.

Conclusion

Cooperative learning offers many positive, affective features which encourage language learning, while also supporting development of prosocial, academic and higher order thinking skills. While it may be difficult for learners with a history of more competitive and individualistic language learning activities, it is worth the effort to introduce cooperative learning, and gradually, over time, to support learners as they work interdependently in groups and move to greater independence as language learners.

Suggestions for further reading

Bennett, B., C. Rolheiser-Bennett and L. Stevahn. 1991. *Cooperative Learning: Where Heart Meets Mind*. Toronto: Educational Connections.

Coelho, E., L. Winer and J. W. Olsen. 1989. *All Sides of the Issue: Activities for Cooperative Groups*. Englewood Cliffs, NJ: Prentice Hall Regents.

DeBolt, V. 1994. *Write! Cooperative Learning & the Writing Process*. San Juan Capistrano, CA: Kagan Cooperative Learning.

Johnson, D. W., R. T. Johnson and E. J. Holubec. 1994. *The New Circles of Learning: Cooperation in the Classroom and School*. Alexandria, VA: Association for Supervision and Curriculum Development.

Putman, J. A. 1997. *Cooperative Learning in Diverse Classrooms*. Upper Saddle River, NJ: Merrill/Prentice Hall.

15 Creating a learning culture to which students want to belong: the application of Neuro-Linguistic Programming to language teaching

Herbert Puchta

Introduction

Neuro-Linguistic Programming (NLP) was founded by John Grinder and Richard Bandler in 1976. By observing behavioural patterns and analysing the thinking skills of people excelling in various fields, Bandler and Grinder created a model of how the mind (Neuro) interacts with language (Linguistic) and the body. They developed explicit skills and techniques – patterns of excellence – that people can learn (Programming) and thus enhance their own performance. NLP soon became popular in various fields: psychotherapy, business, law, counselling and education. In the late eighties, NLP started to become a buzzword in EFL circles, although there seemed to be quite a bit of confusion about what it could contribute to the field of language teaching. Whereas some people thought it was a new language teaching method, others tried to sell it as the answer to all problems. With amusement I remember reading a leaflet promoting a book on NLP and teaching at a language teaching conference – 'Read this book and take a holiday in the classroom' the flyer promised. It seems that NLP was misunderstood and (partly promoted) as a set of techniques that would make it possible for teachers to manipulate their students and thus achieve magic results. Not surprisingly, some language teaching professionals reacted sceptically and were wary of the application of ideas derived from NLP.

Over the last few years reflective practitioners have become increasingly aware that the success of their teaching to a large degree depends on factors that lie beyond the mere methods and materials they are using. It has been acknowledged that if we want to be more successful with our teaching we need to turn our attention to what goes on in the students' minds and hearts when they are or are not learning. Some of the questions focal to such thinking have been: How can I address different learning styles in my classroom? How can I assist my students in developing efficient learning strategies and meta-cognitive awareness? What can I do to help my students access optimal affective learning states? How can I help my students in overcoming learning blocks?

Principles of NLP

NLP is based on a number of principles or presuppositions that I believe can be very helpful in trying to find answers to questions like those above. From a language teaching perspective, the following NLP presuppositions could be seen as the most essential:

1 The map is not the territory

Humans interact with the world around them on the basis of their own inner map, which they make of the world. Our senses (or representational systems), together with our unique experiences, beliefs, culture, language, interests and values act as filters that we use in the creation of our maps. It is because of these individual maps that people have different emotional configurations and therefore react so differently in situations that are the same. If a teacher tells a class that they are to expect a test, for example, some learners might show signs of panic and consequently block themselves from being able to utilise fully their resources, whereas others might see the test as a challenge and even look forward to it as an opportunity to prove how much they know.

2 People already have all the resources that they need

Our mental images, inner voices, body sensations and feelings can be used as modules to construct the thoughts and skills that we need in order to be successful. Not everybody will necessarily have or find the most appropriate conglomerate of these building blocks, in the same way as not every map is as useful as any other. It is, however, possible to use the maps and strategies of people who excel and improve one's own performance through the implementation of these maps and skills. It is the teacher's task to enable the students to develop appropriate skills and strategies more easily.

3 (Learning) experiences have a structure

Our students' thoughts, actions and feelings have a pattern to them. We can help them to find out and utilise more fully their successful patterns and change their less successful ones. Or as an NLP saying goes, 'If you always do what you have always done, you will always get what you have always got'.

4 Underlying all behaviour is a positive intention

Even if a student's behaviour is perceived as disruptive by the teacher and the other students in class, there was initially some positive intention at the root of this behaviour. If, for example, teachers can manage to help their (adolescent) students to become aware of the positive intention behind their behaviour (for example trying to get the teacher's or some classmates' attention), the students can learn other – less hurtful – ways of achieving their purpose.

An example of the application of NLP to language learning

Some time ago I was asked to do work as a consultant for a senior business executive of a large company. He was learning Spanish as a foreign language. His mother tongue was English, and his aim was to develop enough competence in Spanish to be able to communicate with business partners from Spanish-speaking markets both professionally and also socially. After a rather intensive course of about a year or so, his listening as well as speaking skills had reached intermediate level. Both his teacher and he himself were quite pleased with the results. Soon, however, one striking problem arose. Whenever he was supposed to make a phone call in Spanish, and especially, when he was rung up by someone speaking Spanish, he experienced total failure. 'I just don't know what to do,' he commented. 'As soon as I hear the other person's voice, my mind seems to go blank and I have a total blackout. Then I feel like an idiot.'

The man's 'failure' could certainly not be explained with any of the standard arguments. He showed no lack of motivation; quite the contrary, he was highly motivated. He was intelligent and he received up-to-date language teaching. In fact, his teacher tried to do everything she could think of to help, from intensive practising of 'repair strategies' (e.g. asking the other person to repeat what had been said, to speak more slowly, etc.) in the foreign language to simulated phone calls in the classroom. It was obvious that, whenever he was in that situation, he somehow got into an affective state that made it impossible for him to accesss his true potential.

I set up a simulation that came close to the 'real' situation the business executive would normally fail in. We arranged for his teacher to phone him from the next door office and talk Spanish to him, while I was sitting with him in his office in order to be able to observe what was going on. It turned out that he had a very powerful habit of blocking himself from his own resources. The process that he went through was more or less like this: As soon as he heard someone speaking Spanish to him over the phone, he would get a very strong feeling of what he called 'incompetence'. Almost at the same time as this feeling occurred, he would see a picture in his mind's eye which he described as 'very negative'. He found that the picture was a memory of a situation at school. In that situation, he as a twelve- or thirteen-year-old had been ridiculed by a teacher in front of his classmates. Finally, in addition to his feeling incompetent and the memory of that situation at school, he would go into his inner monologue saying to himself something like 'I'll never be able to do that'.

It is commonly known that making a phone call in the foreign language is much more demanding than talking to a person face-to-face, partly because of a lack of visual clues that could assist us in the process of interpreting meaning. Instead of using his undoubtedly rich cognitive resources in a way that would have supported him with the task, the business executive experienced stress that came from a combination of kinaesthetic (his emotions), visual (his memory of a past negative experience) and auditory (his inner monologue) processes. (For a discussion of the effects of anxiety and stress on foreign language performance see Stevick 1996; Oxford this volume; and Young in press.) This complex activation of his neurology led to an emotional block and a limiting belief which he actually verbalised when he said to me 'I'll never be able to do that'. In his research into the supportive and limiting power of beliefs and belief systems, Dilts (1990:22) found that the negative beliefs usually centre around perceived hopelessness ('It's not possible.'), helplessness ('I can't do it.') or worthlessness ('I don't deserve it.').

Metaphorically speaking, the businessman was like a skier who before catapulting himself down the slope feels that he is definitely going to fall. During the first few seconds of the race this skier sees pictures of a time when he went skiing as an adolescent and broke his leg, and these definitely not very supportive memories are further worsened by an inner voice that tells him that he is a failure. It is commonly known that skiers (and other sports professionals) have mental exercises that help them get into a resourceful inner state. (See Arnold, this volume.) Many NLP exercises are similar to such mental techniques.

I suggested the following exercises: First I asked him to relive mentally the key situation from his adolescence from 'first position'[1] and re-experience the situation of being ridiculed as if it was really happening to him now. Then I asked him to dissociate from that experience and imagine that he was watching a movie of himself in that situation from behind a glass screen. In taking a different perception of the problem he was able to dissociate himself from the negative emotions and watch himself in that situation like an outside observer with a neutral attitude. What followed was a visualisation exercise in which I asked him to watch a movie of that situation as a neutral observer up to the point where he was ridiculed. I asked him to hold a still picture of that situation in his mind's eye and finally to get back into the situation as himself again and relive the whole experience backwards, as if it were a movie run from back to front. I asked him to do this very quickly, and to repeat this several times. He ended up laughing about the situation and he commented that he just could not re-access that feeling of being ridiculed any more.

At this point I would like to invite the reader to do a little experiment that can show clearly how our thoughts influence our feelings. I would like you to think of a pleasant experience you have had. As you are thinking of that experience, notice how you are doing this. Are there any pictures in your mind's eye? Are they bright and clear? Are they still pictures or a movie? Are you aware of any sounds that you can hear as you are thinking of that experience? And finally, I would like you to notice your feelings. Can you locate them anywhere in your body? How would you describe them? Now bring that experience closer to yourself. Play around with intensifying the colours in your mind's eye. If there is any sound, make it louder. How does all this change your feelings? Now try to move the experience further away from you. Again, watch how your feelings change . . .

Andreas and Faulkner (1996:32) report that most people who go through this simple activity comment that the intensity of their feelings changes when they change the 'submodalities' of their inner pictures and sounds. What is important to note is that when, for example, a person's feelings intensify as they bring the picture closer, this is a result of a change that the person makes to their map and not a change in the reality of the initial experience. In the case of my client learning Spanish, at the root of his limiting beliefs were his inner representations of a situation he experienced a long time ago. He was able to change his emotions by changing his inner representations of that situation, and

---

[1] NLP names various positions from which a person can perceive a situation or an experience: through his own eyes (from first position), from somebody else's perspective (second position) or from a neutral position of an outside observer (third or meta position).

not the situation itself (which would have been impossible). Once this process was completed, the feeling of incompetence was not there any more. Instead, he commented that he felt 'relieved and confident'.

This was the appropriate moment for him to install a new thought pattern that would create a more supportive affective state that would be better able to assist him when making a phone call in the foreign language. In order to get some examples of what people successfully do when faced with such a task, I used a technique called modelling. The NLP modelling process aims at analysing abilities or skills of people who excel in a certain field and at making these patterns of excellence available to others. Modelling typically consists of the observation and mapping of behavioural and linguistic patterns. I observed a number of people who succeed in this specific context; the outcome of this modelling of successful strategies in making a phone call in a foreign language can be summarised in the following maxims:

1 Have a positive feeling about your own ability to make a phone call in the foreign language. To activate the feeling it could be helpful to think first of a challenging situation that you successfully mastered.
2 As soon as you hear the other person's voice, ask yourself what it is that the other person might want to communicate to you. You might find it useful to remember visually what the other person looks like or (if you have never met the person before) try to make a picture in your mind's eye of what the other person might look like.
3 Be aware that it is not necessary to understand each and every word of the communication. Relax and focus on the words that carry most of the information. They are usually the ones that the other person would stress.
4 Summarise what you have understood in order to check that you have successfully received the message.
5 When you do not understand, make this clear to the other person. Communicate what specifically it is that you do not understand.

Logical levels of thinking and learning

I have seen remarkable effects on some students' learning process and performance through the application of NLP techniques. Some of these changes have worked incredibly fast. Others have taken a lot of time, patience and support. I have also seen NLP techniques applied with little or no success. Following on the work of anthropologist Gregory Bateson, Robert Dilts (1990:60) has developed a model of the complexity of human thinking, communication and change. (See Figure 1.)

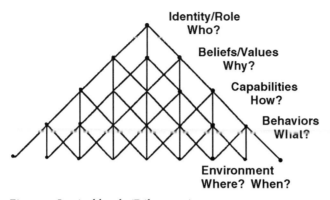

Figure 1 *Logical levels (Dilts 1996)*

The model shows that it takes a lot more than just techniques to facilitate our students' growth. Dilts' research projects in such diverse fields as health (Dilts, Holborn and Smith 1990), leadership (Dilts 1996) and creativity and learning (Dilts 1991) stress the importance of a systemic alignment of all the different logical levels that the human brain (and any biological or social system) is organised into: environment, behaviour, capabilities, belief systems and identity.[2]

The basic level is our *environment*. In a language class, examples of environmental factors that influence the outcome of the learning process are the condition of the furniture in the class, the seating arrangement, the quality of the cassette recorder, the light conditions, the set-up of the timetable and so forth. The teacher and the students (inter)act in that environment through their *behaviour*. Obviously, in the same way as some environmental factors are more supportive to the students' learning than others, so are certain behavioural routines. The students' behaviour depends on their (mental) *capabilities*. A student who has proper mental maps and efficient learning strategies will learn better and faster than a student who lacks them. The students' capabilities in turn are organised by their *belief systems* and these are influenced by their *identity* (their sense of who they are).

Dilts stresses that the model is a hierarchical system. The higher the logical level that we operate on, the more influential it becomes on the outcome of a thinking process or an act of communication and, likewise, the stronger the affective reactions will be. Change on a lower level might influence a higher one, but change on a higher level will always have some effect also on the levels below. Somebody might study

---

[2] The logical levels model (Dilts 1996) is used with permission of Meta Publications, Capitolia, CA.

under very poor environmental conditions and might not have very effective behavioural and mental strategies. The person might still be successful in achieving the planned outcome as long as they have strong and supportive beliefs that they can be successful and/or an identity that is in line with the outcome they want to achieve. This person will probably also gradually develop proper behavioural procedures and find the proper mental strategies that help to achieve the aim.

The argument can also be turned on its head: students in the most comfortable classroom with the most modern equipment, will nevertheless remain unsuccessful if their level of motivation is low or they identify themselves as poor foreign language learners. (Dilts [1990:60] stresses that from a psychological perspective, belief, motivation and permission are all three housed on the same logical level.) This will be the case in spite of attempts by the teacher to teach the students efficient behavioural routines and learning strategies.

Researchers such as Good and Brophy (1986) have shown how influential these two levels of belief and identity are, both from an individual point of view, but also and maybe even more powerfully, from a systemic perspective of the social and psychological interaction between the teacher and the individual student and between students and students. There is without doubt a direct link between these issues and the teacher's leadership qualities and skills. In one study into the patterns of success of visionary leaders, Dilts (1996:3) quotes one of the outstanding business leaders that he had modelled as saying 'Leadership means creating a world to which people want to belong'. The same, I believe, is true of teaching. If we can manage to align the different logical levels in our classrooms, we will be able to establish a learning culture to which our students will want to belong because it offers them a supportive learning environment, helps them establish effective behavioural patterns and mental strategies, fosters facilitating beliefs about themselves and their capability to learn and helps them identify with the foreign language they are learning. Consequently, in the students' perception, the 'foreign-ness' about the language they are learning will be reduced. It is this special classroom culture that I believe is essential for NLP-derived (and in fact any) techniques to work. If this culture is lacking, any technique will be perceived by the students as a gimmick.

Environment and behaviour – two examples: error correction and the use of mother tongue in monolingual classes.

The two lowest logical levels are the classical domains of behavioural learning. As Williams and Burden (1997:10) point out, a mere stimulus – response method is not the most efficient way to teach a foreign language. On the other hand there is evidence from classroom experience that behavioural support can be quite useful when it comes to the teaching of some language forms. This is especially the case with structures the acquisition of which takes a long time and a lot of patience and support from the teacher. In English one such structure (at least for most of the students I have worked with) seems to be the third person singular -s. Although there is research evidence that it is also acquired late by native-speaker children, it seems that teachers often become impatient when a learner makes a third person singular -s error.

It is generally accepted that the way a teacher handles errors in the students' oral performance is a critical issue. Whereas some voices go as far as to claim that error correction does not improve the students' oral performance at all, I am convinced that it can be helpful if it is done in the right way. Discussions with students also show that many of them do want to know when they have made a mistake. Let us imagine that a student in a class of young learners has just made a third person singular -s error. What can easily happen is that the student interprets the teacher's reaction to this error not as a signal how they should change their language *behaviour*, but as communication on the *identity* level. In this case the student might say to him or herself something like, 'Oh, I have made this mistake again. How stupid of me. I'd better keep quiet now'. The likelihood of such reactions is stronger if the learner has a weak self-concept or if the teacher overreacts verbally or non-verbally to the student's error.

I have frequently used the following technique, which is aimed at avoiding confusion of the level of behaviour with the levels of belief and identity. During a phase in which error correction is appropriate, e.g. a short drill aimed at practising the particular form, when a learner makes a third person singular -s error, I take a piece of coloured paper, write an 's' on it, put it somewhere on the walls of the classroom where all the students can see it, point at it, smile at the student and wait. It usually does not take long for the student to correct his sentence. The next time the same error occurs, I point at the sign on the wall, wait and – yes – smile. (I hope that the meta-message of this communication is perceived by the student as 'It's OK to make mistakes'.) I carry on like this for some time, then I remove the card from the wall. The next time a student makes the same mistake, I take a piece of paper of the same colour, do not write anything on it and put it on the same spot on the wall again. Then I wait – and I smile. After this has been done several times, I take the card off the wall. When the error occurs again, I only need to point at the same spot on the wall (this time there is no card on it) and wait – and smile!

This is an example of an anchor. In NLP, an anchor is an external stimulus that triggers off a certain internal state. For children at school, the school bell (an auditory anchor) signals the beginning of the lesson and the end of playtime. A red traffic light (a visual anchor) means stop. Anchors are often created by repetition. Resource anchors are external stimuli that remind us of very pleasant experiences or inner strengths. I have used various such visual anchors, especially with young learners. In monolingual classes, for example, it is very common for students to fall back into their mother tongue even if they already have enough language to express what they want to say. When I discuss the issue with them, they usually agree that it is much better for the development of their foreign language competence if they use the target language as often as possible. So I suggest making this a rule that everybody in class should agree to. As a little reminder of the rule they have agreed to, I bring to class a Union Jack or Stars and Stripes flag with the words ENGLISH SPOKEN written on it. At the beginning of each class, I ask one student to put the flag on the door handle on the outside of the classroom door. This serves as an anchor. When students fall back into their mother tongue, I usually only need to gesture towards where the student has hung the flag outside the door.

Capabilities – developing the students' learning potentials

The NLP modelling process offers a way to help develop the students' cognitive and meta-cognitive strategies. The following is an excerpt from a transcript of a lesson that I was teaching in a class of eight-year-olds whose mother tongue was German. My objective was to teach them the numbers from ten to twenty. I had written the numbers (in digits) on the board, introduced the pronunciation and got the students to repeat the words after me several times. They soon were able to count from ten to twenty without any difficulty. When I pointed at the numbers individually, however, and when I gave them little mathematics problems to solve, some learners in class had difficulties remembering the English word for the number 13. Other learners had no problem recalling the word. So I tried to 'model' those learners who had no problem with the word. The discussion was carried out in German. I have translated it here (with the exception of the German word for 'thirteen'):

> HP: Is there any number that is particularly difficult?
> SS: Yes, dreizehn.
> HP: Uhuh, dreizehn. Is there anybody in class who has no problems finding the English word for 'dreizehn'? (*A few hands go up*).

HP: You don't find this difficult, do you? What I'd like to ask you, and I think this is really interesting for all of us, when I point at number 'dreizehn', and you remember the English word for it, how do you do that?

S1: No idea. (*laughs*)

HP: You have no idea? Just wait a second. When I point at 'dreizehn' (*points at the number on the board*), what happens at this moment that makes it possible for you to know the proper English word for it? Do you see a picture in your mind's eye? Or do you hear anything? Or is there a feeling that helps you to find the word? Or do you use a combination of them?

S2: I see a picture.

HP: A picture?

S2: Yes. It's strange.

HP: You mean you see a strange picture?

S2: Yes, it's a picture of a boy, and he's trying to climb a tree . . .

HP: Really?

S2: Yes, and he can't climb it. So he gives up, and he says [θ :] and goes away. (*S2 makes a sound that is used as a gambit in German to indicate that somebody or something has failed*). And when I hear this, I immediately remember the word <u>thir</u>teen (*stresses first half of the word.*)

The situation described above was interesting for a number of reasons. The discussion was the first one of its kind in that class. It seemed to open up a field of awareness of how our thoughts are formed through our inner visual, auditory and kinaesthetic representations. The more often I involved the students in such conversations, the more natural it seemed for them to speculate about and describe the mental processes they were going through while they were (or were not) learning.

One obvious advantage of such an approach is that students begin to develop a gradual awareness of *how* they think. If a teacher continues this process over a longer period, students can become the managers of their own learning processes. If something does not work, they are more likely to try something else. If someone else has a strategy that works for him or herself, other students could try it out. It might not work for them in the same way, but experimenting with new patterns might lead to new insights and help them find more suitable strategies.

Beliefs – how they are formed and what we can do to support positive beliefs

As we have seen in the initial example of the business executive, beliefs act as very strong filters of reality. If we believe in something, we act as if it were true, regardless of reality. Our students' negative and positive beliefs can be of enormous influence on the success of their learning. Strong supportive beliefs do not automatically guarantee success, but they help students access learning states in which they can more easily utilise their inner resources and become more aware of having a wider range of choices available to them. Negative beliefs influence our students' expectations. Low expectations lead to a low level of motivation and every failure is seen as confirmation of the initial beliefs. Not only the students' beliefs, but also those of the teacher can have a strong systemic influence, in the form of self-fulfilling prophecies, on the students' success.

Beliefs are formed in various ways. One way is through the culture we live in. They are also formed through repetitive experiences. Children frequently form their beliefs through the modelling of significant others. They observe the teacher, compare the teacher's communication with themselves and their classmates, and interpret this communication. Gradually, their interpretations become the foundations of their belief systems. Hence, self-fulfilling prophecies play an important role, especially in young learners' classrooms. When teaching young learners, we should have a high level of expectation of our students' potential learning success. (Realistically) high expectations generally help build competence, low expectations build incompetence.

Our learners' beliefs are often related to past experiences, but they also form blueprints for future behaviour. If learners have a supportive belief, they will more easily learn to overcome problems and less easily become demotivated. This clearly shows from modelling interviews that I held with children who were excellent at learning a foreign language. When I asked Barbara what her reactions were if she noticed that something was going wrong with her learning, for example, when she was not able to remember something, she said, 'It doesn't matter if I'm not able to do it *now*. It just doesn't matter. I just tell myself one day I'll be able to do it. I'm sure I will'. What a wonderful supportive belief!

Our students are directly influenced by their success in learning. Therefore, if emphasis is put on meaning and not just formal aspects of language, students are more likely to develop positive beliefs. In many language classrooms, however, opportunities for students to gain positive feedback beyond linguistic achievement is limited. A very useful model of how students can develop positive beliefs when their linguistic performance is not very high is Howard Gardner's (1983) theory of Multiple Intelligences. There is evidence from classroom research that EFL exercises specifically aimed at acknowledging the students' other intelligence(s), not just the linguistic, can strongly support the forming of positive beliefs in students of all age groups. (An application of

Gardner's theories on multiple intelligences to language teaching can be found in Puchta and Rinvolucri [in preparation].)

Identity

The students' sense of who they are has a powerful impact on their learning. Not surprisingly, the enhancement of the students' self-concept has been at the core of humanistic language teaching ideas for a number of years. Williams and Burden (1997) have taken a social constructivist view of language learning and stress the importance of the individual making meaning of the tasks they are confronted with. They also underline the significance that the learners' positive feelings about themselves have, and, among other things, advocate fruitful interaction in the classroom as the key to learning.

The concept of communicative language teaching, with its high priority on teaching students to express themselves in the target language, has had enormous influence on syllabus design in many countries. Likewise, most modern language teaching materials subscribe to getting students to say what they want, express their emotions, etc. Yet, teaching practice in many classrooms is probably far from achieving these worthwhile goals. There may be many different reasons why this is the case. If we look at this phenomenon from the point of view of its systemic nature, the following metaphor might be useful (Dilts, personal communication):

If someone wants to lead a healthy life (maybe because they have a health problem) and therefore decides that they will start eating organic food (which means change on the behavioural level), they might not achieve their aim if at the same time they live in a very unhealthy environment. If the environment supports the achievement of their aim, but the person, in spite of healthy eating habits, engages in other unhealthy behaviour (e.g. smokes or drinks a lot), they still might not achieve their goal. Even more strongly, the change in the person's eating habits will not lead to success if the person does not have the proper mental maps to support their aim, or does not believe that they will be able to be healthy, or, last but not least, if they identify themselves as an unhealthy person.

Conclusion

In the same way as any goal can be achieved most efficiently if one can manage to utilise all the logical levels congruently, a supportive class-room culture depends on the alignment of the same levels. As Diana

Whitmore (1986:216) says, 'It is not what we do with our students, it is who we are. No great teaching method will be enough, if we ourselves are not at home. We are all teachers and learners. Educators can educate only if they are willing to put themselves into question as well. The answer does not lie in better classrooms, more equipment, new tools and methods, although these things may help. It lies in you'.

Suggestions for further reading

Andreas, S. and C. Faulkner. 1996. *NLP. The New Technology of Achievement*. London: Nicholas Brealey.

Dilts, R. 1996. *Visionary Leadership Skills. Creating a world to which people want to belong*. Capitola, CA: Meta Publications.

O'Connor, J. and J. Seymour. 1990. *Introducing Neuro-Linguistic Programming. The New Psychology of Personal Excellence*. London: HarperCollins.

Revell, J. and S. Norman. 1997. *In Your Hands. NLP in ELT*. London: Saffire Press.

16 Visualization: language learning with the mind's eye

Jane Arnold

Introduction

If someone tells us not to think about Little Red Ridinghood, no matter what, the first thing that probably comes to mind is a mental picture of a little girl dressed in red. If we are asked to describe our kitchen, in order to answer we almost certainly form a mental image. If, after seeing a film, we comment that the book is better, it may in part be due to the greater scope of the written version, but it is also very likely going to be because as we read the novel, we form mental images that satisfy us much more than the images we see on the screen. In this chapter we will be looking at the role that these pictures in our mind can play in the second language learning process. Since our brains cannot deal with all the countless stimuli coming in from the senses, for learning to occur salience is important; we learn better that which attracts our attention, and emotion automatically makes us pay attention. Mental images are strongly connected to the emotional side of life and thus can help to achieve learner engagement and greater assimilation of the language.

What are mental images?

Stevick defines *image* as 'a composite that we perceive (more or less vividly) as a result of the interaction between what we have in storage and what is going on at the moment' (1986:16). The process of forming mental images is often unconscious, although it can be guided and partially domesticated. As I shall be using the term here, visualization refers to mental images called up for some purpose. It is seeing with what is sometimes called the 'mind's eye', creating pictures in the mind, rather ghost-like images which we know exist but we cannot say exactly how or where. It should be noted, however, that images, while very often of a predominantly visual nature, may be associated with all sensory modes.

Neurologist Antonio Damasio has pointed out that the neural basis of knowledge is dependent on image formation, which seems to occur not in one particular site in the brain but rather in a parcellated manner in different neural locations. He states that along with the external responses known as behaviour, complex organisms, such as that which is constituted by our brain and body, 'also generate internal responses, some of which constitute images (visual, auditory, somatosensory, and so on), which I postulate as the basis for mind'; thus an essential condition for mind is 'the ability to display images internally and to order those images in a process called thought' (1994:89–90). In a similar manner Ralph Ellis (1995) notes how thinking is built up by combinations of images in different modalities and patterns, and, in this way, imagery is a more basic event than thinking and can have a significant influence on reasoning.

The importance, then, of images for our mental processes should not be underestimated. They help us make sense of and organize incoming data; they provide us with ways to reason and make decisions and to select or develop a motor response (Damasio 1995:93). Whatever mental activity we have going on, mental images are certain to participate to some extent. They are not bound by time and so may be of moments in the past or of possibilities for the future.

Etymologically, there is an intimate connection between knowing and seeing. As Arendt points out, the Greek word for 'to know' means 'to have seen.' But this does not refer only to seeing with our 'outer' eyes; seeing with the mind's eye, using imagination, is also involved. She refers to the essentiality of imagination: 'Re-presentation, making present what is actually absent, is the mind's unique gift, and drawn from vision's experience, this gift is called imagination' (1978:76). Arendt underlines the usefulness of these inner images for our cognitive functioning. By bringing the external material from our senses into the terrain of our imagination, we are able to utilize it; '... only in this immaterial form can our thinking faculty now begin to concern itself with these data' (1978:87).

Information coming into our consciousness, including information about a second language we are learning, is processed by what Paivio refers to as a dual encoding system composed of imagery and verbal codes. T. Rogers (1983:290) has suggested that this basic model seems incomplete, for when dealing with real world conditions, 'we find an increasing need to begin to inject some aspect of emotion into our theories'. While there is no concrete empirical evidence that a separate third code for emotion exists, it is clear that emotion interacts with the imaginal and verbal codes. The fact that emotional traces are coded with images and words has important implications for language teaching (see below and Stevick 1996 and this volume).

Imagery and creativity in learning

We all have the ability to form mental images. Children have this to a greater degree, as they have more imagination. Kosslyn (1983) points out how research suggests that young children rely strongly on imagery, something which should certainly be taken into account in early education. In fact, Whitmore (1986:25) affirms that 'most learning occurs through imagining what is to be learned. If an individual cannot conceive of something in his mind it may be impossible for him to learn it in a lasting way'. However, most educational systems cater to the logical, analytical 'left brain' and unwisely phase out the imaginal elements very soon. Stimulation of the visualization abilities resident in the mind is generally offered only to the youngest learners, if at all. Giving so much emphasis to verbal thinking means that we deprive learners of a valuable asset for their development. Inactive, our natural ability to use mental images and to develop our imagination greatly declines with age. In our educational systems words and numbers have pushed imagery 'out of the picture', and in the process much is lost. When used appropriately, images can provide a strong impetus for learning. One of the reasons that this is so is that they are related to creativity and to our emotions; and these relationships can greatly empower learning. Neville (1989:93–4) suggests that simple exercises be used to retrain the imagining, 'which, like language, significantly affects the child's ability to learn, to develop peer and adult relationships, to pursue goals and to experience pleasure'. Introduced in teaching programmes, these exercises can bring benefits on diverse levels: 'The children's improved concentration and ability to visualize are a worthwhile goal in themselves. Besides that, they can be exploited for more effective teaching of the curriculum'. (An exercise for developing visualization skills can be found in Appendix A on page 277.)

Visualization is involved in day dreams and fantasy and, as such, in a left-brain world is subject to bad press. As a *guided* process, however, imagery work can provide structure and control for mental images, leading to a reversal of the atrophied sense of creativity and imagination present in many educational settings. We shouldn't forget that the imaginal area of experience is responsible for many of the most important artistic, scientific and technological discoveries of history. The best known perhaps is Einstein's visualization of himself riding a beam of light which led him eventually to formulate the theory of relativity. On one level his genius could be explained by his ability to use first the insights provided by imagery and then rational thinking to develop and explain the images at a later stage. He himself described his process thus: 'The words of the language ... do not seem to play any role in my mechanism of thought. The psychical entities which seem to serve as elements in thought are certain signs and more or less clear images which can be "voluntarily" reproduced and combined ... [These] elements are, in my case, of visual and some of muscular type' (Ghiselin 1952:43).

Creativity springs from greater depths than usual of our mind, from areas alive with imagery which Jean Houston (1982:134) refers to as 'inscapes', regions of inner space and inner time; there, 'by thinking in images, ideas emerge that are otherwise impossible'. She cites an experiment in the 1920s in which children were specifically taught to use imaging processes; years later in their teens they were 'more creative and better able to draw. Also, they scored higher on intelligence tests than comparable children whose imagery was allowed to meet the usual fate of atrophy and inhibition imposed by educational processes too oriented to the verbal' (Houston 1982:140). Some verbal capacities themselves may be compromised by the lack of a well-developed imaginal faculty; data suggest that those who have poor imaging ability may process words analytically less effectively than good imagers (Allen, Wallace and Loschiavo 1994). Campos and González (1995) present research carried out in the 1990s which further supports the idea that creativity is influenced significantly by imaging ability.

Like creativity, general mental ability (as measured by IQ scores) has been shown to increase through a visualization technique called image streaming, developed by Wenger. It consists of starting an 'image stream' of free associations in your mind and describing them aloud to someone or recording them. As several different parts of your brain are being used together, a 'pole bridging' effect is produced, and at some point creative discoveries or solutions to problems can be forthcoming. (For further discussion, see Murphey 1998.)

The use of visualization is becoming more and more common in diverse areas of educational endeavor, whether in science, mathematics, creative writing or second language learning. Majoy (1993:64) predicts that 'visualization will become one of the most powerful, effective, and necessary tools for teachers in the years to come. Harnessing inner space will revolutionize teaching and learning ... We must use it as an essential and basic teaching skill'.

Imagery and affect in language learning

In the language learning process there are significant connections between images and affect. Words are generally encoded with some type of image, making them easier to recall; in Paivio's formulation it is the imaginal representation that contains the affective aspects. In their extensive report on the hemispheric specialization of the brain, Springer and Deutsch (1993:199) conclude that there is good reason to believe that the right hemisphere is dominant in 'both the processing of emotional information and in the production of emotional expressions'. Quoting Borod, they offer a possible explanation for this: 'emotional processing involves strategies and functions for which the right hemisphere is superior: strategies termed nonverbal, synthetic integrative, holistic, and Gestalt, and functions such as pattern perception, visuo-spatial organization, and *visual imaging*' (Springer and Deutsch 1993:201; emphasis added).

Language learning, of course, deals with words; words are not encoded in isolation in our brains. They are present there with many, many associations and images – visual, auditory, kinaesthetic, pleasant, unpleasant … – which play an important role in the learning process. Stevick stresses the diversity of the dimensions of an image and concludes that 'the *spectrum of nonverbal memory items* that are relevant to language teaching is very broad, including particularly items of purpose and emotion' (1986:162).

We could say that a circular relationship exists between imagery and affect. Images are saturated with affect, but in turn mental imagery can influence our affective states and development. Both directions are important for language learning. This bond between affect and imagery in our mental processes points to the usefulness of incorporating visualization into an affective approach to language learning. When positive emotions are involved, learning is reinforced, and an easy way to bring about an association of emotion and language is through images. Words are merely a series of letters, originally without meaning or emotional content. What stimulates the emotional reaction is the image associated in our minds with the words. Thus imagery in the classroom helps us connect the language we teach with the affective side of our learners.

Uses of imagery in language teaching

The possible applications of visualization or guided imagery in language teaching are numerous. Stevick has pointed out how for verbal communication to exist there must be a modification of images in the participants' minds; he adds that images in language study are of use because generating them creates new neural connections and strengthens the old and makes 'the networks more solid, more complete, and more usable' (1986:51).

To begin to explore the world of imagery in language learning, one possibility we might consider is a simple exercise that could be used in a variety of classroom situations, most obviously with material related to rooms of the house and furniture.

> *Imagine yourself in a room you knew very well as a child. What do you see in the room? What furniture is there and where is it placed? Where are the windows? Look out of one window. What do you see? Do you hear any sounds? What do you see on the walls? Is there anything in the room that brings back special memories? How do you feel there? Where do the doors lead?*
> (Adapted from Miller 1981)

A follow-up on this simple visualization would be to have students write a description of the room, which will undoubtedly be richer and more detailed after having returned to it in the mind's eye. A further possibility would be for Student A to describe the room to Student B, who would make a drawing of the room as she understands it from the description. Student A would then check to see if the drawing is correct.

Another example:

> *Think of an object that for one reason or another means something special to you. See it in your mind's eye with all its details. Remember how you got it, the circumstances surrounding this moment ... where you keep it ... how it feels when you touch it ... what shape and colour it has ... what feelings you have when you see it.*

Learners can then be asked to describe it to another person.

To accustom learners to calling up images in their minds, an Image Quiz can be used. Ask a series of questions which will require learners to form mental images in order to answer. *How many windows are there in your home? As you walk in the door to your home, what is in front of you? What do you see on the way to school? What was the first thing you did when you got up this morning? Would you look better in a green sweater or a red one?* This exercise is well-adapted to pair work with students asking each other the questions.

In the above examples imagery work is based on more superficial levels of mental activity. However, the creation of certain types of new mental images can involve deeper levels that connect to very significant learning and to the modification of negative attitudes which place obstacles in our way. It is here that the influence of affect is most strongly felt.

One example of deep imagery work would be with goal setting. Learners can be asked to see themselves as they are now regarding their language learning skills and then to imagine how they would like to be at the end of the course. It is important for them to imagine the possible new state as completely as possible: What would they feel like? What would they be able to do? What doors would be opened? Who might share their satisfaction with them? After they have had enough time to develop and enjoy the second image, have them write down their specific language learning goals and devise plans to reach these goals.

For work with imagery, especially with developing powerful new images, it is often useful to have students close their eyes and relax. A quiet, concentrated mind is a more fertile ground for the growth of mental imagery. Learners can be prepared for this gradually to avoid resistance to what for some may be a very new type of activity: *Close your eyes a moment and imagine a car. What colour is it? ... Imagine a dog. What does it look like?* At a later stage a basic relaxation exercise to precede visualization might be useful. In a slow, calm voice (possibly in their native language) tell students: *Close your eyes and observe your breathing. As you breathe out, notice how all the tension in your body disappears. Breathe in a feeling of calm and well-being, breathe out all your worries, stress, discomfort, any tension you find in your body.* More extensive relaxation exercises which ask learners to relax the body gradually can be introduced when reviewing vocabulary of the parts of the body. (Moskowitz 1978:179–80 is a good example.)

Imaging may be mainly a visual process – *seeing* in the mind's eye. But hearing, feeling, tasting, smelling also enrich our imaginal world, and all senses should be addressed in visualization activities. Murdock (1987:27–8) presents an exercise called 'Multisensory Imagery' which encourages the participation of all the senses, as well as working imaginally with both hemispheres of the brain. It involves experiencing on the left, then the right sides of the brain images of different sensory categories. An example of this type of imaging exercise would be: *On the left of your brain you see a sunny beach ... on the right a snow-covered mountain ... On the left you feel the texture of soft red velvet ... on the right the texture of tree bark ... On the left you smell bread baking ... on the right the scent of a pine tree ...*

Turning to some of the specific areas where visualization can be used in the language classroom, we will be focusing on factors related to language learning processes, on the facilitation of affective states which are more favourable to language learning and on ways to use visualization as a basis for learning materials and activities.

Factors in the language learning process

Memory

Memory is obviously an essential to all learning, and prominently so in second language learning. And essential for the memory system is mental imagery. Marks (1973:23) states that 'images have an important function in memory. Image vividness ... facilitates accurate recall'.

The use of imagery as a conscious memory aid is centuries, even millenniums old. Simonides, Greek poet and orator, and the Roman orators after him, would associate in their mind parts of their speech with sections of a building and then mentally go through the building to bring to mind each part of the speech. Today specialists in learning techniques use a similar device often referred to as the peg system. The idea here is that you learn, say, ten fixed items which are like pegs to hang new items on. (These should be very concrete and, if possible, rhyme with the numbers from one to ten. For example, one–sun, two–shoe ...) Then when you need to memorize, you associate a mental image with the fixed items. If the first word to memorize was feather, you could form an image in your mind's eye of the sun laughing because it is being tickled with a feather. (Buzan 1991 describes this technique in greater depth.) This is somewhat similar to the keyword technique – when learning a new word, associate it with a known word, preferably involving an image, that in some way will remind you of the new word. If the images are unusual, shocking or in some way attention-getting, they may be more effective aids. Research suggests that imagery mnemonics, in addition to improving the cognitive effectiveness of recall, may also influence motivational aspects, possibly making learning easier and more enjoyable (Higbee 1994).

In an exercise described by Earl Stevick (1986), I saw in passing that the Swahili world for crocodile is mamba and immediately formed a mental image of a crocodile dancing the mambo. Though I probably will never learn more Swahili, the fact that I can still remember this word after a relatively long period of time has elapsed with no other reinforcement testifies to the efficiency of the technique, which is one that many good language learners use automatically. As Fogarty (1994:23) has said, 'Images and words together create a more powerful learning episode'.

It has been demonstrated that concrete words (words that have images behind them) are easier to remember; they can be learned in two ways, verbally and with imagery, which gives greater reinforcement to memory. Kosslyn (1983:174) cites Bower's experiment at Stanford University which showed that of three methods for learning pairs of concrete words – repeating the words over and over, constructing separate images of the pairs of objects and constructing an image of the two objects interacting, the latter was definitely the most effective memory strategy. Drose and Allen (1994) comment on how imagery has also been shown to increase retention on the sentence level.

Students can be taught to make mental flash cards to help them assimilate vocabulary. Especially with languages such as English which are not spelled phonetically, it is very useful to be able to picture the word itself and, if possible, an image associated with it. Revell and Norman describe an interesting NLP spelling technique which incorporates visualization. Write the word on the board high enough so learners have to look up, the natural position of the eyes when visualizing. Have students take a mental picture of the word and then close their eyes and see it. Next they write it down from memory. These steps can be repeated until the word is mastered; if one part of a word creates problems, they can imagine that part bigger (Revell and Norman 1997:41).

Rehearsal

McLaughlin (1990:115) points out that for complex cognitive skills, such as those involved in language learning, to become automatic and thus free attention for new learning, practice is a necessary activity: 'A skill must be practiced again and again and again, until no attention is required for its performance'. One type of practice for a second language would be to repeat verb conjugations or do grammar exercises. This type of practice can lead to greater accuracy but may not affect fluency at all. With visualization we can do another type of practice called rehearsal, which is closely linked to what athletes do in many sports. On the purely physiological level, it has been shown that merely activating an image of yourself swimming, for example, can produce minute muscular changes. Several experimental studies (Kendall, Hrycaiko, Martin and Kendall 1990; Vernacchia and Cooke 1993, among others) have shown the effectiveness of mental rehearsal techniques in basketball training. Speaking about perceptual motor skills in general, Richardson (1983) states that if an individual has an adequate inner model of a skill, performance can be significantly improved by mental practice procedures. In the area of self-confidence in athletes, however, results of a Michigan State University study suggest that merely imagining rehearsal is of less significance than the use of imagery of mastery experiences and the emotions involved in the experiences (Moritz, Hall, Martin and Vadocz 1996). Though not particularly concerned with the physical aspects of imagery work,

Assagioli was nevertheless aware that 'vividly imagining an action performed successfully trains our brain and our body to perform it' (Neville 1989:102).

Tharp and Gallimore (1988:48) connect modelling and mental rehearsal:

> ... research has shown that active coding of modeled activities into descriptions or labels or vivid imagery increases learning and retention of complex skills. Through watching others, then a person can form an idea of the components of a complex behavior and can begin to visualize how the pieces could be assembled and sequenced in various other settings. All of this can be achieved through central processing, without having performed the action.

They stress the usefulness of this type of activity as a tool in teacher training.

What first attracted my attention to visualization in language learning was Jean Houston's narration of the case of an American scholar who, before going to a conference in Europe, eliminated blocks about speaking French and Italian by working with imagery. For each language, in a very relaxed state he was told to think of a word that was the essence of the language for him and to let it flow through him. He was then instructed to visualize himself travelling throughout the country, speaking to everyone. In both cases after thirty minutes, in which he reported that he felt he had been travelling for a week, it was found that his fluency improved notably and with Italian his accuracy did also. Houston (1982:153) comments on results such as these: 'it is possible to focus psychic processing so that it seems as if a pathway is being cleared to formerly hidden knowledge'. Similarly, Brown (1991:86) describes what he calls the visualization game: 'Visualize yourself speaking the language fluently and interacting with people. Then when you are actually in such a situation, you will, in a sense, have "been there" before'. In exercises of this nature it is useful to bring in as many of the senses as possible and to emphasize the emotional reactions involved.

Focus on meaning

An important factor in language acquisition is shifting the focus from linguistic form to meaning and, even more, to meaningfulness. Working, as it does, with material which emerges from within each person, visualization brings personal meaning to the learning process. One example, adapted from a presentation by Robert O'Neill based on

Stevick (1986), is to read a short narrative text and then elicit answers to questions based not on the actual text, but on images created in each listener's mind. (If you read *As the rain fell, Mary was looking out the window nervously. She saw John approaching. She ran to him as he entered the door...*', you can ask, *What was Mary wearing? How tall is she? Does she hug John or hit him? ...*) Learners need not fear giving a factually wrong answer since the question is designed for information in their own store of images. Their attention is automatically drawn towards the meaning that they are constructing mentally, which is more like the process of natural language acquisition than many traditional types of language learning activities. Furthermore, a holistic learning situation is provided because meaning and affective evaluation are not separated from the language being learned.

Language learners often do the following: think of what they want to say, convert the proposition into their native language, then translate this into the target language, with consequent difficulties. Working with visualization, learners start with an image and can move directly into the L2, bypassing translation. Speaking of teaching foreign language writing, Mata (1996:60) notes that:

> People write what they see. By 'see' I mean when words in one language are no longer equal to a translation, but are the instantaneous communication of the actual object, feeling, or action. It is quite possible for students to see a movie in their heads as they write, rather than overlaying Spanish translations or English grammar rules.

So, along with encouraging learners of English to 'think in English', we also might do well to ask them to '*see* in English'.

Goodey (1997:8) notes that 'language lives only when meaning breathes life into form and transcends it' and stresses the importance of contextualizing grammar through imagery: 'much of language is the translation of pictures in the mind. As language teachers, we must evoke in the minds of our students a whole series of pictures, for without them there can be no successful language learning'.

Skills development: reading

Discussing reading, Tomlinson notes how L1 readers make much more use of high level top-down skills such as visualization, while in L2 reading much more attention is given over to low level decoding. If visualization is not developed, the reading process and language learning can be rendered more difficult.

> If learners do not see pictures in their minds of the texts they are reading then they will have great difficulty in achieving global understanding and their experience of the texts will be fragmentary and shallow. Not only will they not enjoy reading but they will not transfer reading skills which they have already developed in their L1 and their encounter with the language of the texts is unlikely to be deep and meaningful enough to facilitate language acquisition. (Tomlinson 1998:277–8)

He recommends developing visualization through strategy instruction and the use of visualization strategy activities for reading in a second language and affirms that 'increasing an L2 reader's ability to visualise can facilitate positive engagement with the text and can increase the reader's ability to comprehend and retain what is read' (Tomlinson 1998:270).

When working with reading, the proper choice of texts is important. Tomlinson (1997) recommends the use of literary texts for their facility in engaging the learner both cognitively and affectively. However, they can only be truly effective if they are not studied for the language but rather responded to aesthetically. And for this to happen, it is helpful to use visualization throughout the reading process. (See Appendix B on page 277 for an example of using visualization when reading literary texts.)

In all skills work visualization can prime the existing schema to facilitate comprehension or to enrich production. And in the context of working with literature, it is interesting to note how Shakespeare in *Henry V* recognizes the importance of mental imagery:

> Piece out our imperfections with your thoughts . . .
> Think, when we talk of horses, that you see them
> Printing their proud hoofs i' the receiving earth;
> For 'tis your thoughts that now must deck our kings . . .

Positive affective states

According to Kosslyn (1983), much of what we consider personality is made up of representations, 'images', in memory. At least part of what we conceive of as self and others is stored as images there. Modifying these mental images with the help of visualization, creating more efficient new affective states and replacing inefficient old ones, has a very facilitating effect on language learning. Imagery can bring out the unrecognized and rework the already existing. Neville (1989:103) lists some of the ways learners' affective states can be improved:

Students can deal with learning difficulties by imagining themselves able to handle the task with ease. They can deal with
fatigue and boredom by a visualisation in which they are
refreshed and energised. They can deal with depression and
frustration by a fantasy in which these emotions are symboli-
cally transformed into their opposites.

Drawing on the work of Assagioli and psychosynthesis, Whitmore
(1986) describes ways to help learners recognize their feelings and
recondition those that are not positive through a structured use of
imagery. This type of visualization can provide support for developing
several of Gardner's multiple intelligences, especially the interpersonal
and intrapersonal.

A basic use of visualization in this sense is to help students learn to
leave their problems and worries at the door to the classroom. If they
are centred, learning will be much easier. A simple centring exercise
would be:

*Close your eyes and relax your body and mind. It is a pleasant
spring day. Go in your mind to a place that you enjoy. It may
be a place that you have been before or one that you are
imagining now for the first time. It may be in a forest, on a
mountain, at the sea or some place else. As you walk along,
enjoy the fresh air. Notice the colours around you and listen to
the sounds. Feel the sun warming you and giving you energy.
Enjoy for a moment the peace and well-being surrounding you.*

Guided imagery can lead to a greater integration of the affective and
cognitive functions. An exercise such as 'Feeling and mind integration'
(Whitmore 1986:102–4), designed specifically for adolescents, can
make learners more aware of their feelings and help them to explore
and strengthen the relationship between the two domains. In this
exercise you first develop images for your cognitive and affective sides
(perhaps an owl and a heart, or a computer and a bird) and then take a
pleasant walk up a mountain accompanied by the images, the three of
you experiencing the beautiful day and possibly maintaining three-way
communication leading to greater harmony among the parts. Work of
this nature can prepare the way for more effective language learning to
take place, especially with learners who have difficulty integrating
different aspects of themselves.

The negative influence of anxiety on language learning is very
generally accepted (see Oxford this volume), but working with imagery
can provide solutions. One way to do so is shown in an experiment
carried out at the University of Seville (Arnold 1994) involving two

groups of fifteen students who had expressed significant feelings of anxiety about their listening comprehension exam. With the experimental group, evenly matched on the pretest with the control group, six sessions of relaxation-visualization exercises were used before six practice exams. The control group only did the practice exams. On post-test scores the experimental group showed marked improvement over the control group. More importantly, on open-ended questionnaires a high percentage of the comments from members of the experimental group reflected a definite reduction of anxious feelings: 'At first I felt very nervous but then I began to relax. Now I can even listen to the text and I have time to think.' 'I believe that being calmer is very important because the texts are accessible to everyone as far as vocabulary and the rest; all that is necessary is to recognize what we already know.' 'I feel more confident about listening and about myself.' Though further research with larger samples is necessary, there is a clear indication that anxiety can be reduced by visualization. Likewise, Roberts and Clark (1976:6) mention the case of the German teacher who used relaxation and visualization exercises before an exam, noting significant improvement in the quality of the writing produced. The students involved couldn't understand this change until he explained how 'a lot of their learned knowledge was not able to surface because of the nervousness and fear and the tension, and once they were relaxed, the learned storehouse of information was able to be tapped'.

Systematic desensitization is a technique that uses visualization to reduce phobias, stage fright and diverse types of anxiety. It can be used with anxiety produced by certain situations related to language learning, such as taking exams or speaking before others in the language. The learner makes a list of twenty items related to the task, arranged according to the degree of risk involved. (Pencil, blank paper, desk, classroom, rows of people writing ... going into the exam room, waiting for the exam to start, picking up the exam paper, taking the exam.) In a very relaxed state the learner is told to imagine the least anxiety-provoking. When she feels comfortable with this image, the next is visualized, continuing until the learner can at last calmly evoke an image of taking the exam itself. If anxiety arises at any point, it may be necessary to deepen the state of relaxation or make the list longer (Davies 1986). Research by Tyron (1980) shows that eight one-hour sessions can produce a marked decrease in anxiety in a test situation.

Self-esteem and self-efficacy can be improved through the use of imagery. In a relaxed state, the mind is receptive to a restructuring of one's self-image and the appraisal of one's abilities; NLP has shown that if you can imagine yourself doing something, you are more likely to be able to do it. One example is an exercise suggested by Canfield and Wells (1994:203–4) called 'I have a dream'. After working with Martin Luther King's famous speech, learners select a dream they have. When they are relaxed, they are guided through a visualization in which they experience having actually achieved their dream. All their senses are incorporated, and they register how they are feeling, what they are saying and doing. Afterwards, setting writing tasks about their visualization provides reinforcement for developing the ability to succeed, as well as further work in the second language. (An example of a visualization to increase learners' confidence and to make them more aware of ways to access their knowledge of the language is found in Appendix C on page 278.)

Likewise, empathy, which has been shown to be a useful quality for language learning, is amenable to development with images. Miller (1981:118) proposes that 'using our imagination and intuition we can attempt to perceive the other person's feelings and thoughts'; this is important in communicative behaviour and particularly when language learning also involves culture learning. After all, isn't 'putting yourself into someone else's shoes' *imagining* what it is like to be the other person?

If, as has been proposed in this volume, language classrooms can at times also be a source of values education and of the development of emotional intelligence, then visualization can further this goal. Through imagery it is possible to find creative solutions to problems discussed in the classroom. When dealing with a moral dilemma, Miller (1982:117–8) suggests that students 'could sit quietly for a short period of time and imagine themselves responding to this situation. Perhaps several images and responses would come to mind'. He suggests using this material as a basis for group discussion, but other second language work could be role-plays, composition projects, diary work, debates or further research on the topic. In our images may be contained the energy to bring our dreams into the realm of reality. As Mulligan (1991:185) has said, imagining 'is the precursor to creativity and action ... It helps us transcend current experience of reality and combine the possible with the impossible'.

Teaching materials and activities

The more experience we acquire as teachers, the more we are attracted to diversifying our classroom activities, supplementing the textbook with material that we feel is appropriate and interesting for our particular context. One objection to supplementing the textbook with other materials is that this requires considerable expenditure of time and money. However, with imagery work, we can create very enriching language activities with little time and no money because these activities rely on material that is in each student's mind already.

We cannot assume that all learners are able to visualize well. Precisely because, as we have seen, the imaginal parts of our mind have been allowed to rust, it is often necessary to provide learners with exercises to develop their imaging abilities at the same time as they are working on their language abilities. In addition to the suggestions above, for useful work with the language you can give learners a sentence: '*The girl walked along the road*'. *Add an adjective to* '*girl*'. *Add an adverb to* '*walked*'. *Add a prepositional phrase after* '*road*'. *Follow the girl to see what she does next*. Then debrief, having learners compare their different versions. This is doubly useful, as they provide models for each other's imagination, as well as linguistic input (Adapted from Grinder 1991). When working with less superficial aspects of imagery, it is even more important to process the experience in some way – small group discussion, writing, journal work, drawing and reflection are some of the possibilities.

Moskowitz (1978) has developed guided imagery activities, which she calls fantasy trips. In these, students are guided through jungles, to quaint villages, beneath the sea, back to their own past. The imaginal material produced on these trips can be used for many purposes, ranging from practice with discrete grammar points to integrated skills work.

Music is useful as a stimulus for visualization and as a way to incorporate an affective investment in the language learning situation. One effective activity is to play bits of different types of music and have learners invent a film each piece could be used for. As music tends to open our minds to images, we can expect more highly developed writing than if we simply asked students to write about a film they would like to make.

NLP makes extensive use of visualization. Grinder (1991) suggests using simple exercises such as the following, which can be used to supplement other materials for various purposes. *Consider the top of your desk to be your room. As if looking down from the ceiling, touch what would be the door, where the bed would be*, and so forth. Similarly, ask learners to imagine there is a cat on the desktop. *Which way is it facing? What color is it? How big is it? Is it standing, sitting or lying down? Scratch its ear.* Both of these are especially useful for kinaesthetic learners as an element of movement is involved.

The above examples are offered as a sample of the many ways that imagery can be incorporated into the classroom to support learning.

Both the cognitive and affective aspects of the language learning process can benefit from activating elements of our learners' visual storehouse.

In preparing visualization activities, as when working with any affect-related area in the language class, it is wise to remember that nothing will be right for all students all the time. However, the great majority of learners will find that imagery work is a valuable tool that can, in Murdock's words, help them to 'relax, learn more easily, improve memory skills, get along better and be more creative and productive' (Murdock 1987:14).

Conclusion: extending imagery to teachers

In this chapter several ways of using mental imagery to help language learners have been discussed. However, as teachers we can also benefit from using visualization. I would like to suggest one activity. When you are alone and in a quiet place, relax your body and your mind and visualize a scene: it is a typical class, a few good things, some less good. Problems come up; there are no very effective solutions ... Everyone is anxious for class to be over to go home. When the bell rings, there is a rush for the door. Now, change the scene. You are teaching the best class ever. Everyone is enjoying themselves. The students are learning a lot, both about the language, which they are using enthusiastically, and about themselves and each other. There are many positive feelings toward the experience, and when the class is over, you and the students take a pleasant sensation out of the classroom. Either image can be real; it's up to you to choose.

Suggestions for further reading

Houston, J. 1982. *The Possible Human*. Los Angeles: Jeremy P. Tarcher, Inc.

Moskowitz, G. 1978. *Caring and Sharing in the Foreign Language Class*. Rowley, MA: Newbury House.

Murdock, M. 1987. *Spinning Inward*. Boston: Shambhala.

Revell, J. and S. Norman. 1997. *In Your Hands. NLP in ELT*. London: Saffire Press.

Stevick, E. W. 1986. *Images and Options in the Language Classroom*. Cambridge: Cambridge University Press.

Whitmore, D. 1986. *Psychosynthesis in Education*. Wellingborough: Turnstone Press Limited.

Appendix A Developing the ability to concentrate and to visualize

Sit comfortably, close your eyes and direct your attention to your breathing. As you breathe deeply and slowly, feel yourself becoming very relaxed, yet alert (pause several seconds.) ... Hold the following in your mind for several moments, returning to the image if you become distracted. Try to imagine each as completely as possible, using all your senses: a white dove ... , bells ringing ... , apple pie ... , a cool, clear stream ... , a tall tree ... , a red rose ... , the moon ... , an elephant walking.

Now, visualize a soft white cloud high up in a very blue sky ... make it come nearer ... make it smaller ... make it bigger ... change its shape to resemble a rabbit ... now change it to look like a house with lovely white smoke coming out of the chimney ... Observe how the smoke writes your name in the sky.

(Adapted from an exercise in Neville 1989:93–4)

Appendix B Visualizations with literary texts

For work with a literary text, for example, Edith Wharton's short novel, *Ethan Frome*.

Before reading:

Bring to your mind a picture of life in a poor rural area of New England at the end of the nineteenth century ... If you lived there, what would your life be like? ... Imagine a typical day on the farm in winter, what would you do? ... Who would you see? ... What might you do in the evenings? ... Imagine that your spouse is a person who is always complaining ... What would your meals together be like? ... What hopes and dreams would you have? ...

After reading the text:

Visualize the evening Ethan walks young, joyful Mattie, his wife's cousin, home from the dance ... What do they talk about? ... What is the sound of her voice like? ... How does he feel? ... Imagine how he walks – is there any difference from how he usually walks? ...

Visualize Ethan's life after the accident at the end of the book ... What changes in his appearance do you imagine? ... What atmosphere do you feel in the house now with Mattie crippled and bitter? ... If you were

the narrator and could talk with Ethan, what would you ask him? ...
Discuss with him anything that you may have thought about as you
were reading his story ... Then change roles and imagine you are Ethan
... Explain your experiences and feelings to someone ...

Appendix C Visit with a master teacher

Close your eyes and bring your attention to your breathing. Notice how
with each breath you become more and more relaxed ... It is a warm
spring day and you are in the countryside near a beautiful mountain.
There is a very easy path going up the mountain and you decide to walk
up to the top. As you go, you notice all the sights and sounds and smells
along the way. There is a soft breeze that you feel touching your face as
you walk. You see flowers of all colours along the path and hear the
birds singing in the trees. When you get to the top you can see the
countryside below. As you look around, you notice a shady tree. Under
the tree is a large rock where someone is sitting. It is a person who is
very wise and who can help you learn exactly what you need to know at
this moment. This person is waiting for you to help you with the
process of learning your new language. Ask any questions, seek any
advice you need. This teacher may communicate with you in many
different ways in order to improve your abilities to use the language.
You will have three minutes, which is all the time you need to receive
these teachings.

(After three minutes) Now you must say good-bye, thanking this
person and knowing that you can return for more help whenever you
wish. You walk down the mountain, taking with you everything that
you have learned ... I am going to count to five and when I reach five,
open your eyes, feeling relaxed, alert and conscious of your ability to
learn the language well ...

17 Authentic assessment in affective foreign language education

Viljo Kohonen

Evaluation in the context of a holistic view of language education

Evaluation as part of a paradigm shift towards transformative learning

It is well-known that anticipation of testing procedures has a backwash effect on learning. Learners prepare for examinations and organise knowledge in memory in the light of how they are going to be tested. Evaluation also guides the teacher's pedagogical decisions, particularly when preparing learners for important external tests. Evaluation thus affects the quality and quantity of learning. Therefore, it needs to be examined in terms of both the learning processes and the outcomes of learning.

Process evaluation refers to the reflective assessment that is an integral part of the ongoing learning process. It can provide significant information to:

– Teachers about the progress of individual learners' communicative proficiency, personal development, learning skills and social skills. This helps them to plan instructional interventions.
– Learners about how they are progressing in terms of both their communicative and process skills, helping them to take charge of their learning (Kohonen 1992a, b).

Product evaluation is summative performance testing, aimed at gauging the learner's current language competence, skills and attitudes in relevant communicative tasks and contexts. For this purpose, various criterion-referenced proficiency scales have been developed (cf. Carroll and West 1989; North 1993; O'Malley and Valdez Pierce 1996; Common European Framework Proposal 1996).

There are various levels of formality depending on the purpose and functions of language testing. Tests can be designed and administered by the teacher in the classroom to track student learning and to guide educational practices. For more formal purposes, language tests are usually designed (and sometimes also administered and scored) by educational authorities and other outside experts to evaluate language education programmes or curriculum-related achievements at national levels. Tests are also necessary in various institutional settings for student selection and placement purposes. Proficiency tests are designed and administered commercially by various professional organisations for official certification purposes, regardless of prior language teaching curricula.

Obviously, different kinds of evaluation are needed, given the many purposes and functions of evaluation that exist in the total educational setting. However, the selective system with its product-oriented testing should not be the main intent of educational language assessment. Process evaluation can exercise a powerful effect on affective language learning outcomes by enhancing the learner's competence and confidence as a person. It therefore deserves to be considered seriously by language teaching professionals (cf. Kohonen 1992a, b; 1996).

Evaluation is never carried out in a vacuum. Evaluation practices need to be critically reviewed and developed as part of the whole educational setting and the learning-teaching process.

Nothing less than a major paradigmatic shift is taking place in current educational theory. The shift entails a clear movement away from the models of teaching as transmission of knowledge towards an experiential, more learner-centred approach. In this approach teaching aims at the transformation of knowledge, integrating new knowledge with existing personal constructs and meanings. An important affective goal of the new models is to promote the learner's holistic personal growth. Evaluation can facilitate the learner to become a more skilled, independent and responsible person through a better understanding of the process and of himself. Personal growth is also at the heart of education for democratic citizenship, which is becoming increasingly important in modern learning societies (Ranson 1994:116).

The paradigm shift can be analysed by juxtaposing the polar ends of some pedagogically relevant dimensions (cf. Miller 1988:46–60; Kohonen 1992b:30–33; Järvinen, Kohonen, Niemi and Ojanen 1995; Kohonen 1996:70). However, neither of the paradigms should be seen as the 'right' or 'wrong' way of teaching. They are not mutually exclusive or the only ways of organising instruction. They are just based on different conceptions of the person, learning and knowledge that lead to substantially different instructional decisions. Between the ends described in Figure 1, there is a continuum which allows for various degrees of emphasis on either side. If the teacher decides to

Assumptions in instruction: some dimensions	Traditional approach: teaching as transmission	Experiential approach: transformative learning
1. Dominant conceptions of learning	Behavioristic theories of learning	Socio-constructivistic and humanistic theories of learning
2. Power relation and teacher's role orientation	Authority, teacher to impart knowledge (mainly through frontal instruction); teachers working in isolation	Partnership, teacher to facilitate learning (mainly in various cooperative groups); teachers working in collaboration
3. Learner's role	Relatively passive, with emphasis on individual work	Active participation, both alone and in cooperative teams
4. View of knowledge and curriculum	Knowledge given from outside; sequential grading of subject matter in the curriculum	Construction of personal knowledge in process; dynamic, looser curriculum organisation
5. Learning experiences and outcomes	Emphasis on product: facts, concepts and communication skills	Emphasis on process: self-esteem, learning skills, social and communication skills
6. Control of process and motivation	Teacher in charge; teacher-structured learning; external locus of control, extrinsic motivation	Learner in charge; self-organised learning; internal locus of control, intrinsic motivation
7. Evaluation	Product-oriented; achievement testing; criterion-referencing (and norm-referencing)	Process-oriented; authentic assessment; reflection of process, self-assessment; criterion-referencing

Figure 1 Comparison of two models of learning and teaching

move towards the experiential approach, this means shifting more emphasis towards the right-hand end on the pedagogical dimensions specified.

Reflection enhances teachers' awareness of the extent to which their choices are internally consistent and coherent within the broad paradigmatic position that they have adopted and points to what changes might be desirable. For example, adopting portfolio assessment in a strongly teacher-structured learning environment may not be successful because the learner's self-assessment needs space for self-directed and negotiated learning. Similarly, developing learner-centred classroom practices while adhering strictly to teacher-controlled testing procedures undermines the teacher's authenticity as a learner-centred educator.

Pedagogical coherence needs to be considered at all instructional stages: defining the aims, designing instruction and materials, conducting interactive teaching, and evaluation. Coherence goes, however, beyond the teaching-learning process as such. It is also a matter of the whole learning environment and the affective atmosphere created by the institutional culture with its norms, beliefs and expectations (Kohonen 1992c; 1996).

To evaluate educational processes and their outcomes, teachers need to clarify their understanding of the broad goals of foreign language education. A natural task for language learning is to connect people from various cultural backgrounds and thus increase the tolerance for human diversity. Intercultural communication aims at bridging the diverse cultural values and beliefs that each person brings to the communicative process. The emerging goal of intercultural competence thus provides new challenges that underscore the importance of affective language learning.

Intercultural competence as the broad goal of language education

Lustig and Koester (1993) suggest the concept of *intercultural communication competence* as the overall goal for teaching in intercultural communication situations. They define this concept as follows:

> Intercultural communication is a symbolic, interpretive, transactional, contextual process in which people from different cultures create shared meanings. (Lustig and Koester 1993:51)

Human communication is complex. As personal relationships are made, maintained (and also broken) through talk, communicative misunderstandings will occur even in the closest private encounters in families. People from different cultures have greater differences between them; and these give rise to dissimilar interpretations and expectations about communication behaviours, resulting more easily in breakdowns and failures in communicative transactions. Establishing shared meanings in intercultural communication is consequently a matter of negotiation and tolerance of ambiguity in the process. It is a question of respecting human dignity and otherness in intercultural encounters, assuming the ethical responsibility for attempting to understand the other person (Kaikkonen 1997).

Lustig and Koester (1993: 66–73) provide the following summary of the components of intercultural competence:

1. **Respect:** ability to express respect and positive regard for another person
2. **Orientation to knowledge:** terms people use to explain themselves and their world (e.g. explaining oneself in personal ways, avoiding generalisations)
3. **Empathy:** capacity to behave as though one understands the world as others do
4. **Interaction management:** skill in regulating conversations
5. **Task role behaviour:** initiation of ideas related to group problem-solving
6. **Relational role behaviour:** facilitating interpersonal harmony and mediation
7. **Tolerance for ambiguity:** ability to react to new and ambiguous situations with little visible discomfort
8. **Interaction posture:** ability to respond to others in descriptive, non-evaluative and non-judgmental ways

The components suggest that intercultural competence goes beyond communicative competence in language learning. It manifests the importance of affective foreign and second language education, with an emphasis on personal growth.

Experience and awareness in language learning and teaching

Intercultural competence entails merging learning, evaluation and reflection into a holistic, experiential learning orientation aimed at increasing learner awareness and autonomy. To summarise the essential experiential learning theory briefly, immediate personal experience is seen as the focal point for learning. However, experience also needs to be processed consciously by reflecting on it. In this sense, reflection is a form of evaluation. Experience that is reflected upon yields a full measure of learning in terms of abstract conceptualization and understanding, e.g. of the grammar rules or learning skills. Reflection needs to be followed by active experimentation, risk-taking and social interaction, and more experience (see also Kohonen 1992b:14–17; Legutke and Thomas 1991).

Experiential learning emphasizes that theoretical concepts become part of the individual's personal constructs only when they have been experienced meaningfully on a subjective, emotional level. Reflection plays an important role in this process by providing a bridge, as it were, between experiences, emotions and theoretical conceptualizations. Learning is internalized and transformed in the process of reflecting experience at deeper levels of understanding and interpretation, and using the new meanings in active ways. Learning is thus a continuous, cyclic process that integrates immediate experience, reflection, abstract conceptualization and action.

Towards authentic assessment in foreign language evaluation

What is authentic assessment?

Authentic assessment refers to the procedures for evaluating learner progress using activities and tasks that integrate classroom goals, curricula and instruction and real-life performance. It emphasizes the communicative meaningfulness of evaluation and the commitment to measure that which we value in education. It uses the diverse forms of assessment that reflect student learning, achievement, motivation and attitudes on instructionally-relevant classroom activities. Authentic assessment corresponds to and mirrors good classroom practices. Its results can be used to improve instruction, based on the knowledge of learner progress. Authentic assessment also emphasizes the importance of the teacher's professional judgement and commitment to enhancing student learning. The use of self-assessment promotes the learner's direct involvement in learning and the integration of cognitive abilities with affective learning. (Hart 1994:9; O'Malley and Valdez Pierce 1996:x–6.)

Authentic assessment includes communicative performance assessment, language portfolios and various forms of self-assessment by learners. The following summary provides a list of the basic types of authentic assessment in language learning (O'Malley and Valdez Pierce 1996:12):

- oral interviews (of learners by the teacher)
- story or text retelling (with listening or reading inputs)
- writing samples (with a variety of topics and registers)
- projects and exhibitions (presentation of a collaborative effort)
- experiments and demonstrations (with oral or written reports)
- constructed-response items (to open-ended questions)
- teacher observation (of learners' work in class, making notes)
- portfolios (focused collection of learner's work to show progress)

Essential to the different forms of authentic assessment is that they (1) focus on important curriculum goals, (2) aim at enhancing individual competence, and (3) are carried out as an integral part of instruction.

The developments in evaluation can be highlighted by comparing authentic assessment with traditional standardized testing. Standardized tests are usually based on multiple choice items, fill-in items and short, restricted-response tasks. They are administered to large numbers of testees with consistent scoring results and thus a high degree of reliability. The need to go beyond the standardized tests has recently given prominence to the concept of 'alternative' assessment. Other terms of the new approaches include such labels as performance assessment, dynamic assessment, portfolio assessment and instructional assessment. (Wolf, Bixby, Glenn and Gardner 1991; Wiggins 1993; Darling-Hammond 1994; Hart 1994; Fradd and Larrinaga McGee 1994). Though the emphasis may be different, they all imply an approach that aims at integrating learning, teaching and evaluation.

Standardized testing can be contrasted to authentic assessment as follows (Figure 2, adapted from Armstrong 1994, 117–118):

Standardized testing	*Authentic assessment*
1 Testing and instruction are regarded as separate activities	Assessment is an integral part of instruction
2 Students are treated in a uniform way	Each learner is treated as a unique person
3 Decisions are based on single sets of data (test scores)	Provides multiple sources of data, a more informative view
4 Emphasis on weaknesses/failures: what students cannot do	Emphasis on strengths/ progress: what learners can do
5 One-shot exams	Ongoing assessment
6 Cultural/socio-economic status bias	More culture-fair
7 Focus on one 'right answer'	Possibility of several perspectives
8 Judgement without suggestions for improvement	Useful information for improving/ guiding learning
9 Pressures teachers to narrow teaching to what is tested	Allows teachers to develop meaningful curricula
10 Focus on lower-order knowledge and skills	Emphasis on higher-order learning outcomes and thinking skills
11 Forbids students to interact; promotes comparisons between students (norm-referencing)	Encourages collaborative learning; compares learners to their own past performances and the aims
12 Extrinsic learning for a grade	Intrinsic learning for its own sake

Figure 2 Comparison of standardized testing and authentic assessment

As with the comparison of the general instructional paradigms, the two evaluation paradigms are *not* mutually exclusive in practice. Rather, they are based on different philosophies of learning, teaching and evaluation and address different educational needs and goals. So they might be seen as supplementing each other, depending on the purpose of testing. Authentic assessment entails a movement towards a new culture of evaluation in the service of learning. Only portfolio assessment is discussed in this chapter in more detail since it can combine several types of authentic assessment mentioned above.

The portfolio as a tool in authentic assessment

A portfolio is defined as a purposeful, selective collection of learner work and reflective self-assessment that is used to document progress and achievement over time with regard to specific criteria (cf. Wolf, Bixby, Glenn and Gardner 1991; Kohonen 1992b, c, 1996; Gottlieb 1995; O'Malley and Valdez Pierce 1996). In the course of the learning process the portfolio becomes a kind of autobiography of the learner.

The language portfolio combines the twin goals of the learner-centred curriculum by facilitating language learners to develop (Nunan 1988:134–135; McNamara and Deane 1995:17):

1 the necessary language skills and attitudes, and
2 a critical self-consciousness of their own role as active agents within the learning process, with an ability to assess their own progress and the learning arrangements.

The language portfolio serves two main functions in the total learning process:

– *pedagogic function*: a tool for self-organised language learning. Learners learn to collect authentic data of their own work, record it in suitable ways and reflect on their language learning biography.
– *reporting function*: a tool for reporting language learning outcomes to teachers, institutions and other relevant stakeholders (parents, administrators, other educational institutions, employers, etc.)

The learning portfolio and the showcase portfolio

The learner uses the *learning* (working) *portfolio* to store relevant, authentic documentation of language learning processes over time. Learners are also guided to reflect on their learning and to assess their learning contents and processes. For self-assessment to be meaningful, it is essential that there is an element of learner choice regarding the learning process. This entails the idea of at least a partially open, negotiated curriculum, e.g. through learner-initiated and monitored project work. The teacher negotiates the learning contracts and teaches the learners the evaluation criteria for acceptable learning outcomes (Kohonen 1996).

The learning portfolio thus constitutes an interface, as it were, between learning and evaluation. It helps learners to develop a reflective orientation to their learning. This is the first step in the process of learning to learn, evident in a recent study (McNamara and Deane 1995), in which university ESL students were taught self-assessment in writing activities as part of their English portfolio. They were instructed to write a letter to the teacher at the beginning and end of the semester, and keep a daily language learning log. In the first letter, the students assessed their strengths and weaknesses in English and described specific areas that they wanted to improve. The letters gave the teachers a window into their students' language learning processes and helped them to facilitate learner growth, based on the knowledge of their students. They could help their students establish realistic expectations about the language skills they needed in order to achieve their goals.

During the two-month course, the students recorded in their learning logs their experiences with English over and above their classwork and homework, as well as their extracurricular uses of English. They also recorded their use of specific language learning strategies and their successes and failures with each one. In their weekly evaluations they reread their entries for the week analysing and describing their progress, and made plans for moving ahead. The process facilitated the students to gain a better understanding of their learning processes. The language learning log provided authentic self-observations to be used in the reflective second letter.

At the end of the semester, the students wrote a second letter for the teacher, to be included in their portfolio. In this letter they assessed their efforts on the course and gave themselves a letter grade. They described the area in which they felt they had improved most, reflecting also on why they had progressed so well. Further, they identified a strong and a weak area in their English, discussed the reasons for each, and made a plan for improving the weak areas. The analysis of the entire portfolios suggested that students could take charge of their learning, assuming a greater voice in their language learning process.

To assess their own progress, learners need to be taught how to identify their goals clearly and how to monitor their progress in language learning. The importance of learner guidance has repeatedly come up in the ongoing Finnish experiments on portfolio assessment. Similarly, in an American portfolio study of learning reading in ESL in the middle school (Smolen, Newman, Wathen and Lee 1995), learners were taught to write their weekly goals on small goal cards (index cards) every Monday morning. The cards were on their desks during the week to remind them of what they had chosen to accomplish. An explicit teaching of good reading strategies helped them to identify appropriate strategies in their reading, and when to use them. Discussions in cooperative teams helped them to classify their reading strategies (such as making predictions and confirming them). They were able to develop their metacognitive skills in analysing their own reading behaviour. On Fridays they wrote a reflective statement on the reverse side of the card describing how well they thought they had achieved their goals during the week. In addition, learners had a time planning sheet and a daily learning log available to negotiate with the teacher and to monitor their work. Each Friday the learners selected a sample of their work for inclusion in the showcase portfolio, with a reflective statement explaining why that piece was important for them and why they chose it for the portfolio.

In a Finnish portfolio experiment in the upper secondary school English teaching (Pollari 1997), portfolios were used as a means for learners to negotiate their own syllabuses within a given framework. The contents of the six-week intensive course dealt with culture in English-speaking countries. A central goal in the project was to promote self-directed learning. The learners had the freedom and power to make decisions concerning their own learning and thereby to develop an ownership of their learning. The basic requirements were as follows. The pieces of portfolio work were expected to be diverse both in content and in form, including both oral and written documents. Self-assessment was taught explicitly and regular class conferences were organised to supervise learner work. Learners were expected to choose two or three pieces of work for their showcase portfolios, which were presented in the class. The products were evaluated holistically by the teacher for the grades on that particular course; no other language tests were used. The assessment criteria emphasised learner effort, responsibility, involvement and the ability to communicate meanings, regardless of language errors.

An analysis of the learner portfolios (about 100 learners) indicated that nearly 80 per cent of the students had taken an active and responsible learner role. They set their own goals and generally worked hard to reach them. They also had a positive attitude to portfolios as a vehicle of their learning. Self-direction enhanced the meaningfulness of language learning for them. Feelings of personal satisfaction and accomplishment were evident in a number of learners' comments on their own work, as in the following (Pollari 1997):

... I enjoyed writing and doing my portfolio. ... I have already given myself a 10 [highest grade] from trying and crossing my limits. And the most important thing is I am satisfied with my work and proud of it.

In the teacher's assessment, these students also learned English at least as well as on the earlier, more traditional courses. A number of students who were already high achievers did extremely well. About 20 students who were low achievers clearly improved their grades. However, 14 students (all boys) did not assume an active role during the course and they also found the portfolios too distressing or too demanding, requiring too much work. They considered teacher-directed work more effective and suitable for them (Pollari 1997). This suggests that we need to be sensitive to the diverse learner needs, beliefs and expectations and see how far self-assessment is viable for the different learners. It certainly needs explicit learner guidance and support, and time for acquiring the new attitudes and skills of self-management.

If the portfolio needs to be used for more formal grading purposes, the learning portfolio can become a *showcase* (exhibition) *portfolio*. For different purposes, learners can make different choices of the documents contained in their learning portfolio for presentation in their showcase portfolios (Gottlieb 1995; Smolen, Newman, Wathen and Lee 1995).

Margo Gottlieb (1995:13) suggests the acronym 'CRADLE approach' for the portfolio development, coming from:

C = Collecting learning documents
R = Reflecting on own learning, based on documents
A = Assessing and analysing the documentary material
D = Documenting learning outcomes to others
L = Linking learning with curriculum goals
E = Evaluating learning for grading purposes

Towards the more formal end of reporting learning by personal documents and reflections, increasingly formal criteria for evaluation need to be introduced. Learners are taught how to analyse their work in terms of check-lists and/or criterion-based descriptions. They are taught to choose certain pieces out of the learning portfolio to include in the showcase portfolio and justify their choices by evidence of learning. By developing systematic guidelines, greater uniformity can be achieved within the learning institution. Learning outcomes can be linked to the institutional (and national) curriculum goals (Gottlieb 1995).

The accumulated evidence of language learning can also be demonstrated beyond the individual and classroom levels. In the expanded notion, portfolios can be used at the levels of programme, school or district, and even state evaluation. This entails moving towards a more restrictive, externally imposed portfolio system. Private documents become public and legal and can be used for educational decision-making, with appropriate caution (Gottlieb 1997). However, more research and development work needs to be conducted to explore the viability of portfolios for grading purposes, particularly beyond the classroom level.

Validity and reliability in authentic assessment

Product-oriented performance evaluation will inevitably indicate what we regard in our syllabuses as 'worth learning'. In communicative thinking this is essentially the ability and willingness to put into communicatively meaningful use whatever amount of language the learner has acquired. The evaluation criteria must therefore emphasize the opportunities for the learners to show what they can do with their language. Authentic assessment needs to be sensitive to real-life tasks of language use. For this reason the context is essential, as communication takes place in relevant contexts. Information must thus be provided about the audience, setting and purpose of the tasks. This enables the learner to activate relevant background information and expectancies associated with the topic and setting. The demand for contextual relevance is also important because of the backwash effect of tests on teaching; evaluation procedures need to encourage communicatively oriented classroom and homework (Kohonen 1992b).

Communicative thinking involves a criterion-referenced orientation, with communicative efficiency in the given context as the criterion. The specification of a sufficient level of mastery in relation to the objectives remains a difficult task. The application of the criteria to the evaluation of the learner performance is thus always a matter of subjective interpretation. This brings in the problems of reliability. It is well-known that validity and reliability are difficult to maximize in the same test. Thus, for example, while multiple-choice items eliminate problems of scorer reliability, their validity is restricted as a measure of the communicative use of the foreign language.

Valuable goals are worth evaluating. This is a question of the validity and credibility of evaluation. An important validity construct has been suggested recently by Glaser (1990): consequential validity. The concept describes the extent to which an assessment tool and the ways in which it is used can produce positive consequences for the teaching and learning process and the learners. Darling-Hammond (1994:11) makes an important point when she argues that the emerging validity standard places a burden on assessment developers and users to demonstrate that what they are doing works to the benefit of those who are assessed and to the society at large. Assessment needs to support challenging and authentic forms of teaching and learning. This is again a matter of coherence between the educational goals and assessment practices (North 1992; Kohonen 1996).

Validity must, therefore, be given the first priority in communicative evaluation. Still, evaluation must also meet sufficient requirements of reliability in order to be valid. As the test format is made more open by introducing choices and alternatives, ensuring sufficient scorer reliability becomes increasingly important. In addition to the descriptive scoring criteria, specimens of learner work at the various levels of proficiency will be necessary to ensure sufficient reliability.

Discussion: assessment reform and professional development

Possibilities and problems in authentic assessment

From the teacher's point of view, process evaluation means a conscious effort to collect information about learner progress and the social learning environment in the class. This can be based on a variety of sources: learner portfolios, observation of learners in the class, formative tests, field notes and learner interviews. This is done, of course, by all teachers in varying degrees of detail, but what is involved in authentic assessment is a more conscious and systematic approach to classroom and learner observation and document analysis, at a greater level of professional awareness and sophistication. It entails developing 'an eye' for classroom processes and becoming sensitive to individual learners. The teacher needs to invite learners to become reflective about their learning by asking proactive questions, e.g. Why might this be so? How could you justify your idea? How can you proceed from here? Such questions help them to become critically aware of their own learning (Kohonen 1992b). Informed observation and reflection can act as an important link between language learning theory and pedagogical practices.

The learner's own reflection is an important part of his learning, functioning as a bridge between practical experience and various ways of conceptualizing it. As Henry Holec (1987) pointed out, learners need to learn how to manage their learning, rather than just managing to learn. Reflective awareness is thus a significant key to develop learner autonomy. It involves self-assessment and peer assessment (in pairs or in small groups) and an attitudinal development towards self-direction.

In summary, authentic assessment can enhance learning in the following ways:

1 Assessment is an integral part of the new 'thinking' curriculum goals: complex reasoning (using ambiguous, open-ended tasks); posing questions, making judgements, considering evidence.
2 Assessment focuses on educationally and communicatively worthwhile tasks, emphasizing important learning goals.
3 Assessment is based on multiple sources of data, with a possibility of several perspectives, providing more detailed information about learner progress.
4 Assessment recognizes the learner as a unique person having multiple intelligences.
5 Assessment is ongoing and emphasizes learner strengths and initiative.
6 Assessment encourages collaboration between learners; classrooms are seen as learning communities.
7 Assessment procedures and criteria are known to learners in advance, allowing choices and preparation (exhibition portfolios).
8 Assessment encourages teachers to develop meaningful curricula, providing detailed information to guide student learning.
9 Assessment fosters intrinsic learning motivation.
10 Assessment promotes responsible, self-regulated learning.

Authentic assessment can also improve the learning atmosphere by introducing a shared management of learning and by increasing mutual trust and partnership among learners and teachers. It will increase learners' involvement and their responsibility for and ownership of their learning. It can also open an important avenue for enhancing the learner's self-esteem and feelings of efficacy as a growing person. Self-esteem is based on the learner's personal feelings of identity, belonging, security, sense of purpose and individual competence (Reasoner and Dusa 1991). Self-esteem affects learning in several ways: relating to others, taking risks, tolerating uncertainty and anxiety, and feeling able and willing to assume responsibility for life-long learning. Promoting such goals is at the heart of affective language learning. (See Wolf, Bixby, Glenn and Gardner 1991; Kohonen 1992b; Wiggins 1993; Gardner 1993; Darling-Hammond 1994; Gottlieb 1995; O'Malley and Valdez Pierce 1996.)

Authentic assessment undoubtedly has many advantages, but it also poses new problems for all the partners. While learning documentation provides rich data about learning, it is labour-intensive for the teacher to analyse thoughtfully in order to give accurate feedback to the learner. This is a problem particularly in large classes. Another difficulty is related to the learner guidance; to become more skilful in taking charge of their own learning, learners need clear guidelines and a great deal of personal supervision. In addition, learners may also resist the new practices, being accustomed to traditional language tests. They certainly need time and encouragement to learn the new skills of self-assessment.

Further questions are raised by the problem of how to grade the portfolios with sufficient reliability and consistency, owing to the variety of the learner documents and reflective abilities. By what criteria can the different documents be graded in a comparable way? How to communicate the standards of assessment to the learners? What kind of balance should there be between language proficiency, and the learner's personal and social development and the learning skills? How to assess attitudinal elements of intercultural competence, such as ambiguity tolerance, risk-taking and respect for diversity? Obviously, there are no easy answers to such questions, and the decisions need to be considered thoughtfully in the light of the instructional and educational goals in the given context.

Authentic assessment through teacher development

A recurrent theme in this chapter has been that there is an integral connection between language learning, instruction and evaluation. This entails a view of evaluation as part of a process in which the learner moves toward growth as an autonomous person. Education to enhance learner autonomy and self-esteem is part of a more general concept of values education in school. This is an ethical question of the respect for human dignity in the school community. Values education is inherent in all encounters between the learners and the school staff (Kohonen 1993).

The emerging concept of teacher professionalism emphasizes teacher autonomy and the moral nature of teaching. Professionalising teaching involves a new collegial culture in school. It involves a commitment by teachers to their own learning and the learning of others (Hargreaves 1994; Järvinen, Kohonen, Niemi and Ojanen 1995; Niemi and Kohonen 1995; Kohonen 1996). Authentic assessment provides new ways of guiding, supervising and reporting learning with an emphasis on the learner's holistic growth. It needs to be nurtured by educators working towards a community of teachers and learners.

Suggestions for further reading

Gardner, H. 1993. *Multiple Intelligences: Theory in Practice*. New York: Basic Books.

Gottlieb, M. 1995. Nurturing student learning through portfolios. *TESOL Journal*, 5, 1, 12–14.

O'Malley, M. and L. Valdez Pierce. 1996. *Authentic Assessment for English Language Learners*. New York: Addison Wesley.

Wiggins, G. 1993. *Assessing Student Performance*. San Francisco: Jossey Bass Publishers.

Wolf, D., J. Bixby, J. Glenn III and H. Gardner. 1991. To use their minds well: investigating new forms of student assessment. In G. Grant, (Ed.), *Review of Research in Education*, vol. 17. Washington, DC: American Educational Research Association, 31–74.

Part D: Questions and tasks

1 This book has presented many areas of language learning that have to do with the affective domain. Think of one aspect that is a particular concern of yours and reflect on how you might design an informal research inquiry related to this aspect which would be appropriate for your teaching situation or a situation you are familiar with.

2 If you are presently teaching, do a non-communicative exercise with your class, a pseudo-communicative exercise, and one in which there is real, meaningful communication. Observe students' behaviour during the activities, noting any significant differences. After completing the three activities, give the students an open-ended questionnaire to elicit their opinions about each. What conclusions do you come to? What new questions are raised?

3 Working alone or in a group, brainstorm ideas on how to bring aspects of the aesthetic experience into the language classroom. Choose one of these and develop it as a complete activity. Try it out with your students or present it to the group.

4 How does cooperative learning differ from traditional small-group instruction? In which language learning contexts would cooperative learning be most useful?

5 In Chapter 14 Crandall discusses possible difficulties in implementing cooperative language learning. Make a list of some of these problems that might exist in a teaching situation you know and think of a solution for each.

6 Why should language classes aim at developing social proficiency? How can cooperative learning be used to help learners develop both social and academic language proficiency? Describe how you might use some of the activities described in Chapter 14 for both of these purposes.

7 Think of a problem situation you have experienced as a teacher or student. Which of the logical levels (environment, behaviour, capabilities, belief systems, identity) discussed in Chapter 15 do you

think the problem related to? What was your evidence for that? What changes would have been helpful to correct the problem?

8 Develop a guided imagery exercise designed to help students relax, forget their problems and worries and become more centred. Try it out with a colleague or friend. Inquire about the friend's reactions and how the exercise might be improved.

9 Imagine yourself teaching a very successful class. Stay with the visualization for a few minutes, observing what happens and how you and your students feel. Afterwards, write down what you think made it so successful. What could you do to bring your present teaching closer to that ideal state?

10 What possibilities for the development of your evaluation practices are suggested to you by the concept of authentic assessment as discussed in Chapter 17? What problems might you foresee and how might you tackle them? What kind of an action plan might you outline for yourself? How could you ensure support for your action plan?

11 Imagine you are teaching in a setting that requires very traditional forms of assessment. Within such a structure, how could you incorporate aspects of authentic assessment?

12 Design an instrument for student self-evaluation for a level you know. If you are teaching now, use it with your students at two or more different moments, observing any changes in the group that might be attributed to its use.

13 Ask your students to design some forms of authentic assessment for themselves. Try them out in your class. Afterwards, discuss their effectiveness with your students.

Part E Epilogue

18 Affect in the classroom: problems, politics and pragmatics

Joy Reid

NO FEAR. I see this phrase on T-shirts, and while I do not know what it references in the lives of the young people who wear the T-shirts, for me it relates directly to teaching. If we define fear as the feelings we have and the physical responses that are triggered ('fight or flight') when we believe that we face threat to our security – public humiliation, emotional attack, or failure – it is easy to see why fear closes us to learning. Fear of the unknown abounds in the classroom, especially for students of another language, because language is so integrally related to self-confidence and self-esteem. Even in optimum conditions, students can experience destructive forms of anxiety. For example, in a linguistics class, my colleague arrives and begins teaching entirely in Greek. The students know that they are 'safe' because they know this is an experiment, it will not affect their grades, and it is very temporary, so they are happy to 'play', to learn a few words in Greek by the inductive method. However, the fatigue factor is great, and within a few minutes, the class grows quieter; then irritation and withdrawal from the experience follow.

More than thirty years of teaching English as a second language (ESL) have taught me that students studying a foreign language respond better in a positive classroom community. And the more 'fearsome' the course content, the more support and the more community building is needed to establish a positive learning environment. This chapter outlines and discusses some of the issues we must confront if we are to persuade our colleagues to implement appropriate changes in traditional, teacher-centered and test-dependent classrooms, and speculates on solutions to some of the problems, politics and pragmatics involved in affect and language learning.

Perhaps the first problem is that a positive classroom environment and students who are open to learning may not be nearly enough. For example, in a class of 25 students, usually only a handful is completely immersed in the task (what Csikszentmihalyi [1990] calls 'in the flow channel') at any one time. About half the class is attentive, but only partially involved, and half a dozen are, for a variety of reasons, 'tuned out' because they are, for example, ahead or behind the rest of the class; they are uninterested in the topic; they are suffering from cultural stress; or they didn't get enough sleep the night before. What are clear goals and 'involving materials' for some students may not be for others in the same class, and whether or not students have control over the outcomes of their learning processes may well depend, at least in part, on variables that exist outside the classroom.

So, despite the fact that I am committed to establishing and maintaining a positive atmosphere, and to building and extending a classroom community, affect alone has not been the panacea for my language learning or language teaching. Indeed, in all my years of teaching, I have had only one class in which all the students were caught up in the flow. The class went half an hour late, and not one student made a move to leave; students and the professor for the next class entered and sat on the floor, cognitively and emotionally spellbound. The content of that amazing class had nothing to do with the course; students from the class were in the front of the room, spontaneously discussing the Palestinian 'problem'; I was not the facilitator or even a participant – just a delighted observer.

Consequently, I believe that while affect seems, intuitively, to play an important part in the learning process, we need to recognize other variables, both internal and external to the classroom, to continue to investigate affect empirically, and, at the same time, to work toward changing current mindsets that prevent affect from being integrated into language programs, curricula, and lesson plans.

Problem: more research needed

Given the enormous complexity and number of variables involved in language learning, it is little wonder that our knowledge is still so limited. One problem that exists in the implementation of affect in the language classroom is that there is still basic research needed to determine the value of the entire field of study. Included would be the continued studies in the validity and reliability of self-report (and other) instruments, the neurophysiological bases for cognitive and affective learning styles and strategies, and even the commonly accepted definitions for such terms as *learning* (e.g. is it different from acquiring?), *motivation* (e.g. does intrinsic motivation exclude the teacher 'motivating' students?), *student-centered* (e.g. what level of decision-making is most effective?), and even *anxiety* (how about the 'stress for success' satisfaction that comes from doing well on an examination?). Many basic questions about the practical use of affect in teaching and learning language remain, among them:

- How can teachers 'touch' the affective and cognitive language learning styles and strategies of each student in every class?
- Can all students learn to 'flex' their language learning approaches – that is, to adopt alternate learning strategies and styles – when the need arises?
- Do students from different language and cultural backgrounds need different types of classroom environments and/or different levels of positive affect?
- Is intrinsic motivation always intrinsically better? Is it too cynical to say that real-world motivation is often based on pragmatic and extrinsic motivation?
- Is equal opportunity for a variety of learners available in foreign language classrooms?
- What about affective and cognitive styles and strategies in distance learning and on-line classes? How can we set up a community in a class that never meets face-to-face?
- Is student awareness of affect, of cognitive and affective learning styles and strategies, essential for effective learning? If so, how do teachers raise student awareness?
- What do we 'learn' at different levels? That is, in terms of the Triune Brain, what do we learn at a most basic, 'reptilian' level, from pain, flight and fight; at an emotional, 'limbic' level; as well as at the cognitive, 'neo-cortical' level, in which positive affect is most important?
- Do all students function better in a fully positive environment? Do some students learn more effectively when some anxiety or pressure is present sometimes? Is 'No pain, No gain' merely a puritan platitude?
- Is there such a thing as 'stress for success'? Might a totally positive atmosphere breed boredom rather than effective learning?
- Are some self-report (or other) affective instruments more or less effective and/or enlightening for some students?
- What do language learning students do to cope in classes that are not conducted in ways conducive to their learning and affective preferences?
- Are there affective language learning differences between different age groups?
- How (and how much) should preparation programs for language teachers teach their students about the role(s) of affect in the classroom?
- What are the best ways to provide opportunities for teachers-in-training to learn about and apply information about affect during their preparation programs?

This chapter does not answer these questions. Rather, it provides a base for understanding the problems, the politics, and the pragmatics – that is, the practical considerations – that should be confronted as future researchers encounter these issues. My hope is that many teachers will become these front-line action researchers. Because the questions surrounding the focus on positive affect in language learning are based in the classroom, who better to investigate the effects than teachers ourselves?

Fortunately, our definition of 'research' has expanded in the last decade. No longer do we confine the term to work with statistical analyses and empirical methods (although those can, of course, offer valuable insights and information). Instead, teachers are observing, making notes, identifying and testing hypotheses (regardless of what we call them) by using classroom experiences, asking students for input concerning curricular processes and for evaluation of methods and materials, using informal as well as formal survey instruments to collect information, keeping reflective journals, and sharing ideas orally.

Problem: learning styles and affect

My own classroom research in learning styles began when I recognized the diversity of learning approaches in my ESL classes. Over the last fifteen years, I have discovered the benefits of raising students' awareness about their individual learning strengths: higher interest and motivation in the learning process, increased student responsibility for their own learning, and greater classroom community. These are affective changes, and the changes have resulted in more effective learning. So I hypothesize that using learning styles can be instrumental in establishing a positive affective environment in the language learning classroom. Figure 1 provides a brief introductory overview of some learning styles that have been investigated for language learners in the last decade.

Much learning style research has demonstrated that there are substantial individual differences among students' preferred styles and their selected use of learning strategies (Reid 1987, 1995). For example, for a student who is strongly field independent, analytic and reflective (Chapelle 1995; Ehrman 1996), the audio-lingual method of teaching ESL might well hold much comfort and success. Oral fluency may be delayed, but decades of language teaching the world over has demonstrated that some students learn languages exceedingly well with that approach. In contrast, a student who is a strongly field dependent (field sensitive), global, and impulsive learner might suffer serious anxiety and

The Seven Multiple Intelligences

Verbal/Linguistic	ability with and sensitivity to words, orally and in writing
Musical	sensitivity to rhythm, pitch and melody
Logical/Mathematical	ability to use numbers effectively and reason well
Spatial/Visual	sensitivity to form, space, color, line and shape
Bodily/Kinesthetic	ability to use the body to express ideas and feelings
Interpersonal	ability to understand another person's moods and intentions
Intrapersonal	ability to understand yourself, your strengths and weaknesses

Perceptual Learning Styles

Visual	learns more effectively through the eyes (seeing)
Auditory	learns more effectively through the ear (hearing)
Tactile	learns more effectively through touch (hands-on)
Kinesthetic	learns more effectively through complete body experience
Group	learns more effectively through working with others
Individual	learns more effectively through working alone

Field Independent / Field Dependent (Sensitive) Learning Styles

Field Independent	learns more effectively sequentially, analyzing facts
Field Dependent	learns more effectively in context, holistically and is sensitive to human relationships

Analytic/Global Learning Styles

Analytic	learns more effectively individually, sequentially, linearly
Global	learns more effectively through concrete experience and through interaction with other people

Reflective/Impulsive Learning Styles

Reflective	learns more effectively when s/he has time to consider options
Impulsive	learns more effectively when s/he is able to respond immediately

Figure 1 Overview of Some Learning Styles

even failure in an audio-lingual classroom (Oxford 1997; Oxford and Green 1996).

Furthermore, although each of the styles is presented dichotomously (i.e. field independence vs. dependence, analytic vs. global, reflective vs. impulsive), the opposing pairs exist by definition on a long continuum. As students learn about their styles, they realize that they are, for instance, more or less field sensitive, global or impulsive. In another area of learning styles being currently studied, students who excel in one area of multiple intelligences (Christison 1996; Gardner 1995) – interpersonal or verbal intelligences, for example – may struggle with others, such as spatial or mathematic intelligences.

We can say the following about learning styles:

- Every person, student and teacher alike, has a learning style and learning strengths and weaknesses;
- learning styles exist on wide continuums, although they are often described as opposites;
- learning styles are value neutral; that is, no one style is better than others (although clearly students will be affected by their school systems, most of which value some learning styles over others);
- students can be encouraged to 'stretch' their learning styles so that they will be more empowered in a variety of learning situations; and
- often, students' strategies can be linked to their learning styles.

Politics: educational values and affect

There are politics related to second language learning, attitudes and cultural assumptions that impinge on the educational system: who should learn? what should be taught? how? when? where? why? Should all students learn a second language? Why or why not? What educational and cultural values underlie this answer? Should second language learning begin in elementary school? Should second language learners be taught in their first language? Should whole families (of, for instance, immigrant families) be involved in the child's second language learning? Importantly, if funds are needed for teaching this second (or additional) language (as they almost certainly are), where can they originate?

Affect and learning styles have their own ethical questions. Particularly in ESL, teachers must become sensitive to the difference between *typical* behavior and preferences and *stereotyping* students according to widely held sociocultural assumptions. After all, within a cultural group, almost certainly the variations among individuals are as great as their commonalties. However, tendencies toward classroom behavior which are culturally based are often identifiable in groups of students. For example, Japanese EFL students have been described as group-oriented, focused on consensual decision-making, reserved, formal and cautious; these characteristics emerge from schooling – they are stressed even in Japanese pre-schools (Anderson 1995; Lewis 1991; Peak 1991). The characteristics preferred by North American educators and students – self-reliance, frankness, informality, spontaneity, and gregariousness (Barnlund 1975) – seem in direct contrast. Yet we all know US students who are reserved planners, who interact with difficulty in the classroom, and who prefer cooperation and harmony to conflict and confrontation. And we know Japanese students who are gregarious and self-confident, direct and decisive, who enjoy arguing more than consensus building.

Then there are the politics of higher education: the old saying, 'It's easier to move a graveyard than it is to change anything in academe' holds. In the US, for example, most university classes are teacher-fronted and teacher-centered; students are graded on paper performance (tests and projects), and perhaps on class participation. Cooperative and collaborative work has gained some popularity among professors (sometimes for the wrong reasons, such as having fewer written projects to grade), but students are often resistant, even recalcitrant, about working with others for a single grade. Student achievement is based almost solely on grades, and examinations for college and professional schools are indirect, discrete-point tests that measure (and reflect the educational values of) the objective and accurate information of independent, analytic learners.

Despite all these potential barriers to the implementation of education values that include the use of affect and of individual language learning preferences in the classroom, in recent years I've grown increasingly aware of how much my students know, how eager they are to learn more about themselves and their language learning strengths and strategies, and how much responsibility they are capable of taking for their own learning. As a result, I have focused specifically on student responsibility and classroom community; however, the politics of the classroom impinge on the success or failure of my efforts.

In my international student ESL writing classes, I have been dramatically successful. These students, many of whom are risk-takers and flexible learners (else they might not have chosen to study in a second language environment), understand that the culture may make unusual demands on them; moreover, they have a need for community (in this strange country). They therefore adapt to my requests to establish a community, to work in pairs and groups, to make use of multiple audiences like writing center personnel and peer tutors, and even to interview university officials about campus problems. In my senior-level native English speaker classes, however, I have been a dismal failure. My Introduction to Linguistics students are more than reluctant to participate in classroom group work and collaborative presentations, and to meet with an international student weekly to discuss language and culture. Most of these students are in their final semester of university work; they are taking the course as a requirement and would never choose it as an elective; most have experienced teacher-fronted classes throughout their academic careers, and most have flourished, independently and analytically, in that classroom environment. As a consequence, they have not developed flexible learning styles and a spirit of experimentation. Rather, they focus on completing the class with the best possible grade in the most expedient way. They are interested neither in the community of the classroom nor in taking responsibility for their own learning.

I must say that I can hardly blame them. Only a rare student would enter a required class in a field in which she has little interest and be willing to make seminal changes in what previously has been a successful learning career. Indeed, I have begun to modify my organization of that class, returning to my more teacher-fronted, teacher-responsible classrooms of the past. In practical terms, one cannot, after all, change the world in a semester, and student needs in this class clearly differ from my current philosophy of teaching.

Pragmatics: the change process

My work with the processes of change has provided me with rather clear explanations for the problems in my linguistics class (Reid 1992, 1994). I have learned that education is change, but change, in reality, is not easy, and the more numerous or complex the changes, the more time and resources are needed. It is clear, for instance, that I need to slow the pace of change in my linguistics class if I am to persuade the students to be more responsible and community-minded.

As change agents, teachers need to understand that change occurs in individuals first, and only then in classrooms, institutions and countries. If, for example, we want to 'educate' students, administrators and curriculum/materials designers to integrate knowledge of affect into their work, we must consider the complexity of such a change, taking into account the essential time, patience and resources needed to bring it about.

Research has also demonstrated that people do not change unless they can see the benefit of that change, whether we are talking about taking a different route to school, learning to use topic sentences, or

Stage	Typical reaction	Intervention strategy
Awareness (Yawn)	'I'm not really interested.'	Introduce; don't push
Information	'What does it mean?'	Answer questions
Personal	'How will it benefit me?'	(Crucial stage) Empathy
Management	'How can I do it?'	Time, resources support
Consequences	'How do others do it?'	Opportunities for sharing
Collaboration	'I did it and it works!'	Use to persuade others
Refocusing	'I've got a better way to do it.'	Encourage

Figure 2 Overview of the Change Process

implementing research results in a classroom. Of course, people may appear to change: they *behave* – temporarily – but they do not *become*. If we want our students to become lifelong learners, then we must aim for long-term cognitive and affective change. Therefore, we must learn more about the stages of change and about appropriate intervention during the change processes. Figure 2 gives an overview of one model of the stages of change.

Conclusion

Knowledge is power. For teachers, learning more about the complexities of learning, both cognitive and affective, can only help our professional growth and personal satisfaction. A teacher who truly understands the importance of affect in the classroom, and who believes that all students can learn, can offer opportunities for success to all students (Guild 1994). Teachers also have the responsibility to ask students about their learning strengths and then to listen. My own experience is that informed students are able to articulate their needs, both affective and cognitive, to summarize their styles and strategies, and to offer suggestions that are in their best language learning interests.

Raising student awareness of affect in the language learning classroom can provide the scaffolding for more effective and efficient learning. A broad understanding of learning environments, learning styles and learning strategies can allow students to take control of their learning and maximize their potential for learning. Asking students to evaluate their language learning experiences and to be accountable for their own learning increases their sense of both freedom and responsibility. Students need time to investigate and experience resources that enable them to experiment and discuss, and they need the opportunity to evaluate what they are learning about learning. Moreover, students can comprehend (and are generally fascinated by) how learning processes occur, what choices they have in these processes, and how they can identify their learning strengths and weaknesses. They become self-motivators who are supported by their classroom community. The result can be educated students who are able to participate fully in society, both freely and responsibly: students ready for change.

References

Aaronson, E. 1978. *The Jigsaw Classroom*. Beverly Hills, CA: Sage Publications.

Adler, R. S. 1987. Culture shock and the cross-cultural learning experience. In L. F. Luce and E. C. Smith (Eds.) *Toward Internationalism: Readings in Cross-cultural Communication* (2nd ed.) New York: Newbury House.

Aida, Y. 1994. Examination of Horwitz, Horwitz and Cope's construct of foreign language anxiety: The case of students of Japanese. *Modern Language Journal*, 78, 155–168.

Allen, P., B. Wallace and F. Loschiavo. 1994. Influence of imaging ability on word transformation. *Memory and Cognition*, 22/5, 565–574.

Allwright, R. L. 1983. Classroom-centered research on language teaching and learning: a brief historical overview. *TESOL Quarterly* 17, 191–204.

Anderson, J. A. 1995. Toward a framework for matching teaching and learning styles for diverse populations. In R. S. Sims and S. J. Sims (Eds.) *The Importance of Learning Styles: Understanding the Implications for Learning, Course Design, and Education*. Westport, Connecticut: Greenwood Press.

Anderson, J. R. 1984. Spreading activation. In Anderson, J. R. and S. Kosslyn (Eds.) *Tutorials in Learning and Memory*. San Francisco: Freeman.

Andreas, S. and C. Faulkner. 1996. *NLP. The New Technology of Achievement*. London: Nicholas Brealey.

Andrini, B. 1990. *Cooperative Learning and Mathematics: A Multi-structural Approach*. San Juan Capistrano: Kagan Cooperative Learning.

Ard, J. 1989. A constructivist perspective on non-native phonology. In S. M. Gass and J. Schachter (Eds.) *Linguistic Perspectives on Second Language Acquisition*. New York: Cambridge University Press.

Arendt, H. 1978. *The Life of the Mind. Thinking*. Vol. 1. New York: Harcourt Brace Jovanovich.

Armstrong, T. 1994. *Multiple Intelligences in the Classroom*. Alexandria, VA: Association for Supervision and Curriculum Development.

Arnold, J. 1994. La ansiedad en la comprensión auditiva: una posible solución. In A. Bruton and J. Arnold (Eds.) *Lingüística Aplicada al Aprendizaje del Inglés*. Alcalá de Guadaira: CEP.

1998. Towards more humanistic language teaching. *ELT Journal*, 52, 3, 235–242.

References

Asher, J. 1977. *Learning Another Language through Actions: The Complete Teacher's Guidebook*. Los Gatos, CA: Sky Oaks Productions.

Assagioli, R. 1968. *Come si imparano le lingue con il inconscio*. Firenze: Istituto di Psicosintesi.

Avila, J. 1997. La motivación en la lectura en una segunda lengua: Preferencias en los temas de lectura. Unpublished Master's thesis, University of Seville.

Bailey, F. 1996. The role of collaborative dialogue in teacher education. In Freeman, D. and J. Richards, *Teacher Learning in Language Teaching*. Cambridge: Cambridge University Press.

Bailey, K. M. 1983. Competitiveness and anxiety in adult second language learning: Looking at and through the diary studies. In H. W. Seliger and M. H. Long (Eds.) *Classroom-oriented Research in Second Language Acquisition*. Rowley, MA: Newbury House.

1991. Diary studies of classroom language learning: The doubting game and the believing game. In E. Sadtons (Ed.) *Language Acquisition and the Second/Foreign Language Classroom*. Singapore: SEAMEO Regional Language Centre.

Bailey, K. M. and R. Ochsner. 1983. A methodological review of the diary studies: Windmill tilting or social science? In K. M. Bailey, M. H. Long and S. Peck (Eds.) *Second Language Acquisition Studies*. Rowley, MA: Newbury House, 188–198.

Barber, E. 1980. Language acquisition and applied linguistics. *ADFL Bulletin*, 12, 26–32.

Barbou, A. 1972. The self-disclosure aspect of the psychodrama sharing session. *Group Psychotherapy and Psychodrama*, 25, 132–138.

Barnlund, D. C. 1975. *Communicative Styles of Two Cultures*. Tokyo: Kinseido.

Bartlett, F. C. 1932. *Remembering: a Study in Experimental and Social Psychology*. London: Cambridge University Press.

Bedford, D. 1985. Spontaneous playback of the second language. *Foreign Language Annals*, 18, 279–287.

Beebe, L. M. 1983. Risk-taking and the language learner. In H. W. Seliger and M. H. Long (Eds.) *Classroom-oriented Research in Second Language Acquisition*. Rowley, MA: Newbury House.

Bejarano, Y. 1987. A cooperative small-group methodology in the language classroom. *TESOL Quarterly*, 21, 483–504.

Bell, D. 1997. Dance and the power of kinesthetic learning. Paper at TESOL Conference, March, Orlando, USA

Bennett, B., C. Rolheiser-Bennett and L. Stevahn. 1991. *Cooperative Learning: Where Heart Meets Mind*. Toronto: Educational Connections.

Benson, H. 1975. *Relaxation Response*. New York: William Morrow.

1996. *Timeless Healing*. New York: Scribner.

Benson, P. 1996. Concepts of autonomy in language learning. In R. Pemberton, E. S. L. Li, W. W. F. Or and H. D. Pierson (Eds.) *Taking Control: Autonomy in Language Learning*. Hong Kong: Hong Kong University Press.

1997. The philosophy and politics of learner autonomy. In P. Benson and P. Voller (Eds.) *Autonomy and Independence in Language Learning*. New York: Addison Wesley Longman.

Benson, P. and P. Voller (Eds.) 1997. *Autonomy and Independence in Language Learning*. New York: Addison Wesley Longman.

Bentov, I. 1978. *Stalking the Wild Pendulum*. London:Wildwood House.

Berger, P. L. and T. Luckmann. 1966. *The Social Construction of Reality: A Treatise In the Sociology of Knowledge*. New York: Doubleday.

Bernstein, D. A., E. J. Roy, T. K. Srull and C. D. Wikens. 1991. *Psychology* (2nd ed.) Boston: Houghton Mifflin.

Bernstein, H. 1989. The courage to try: Self-esteem and learning. In K. Field, B. J. Cohler and G. Wool (Eds.) *Learning and Education: Psychoanalytic Perspectives*. Madison, CT: International Universities Press.

Besnier, N. 1990. Language and affect. *Annual review of Anthropology*, 19, 419–51.

Bloom, B. 1964. *Stability and Change in Human Characteristics*. New York: John Wiley & Sons.

Blubaugh, J. A. 1969. Effects of positive and negative audience feedback on selected variables of speech behavior. *Speech Monographs*, 36, 131–137.

Borba, M. 1989. *Esteem Builders*. Rolling Hills Estates, CA: Jalmar Press.

Borba, M. and C. Borba. 1978. *Self-Esteem: A Classroom Affair: 101 Ways to Help Children Like Themselves*. Vol 1. San Francisco: HarperCollins.

1982. *Self-Esteem: A Classroom Affair: More Ways to Help Children Like Themselves*. Vol 2. San Francisco: HarperCollins.

Boud, D. 1981. Toward student responsibility for learning. In D. Boud (Ed.) *Developing Student Autonomy in Learning*. London: Kogan Page.

Branden, N. 1987. *How to Raise your Self-Esteem*. New York: Bantam Books.

Brandes, D. and P. Ginnis. 1986. *A Guide to Student-Centered Learning*. Oxford: Basil Blackwell.

Breen, M. P. and S. J. Mann. 1997. Shooting arrows at the sun: perspectives on a pedagogy for autonomy. In P. Benson and P. Voller (Eds.) *Autonomy and Independence in Language Learning*. New York: Addison Wesley Longman.

Brickner, R. M. 1936. *The Intellectual Functions of the Frontal Lobes: Study Based upon Observation of a Man after Partial Bilateral Frontal Lobectomy*. NY: Macmillan.

Brookfield, S. 1993. Self-directed learning, political clarity and the critical practice of adult education. *Adult Education Quarterly*, 43/4, 227–242.

Brothers, L. 1995. Neurophysiology of the perception of intentions by primates. In M. S. Gazzaniga (Ed.) *The Cognitive Neurosciences*. Cambridge, MA: MIT Press.

Brown, G. 1971. *Human Teaching for Human Learning. An Introduction to Confluent Education*. New York: The Viking Press.

Brown, H. D. 1990. M & Ms for language classrooms? Another look at motivation. In J. E. Alatis (Ed.) *Georgetown University Round Table on Languages and Linguistics 1990*. Washington, DC: Georgetown University Press.

1991. *Breaking the Language Barrier*. Yarmouth, ME: Intercultural Press.

1994a. *Principles of Language Learning and Teaching*, (3rd ed.) Englewood Cliffs, NJ: Prentice Hall Regents.

1994b. *Teaching by Principles: Interactive Language Teaching Methodology*. New York: Prentice Hall Regents.

Brown, N. W. 1994. *Group Counseling for Elementary and Middle School Children*. Westport, CT: Praeger.

Brundage, D. and D. MacKeracher. 1980. *Adult Learning Principles and their Application to Program Planning*. Ontario: Ontario Institute for Studies in Education.

Bruner, J. 1962. *On Knowing: Essays for the Left Hand*. Cambridge, MA: Harvard University Press.

Bruner, J. 1996. *The Culture of Education*. Cambridge, MA: Harvard University Press.

Burbidge, N., P. Gray, S. Levy and M. Rinvolucri. 1996. *Letters*. Oxford: Oxford University Press.

Buxton, L. 1981. *Do You Panic About Maths?* London: Heinemann.

Buzan, T. 1991. *Use Both Sides of Your Brain*. New York: Plume.

Calderon, M., R. Hertz-Lazarowitz and J. Tinajero. 1991. Adapting CIRC to multiethnic and bilingual classrooms, *Cooperative Learning*, 12, 17–20.

Campos, A. and M. A. González. 1995. Effects of mental imagery on creative perception. *Journal of Mental Imagery*, 19, 67–76.

Candlin, C. 1987. Towards task-based language learning. In C. Candlin and D. Murphy (Eds.) *Language Learning Tasks*. Englewood Cliffs, NJ: Prentice Hall, Inc.

Canfield, J. and H. C. Wells. 1976. *One Hundred Ways to Enhance Self-Concept in the Classroom: A Handbook for Teachers and Parents*. Englewood Cliffs, NJ: Prentice-Hall.

1994. *100 Ways to Enhance Self-Concept in the Classroom*. Boston: Allyn and Bacon.

Capra, F. 1982. *The Turning Point: Science, Society and the Rising Culture*. New York: Simon & Schuster.

Carroll, B. and R. West. 1989. *ESU Framework. Performance scales for English language examinations*. London: Longman.

Castillo, G. 1973. *Left-handed Teaching. Lessons in Affective Education*. New York: Holt.

Chamot, A. 1995. Creating a community of thinkers in the ESL/EFL classroom. *TESOL Matters*, 1, 4.

Chamot, A. and J. M. O'Malley. 1987. The cognitive academic language learning approach: A bridge to the mainstream. *TESOL Quarterly*, 21, 227–249.

Chapelle, C. A. 1995. Field-Dependence/Field Independence in the L2 classroom. In J. Reid (Ed.) *Learning Styles in the ESL/EFL Classroom*. Boston: Heinle & Heinle.

Chapelle, C. A. and C. Roberts. 1986. Ambiguity tolerance and field independence as predictors of proficiency in English as a second language. *Language Learning*, 36, 27–45.

Chaplin, J. P. 1975. *Dictionary of Psychology*, Revised Edition. New York: Dell.

Chastain, K. 1975. Affective and ability factors in second language learning. *Language Learning*, 25, 153–161.

Chomsky, N. 1988. *Language and Problems of Knowledge*. Cambridge, MA: MIT Press.

Christison, M. A. 1996. Teaching and learning languages through Multiple Intelligences. *TESOL Journal 6*, 1, 10–14.

　1997. Emotional intelligence and second language teaching. *TESOL Matters*, 7, 3, 3.

Clarke, M. A. 1976. Second language acquisition as a clash of consciousness. *Language Learning*, 26, 377–389.

Claxton, G. 1989. *Being a Teacher*. London: Cassell.

Clément, R., Z. Dörnyei and K. Noels. 1994. Motivation, self-confidence and group cohesion in the foreign language classroom. *Language Learning*, 44, 417–448.

Clynes, M. 1982. *Music, Mind and Brain: The Neuropsychology of Music*. New York: Plenum Press.

　1991. On Music and Healing. In D. Campbell (Ed.) *Music: Physician for Times to Come*. New York: Quest Books.

Coelho, E. 1992. Cooperative learning: Foundation for a communicative curriculum. In C. Kessler (Ed.) *Cooperative Language Learning*. Englewood Cliffs, NJ: Prentice Hall Regents.

Coelho, E., L. Winer and J. W. Olsen. 1989. *All Sides of the Issue: Activities for Cooperative Groups*. Englewood Cliffs, NJ: Prentice Hall Regents.

Cohen, E. G. 1987. *Can Classrooms Learn?* Palo Alto, CA: Stanford University Press.

　1994a. *Designing groupwork: Strategies for the Heterogeneous Classroom* (2nd ed.). New York: Teachers College, Columbia University.

　1994b. Restructuring the classroom: Conditions for productive small groups. *Review of Educational Research*, 64, 1–35.

Cohen, E. G. and J. K. Intili. 1981. *Interdependence and Management in Bilingual Classrooms: Final Report 1*. Stanford, CA: Center for Educational Research.

Cohen, L. and L. Manion. 1994. *Research Methods in Education* (4th ed.). London: Routledge.

Cohler, B. J. 1989. Psychoanalysis and education: Motive, meaning, and self. In K. Field, B. J. Cohler and G. Wool (Eds.) *Learning and Education: Psychoanalytic Perspectives*. Madison, CT: International Universities Press.

Common European Framework of reference for modern languages: learning, teaching, assessment, 1996. Draft 2 of a Framework proposal. Strasbourg: Council of Europe, Council of Cultural Cooperation.

Coopersmith, S. 1967. *The Antecedents of Self-Esteem*. San Francisco: Freeman & Co.

Crandall, J. A. (Ed.) 1987. *ESL through Content-area Instruction: Mathematics, Science, and Social Studies*. Englewood Cliffs, NJ: Prentice Hall Regents.

References

Crandall, J. A. and G. R. Tucker. 1990. Content-based language instruction in second and foreign languages. In A. Sanivan (Ed.) *Language Teaching Methodology for the Nineties*. Singapore: SEAMEO Regional Language Centre.

Crookes, G., and R. Schmidt. 1991. Motivation: Reopening the research agenda. *Language Learning*, 41, 469–512.

Cruickshank, D. 1987. *Reflective Teaching*. Reston, VA: Association of Teacher Educators.

Csikszentmihalyi, M. 1990. *Flow. The Psychology of Optimal Experience*. New York: Harper Perennial.

Csikszentmihalyi, M. and I. Csikzsentmihalyi. 1988. *Optimal experience: Psychological Studies of Flow in Consciousness*. New York: Cambridge University Press.

Cummins, J. 1991. Interdependence of first- and second-language proficiency in bilingual children. In E. Bialystok (Ed.) *Language Processing in Bilingual Children*. New York: Cambridge University Press.

Curran, C. A. 1972. *Counseling-Learning: A Whole Person Model for Education*. New York: Grune & Stratton.

1976. *Counseling-Learning in Second Languages*. Apple River, IL: Apple River Press.

Dam, L. 1994. How do we recognize an autonomous classroom? *Die Neueren Sprachen*, 93, 5, 503–527.

1995. *Learner Autonomy 3: From Theory to Classroom Practice*. Dublin: Authentik.

Damasio, A. 1994. *Descartes' Error: Emotion, Reason and the Human Brain*. New York: Avon.

Darling-Hammond, L. 1994. Performance-based assessment and educational equity. *Harvard Educational Review*, 64, 1, 5–30.

Davies, D. 1986. *Maximizing Examination Performance*. London: Kogan Page.

Dawkins, R. 1988. *The Blind Watchmaker*. London: Longman.

de Andrés, V. 1993. *Self-Esteem in the Classroom*. Unpublished classroom research. College of Preceptors.

1995. *Developing Self-Esteem in the Primary School: A Pilot Study*. Unpublished study. Oxford Brookes University.

De Avila, E. A., S. E. Duncan and C. Navarrete. 1987. *Finding out/Descubrimiento*. Northvale, NJ: Santillana.

De Porter, B. with M. Hernacki. 1995. *Quantum Learning*. London: Piatkus.

de Guerrero, M. 1987. The din phenomenon: Mental rehearsal of the second language. *Foreign Language Annals*, 20, 537–548.

DeBolt, V. 1994. *Write! Cooperative Learning & the Writing Process*. San Juan Capistrano, CA: Kagan Cooperative Learning.

Deci, E. 1992. The relation of interest to the motivation of behavior: A self-determination theory perspective. In Renniger, K., S. Hidi. and A. Krapp (Eds.), *The Role of Interest in Learning and Development*. Hillsdale, NJ: Lawrence Erlbaum.

Deci, E. and R. Ryan. 1985. *Intrinsic Motivation and Self-Determination in Human Behavior.* New York: Plenum.

Delpit, L. 1988. The silenced dialogue: power and pedagogy in educating other people's children. *Harvard Educational Review,* 58, 3, 280–298.

Desrochers, A. and R. C. Gardner. 1981. *Second language acquisition: An investigation of a bicultural excursion experience.* Quebec: International Centre for Research on Bilingualism.

Dewey, J. 1916. *Democracy and Education.* New York: The Free Press.

1933. *How We Think.* Chicago: Henry Regnery and Co.

1963. *Experience and Education.* New York: Collier Books.

Dhority, L. 1984. *Acquisition Through Creative Teaching: ACT.* Sharon, MA: Center for Continuing Development.

Diamond, M. 1988. *Enriching Heredity: The Impact of the Environment on the Anatomy of the Brain.* New York: Free Press.

Dilts, R. 1990. *Changing Belief Systems with NLP.* Capitola, CA: Meta Publications.

1991. *Tools for Dreamers. Strategies for Creativity and the Structure of Innovation.* Capitola, CA: Meta Publications.

1996. *Visionary Leadership Skills. Creating a world to which people want to belong.* Capitola, CA: Meta Publications.

Dilts, R., T. Holborn and S. Smith. 1990. *Beliefs: Pathways to Health and Well-Being.* Portland, Oregon: Metamorphous Press.

Dixon, N. F. 1981. *Preconscious Processing.* Chichester: John Wiley & Sons.

Donahue, M. and A. Parsons. 1982. The use of roleplay to overcome cultural fatigue. *TESOL Quarterly,* 16, 359–65.

Dörnyei, Z. 1990. Conceptualizing motivation in foreign language learning. *Language Learning,* 40, 45–78.

1994. Motivation and motivating in the foreign language classroom. *Modern Language Journal,* 78, iii, 273–284.

1996. Ten commandments for motivating language learners. Paper presented at TESOL, Chicago.

In press. Psychological processes in cooperative language learning: Group dynamics and motivation. *Modern Language Journal,* 81.

Dörnyei, Z. and A. Malderez. 1997. Group dynamics and foreign language teaching. *System,* 25, 65–81.

Drose, G. and G. Allen. 1994. The role of visual imagery in the retention of information from sentences. *Journal of General Psychology,* 121/1, 37–60.

Dufeu, B. 1994. *Teaching Myself.* Oxford: Oxford University Press.

1996. *Les Approches non conventionnelles des Langues étrangères.* Paris. Hachette Livre.

Dulay, H., M. Burt and S. Krashen. 1982. *Language Two.* Oxford: Oxford University Press.

Edelman, G. M. 1992. *Bright Air Brilliant Fire: On the Matter of the Mind.* NY: Basic Books.

Edwards, C. H. 1997. *Classroom Discipline and Management.* Upper Saddle River, NJ: Prentice Hall.

References

Ehrman, M. 1993. Ego boundaries revisited: Toward a model of personality and learning. In J. E. Alatis (Ed.) *Strategic Interaction and Language Acquisition: Theory, Practice, and Research*. Washington, DC: Georgetown University.

1994. Weakest and strongest learners in intensive language training: A study of extremes. In C. Klee (Ed.) *Faces In a Crowd: Individual Learners in Multisection Programs*. Boston: Heinle & Heinle.

1995. Personality, language learning aptitude, and program structure. In J. Alatis (Ed.) *Linguistics and the Education of Second Language Teachers. Ethnolinguistic, Psycholinguistic, and Sociolinguistic Aspects*. Washington, DC: Georgetown University.

1996. *Understanding Second Language Learning Difficulties: Looking Beneath the Surface*. Thousand Oaks, CA: Sage.

1998. The learning alliance: conscious and unconscious aspects of the second language teacher's role. *System*, 26, 1, 93–106.

In press Affect and cognition in learner self-regulation in language learning. In O. Kagan and B. Rifkin (Eds.) The Learning and Teaching of Slavic Languages and Cultures: Towards the 21st Century. Bloomington, IN: Slavica.

Ehrman M. and R. Oxford. 1990. Adult language learning styles and strategies in an intensive training setting. *Modern Language Journal*, 74, 3, 311–327.

1995. Cognition plus: Correlates of adult language proficiency. *Modern Language Journal*, 79, 67–89.

Ehrman, M. and Z. Dörnyei. 1998. *Interpersonal Dynamics in Second Language Education: The Visible and Invisible Classroom*. Thousand Oaks, CA: Sage.

Ellis, R. 1995. *Questioning Consciousness: The Interplay of Imagery, Cognition and Emotion in the Human Brain*. Amsterdam: John Benjamins.

Ellsworth, E. 1992. Why doesn't this feel empowering? Working through the repressive myths of critical pedagogy. In C. Luke and J. Gore (Eds.) *Feminisms and Critical Pedagogy*. New York: Routledge.

Elson, M. 1989. The teacher as learner, the learner as teacher. In K. Field, B. J. Cohler and G. Wool (Eds.) *Learning and Education: Psychoanalytic Perspectives*. Madison CT: International Universities Press.

Ely, C. 1986. An analysis of discomfort, risktaking, sociability, and motivation in the L2 classroom. *Language Learning*, 36, 1–25.

1989. Tolerance of ambiguity and use of second language strategies. *Foreign Language Annals*, 22, 437–446.

Evans, C. R. and K. L. Dion. 1991. Group cohesion and performance: A meta-analysis. *Small Group Research*, 22, 175–186.

Eysenck, M. W. 1979. Anxiety, learning and memory: A reconceptualization. *Journal of Research in Personality*, 13, 363–385.

Fancelli, V. and A. Vidal-Folch. 1997. Yehudi Menuhin. *El País Semanal* (May 4), 32–37.

Fehr, B. and J. A. Russell. 1984. Concept of emotion viewed from a prototype perspective. *Journal of Experimental Psychology: General*, 113, 464–86.

Feuerstein, R., P. S. Klein and A. J. Tannenbaum. 1991. *Mediated Learning Experience: theoretical, psychological and learning implications*. London: Freund.

Flanders, N. A. 1970. *Analyzing Teacher Behavior*. Reading, MA: Addison Wesley.

Fogarty, R. 1994. *The Mindful School. How to Teach for Metacognitive Reflection*. Palantine, IL: IRI/ Skylight.

Fontana, D. 1988. *Psychology for Teachers* (2nd ed.) London: The British Psychological Society in association with Macmillan Publishers Ltd.

Forsyth, D. R. 1990. *Group Dynamics* (2nd ed.) Pacific Grove, CA: Brooks/ Cole Publishing Company.

Foss, K. A. and A. C. Reitzel. 1988. A relational model for managing second language learning anxiety. *TESOL Quarterly*, 22, 437–454.

Foster, R. P. 1992. Psychoanalysis and the bilingual patient: some observations on the influence of language choice on the transference. *Psychoanalytic Psychology*, 9 (1), 61–76.

Fradd, S. H. and P. Larrinaga McGee with D. K. Wilen. 1994. *Instructional Assessment*. Reading, MA: Addison Wesley.

Frank, C. and M. Rinvolucri. 1987. *Grammar in Action Again*. Hemel Hempstead: Prentice Hall International, in association with Pilgrims.

Fraser, B. J. 1994. Classroom environments. In *The International Encyclopedia of Education* (2nd ed., Vol. 2) Oxford: Pergamon Press.

Fraser, B. J. and H. J. Walberg (Eds.) 1991. *Educational Environments: Evaluation, Antecedents and Consequences*. Oxford: Pergamon Press.

Freeman, D. 1992. Collaboration: Constructing shared understandings in a second language classroom. In D. Nunan (Ed.) *Collaborative Language Learning and Teaching*. Cambridge: Cambridge University Press.

Freire, P. 1972. *The Pedagogy of the Oppressed*. Harmondsworth: Penguin.

Freud, S. 1900. *The Interpretation of Dreams*. Standard edition, Vol. 4. London: Hogarth Press and the Institute of Psycho-Analysis.

Freudenstein, R. 1992. Communicative peace. *English Today, 31*, 3–8.

Gaffan, D. 1992. Amygdala and memory of reward. In J. P. Aggleton (Ed.), *The Amygdala*. New York: Wiley-Liss.

Gaies, S. 1983. *Peer Involvement in Language Learning*. Orlando, FL: Harcourt Brace Jovanovich.

Galyean, B. 1977a. *The Effects of a Confluent Language Curriculum on the Oral and Written Communication Skills, Self-Identity and Esteem, Attitudes, and Interpersonal Relationships of Junior and Senior High School French and Spanish Students*. Research report, Confluent Education Research Center, Santa Barbara, CA.

1977b. *The Effects of a Confluent Language Curriculum on the Oral and Written Communication Skills and Various Aspects of Personal and Interpersonal Growth on a College French Level One Class*. Diss., Univ. of California, Santa Barbara.

Ganschow, L., R. L. Sparks, R. Anderson, J. Javorsky, S. Skinner and J. Patton. 1994. Differences in language performance among high-, average-, and low-anxious college foreign language learners. *Modern Language Journal*, 78, 41–55.

Gardner, H. 1983. *Frames of Mind: The Theory of Multiple Intelligences*. New York: Basic Books.

1993. *Multiple Intelligences: The Theory in Practice*. New York: Basic Books.

1995. Reflections on multiple intelligences: Myths and messages. *Phi Delta Kappa* 77, 200–209.

Gardner, R. C. 1985. *Social Psychology and Second Language Learning: The Role of Attitudes and Motivation*. London: Edward Arnold.

1988. Attitudes and motivation. *Annual Review of Applied Linguistics*, 9, 135–148.

Gardner, R. C., R. N. Lalonde, R. Moorcroft and F. Evers. 1987. Second language attrition: The role of motivation and use. *Journal of Language and Social Psychology*, 6, 29–47.

Gardner, R. C. and W. Lambert. 1972. *Attitudes and Motivation in Second Language Learning*. Rowley, MA: Newbury House.

Gardner, R. C. and P. D. MacIntyre. 1993. On the measurement of affective variables in second language learning. *Language Learning*, 43, 157–194.

Gattegno, C. 1972. *Teaching Foreign Languages in Schools: The Silent Way*. New York: Educational Solutions.

1976. *The Common Sense of Teaching Foreign Languages*. New York: Educational Solutions.

Ghiselin, B. 1952. *The Creative Process*. New York: Mentor.

Glaser, R. 1990. *Testing and assessment: O tempora! O mores!* Pittsburgh, PA: University of Pittsburgh.

Goleman, D. 1995. *Emotional Intelligence*. New York: Bantam Books.

1997. *Healing Emotions*. Boston: Shambhala.

Good, T. L. and J. E. Brophy. 1986. School Effects. In M. Wittrock (Ed.) *Handbook for Research on Teaching*. New York: John Wiley & Sons.

Goodey, N. 1997. Grammar practice and presentation in context. *English Teaching Professional*, 5, 7–8.

Goodlad, J. 1984. *A Place Called School*. New York: McGraw Hill.

Gottlieb, M. 1995. Nurturing student learning through portfolios. *TESOL Journal*, 5, 1, 12–14.

1997. A peek into portfolio practices. In A. Huhta, V. Kohonen, L. Kurki-Suonio and S. Luoma (Eds.) Current developments and alternatives in language assessment: proceedings of the LTRC 1996 in Tampere. University of Jyväskylä: Center for Applied Language Studies.

Greenson, R. R. 1978a. The mother tongue and the mother. In R. R. Greenson, *Explorations In Psychoanalysis* (31–43) (collected papers). New York: International Universities Press. Reprinted from *International Journal of Psycho-Analysis*, 31, 18–23 (1950).

1978b. The origin and fate of new ideas in psychoanalysis. In R. R. Greenson. *Explorations in Psychoanalysis* (333–357) (collected papers). New York: International Universities Press. Reprinted from *International Journal of Psycho-Analysis*, 50, 503–515 (1969).

Greenspan, S. 1989. Emotional intelligence. In K. Field, B. J. Cohler and G. Wool (Eds.) *Learning and Education: Psychoanalytic Perspectives.* Madison, CT: International Universities Press.

Gremmo, M. J. and P. Riley. 1995. Autonomy, self-direction and self-access in language teaching and learning: The history of an idea. *System,* 23, 2, 151–164.

Griggs, D. 1996. Spirit of learning: An exploration into personal/spiritual development within the learning/teaching process. Unpublished MSc. thesis, University of Hawkesbury.

Grinder, M. 1991. *Righting the Educational Conveyor Belt.* Portland, OR: Metamorphous Press.

Gross, R. 1992. Lifelong learning in the learning society of the twenty-first century. In C. Collins and J. Mangieri (Eds.) *Teaching Thinking: An Agenda for the Twenty-First Century.* Hillsdale, NJ: Lawrence Erlbaum.

Gudykunst, W. and S. Ting-Toomey. 1988. *Culture and Interpersonal Communication.* Newbury Park: Sage Publications.

Guild, P. 1994. The culture/learning style connection. *Educational Leadership,* May, 126–21.

Guiora, A. 1972. Construct validity and transpositional research: Toward an empirical study of psychoanalytic concepts. *Comprehensive Psychiatry,* 13, 139–150.

1981. Language, personality, and culture, or the Whorfian hypothesis revisited. In M. Hines and W. Rutherford (Eds.) *On TESOL '81.* Detroit, MI: Teachers of English to Speakers of Other Languages.

1984. The dialectic of language acquisition. *Language Learning,* 34 1, 3–12.

Guiora, A., W. Acton, R. Erard, and F. Strickland. 1980. The effects of benzodiazepine (Valium) on permeability of ego boundaries. *Language Learning,* 30, 351–363.

Guiora, A., B. Beit-Hallami, R. Brannon, C. Dull, and T. Scovel. 1972. The effects of experimentally induced changes in ego states on pronunciation ability in second language: An exploratory study. *Comprehensive Psychology,* 13.

Guiora A., R. Brannon and C. Dull. 1972. Empathy and second language learning. *Language Learning,* 22, 111–130.

Gully, S. M., D. J. Devine and D. J. Whitney. 1995. A meta-analysis of cohesion and performance: Effects on level of analysis and task interdependence. *Small Group Research,* 26, 497–520.

Gurney, P. 1987. Self-Esteem Enhancement in Children: a review of research findings, *Educational Research,* 29.

Hadfield, J. 1992. *Classroom Dynamics.* Oxford: Oxford University Press.

Hamilton, V. 1983. *The Cognitive Structures and Processes of Human Motivation and Personality.* Chichester: John Wiley and Sons.

Hammond, M. and R. Collins. 1991. *Self-directed Learning: Critical Practice.* London: Kogan Page.

Hannaford, C. 1995. *Smart Moves.* Arlington, VA: Great Ocean Publishers.

Harel, Y. 1992. Teacher talk in the cooperative classroom. In C. Kessler (Ed.)

Cooperative Language Learning. Englewood Cliffs, NJ: Prentice Hall Regents.

Hargreaves, A. and E. Tucker. 1991. Teaching and guilt: exploring the feelings of teaching. *Teaching and Teacher Education*, 7, 5/6, 491–505.

Hargreaves, D. H. 1994. The new professionalism: the synthesis of professional and institutional development. *Teaching and Teacher Education*, 10, 4, 423–438.

Hart, D. 1994. *Authentic assessment: a handbook for educators*. New York: Addison Wesley.

Hartmann, E. 1991. *Boundaries In the Mind: A New Psychology of Personality*. New York: Basic Books.

Hartmann, H. 1950. Comments on the psychoanalytic theory of the ego. *Psychoanalytic Study of the Child*, 5, 74–96.

Hatton, N. and D. Smith. 1995. Reflection in teacher education: towards definition and implementation. *Teaching and Teacher Education*, 11, 1, 33–49.

Head, K. and P. Taylor. 1997. *Readings in Teacher Development*. Oxford: Heinemann.

Heron, J. 1989. *The Facilitator's Handbook*. London: Kogan Page.

1990. *Helping the Client*. London: Sage.

1992. *Feeling and Personhood: Psychology in Another Key*. London: Sage.

Hertz-Lazarowitz, R. and H. Shachar. 1990. Changes in teachers' verbal behavior in cooperative classrooms. *Cooperative Learning*, 11, 13–14.

Heyde, A. 1979. The relationship between self-esteem and the oral production of a second language. Unpublished doctoral dissertation, University of Michigan.

Higbee, K. 1994. More motivational aspects of an imagery mnemonic. *Applied-Cognitive Psychology*, 8, 1, 1–12.

High, J. 1993. *Second Language Learning through Cooperative Learning*. San Juan Capistrano: Kagan Cooperative Learning.

Hilgard, E. 1963. Motivation in learning theory. In S. Koch (Ed.) *Psychology: A Study of Science*. Vol. 5. New York: McGraw-Hill Book Company.

Hilgard, E., R. L. Atkinson and R. C. Atkinson. 1979. *Introduction to Psychology* (7th ed.) New York: Harcourt Brace Jovanovich.

Hoffman, E. 1989. *Lost in Translation: A Life in a New Language*. New York: Penguin Books.

Hofstede, G. 1991. *Cultures and Organizations*. London: HarperCollins.

Hogan, R. 1969. Development of an empathy scale. *Journal of Consulting and Clinical Psychology*, 33, 307–316.

Holec, H. 1981. *Autonomy and Foreign Language Learning*. Oxford: Pergamon Press.

1985. On autonomy: Some elementary concepts. In P. Riley (Ed.) *Discourse and Learning*. New York: Longman.

1987. The learner as manager: managing learning or managing to learn? In A. Wenden and J. Rubin (Eds.) *Learner Strategies in Language Learning*. Englewood Cliffs, NJ: Prentice Hall Inc.

Holt, D. (Ed.) 1994. *Cooperative Learning: A Response to Linguistic and Cultural Diversity*. Mothery, IL: Delta Systems.

Hooks, B. 1994. *Teaching to Transgress: Education as the Practice of Freedom*. New York: Routledge.

Horwitz, E. K. 1986. Preliminary evidence for the reliability and validity of a foreign language anxiety scale. *TESOL Quarterly*, 20, 559–562.

1988. The beliefs about language learning of beginning university foreign language students. *Modern Language Journal*, 72, 283–294.

1990. Attending to the affective domain in the foreign language classroom. In S. S. Magnan (Ed.) *Shifting the Instructional Focus to the Learner*. Middlebury, VT: Northeast Conference on the Teaching of Foreign Languages.

Horwitz, E. K., M. B. Horwitz and J. A. Cope. 1986. Foreign language classroom anxiety. *Modern Language Journal*, 70, 125–132. Also 1991. In E. K. Horwitz and D. J. Young (Eds.) *Language Anxiety: From Theory and Research to Classroom Implications*. Englewood Cliffs, NJ: Prentice Hall.

Horwitz, E. K. and D. Young (Eds.) 1991. *Language Anxiety: From Theory and Research to Classroom Implications*. Englewood Cliffs, NJ: Prentice Hall.

Houston, J. 1982. *The Possible Human*. Los Angeles: Jeremy P. Tarcher, Inc.

Höweler, M. 1972. Diversity of word usage as a stress indicator in an interview situation. *Journal of Psycholinguistic Research*, 1, 3, 243–248.

Illich, I. 1970. *Deschooling Society*. New York: Harper & Row.

Jacobs, B. 1988. Neurobiological differentiation of primary and secondary language acquisition. *Studies in Second Language Acquisition*, 10, 303–337.

Jacobs, B. and J. Schumann. 1992. Language acquisition and the neurosciences: Towards a more integrative perspective. *Applied Linguistics*, 13, 3, 282–301.

Jacobs, E., L. Rottenberg, S. Patrick and E. Wheeler. 1996. Cooperative learning: Context and opportunities for acquiring academic English. *TESOL Quarterly*, 30, 253–280.

Jacobs, G. M. 1996. Cooperative learning and group activities: Is there a difference? If so, does the difference make a difference? Plenary address at the 44th TEFLIN (Teaching English as a Foreign Language in Indonesia) Seminar, Surabaya, East Java, Indonesia, October 1996.

Jacobs, G. M. and S. J. Hall. 1994. Implementing cooperative learning. *English Teaching Forum*, 32, 2–5,13.

Järvinen, A., V. Kohonen, H. Niemi and S. Ojanen. 1995. Educating critical professionals. *Scandinavian Journal of Educational Research*, 39, 2, 121–137.

Jersild, D. 1955. *When Teachers Face Themselves*. New York: Columbia University Press.

Johnson, D. W. and R. T. Johnson. 1989. *Cooperation and Competition: Theories and Research*. Edina, MN: Interaction Book Co.

1992. *Structuring Academic Controversies: Creative Conflict in the Classroom*. Edina, MN: Interaction Book Co.

1994. *Learning Together and Alone: Cooperative, Competitive, and Individualistic Learning*. Boston: Allyn and Bacon.

1995. Cooperative learning and nonacademic outcomes of schooling. In J. E. Pedersen and A. D. Digby (Eds.) *Secondary Schools and Cooperative learning*. New York: Garland.

Johnson, D. W., R. T. Johnson and E. J. Holubec. 1993. *Circles of Learning*. (4th ed.) Edina, MN: Interaction Book Co.

Johnson, D. W., R. T. Johnson and L. Scott. 1978. The effects of cooperative and individualized instruction on student attitudes and achievement. *The Journal of Social Psychology*, 104, 207–216.

Johnson, D. W., R. T. Johnson and K. A. Smith. 1995. Cooperative learning and individual student achievement in secondary schools. In J. E. Pedersen and A. D. Digby (Eds.) *Secondary schools and cooperative learning*. New York: Garland.

Johnson, W. 1997. Jack Millett. *TESOL Matters*, 7, 5, 20.

Jones, J. F. 1995. Self-access and culture: Retreating from autonomy. *ELT Journal*, 49, 3, 228–234.

Jones, V. F. and L. S. Jones. 1995. *Comprehensive Classroom Management: Creating Positive Learning Environments for All Students*. Needham Heights, MA: Allyn & Bacon.

Jourard, S. 1964. *The Transparent Self*. New York: Van Nostrand Reinhold.

1971. *Self-Disclosure: An Experimental Analysis of the Transparent Self*. New York: John Wiley and Sons.

Joyce B. and M. Weir. 1986. *Models of Teaching*. (3rd ed.) Englewood Cliffs, NJ: Prentice Hall.

Jung, C. 1923. *Psychological Types*. New York: Harcourt Brace Company.

Kachru, B. 1992. World Englishes: Approaches, issues, and resources. *Language Teaching*, 25, 1–14.

Kagan, S. 1986. Cooperative learning and sociocultural factors in schooling. In California State Department of Education (Ed.) *Beyond Language: Social and Cultural Factors in Schooling Language Minority Students*. Los Angeles: Evaluation, Dissemination and Assessment Center, California State University.

1989. The structural approach to cooperative learning. *Educational Leadership*, 47, 12–15.

1994. *Cooperative Learning*. San Juan Capistrano, CA: Kagan Cooperative Learning.

Kaikkonen, P. 1997. Learning a culture and a foreign language at school – aspects of intercultural learning. *Language Learning Journal*, 15, 47–51.

Keirsey, D. and M. Bates. 1984. *Please Understand Me: Character and Temperament Types*. Del Mar, CA: Prometheus Nemesis.

Kellerman, H. 1981. The deep structures of group cohesion. In: H. Kellerman (Ed.) *Group Cohesion: Theoretical and Clinical Perspectives*. New York: Grune and Stratton.

Kelly, R. 1996. Language Counselling for learner autonomy: the skilled helper in self-access language learning. In R. Pemberton, E. S. L. Li, W. W. F. Or and H. D. Pierson (Eds.) *Taking Control: Autonomy in Language Learning.* Hong Kong: Hong Kong University Press.

Kemmis, S. 1985. Action research and the politics of reflection. In D. Boud, R. Keogh and D. Walker (Eds.) *Reflection: Turning Experience into Learning.* London: Croom Helm.

Kemmis, S. and R. McTaggart. 1982. *The Action Research Planner.* Victoria, Australia: Deakin University Press.

Kendall, G., D. Hrycaiko, G. L. Martin and T. Kendall. 1990. The effects of an imagery rehearsal, relaxation and self-talk package on basketball game performance. *Journal of Sport & Exercise Psychology.* 12, 2, 157–166.

Kessler, C. (Ed.) 1992. *Cooperative Language Learning.* Englewood Cliffs, NJ: Prentice Hall Regents.

Kleinmann, H. 1977. Avoidance behavior in adult second language acquisition. *Language Learning,* 27, 93–107.

Klippel, F. 1984. *Keep Talking: Communicative Fluency Activities for Language Teaching.* Cambridge: Cambridge University Press.

Koch, A. and T. Terrell. 1991. Affective reactions of foreign language students to Natural Approach activities and teaching techniques. In E. K. Horwitz and D. J. Young (Eds.) *Language Anxiety: From Theory and Research to Classroom Implications.* Englewood Cliffs, NJ: Prentice Hall.

Kohn, A. 1990. Rewards hamper creativity. *San Francisco Chronicle* (June 21), B3–B4.

1994. The Truth about Self-Esteem. *Phi Delta Kappa,* December 1994, 272–283.

Kohonen, V. 1992a. Experiential language learning: second language learning as cooperative learner education. In D. Nunan (Ed.) *Collaborative Language Learning and Teaching.* Cambridge: Cambridge University Press.

1992b. Evaluation in relation to learning and teaching of languages for communication. In J. Trim (Ed.) *Language Learning and Teaching Methodology for Citizenship in a Multicultural Europe.* Strasbourg: Council of Europe.

1992c. Foreign language learning as learner education: facilitating self-direction in language learning. In B. North (Ed.) 1992. *Transparency and Coherence in Language Learning in Europe.* Strasbourg: Council of Europe.

1993. Language learning as learner education is also a question of school development. In L. Lösfman, L. Kurki-Suonio, S. Pellinen and J. Lehtonen (Eds.) *The Competent Intercultural Communicator.* Tampere: AFinLA Series of Publications 51, 267–287.

1996. Learning contents and processes in context: towards coherence in educational outcomes through teacher development. In H. Niemi and K. Tirri (Eds.) Effectiveness of teacher education: new challenges and approaches to evaluation. Tampere: Reports from the Department of Teacher Education in Tampere University A 6, 63–84.

Kosslyn, S. 1983. *Ghosts in the Mind's Machine. Creating and Using Images in the Brain.* New York: W W Norton.

Krashen, S. 1982. *Principles and Practice in Second Language Acquisition.* Oxford: Pergamon Press.

1983. The din in the head, input, and the Second Language Acquisition Device. *Foreign Language Annals*, 16, 41–44.

1985. *The Input Hypothesis: Issues and Implications.* New York: Longman.

Krashen, S. and T. Terrell. 1983. *The Natural Approach: Language Acquisition in the Classroom.* Oxford: Pergamon Press.

Kris, E. 1952. *Psychoanalytic Explorations In Art.* New York: International Universities Press.

Kuhn, T. 1973. *The Structure of Scientific Revolutions.* Chicago: University of Chicago Press.

Lambert, W. 1967. A social psychology of bilingualism. *The Journal of Social Issues*, 23, 91–109.

Larsen-Freeman, D. 1986. *Techniques and Principles in Language Teaching.* New York: Oxford University Press.

Larson, D. and W. Smalley. 1972. *Becoming Bilingual: A Guide to Language Learning.* New Canaan, CN: Practical Anthropology.

Lave, J. and E. Wenger 1991. *Situated Learning: Legitimate Peripheral Participation.* New York: Cambridge University Press.

Lazear, D. 1991. *Seven Ways of Knowing.* Palatine, IL: IRI/Skylight Training and Publishing.

Leary, M. 1983. *Understanding Social Anxiety: Social, Personality, and Clinical Perspectives.* Beverly Hills: Sage.

LeDoux, J. 1996. *The Emotional Brain.* New York: Simon & Schuster.

Legutke, M. and H. Thomas. 1991. *Process and Experience in the Language Classroom.* Harlow: Longman.

Lehmann, D. 1988. Music in Suggestopedia, pamphlet translated by Sigrid Gassner Roberts. Adelaide: University of Adelaide Press.

Levin. R. 1990. Ego boundary impairment and thought disorder in frequent nightmare sufferers. *Psychoanalytic Psychology*, 7, 4, 529–543.

Levine, J. M. and R. L. Moreland. 1990. Progress in small group research. *Annual Review of Psychology, 41*, 585–634.

Lewin, K., R. Lippitt and R. White. 1939. Patterns of aggressive behavior in experimentally created 'social climates'. *Journal of Social Psychology*, 10, 271–299.

Lewis, J. 1991. Nursery schools: The transition from home to school. In B. Finkelstein, A. E. Imamura and J. J. Tobin (Eds.) *Transcending Stereotypes: Discovering Japanese Culture and Education.* Yarmouth, ME: Intercultural Press.

Lindstromberg, S. (Ed.) 1990. *The Recipe Book.* Harlow and Canterbury: Pilgrims Longman.

Little, D. 1991. *Learner Autonomy 1: Definitions, Issues and Problems.* Dublin: Authentik.

1996a. The politics of learner autonomy. Learning Learning: JALT Learner Development N-SIG Forum, 2/4, 2–7.

1996b. Freedom to learn and compulsion to interact: Promoting learner autonomy through the use of information systems and information technologies. In R. Pemberton, E. S. L. Li, W. W. F. Or and H. D. Pierson (Eds.) *Taking Control: Autonomy in Language Learning*. Hong Kong: Hong Kong University Press.

Lofgren, L. B. 1975. Organizational design and therapeutic effect. In A. D. Colman and W. H. Bexton (Eds.) *Group Relations Reader* 1 (185–192). Washington, DC: A. K. Rice Institute.

Long, M. H. 1981. Input, interaction, and second language acquisition. *Annals of the New York Academy of Sciences*, 379, 259–278.

Long, M. H. and P. A. Porter. 1985. Group work, interlanguage talk, and second language learning. *TESOL Quarterly*, 19, 207–228.

Lotan, R. A. and J. Becton. 1990. Finding out about complex instruction: Teaching math and science in heterogeneous classrooms. In N. Davidson (Ed.) *Cooperative Learning in Mathematics*. Menlo Park, CA: Addison Wesley.

Lou, Y., P. C. Abrami, J. C. Spence, C. Poulsen, B. Chambers and S. d'Apollonia. 1996. Within-class grouping: A meta-analysis. *Review of Educational Research*, 66, 423–458.

Lozanov, G. 1979. *Suggestology and Outlines of Suggestopedy*. New York: Gordon & Breach.

Lozanov, G. and E. Gateva. 1988. *The Foreign Language Teacher's Suggestopedic Manual*. New York: Gordon & Breach.

Luke, C. and J. Gore (Eds.) 1992. *Feminisms and Critical Pedagogy*. New York: Routledge.

Lustig, M. and J. Koester. 1993. *Intercultural Competence. Interpersonal Communication across Cultures*. New York: HarperCollins College Publishers.

McCollom, M. 1990a. Reevaluating group development: A critique of the familiar models. In J. Gilette and M. McCollom (Eds.) *Groups in Context: A New Perspective on Group Dynamics*. Reading, MA: Addison Wesley.

1990b. Group formation: Boundaries, leadership and culture. In J. Gilette and M. McCollom (Eds.) *Groups in Context: A New Perspective on Group Dynamics*. Reading, MA: Addison Wesley.

McCoy, I. 1979. Means to overcome the anxieties of second language learners. *Foreign Language Annals*, 12, 185–9.

McCroskey, J.C. 1984. The communication apprehension perspective. In J. A. Daly and J. C. McCroskey (Eds.) *Avoiding Communication: Shyness, Reticence, and Communication Apprehension*. Beverly Hills: Sage.

McCroskey, J. C., J. M. Fayer and V. P. Richmond. 1985. Don't speak to me in English: Communication apprehension in Puerto Rico. *Communication Quarterly*, 33, 185–192.

McGroarty, M. 1989. The benefits of cooperative learning arrangements in second language acquisition. *NABE Journal*, 13, 127–143.

MacIntyre, P. D. and R. C. Gardner. 1989. Anxiety and second-language learning: toward a theoretical clarification. *Language Learning*, 39, 2, 251–275.

References

1991. Language anxiety: Its relation to other anxieties and to processing in native and second languages. *Language Learning*, 41, 513–534.

McLaughlin, B. 1990. Restructuring. *Applied Linguistics*, 11/2, 113 128.

McLeod, B. and B. McLaughlin. 1986. Restructuring or automaticity? Reading in a second language. *Language Learning*, 33, 135–158.

McNamara, M. and D. Deane. 1995. Self-assessment activities: toward autonomy in language learning. *TESOL Journal*, 5, 1, 17–21.

Majoy, P. 1993. *Doorways to Learning*. Tucson, AR: Zepher Press.

Maley, A. and A. Duff. 1982. *Drama Techniques in Language Learning: A Resource Book of Communication Activities for Language Teachers*. Cambridge: Cambridge University Press.

Mandler, G. 1982. The structure of value: Accounting for taste. In M. S. Clark and S. T. Fiske (Eds.) *Affect and Cognition*. Hillsdale, NJ: Lawrence Erlbaum.

Marks, D. 1973. Visual imagery differences in the recall of pictures. *British Journal of Psychology*, 64/1, 17–24.

Maslow, A. 1968. *Toward a Psychology of Being*. New York: Van Nostrand Reinhold.

1970. *Motivation and Personality*. New York: Harper & Row.

Mata, K. 1996. See it! Tell it! Write it! *The Journal of the Imagination in Language Learning*, III, 60–65.

Miller, J. 1981. *The Compassionate Teacher*. Englewood Cliffs, NJ: Prentice Hall.

Miller, J. 1988. *The Holistic Curriculum*. Toronto: OISE Press.

Morgan, J. and M. Rinvolucri. 1983. *Once Upon a Time*. Cambridge: Cambridge University Press.

Moritz, S., C. Hall, K. Martin and E. Vadocz. 1996. What are confident athletes imaging? An examination of image content. *Sport-Psychologist*, 10, 2, 171–79.

Morrison, A. P. 1989. *Shame: The Underside of Narcissism*. Hillsdale, NJ: Analytic.

Moskowitz, G. 1978. *Caring and Sharing in the Foreign Language Class: A Sourcebook on Humanistic Techniques*. Boston, MA: Heinle & Heinle.

1981. Effects of humanistic techniques on the attitude, cohesiveness, and self-concept of foreign language students. *Modern Language Journal*, 65, 2, 149–157.

In preparation. The effects of humanistic activities on the personal growth of foreign language students and teachers.

Mullen, B. and C. Copper. 1994. The relationship between group cohesiveness and performance: An integration. *Psychological Bulletin*, 115, 210–227.

Mulligan, J. 1991. Internal processors in experiential learning. In J. Mulligan and C. Griffin (Eds.) *Empowerment through Experiential Learning*. London: Kogan Page.

Murdock, M. 1987. *Spinning Inward*. Boston: Shambhala.

Murphey, T. 1995. Identity and beliefs in language learning. *The Language Teacher*, 19, 4, 34–36.

1998. A room with a view – to move: what image are you streaming now? *English Teaching Professional*, 9.

Murphy, G. 1968. Psychological views of personality and contributions to its study. In E. Norbeck, D. Price-Williams and W. M. McCord (Eds.) *The Study of Personality: An Interdisciplinary Appraisal*. New York: Holt, Rhinehart and Winston.

Myers, I. B. and M. McCaulley. 1985. *Manual: A Guide To the Development and Use of the Myers-Briggs Type Indicator*. Palo Alto, CA: Consulting Psychologists.

Nash, M. J. 1997. Fertile Minds. *Time*, 146, 5, 48–56.

Nedelsky, J. 1989. Reconceiving autonomy: Sources, thoughts and possibilities. *Yale Journal of Law and Feminism*, 1, 7–36.

Neves, A. 1983. The effect of various input on second language acquisition of Mexican American children in nine Elementary school classrooms. Ph.D. thesis, Stanford University.

Neville, B. 1989. *Educating Psyche: Emotion, Imagination and the Unconscious in Learning*. Victoria: Collins Dove.

Niemi, H. and V. Kohonen. 1995. Towards new professionalism and active learning in teacher development: empirical findings on teacher education and induction. Tampere: Reports from the Department of Teacher Education in Tampere University A2 1995.

North, B. (Ed.) 1992. *Transparency and Coherence in Language Learning in Europe*. Strasbourg: Council of Europe.

1993. *The Development of Descriptors on Scales of Language Proficiency*. Washington, DC: The National Foreign Language Center.

Norton, R. W. 1975. Measurement of ambiguity tolerance. *Journal of Personality Assessment*, 39, 608–619.

Nunan, D. (Ed.) 1992. *Collaborative Language Learning and Teaching*. Cambridge: Cambridge University Press.

1988. *The Learner-Centred Curriculum*. Cambridge: Cambridge University Press.

O'Connor, J. and J. Seymour. 1990. *Introducing Neuro-Linguistic Programming. The New Psychology of Personal Excellence*. London. HarperCollins.

O'Malley, M. and L. Valdez Pierce. 1996. *Authentic Assessment for English Language Learners*. New York: Addison Wesley.

Oatley, K., and J. Jenkins. 1996. *Understanding Emotions*. Cambridge, MA: Blackwell.

Odent, M. 1984. *Birth Reborn*. London: Fontana.

1986. *Primal Health: A Blueprint for Our Survival*. London: Century.

Oliver, R. 1995. Negative feedback in child NS–NNS conversation. *Studies in Second Language Acquisition*, 17, 4, 459–481.

Ortony, A., G. L. Clore and A. Collins. 1988. *The Cognitive Structure of Emotions*. New York: Cambridge University Press.

Oxford, R. L. 1990a. Language learning strategies and beyond: A look at strategies in the context of styles. In S. S. Magnan (Ed.), *Shifting the instructional focus to the learner.* Middlebury, VT: Northeast Conference on the Teaching of Foreign Languages. 35–55.

1990b. *Language Learning Strategies: What Every Teacher Should Know.* New York: Newbury House.

1997. *Language Learning Strategies Around the World: Crosscultural Perspectives.* Manoa: University of Hawaii Press.

Oxford, R. L. and M. Ehrman. 1993. Second language research on individual differences. *Annual Review of Applied Linguistics,* 13, 188–205.

Oxford, R. L., M. Ehrman and R. Z. Lavine. 1991. Style wars. Teacher–student style conflicts in the language classroom. In S. S. Magnan (Ed.) *Challenges in the 1990s for College Foreign Language Programs.* Boston: Heinle & Heinle.

Oxford, R. and J. M. Green. 1996. Language learning histories: Learners and teachers helping each other understand learning styles and strategies. *TESOL Journal,* 6, 1, 22–24.

Oxford, R. and J. Shearin. 1994. Language learning motivation: Expanding the theoretical framework. *Modern Language Journal,* 78, i, 12–28.

Peak, L. 1991. Training learning skills and attitudes in Japanese early education settings. In B. Finkelstein, A. E. Imamura and J. J. Tobin (Eds.) *Transcending Stereotypes: Discovering Japanese Culture and Education.* Yarmouth, ME: Intercultural Press.

Peirce, B. N. 1995. Social identity, investment and language learning. *TESOL Quarterly,* 29, 1, 9–31.

Pemberton, P., E. S. L. Li, W. W. F. Or and H. D. Pierson (Eds.) 1996. *Taking Control: Autonomy in Language Learning.* Hong Kong: Hong Kong University Press.

Pennycook, A. 1997. Cultural alternatives and autonomy. In P. Benson and P. Voller (Eds.) *Autonomy and Independence in Language Learning.* New York: Addison Wesley Longman.

Piaget, J. 1967. *Six Psychological Studies.* New York: Random House.

1973. The affective unconscious and the cognitive unconscious. *Journal of the American Psychoanalytic Association,* 21, 249–261.

Pica, T. and C. Doughty. 1985. The role of group work in classroom second language acquisition. *Studies in Second Language Acquisition,* 7, 233–248.

Pine, G. J. and A. V. Boy. 1997. *Learner Centred Teaching: A Humanistic View.* Denver, CO: Love Publishing.

Pollari, P. 1997. Could portfolio assessment empower EFL learners? In A. Huhta, V. Kohonen, L. Kurki-Suonio and S. Luoma (Eds.) Current developments and alternatives in language assessment: proceedings of the LTRC 1996 in Tampere. University of Jyväskylä: Center for Applied Language Studies, 37–54.

Porter, P. A. 1983. Variations in the conversations of adult learners of English as a function of the proficiency level of the participants. Ph.D. thesis, Stanford University.

Price, M. L. 1991. The subjective experience of foreign language anxiety interviews with high-anxious students. In E. K. Horwitz and D. J. Young

(Eds.) *Language Anxiety: From Theory and Research to Classroom Implications*. Englewood Cliffs, NJ: Prentice Hall.

Puchta, H. and M. Rinvolucri. In preparation. *Multiple Intelligences in Foreign Language Teaching*.

Puchta, H. and M. Schratz. 1993. *Teaching Teenagers*. Canterbury and Harlow: Pilgrims Longman. First published in German in 1984. Munich: Max Hueber Verlag.

Pulvermüller, F. and J. H. Schumann. 1994. Neurobiological mechanisms of language acquisition. *Language Learning*, 44, 4, 681–734.

Purkey, W. 1970. *Self-Concept and School Achievement*. New York: Prentice Hall.

Putnam, J. A. 1997. *Cooperative Learning in Diverse Classrooms*. Upper Saddle River, NJ: Merrill/Prentice Hall.

Ranson, S. 1994. *Towards the Learning Society*. London: Cassell.

Rapaport, D. 1958. The theory of ego autonomy: A generalization. *Bulletin of the Menninger Clinic*, 22, 13–35.

Reasoner, R. 1982. *Building Self-Esteem: A Comprehensive Program for Schools*. Palo Alto: Consulting Psychologists Press, Inc.

1992. You Can Bring Hope to Failing Students. *School Administrator*. April 92, 24.

Reasoner, R. and G. Dusa. 1991. *Building Self-esteem in Secondary Schools*. Palo Alto, CA: Consulting Psychologists Press, Inc.

Reid, J. 1987. The perceptual learning style preferences of ESL students. *TESOL Quarterly*, 21, 1, 87–111.

1992. Implementing change in the ESL classroom. *Contact* 17, 1, 1–3.

1994. Change in the language classroom: Process and intervention. *English Teaching Forum*, 32, 1, 8–11, 38.

1995. *Learning Styles in the ESL/EFL Classroom*. Boston: Heinle & Heinle.

Revell, J. and S. Norman. 1997. *In Your Hands – NLP in ELT*. London: Saffire Press.

Richards, J. and D. Freeman. 1996. *Teacher Learning in Language Teaching*. Cambridge: Cambridge University Press.

Richards, J. and C. Lockhart. 1994. *Reflective Teaching in Second Language Classrooms*. New York: Cambridge University Press.

Richards, J. and T. Rodgers. 1986. *Approaches and Methods in Language Teaching*. Cambridge: Cambridge University Press.

Richardson, A. 1983. The voluntary use of memory imagery as an aid to learning and performance. In Fleming, M. and D. Hutton (Eds.) *Mental Imagery and Learning*. Englewood Cliffs, NJ: Educational Technology Publications.

Riley, P. (Ed.) 1985. *Discourse and Learning*. New York: Longman.

Rinvolucri, M. 1982. Awareness activity for teaching structures. In The British Council (Ed.) *ELT Documents 113: Humanistic Approaches. An Empirical View*. London: The British Council.

1984. *Grammar Games*. Cambridge: Cambridge University Press.

Roberts, T. and F. Clark. 1976. Transpersonal psychology in education. In

G. Hendricks and J. Fadiman (Eds.) *Transpersonal Education*. Englewood Cliffs, NJ: Prentice Hall.

Rodgers, T. S. 1988. Co-operative language learning: What's news? In B. K. Das (Ed.) *Materials for Language Learning and Teaching*. Singapore: SEAMEO Regional Language Centre.

Rogers, C. 1956. What it means to become a person. In C. Moustakas (Ed.) *The Self: Explorations in Growth*. New York: Harper & Row.

1961/1995. *On Becoming a Person*. Boston: Houghton Mifflin.

1969. *Freedom to Learn: A View of What Education Might Become*. Columbus, OH: Charles E. Merrill.

1975. Bringing together ideas and feelings in learning. In D. A. Read and S. B. Simon (Eds.) *Humanistic Education Sourcebook*. Englewood Cliffs, NJ: Prentice Hall, 40–41.

1980. *A Way of Being*. New York: Houghton Mifflin. (Quotations are from the new edition published in 1995.)

1983. *Freedom to Learn for the 80s*. Columbus, Ohio: Charles E. Merrill.

1994. *Freedom to Learn*. New York: Merrill.

Rogers, T. 1983. Emotion, imagery, and verbal codes: A closer look at an increasingly complex interaction. In J. Yuille (Ed.) *Imagery, Memory and Cognition*. Hillsdale, NJ: Lawrence Erlbaum Associates.

Rogoff, B. 1995. Observing sociocultural activity on three planes: participatory appropriation, guided participation, and apprenticeship. In J. V. Wertsch, P. Del Rio and A. Alvarez (Eds.) *Sociocultural Studies of Mind*. New York: Cambridge University Press.

Rolls, E. 1995. A theory of emotion and consciousness, and its application to understanding the neural basis of emotion. In M. S. Gazzaniga (Ed.) *The Cognitive Neurosciences*. Cambridge, MA: MIT Press

Rossi, E. L. 1986. *The Psychobiology of Mind–Body Healing*. New York: W. W. Norton & Co. Inc.

Rubio, F. D. 1995. Ansiedad en los exámenes orales de inglés. Unpublished Master's thesis, University of Seville.

Rybash, J. M., W. Hoyer and P. Roodin. 1986. *Adult Cognition and Aging*. New York: Pergamon Press.

Sacks, O. 1995. *An Anthropologist on Mars*. New York: Knopf.

Salzberger-Wittenberg, I., G. Henry and E. Osborne. 1983. *The Emotional Experience of Learning and Teaching*. New York: Routledge Kegan Paul.

Samimy, K. and J. P. Rardin. 1994. Adult language learners' affective reactions to Community Language Learning: A descriptive study. *Foreign Language Annals*, 27, 3, 379–390.

Sarason, I. G. 1984. Stress, anxiety, and cognitive interference: Reactions to tests. *Journal of Personality and Social Psychology*, 46, 929–938.

Sartre, J. P. 1956. *Being and Nothingness*. New York: Philosophical Library.

Savitch, J. and L. Serling. 1995. Paving a path through untracked territory. *Educational Leadership*, 52, 72–74.

Scarcella, R. C. and R. L. Oxford. 1992. *The Tapestry of Language Learning:*

The Individual in the Communicative Classroom. Boston: Heinle & Heinle.

Schein, E. H. 1986. The individual, the organization, and the career: A conceptual scheme. In D. A. Kolb, I. M. Rubin and J. M. McIntyre (Eds.) 1984. *Organizational Psychology: Readings On Human Behavior In Organizations* (4th ed.) (87–103). Englewood Cliffs, NJ: Prentice-Hall. Reprinted from Sloan School of Management, MIT, Working Paper No. 326–68.

Scherer, K. R. 1984. Emotion as a multi-component process: A model and some cross-cultural data. In P. Shaver (Ed.), *Review of Personality and Social Psychology: Vol. 5. Emotions, Relationships and Health*. Beverly Hills, CA: Sage.

Schmidt, R. and W. Savage. 1992. Challenge, skill, and motivation. *PASAA*, 22, 14–28.

Schmidt, R., D. Boraie and O. Kassagby. 1996. Foreign language motivation: Internal structure and external connections. In R. L. Oxford (Ed.) *Language Learning Motivation: Pathways to the New Century*. University of Hawaii at Manoa: Second Language Teaching & Curriculum Center.

Schmuck, R. A. and P. A. Schmuck. 1988. *Group Processes in the Classroom*. (5th ed.) Dubuque, IA: Wm. C. Brown.

Schön, D. A. 1983. *The Reflective Practitioner*. New York: Basic Books.

1987. *Educating the Reflective Practitioner*. San Francisco: Jossey-Bass.

1991. *The Reflective Turn: Case Studies in Educational Practice*. New York: Teachers College Press.

Schumann, J. H. 1986. Research on the acculturation model for second language acquisition. *Journal of Multilingual and Multicultural Development*, 7, 5, 379–392.

1994. Where is cognition? Emotion and cognition in second language acquisition. *SSLA*, 16, 231–242.

1997. *The Neurobiology of Affect in Language*. Boston: Blackwell.

Scovel, T. 1978. The effect of affect on foreign language learning: A review of the anxiety research. *Language Learning*, 28, 129–142.

Seligman, M. E. P. 1991. *Learned Optimism*. New York: Knopf.

Shambough, P. W. 1978. The development of the small group. *Human Relations, 31,* 283–295.

Sharan, S. 1980. Cooperative learning in small groups: Recent methods and effects on achievement, attitudes, and ethnic relations. *Review of Educational Research*, 50, 241–271.

Sharan, S. (Ed.) 1990. *Current Research on Cooperative Learning*. New York: Praeger.

Sharan, S., Y. Bejarano, P. Kuissell and R. Peleg. 1984. Achievement in English language and literature. In S. Sharan, P. Kuissell, R. Hertz-Lazarowitz, Y. Bejarano, R Shulamit and Y. Sharan (Eds.) *Cooperative Learning in the Classroom: Research in Desegregated Schools*. Hillsdale, NJ: Lawrence Erlbaum.

Sharan, S. and R. Hertz-Lazarowitz. 1980. A group investigation method of cooperative learning in the classroom. In S. Sharan, P. Hare, C. Webb and R. Hertz-Lazarowitz (Eds.) *Cooperation in Education.* Provo, UT: Brigham Young University Press.

Sharan, S. and H. Shachar. 1988. *Language and Learning in the Cooperative Classroom.* New York: Springer-Verlag.

Sharan, Y. and S. Sharan. 1992. *Expanding Cooperative Learning through Group Investigation.* New York: Teachers College Press.

Shaw, M. E. 1981. *Group Dynamics: The Psychology of Small Group Behavior.* (3rd ed.) New York: McGraw-Hill.

Skinner, B. 1957. *Verbal Behavior.* New York: Appleton-Century-Crofts.

Slavin, R. E. 1983a. When does cooperative learning increase student achievement? *Psychological Bulletin,* 94, 429–445.

1983b. *Cooperative Learning.* New York: Longman.

1990. *Cooperative Learning: Theory, Research, and Practice.* Englewood Cliffs, NJ: Prentice Hall.

Sloan, S. 1992. *The Complete ESL/EFL Cooperative Communicative Activity Book: Learner Directed Activities for the Classroom.* Lincolnwood, IL: National Textbook Co.

Smolen, L., C. Newman, T. Wathen and D. Lee. 1995. Developing student self-assessment strategies. *TESOL Journal,* 5, 1, 22–26.

Smyth, J. 1989. Developing and sustaining critical reflection in teacher education. *Journal of Teacher Education,* 40, 2, 2–8.

Spolsky, B. 1988. Bridging the gap: A general theory of second language learning. *TESOL Quarterly,* 22, 3, 377–406.

Springer, S. and G. Deutsch. 1993. *Left Brain, Right Brain.* New York: WH Freeman.

Stengal, E. 1939. On learning a new language. *International Journal of Psychoanalysis,* 2, 471–79.

Stern, H. H. 1983. *Fundamental Concepts of Language Teaching.* Oxford: Oxford University Press.

Stevens, R. J., N. A. Madden, R. E. Slavin and A. M. Farnish. 1987. *Cooperative Integrated Reading and Composition.* Baltimore, MD: Center for Research on Elementary and Middle Schools, The Johns Hopkins University.

Stevick, E. W. 1976. *Memory, Meaning & Method.* Rowley, MA: Newbury House.

1980. *Teaching Languages: A Way and Ways.* Rowley, MA: Newbury House.

1986. *Images and Options in the Language Classroom.* Cambridge: Cambridge University Press.

1990. *Humanism in Language Teaching.* Oxford: Oxford University Press.

1996. *Memory, Meaning and Method: A View of Language Teaching* (2nd ed.) Boston, MA: Heinle & Heinle.

1998. *Working with Teaching Methods: What's at Stake?* Boston: Heinle & Heinle.

Straight, H. S. 1993. Persistent fallacies in psycholinguistic metatheory and how to overcome them. In Harré and Harris (Eds.) *Linguistics and Philosophy*. Oxford: Pergamon Press.

Sussman, R. 1989. Curiosity and exploration in children: Where affect and cognition meet. In K. Field, B. J. Cohler, and G. Wool (Eds.) *Learning and Education: Psychoanalytic Perspectives*. Madison, CT: International Universities Press.

Swain, M. 1985. Communicative competence: Some roles of comprehensible input and comprehensible output in its development. In S. Gass and C. Madden (Eds.) *Input in Second Language Acquisition*. Rowley, MA: Newbury House.

Swain, M. and S. Lapkin. 1989. Canadian immersion and adult second language teaching: What is the connection? *Modern Language Journal*, 73, 150–159.

Tajfeld, H. (Ed.) 1978. *Differentiation between Social Groups: Studies in Intergroup Behaviour*. London: Academic Press.

Tharp, R. G. and R. Gallimore. 1988. *Rousing Minds to Life. Teaching, Learning and Schooling in Social Context*. Cambridge: Cambridge University Press.

Thomas, L. and E. Hari-Augstein. 1985. *Self-organised Learning*. London: Routledge and Kegan Paul.

Tiberius, R. G. 1990. *Small Group Teaching: A Trouble-Shooting Guide*. Toronto: OISE Press/The Ontario Institute for Studies in Education.

Tomlinson, B. 1997. The role of visualisation in the reading of literature by learners of a foreign language. Unpublished doctoral dissertation, University of Nottingham.

1998. *Materials Development in Language Teaching*. Cambridge: Cambridge University Press.

Tremblay, P. F. and R. C. Gardner. 1995. Expanding the motivation construct in language learning. *Modern Language Journal*, 79, 505–518.

Trylong, V. 1987. Aptitude, attitudes, and anxiety: A study of their relationships to achievement in the foreign language classroom. Unpublished doctoral dissertation, Purdue University.

Tudor, I. 1997. *Learner-centredness as Language Education*. Cambridge: Cambridge University Press.

Turner, J. C. 1984. Social identification and psychological group formation. In H. Tajfel (Ed.) *The Social Dimension: European Studies in Social Psychology*. Cambridge: Cambridge University Press.

Tyron, G. S. 1980. The measurement and treatment of test anxiety. *Review of Educational Research*, 50/2, 343–72.

Underhill, A. 1989. Process in humanistic education. *ELT Journal*, 43/4, 250–60.

Ur, P. 1996. *A Course in Language Teaching*. Cambridge: Cambridge University Press.

Valli, L. 1992. *Reflective Teacher Education: Cases and Critiques*. Albany: State University of New York Press.

van Lier, L. 1994. Forks and hope: Pursuing understanding in different ways. *Applied Linguistics, 15*, 3, 328–346.

1996. *Interaction in the Language Curriculum: Awareness, Autonomy and Authenticity*. London: Longman.

Vernacchia, R. A. and D. L. Cooke. 1993. The influence of a mental training technique upon the performance of selected intercollegiate basketball players. *Applied Research in Coaching and Athletics Annual*, 188–200.

Vigil, N. and J. Oller. 1976. Rule fossilization: a tentative model. *Language Learning, 26, 2, 281–296.*

Voller, P. 1997. Does the teacher have a role in autonomous language learning? In P. Benson and P. Voller (Eds.) *Autonomy and Independence in Language Learning*. New York: Addison Wesley Longman.

Vygotsky, L. S. 1956. *Izbrannie Psibhologicheskie Issledovania*. Moscow: Izdatelstvo Akademii Pedagogicheskikh Nauk.

1978. *Mind in Society*. Cambridge, MA: Harvard University Press.

Wagner, A. C. 1987. 'Knots' in teachers' thinking. In J. Calderhead (Ed.) *Exploring Teachers' Thinking*. London: Cassell Education.

Waltz, G. and J. Bleuer. 1992. *Students' Self-Esteem: A Vital Element of School Success*. Ann Arbor, MI: Counseling and Personnel Services.

Waters, A. 1998. Managing monkeys in the ELT classroom. *ELT Journal, 52*, 11–18.

Watson, L. 1973. *Supernature*. New York: Hodder & Stoughton.

Wattenberg, W. W. and C. Clifford. 1962. Relationship of self concept to beginning achievement in reading. US Office of Education, Cooperative Research Project, no 377.

Weiner, B. 1985. An attributional theory of achievement, motivation and emotion. *Psychological Review, 92*, 548–573.

1992. Motivation. *Encyclopedia of Educational Research*. (6th ed., vol. 3) New York: Macmillan: 860–65.

Wertsch, J. V. and C. A. Stone. 1985. The concept of internalization in Vygotsky's account of the genesis of higher mental functions. In. J. V. Wertsch (Ed.) *Culture, Communication, and Cognition: Vygotskian perspectives*. Cambridge: Cambridge University Press.

Wertsch, J. V., P. Del Rio, and A. Alvarez (Eds.) 1995. *Sociocultural Studies of Mind*. New York: Cambridge University Press.

Wheelan, S. A. and R. L. McKeage. 1993. Development patterns in small and large groups. *Small Group Research, 24*, 60–83.

White, M. 1992. *Self-Esteem: Its Meaning and Value in Schools*. Sets A and B. Dunetable: Folens.

1994. Developing Self-Esteem. In K. Bovair and C. McLaughlin (Eds.) *Counselling in Schools: A Reader*. London: David Fulton Publishers.

Whitmore, D. 1986. *Psychosynthesis in Education*. Wellingborough: Turnstone Press Limited.

Widdowson, H. 1978. *Teaching Language as Communication*. Oxford: Oxford University Press.

Wiggins, G. 1993. *Assessing Student Performance*. San Francisco: Jossey Bass Publishers.

Wildman, T. M. and J. Niles. 1987. Reflective teachers: tensions between abstractions and realities. *Journal of Teacher Education*, 38, 4, 25–31.

Williams, M. and R. L. Burden. 1997. *Psychology for Language Teachers*. Cambridge: Cambridge University Press.

1988. Motivation in language learning: A social constructivist perspective. Paper presented at TESOL, Seattle.

Witkin, H. A. and D. R. Goodenough. 1981. *Cognitive styles: Essence and origins: Field dependence and field independence*. New York: International Universities.

Wolf, D., J. Bixby, J. Glenn III and H. Gardner. 1991. To use their minds well: investigating new forms of student assessment. In G. Grant (Ed.) *Review of Research in Education*, vol. 17. Washington, DC: American Educational Research Association, 31–74.

Woods, D. 1996. *Teacher Cognition in Language Teaching*. Cambridge: Cambridge University Press.

Wright, T. 1987. *The Role of Teachers and Learners*. Oxford: Oxford University Press.

Young, D. 1986. The relationship between anxiety and foreign language oral proficiency ratings. *Foreign Language Annals*, 19, 439–445.

1990. An investigation of students' perspectives on anxiety and speaking. *Foreign Language Annals*, 23, 539–553.

1991. Creating a low-anxiety classroom environment: What does language anxiety research suggest? *Modern Language Journal*, 75, iv, 426–438.

1992. Language anxiety from the foreign language specialist's perspective: Interviews with Krashen, Omaggio Hadley, Terrell, and Rardin. *Foreign Language Annals*, 25, 157–172.

In press. *Affect in L2 Learning: A Practical Guide to Dealing with Learner Anxieties*. Englewood Cliffs, NJ: Prentice Hall.

Zeichner, K. 1993. Connecting genuine teacher development to the struggle for social justice. *Journal of Education for Teaching*, 19, 1, 5–20.

Zeichner, K. and D. Liston. 1996. *Reflective Teaching: An Introduction*. Mahwah, NJ: Lawrence Erlbaum Associates.

Subject index

acceleration of learning 217, 224
acculturation 21–2
action research 89, 300
  collaborative action research, definition 90
active listening 114
activities 173, 174, 175, 194–210, 223, 244,
    283, 295
  see also exercises
  cognitive and affective 193, 199
  didactic purpose of 223
  Lozanov approach to 223
aesthetics in language learning 174, 175,
    199, 218, 271
  art in the classroom 221
  dance and movement 221
  endorphins and aesthetics 221, 295
  harmonizing function of 219
  landscapes 221
  music 219–20, 221
  painting 220–1
  poetry 222
affect, definition of xi, 44
affect and cognition xii, 7, 16, 19, 173, 178
affect and cognition encoded in memory 47
affective and cognitive needs 3, 212, 276,
    284, 305
affect and cognitive styles 299
affect and imagery in language learning 264
affective base for group dynamics 157
affective filter 56, 64, 113
affect-sensitive professions 210
analytic/global learning styles 301
anchors 254–5
anxiety 2, 15, 26, 58–67, 79, 80, 84, 102,
    140, 150, 159, 174, 227, 229, 233, 234,
    249, 272, 273, 292, 297, 298, 299, 300
  debilitating anxiety 60
  existential anxiety 8–9
  facilitating anxiety 61–2

FLCAS (Foreign Language Classroom
    Anxiety Scale) 66
  language anxiety, definition of 59
  self-esteem and anxiety 61, 62
  signs of anxiety in students 66
  social anxiety 63
  state or trait anxiety 60
  test anxiety 64
assessment 67, 279–94, 296
  see also evaluation
  authentic assessment 284–6
  authentic assessment vs. standard
    assessment 285–6
  in new educational paradigm 280
  process evaluation 279–80, 281
  process evaluation and affect in language
    learning 280
  product evaluation 279–80
  traditional vs. experiential approach 281
  types of authentic assessment 284, 291
  validity and reliability 290–2
attitudes 156, 174–5, 180, 181, 183, 184,
    186, 188, 187, 191, 192, 198, 200, 265,
    279, 284, 286, 288, 289, 293, 302
attribution theory 16
audiolingualism 6
automatic responses 214
autonomy 14–15, 105, 106, 107–8, 126,
    131, 135, 140, 142–154, 168, 169, 170,
    216, 217, 222, 231, 239–40, 244, 283,
    291, 293
  affect and cognition in 154
  learner autonomy, definition of 142, 144
  participation 145
  practice of, 145, 146
  politics and affect in 154
  teacher as resource 151–2
  teacher roles in 147, 151
autonomy and collective effort 143

334

Subject index

exercises 173, 194, 295
   see also activities, humanistic activities,
     humanistic exercises
   choral reading 195, 210
   communicative 195, 196, 200
   form-focused 196
   gap-fill 194, 210
   grammar-translation 194–5, 210
   information gap 196
   psychological vacuity of exercises 196
   role-play 197
   rehearsal 196
   semi-communicative 195, 200
   strings of words 194
experiential learning 199, 200, 280 283–4
extroversion 11, 18

facilitation 20, 107, 125–141, 170, 216,
   238, 281
fantasy trips 275
fear 149, 215, 297
   neural aspects of, 215–6
feedback 137, 217, 229, 233, 235, 236, 237,
   242, 243, 257
feedback, affective and cognitive 51
field independent / field dependent learning
   styles 301
first language influence 242, 255
flow 2, 15–16, 297, 298
   see also intrinsic motivation
focus on meaning 269
Foreign Service Institute 68
Foreign Language Attitude Questionnaire
   (FLAC) 180–1, 182, 183
fossilization 53

Gestalt 208
goal setting 265
goals 29, 30, 31, 32, 282, 285, 286, 287,
   288, 289, 292, 298
grammar 53, 204, 268, 270, 283
Greek tragedy 219
group cohesiveness 163–5, 167, 168–9, 179,
   181, 192
group dynamics 20–1, 107, 108, 150,
   155–69, 170, 197, 198, 202, 204, 205,
   211
   history of 157
group dynamics in education 157–8
group goals 162, 168
group intermember relations 159–60
attraction vs. acceptance 159

group leader 165
group leadership styles 165–7
group legends 164, 167
group norms 160–1, 167
group productivity 164
group roles 137–8
group stages
   dissolution 163, 171
   group formation 158, 159–62, 171
   performing 163
   transition 162–3
group work 235
group work and language proficiency 236

Hartmann Boundary Questionnaire (HBQ)
   69, 74, 80, 84, 85
here and now 199, 204, 205, 206, 207
hierarchy of needs 14, 88, 200
holistic learning 270, 283
Human Potential Research Project 5
humanistic activities 174, 178, 179, 180,
   184, 185, 188, 192, 211
   positive focus 188, 189, 192
   research on, 179–89, 191–2
humanistic areas of focus 203–6
humanistic exercises 175, 197–210
   characteristics 199–200
   criticism of 201–3
   sources of 207–10
humanistic language teaching 175, 210,
   258
humanistic philosophy 212, 281
hypnotherapy 212, 213, 217
   physiological base of 213

icebreakers and warmers 150, 167
identity 64, 70, 79, 149, 252, 254, 258, 292
image streaming 263
imagery 175, 197, 218, 251, 256, 296
   see also visualization
   image, definition of 260
   integration of affective and cognitive
     domains in, 272
   importance of imagery for thinking 261
   importance of imagery in education 262
   mental images and emotion 55, 260
   neurobiology of images 55, 261
   sensory modes of 260, 261, 266, 274
imagery and affective states 271–2
imagery and creative discoveries 262–3
imagery and memory 217, 267
   mnemonics 267

336

Subject index

Author index

341

Author index